More praise fo[r]

INVISIBLE HANDS

"The riveting story of how economic conservatism became one of the leading strands in American political thought. . . . Engaging history from a talented new scholarly voice." —*Kirkus Reviews*, starred review

"Kim Phillips-Fein's *Invisible Hands* persuasively shows how anti–New Deal business interests helped create a new political conservatism after 1945. It is essential reading on the history of contemporary American politics, and especially on the origins of Ronald Reagan's ascendancy."
—Sean Wilentz, Princeton University,
author of *The Age of Reagan: A History, 1974–2008*

"A compelling and readable story of resistance to the new economic order." —*Boston Globe*

"A fascinating account of how important wealthy donors were to the rise and success of conservatism. . . . While many historians have focused on the role of ideas, activists, and politicians, this work takes us to the people who put their money where their mouths were."
—*Huffington Post*

"With ferocious archival spadework and a sharply honed critical intelligence, this study shifts the agenda of history-writing about American conservatism and marks a new stage in its maturity. A very important book." —Rick Perlstein, *Nixonland*

"Highly readable for its absorbing historical background. . . . A valuable addition to the history of conservatism." —Gilbert Taylor, *Booklist*

"Readable and engaging. . . . As certain topics remain at the forefront of the political conversation—the economy, increasing government programs, the future of the conservatism and the influence of business in politics, to name a few—*Invisible Hands* lays the groundwork for anyone trying to grasp where some of these issues began and what they mean."

—*Roll Call*

"*Invisible Hands* is a brilliant, lucid, meticulously researched account of the politics of business conservatism. Kim Phillips-Fein's work is pathbreaking. For anyone who wants to understand the triumph of the conservative order during the past quarter century, *Invisible Hands* is a must read."

—Steve Fraser, author of *Wall Street: America's Dream Palace*

"A cogently argued, densely researched book. . . . Phillips-Fein arranges her material into a new synthesis, using archival research to date and describe the exact set of connections that formed at mid-century and that went on to precipitate the Reagan Revolution. She does this with an eye for the vivid—and at times for the entertaining—detail. She moves among the history of ideas, movements, institutions, and political change in prose that is clear and engaging." —*Dissent*

"No one has spanned the decades with such an ironic sensibility and clear style. The book will be an eye-opener for those unfamiliar with the steady growth of the ideological right in the years before 1950. . . . *Invisible Hands* is an incredible achievement. The story Phillips-Fein tells is one of the most politically and religiously significant of our day."

—Randall J. Stephens, *The Christian Century*

INVISIBLE HANDS

INVISIBLE HANDS

The Businessmen's Crusade Against the New Deal

KIM PHILLIPS-FEIN

W. W. NORTON New York • London

Printed in the United States of America
First published as a Norton paperback 2010

For information about permission to reproduce selections from this book, write to Permissions, W. W. Norton & Company, Inc., 500 Fifth Avenue, New York, NY 10110

For information about special discounts for bulk purchases, please contact W. W. Norton Special Sales at specialsales@wwnorton.com or 800-233-4830

Manufacturing by LSC Harrisonburg
Book design by Dana Sloan
Production manager: Julia Druskin

The Library of Congress has cataloged the hardcover edition as follows:

Phillips-Fein, Kim.
Invisible hands : the making of the conservative movement from the New Deal to Reagan / Kim Phillips-Fein.—1st ed.
p. cm.
Includes bibliographical references and index.
ISBN 978-0-393-05930-4 (hardcover)
1. Conservatism—United States—History—20th century. 2. United States—Politics and government—1933–1945. 3. United States—Politics and government—1945–1989. I. Title.
JC573.2.U6P49 2009
320.520973'0904—dc22

2008043050

ISBN 978-0-393-33766-2 pbk.
W.W. Norton & Company, Inc.
500 Fifth Avenue, New York, N.Y. 10110
www.wwnorton.com

W.W. Norton & Company Ltd.
15 Carlisle Street, London W1D 3BS

6 7 8 9 0

For Greg

Contents

Introduction

Late in the spring of 1981, only a few months after being sworn in as president, Ronald Reagan mailed his old friend Lemuel Ricketts Boulware a set of autographed golf balls for his eighty-sixth birthday, accompanied by a personal note: "Dear Lem—in case I do something wrong—hit one of these with a 9 iron or a 'wedge' and I'll feel it."[1]

The two men had known each other for almost thirty years, ever since they met at General Electric in the 1950s. Reagan had gone to work as a spokesman for the industrial giant after his Hollywood film career began to wane, hosting the company's hour-long television drama program and touring plants to give pep talks to workers, while Boulware was in charge of labor relations and community affairs for the company. But even in the 1950s, Reagan and Boulware were not only colleagues and acquaintances; as Reagan's note suggests, they were also political allies. During the years when Reagan worked at the company, Boulware believed that GE was in grave danger, threatened—as was all American capitalism—by the power of the labor unions and the expanded federal government that had been created by the New Deal. From his position, he tried to work toward a goal that seemed impossible at the time: to turn back the central institutions and the reigning ideas of New Deal liberalism, and revive an age of laissez-faire.

In 1981, with Reagan in office, it seemed to Boulware as though the agenda he had sought to establish for decades might finally be on the verge of success. He wrote back to the president thanking him for the gift: "Here's to your creative and courageous program of correction continuing to live up to its great promise—for you and all the rest of us."[2]

THIS IS a book about conservative politics. But it isn't a book about the political leaders of the movement, the men like Reagan whose names and faces everyone knows. It is a book about businessmen like Lemuel Boulware, who supported and helped to build the conservative movement that brought Reagan to power in 1980.

The rise of conservative politics in postwar America is one of the great puzzles of American political history. For much of the period that followed the end of World War II, conservative ideas about the primacy of the free market and the dangers of too-powerful labor unions, government regulation, and an activist, interventionist state seemed to have been thoroughly rejected by most intellectual and political elites. Scholars and politicians alike dismissed those who adhered to such faiths as a "radical right," for whom (to quote the Columbia University historian Richard Hofstadter) politics "becomes an arena into which the wildest fancies are projected, the most paranoid suspicions, the most absurd superstitions, the most bizarre apocalyptic fantasies." How, then, did such ideas move from their marginal position in the middle years of the twentieth century to become the reigning politics of the country by the century's end?[3]

Historians and social critics often explain the successes of conservative politics by pointing to the backlash against the victories of the social movements of the 1960s, the cultural reaction against the radicals who fought for civil rights, feminism, and gay and lesbian rights and who protested against the Vietnam War. The 1970s defection of white working-class people alienated and frightened by the liberal program shifted the politics of the country far to the right. The argument is that in the days before the onset of the culture wars, a "liberal consensus" dominated American politics, especially around economics. During the thirty-odd years between the rise of the New Deal and the election of Richard Nixon in 1968, when the Democratic Party held the White House for all but eight years, many political leaders and social critics believed that there existed a general consensus that the federal government—and other collective institutions, like labor unions—had an important role to play in shaping economic life and helping to redress the ordinary inequalities of a capitalist economy. The fierce and open conflict between rich and poor that had dominated American politics in the early years of the twentieth century had largely disappeared. Businessmen responded to this era of liberal dominance in a variety of ways. Many supported the New Deal order inaugurated by Franklin D. Roosevelt (whom some of them saw as one of their own)—and not without reason, as it fostered a period of relative prosperity and peace. They accepted the general framework of Keynesian economics, acknowledging that government spending could help counterbalance destructive recessions; they saw the welfare state as a necessary social safety net. And indeed, despite the persistence of divisions of class and race, those years saw dramatic improvements in the standard of living for most Americans, as the economy grew without accelerating the inequality between rich and poor.[4]

But if one looks beneath the surface of the postwar years, it is clear that the "liberal consensus" on matters of political economy was never absolute. Even at its zenith, liberalism was far less secure than it appeared to be. And one of the main challenges it faced began with those few prominent business leaders who were outraged by the New Deal, which they saw as a fundamental challenge to their power and their place in American society. Their antagonism toward the economic order it created never fully abated. Rather, these impassioned, committed individuals found ways to nourish their opposition, to resist liberal institutions and ideas, and to persuade others to join in fighting back, until the liberal order began to falter and they could help to bring about the slow and pervasive revolution that would culminate in Reagan's victory in 1980.[5]

This book is about those determined few, those ordinary businessmen (and I use the word advisedly, for they were mostly men) from companies of different sizes and from various industries, who worked for more than forty years to undo the system of labor unions, federal social welfare programs, and government regulation of the economy that came into existence during and after the Great Depression of the 1930s. These were the men who supported and helped to formulate the economic agenda of the conservative movement. They are not the all-knowing, all-seeing caricatures of conspiracy theory; they were people who sought to build a political movement, who faced difficulties and setbacks, who often disagreed with each other about the right course of action, and who could not control the circumstances under which they worked. But it is essential to understand them, their ideas, their motivations, and their strategies, since, after all, the most striking and lasting victories of the right have come in the realm of political economy rather than that of culture. By the early twenty-first century, the conservative movement in power had transformed the tax code, government regulation of business, and the relationship between the federal government and the states; in the private sector, the proportion of the working population represented by labor unions had fallen to levels not seen since before the New Deal. The political economy of the postwar period was sustained by the Keynesian belief that consumption is the key determinant of economic growth, and that therefore public policies should primarily seek to stimulate consumption while encouraging some income redistribution. This vision of the economy no longer enjoys wide support in either political party.

If we shift focus from cultural to economic issues, it becomes clear that the origin of modern conservative politics and ideology predates the 1960s. And in this sense the roots of the movement's triumph can be found in the disaffection of people very different from the white working-class conservatives who are so often seen as central to its rise. It begins instead in the reaction against the New Deal.

INVISIBLE HANDS

1 Paradise Lost

IT WAS IN THE summer of 1934 that the three du Pont brothers—Pierre, Irénée, and Lammot—decided the United States was poised on the brink of collapse. The country, as Irénée wrote, was losing the "freedom granted by the Constitution"; without this guarantee, there was no doubt that it would "rapidly decline in its civilization and happiness."[1]

At first the du Ponts had been content tacitly to support Franklin D. Roosevelt as president; Pierre, the oldest of the three, had even endorsed him over the Republican incumbent, Herbert Hoover, in the 1932 election. Roosevelt had promised to repeal the Prohibition amendment, to which the du Ponts had always been deeply opposed—not because they were hedonistically fond of liquor, but because they feared increased income taxes in the absence of the tax on alcohol. "The liquor tax would be sufficient to pay off the entire debt of the United States, interest and principal, in a little less than fifteen years," Pierre wrote in a fund-raising circular for the anti-Prohibition crusade of the 1920s.[2]

But by 1934 it was clear that Roosevelt would do much more than end Prohibition, and very few of his plans were at all appealing to the du Ponts. Irénée, the middle of the three brothers and the most politically passionate, complained that the new Securities and Exchange Commission, created to regulate the financial markets, marked an attempt to change human nature, disrupting the inevitable risks at the heart of life: "Men are by nature speculators, and Nature enforces the necessity of speculation on all of us." Pierre argued that the Roosevelt administration's opposition to child labor meant government interference with the intimate details of domestic life: "No Federal law or constitutional amendment will abolish child labor unless the parents in the community are convinced that child labor should not exist." The du Ponts were troubled as well by an impending congressional investigation into the role of munitions makers—like the DuPont company—in the decision to enter World War I. And in 1934, Pierre quit the National Labor Board, a new agency that Roosevelt had created to try to manage labor relations, angry at its support for the principle that workers should be able to decide on union representation by majority vote. "Abuse of the strike privilege," he wrote, "has become a national evil."[3]

Great strikes were indeed beginning to ripple through the nation that summer. On the Embarcadero of San Francisco, a strike of dockworkers turned into an open battle with the city police, and when two workers were killed, the funeral procession of thousands began a citywide uprising. In Minneapolis, a strike of truck drivers led by Trotskyist radicals shut down the entire city in what some businessmen were convinced was a harbinger of revolution. In Toledo, unemployed workers picketed along with striking auto-parts plant workers, demonstrating in defiance of an injunction and fighting with police. Over the course of the year, there would be more than 1,800 work stoppages involving more than 1.4 million workers—everyone from the southern garment workers striking for the most basic questions of union recognition and wage increases to the editors and secretaries of the New York publishing house Macauley's, who walked out when one of their coworkers was fired for organizing a union.[4]

While they watched the events unfolding in workplaces across the country, the friends and acquaintances of the du Ponts were facing more intimate difficulties as well. One retired company vice president complained that it was getting harder to maintain a good staff, since his housekeeping workers kept leaving for employment on public works projects: "Five Negroes on my place in South Carolina refused work this spring . . . saying they had easy jobs with the government. A cook on my houseboat at Fort Myers quit because the government was paying him a dollar an hour as a painter."[5]

In a letter to a friend a year later, Irénée du Pont described the family's changing relationship with the Roosevelt administration. At first, he wrote, "large businesses . . . followed the President in the belief that he was sincere and that experiments which he might initiate would be discarded if they were unsuccessful." But things had changed. "It must have now become clear to every thinking man that the so-called 'New Deal,' advocated by the Administration, is nothing more or less than the Socialistic doctrine called by another name."[6]

The du Ponts in the early 1930s were one of the wealthiest families in the nation, blending high-tech commerce with Old World gentility. Unlike the other American dynasties of the day, such as the Morgans and the Rockefellers, who had accumulated the bulk of their wealth in the late nineteenth century, the du Ponts had substantially increased their fortune during World War I and the 1920s. The goods that rolled out of the DuPont factories were the emblems of modernity. Almost every new line of consumer trinkets incorporated a DuPont product. Packaged food needed cellophane wrap. Radios demanded DuPont plastic. Bright, shiny cars required paints produced by DuPont. Hollywood filmed its movies on DuPont cellulose, and the radicals who accused the company of war profiteering told the truth: the Great War had been fought with munitions made in DuPont factories. After the war the family bought out the founder of General Motors, adding one of the leading automobile manufacturers in the nation to the jewels of their industrial empire.[7]

Still, no matter how modern their products, in their private lives the three du Pont brothers hearkened back to the ancien régime. Their lavish estates, with names like Longwood and Granoque (one Cuban vacation home bore the title Xanadu), sprawled through Delaware and southern Pennsylvania, their mansions furnished with Japanese waterfalls and greenhouses designed to coax tropical flowers to bloom in the midatlantic states. These extravagant homes reflected an aristocratic self-image; within their factories, the du Ponts practiced benevolent paternalism, granting death and disability benefits and providing rental homes for workers. Pierre even donated over $4 million to build new schools for black children in the Jim Crow state of Delaware. "In Delaware schools," one observer claimed, "the children chirp George Washington, Abraham Lincoln and Pierre du Pont in the same breath."[8]

FOR MEN like the du Ponts, the leaders of the American business class, the Great Depression was a political disaster as much as it was an economic one. Just a few years earlier, businessmen had been the heroes of American politics. They had been celebrated as the leaders of the nation. The old hostility to big business had finally been defeated, as the revolutionaries and anarchists of earlier generations were deported and driven underground in the wave of repression that followed World War I. The labor movement crumbled: after representing 19.4 percent of the workforce in 1920, its ranks dwindled to 10.2 percent by 1930. One academic commentator exclaimed early in 1929, "The common folk believe in their leaders. We no longer look upon the captains of industry as magnified crooks. Have we not heard their voices over the radio? Are we not familiar with their thoughts, ambitions and ideals as they have expressed them to us almost as a man talks to his friend?" The veneration of business, the promise of easy riches through the magic of the stock market, and the virtual absence of a political challenge to capitalism—nearly a first, since the nation had been shaken by battles between labor and capital for most of the previous thirty years—made the decade an ideal one for enterprise. As one foreign visitor to the United States remarked in 1928, "America is an employer's paradise."[9]

Historians have offered many different diagnoses for the economic malady that swept the nation beginning in the fall of 1929. But whatever its cause, in the early 1930s, the American upper classes suddenly awakened from the bright dreams of the previous decade to discover themselves in the midst of a cataclysm. "Out of the depression we have been going through, we shall have learned something of high importance," mused Myron Taylor, the president of U.S. Steel. But "it is too soon to say just what we are learning." The once-confident corporate leaders of the nation stood speechless and confused, their old wisdom proven hollow.[10]

At first, the leaders of American industry dismissed the crisis as a mere cyclical downturn. They suggested that it was the inevitable price to be paid for the phenomenal abundance of the previous decade, a temporary aberration that was sure to correct itself before too long. A few argued that the decline might purify the economy by slowing the crazed consumption of the nouveaux riches and clearing the way for profitable new investments. "The fact that we have let nature take its course may augur well for the ultimate prosperity of the country," explained Richard Whitney of the New York Stock Exchange. Even as matters worsened, others flatly refused to admit the Depression's severity: one Maryland building contractor wrote to President Hoover in 1931, "There is *not five percent* of the poverty, distress and general unemployment that many of your enemies would have us believe." Charles M. Schwab, the president of Bethlehem Steel, an extravagant gambler who died in the late 1930s, a few years after losing most of his fortune in the Depression, helpfully encouraged the nation: "Just grin, go on working, stop worrying about the future, and go ahead as best we can."[11]

President Hoover, always confident in the ability of reasonable men to solve any problem, initially treated the economic crisis as a matter of public relations. He held conferences of businessmen at the White House, where he begged them to maintain wage rates and hold payrolls steady. Believing that bolstering business confidence was the primary problem and that declarations of surety and faith would eventually inspire the real thing, the president cheerfully told the American people in 1930 that they had "passed the worst and with continued effort we shall rapidly recover." He urged reporters not to write too negatively about the crash, for fear that "we may create a sense that the situation is worse than it really is." He hoped that municipalities would take responsibility for aiding those out of work. Late in his presidency, he did take some action: he created the Reconstruction Finance Corporation to provide emergency loans to failing banks and local governments, he encouraged public works projects, and he signed a bill providing for some federal relief for the poor.[12]

But it was too little, and over time the glib reassurances that nothing was wrong made America's business leaders appear not only incompetent but absurd. They had been trusted with the future of the nation, and not only had they gambled it away, they refused even to admit that they had done so. Even the staunchest Republicans had trouble supporting Hoover with enthusiasm in 1932; one of the few moments of excitement in the Republican Party that year came when there was a brief flurry of interest in drafting Calvin Coolidge to run instead.[13]

The election of a new president seemed to many businessmen like a chance to redeem themselves. Franklin D. Roosevelt, the scion of one of the oldest and most elite families of the Hudson River Valley, educated at the best private schools in the country, immediately reached out, coaxing them to lend their support to his agenda. Executives from the nation's leading industrial companies participated in the new Business Advisory Council. They appreciated the idea behind the National Recovery Administration, which allowed them to cooperate and set industry-wide standards in an attempt to maintain prices and wages in the midst of the economic collapse. The most farsighted and liberal of the business leaders, particularly those in consumer-oriented industries such as electronics and garments, supported the Keynesian New Deal programs that they thought would raise the wages of workers and hence create more disposable income, stimulating mass consumption. And the free-trade agenda of the Democrats appealed to some financiers and oil barons, whose labor costs were low enough that higher wages did not seriously endanger their profit margins.[14]

The New Deal did not mark a break with capitalism; on the contrary, Roosevelt always believed that he was acting to save private property. He was at times quite surprised by how much anger his policies aroused. Nor did the New Deal represent a headlong rush to the welfare state: Roosevelt was wary about expanding the dole, and well into the late 1930s he continued to believe in the paramount importance of balancing the federal budget. The New Deal did not end the Great Depression; only World War II accomplished that, with the result that for the rest of the century there would be a deep connection between economic stimulus and the military.[15]

But as the New Deal began to unfold, American businessmen began to realize just how much had changed since the 1920s. Although the story of the 1930s is often told through the lens of Washington politics, in reality both the president and the legislature were pushed throughout the decade by economic circumstances and political movements that they neither created nor controlled. The New Deal, as historian Lizabeth Cohen has argued, was in large part "made" by the people across the country who responded to the constraints of the Depression by taking part in strikes, in protests, and in politics more generally in ways that previously they would never have believed possible. Their actions, along with the initiatives that came from Washington, came to symbolize the rejection of the old order of laissez-faire economics. During the New Deal years, American workers won the legal right to be protected from the retaliation of their employers when they tried to organize unions. They gained a national minimum wage and a maximum workweek. The federal government distributed monetary relief, employed people in public works programs, established unemployment insurance, and even created a national pension program for the elderly, Social Security. It also began to regulate the financial markets in an attempt to prevent a reprise of the chicanery and fraud of the late 1920s. The Public Works Administration built new roads, schools, bridges, and post offices; the Tennessee Valley Authority electrified the countryside; the Works Progress Administration hired actors, artists, and writers to paint murals, perform in plays, write travel guides, and conduct oral histories. And even the role of the war in ending the Depression served to legitimate the idea that at times the market could not guarantee prosperity; the government had to play a role. Many of these programs were measures that America's business class had resisted for a generation, and the government enacted them at a moment when the power and prestige of business was at its nadir. The employer's paradise had been lost.[16]

. . .

In July 1934, the du Ponts gathered a group of their business friends for a series of meetings in New York City, at such locales as the Empire State Building offices of disaffected Democratic politicians like the former New York State governor Al Smith (whom Roosevelt had beat out for the party's nomination in 1932) and the General Motors offices in Columbus Circle. The main topic of discussion was creating a "propertyholders' association," as Irénée put it, to disseminate "information as to the dangers to investors" posed by the New Deal. The group decided that the name of their association should not refer directly to property—it would be better to frame their activities as a broad defense of the Constitution. The organization should be "liberal," never "reactionary or rigid," let alone paternalistic, wrote Stephen DuBrul, one General Motors executive. It should speak out for the rule of law, not the rights of the rich. Its officers should be "drawn from nationally known persons whose public position is above reproach," not from the "leaders of industry and finance," and it should try to obtain as broad support as possible. Irénée hoped that it would be able to make an alliance with other organizations that in his view defended the Constitution, such as the American Legion and "even the Ku Klux Klan." Each participant in the early meetings took a list of names of executives to call to discuss the idea, and in August the group incorporated itself as the American Liberty League.[17]

The Liberty League sought to rectify what its members perceived as an imbalance in the body politic: that "business, which bears the responsibility for the paychecks of private employment, has little voice in government." The organization presented itself as a "non-partisan" educational group of Democrats and Republicans who had combined to "combat radicalism, preserve property rights, uphold and preserve the Constitution." It would not be an elitist organization. Rather, its spokesman insisted, the league would "unite several millions of people from all walks of life who are now without organized influence in legislative matters," in defense of the "principles upon which our government was formulated." The new organization promised to welcome "every citizen, man or woman, in the shop, in the field, in the mill, in the counting house, in the business world, in the home or in any walk of life." By no means was it "anti-Roosevelt," and certainly its leaders did not intend to be "antagonistic" to the administration—in fact, the spokesman suggested that if a "tendency to extreme radicalism" developed in the country, the Roosevelt administration might well find helpful allies in the millions of people soon to be organized in the league.[18]

The *New York Times* greeted the creation of the league with tentative enthusiasm: "If [the league] will stand firmly for policies and principles, and eschew politics and personalities, it has a real chance to be useful." On Wall Street, the *Times* reported, the league "was little short of an answer to a prayer . . . Nowhere in the country has the lack of any organization of conservative interests been more acutely felt than in the financial community." The *Washington Post* suggested that the league was "unique" in American political history, because it promised to unite "laborers and farmers, stockholders and bondholders" into a single organization. Meanwhile, Roosevelt played the diplomat, insisting that he was in complete agreement with the aims of the league when it came to protecting property and the Constitution—although he could not resist pointing out that for all the league's fine talk of liberty, it was notably silent "about the protection of the individual against elements in the community that seek to enrich themselves at the expense of their fellow man."[19]

The thin veneer of civility between Roosevelt and the Liberty League did not last long. In dozens of speeches and pamphlets, the organization depicted the "ravenous madness" of the New Deal as a monstrous usurpation of power: "Businessmen are denounced officially as 'organized greed,' 'unscrupulous money changers' who 'gang up' on the liberties of the people . . . The dragon teeth of class warfare are being sown with a vengeance." The New Deal thwarted the Constitution, the league claimed, by elevating the federal government over the state governments, leading to a frightening, even "totalitarian" centralization of power. The policies of the New Deal were only exacerbating the economic downturn. As the chairman of the Illinois division insisted, "You can't recover prosperity by seizing the accumulation of the thrifty and distributing it to the thriftless and unlucky." The league asserted that the federal government should keep out of the relief business, leaving it all to the Red Cross. Indeed, the New Deal bureaucracy—"a vast organism spreading its tentacles over the business and private life of the citizens of the country"—would ultimately prevent the return of any prosperity at all.[20]

The league took special pleasure in attacking Social Security, arguing that the hastily planned system infringed on the rights of states, that it was fiscally unsound, and that it would hurt the economy. Social Security, said the president of the league, was far too heavy a burden for the delicate economy to bear. In 1936 one lawyer associated with the league sought to mount a legal challenge to Social Security, suing on behalf of a New Jersey milk company. His argument was that the effect of the law was "to take the property of employers and of certain employees for the benefit of a class," resulting in the "taking of property without due process of law."[21]

Despite the league's claims to be coordinating a mass movement of the common man, when the du Ponts sought to build their organization, they turned to other executives. "There is no secret that one of the 'experiments' is to endeavor to redistribute wealth, in fact, that is what the 'New Deal' really means," Irénée wrote to the president of Eastman Kodak. "It is built on the misconception that the wealthy have either hoards of gold in their cellar or a spring on the hillside which pours forth wealth and that this should be taken possession of and distributed among their less fortunate, or less competent, fellowmen." They encouraged their friends at other companies to send letters about the league to their stockholders, asking them to join. More than half the league's funds for 1935 came from fewer than two dozen bankers, industrialists, and businessmen, and various members of the du Pont family contributed 30 percent of the total. In 1936, a full two thirds of the organization's money came from thirty men giving $5,000 each.[22]

For other organizations in different times and places, perhaps the disproportionate role played by a handful of wealthy men wouldn't have seemed so damning. But in the depths of the Depression, the league's dependence on a small cadre of rich donors was a fatal weakness. The league rapidly became the symbol of the recalcitrance of those reactionaries whom Roosevelt dubbed "economic royalists" in his 1936 reelection campaign. In the eyes of the press, it served as the perfect symbol of opposition to the New Deal—a rearguard fight by a handful of short-sighted, small-minded, self-interested rich men against the programs that were feeding the hungry, succoring the suffering, and saving the nation. The group became the butt of a thousand jokes. Democrats named it the "Millionaires Union." The chairman of the Democratic Party quipped that the league "ought to be called the American Cellophane League" because "first, it's a Du Pont product, and second, you can see right through it." The league could not effectively defend capitalism in the midst of the Great Depression because the contrast between the lives of its members and those of the working population of the United States had simply grown too vast. As one Texas businessman noted, "The capitalist system can be destroyed more effectively by having men of means defend it than by importing a million Reds from Moscow to attack it."[23]

THE LIBERTY LEAGUE was not the only business attempt to stop the New Deal. As the Roosevelt administration's focus shifted from its early attempts to end the Depression through self-action on the part of industry through the National Recovery Administration to its later commitments to labor union rights and the creation of a limited welfare state, the opposition of corporations widened.

The National Association of Manufacturers (NAM), formed in the late nineteenth century in order to coordinate business opposition to labor unions, emerged as the leading organization of anti–New Deal industrialists. In the early 1920s the NAM had led the Open Shop Campaign, a national campaign against labor unions that attempted to quell the labor radicalism that had flared across the country in the wake of World War I. But many companies found their NAM memberships easy expenses to cut as depression engulfed the economy; the number of members dropped from more than 5,000 in the early 1920s to 1,500 in 1933, with resignations flooding in at a rate of 65 per month. The NAM might have dwindled away altogether if not for the devoted leadership of a new group of executives, who, in the words of one of their number, resolved that the NAM was needed to "serve the purposes of business salvation." Big companies replaced the small businessmen that had headed the NAM in the late 1920s. By 1935, close to 60 percent of the board members came from the upper ranks of major manufacturing firms (companies with more than 2,000 employees and sales exceeding $10 million a year).[24]

The NAM suggested that the image of business was suffering during the Depression because of the American public's lack of understanding of the central role of business in the economy. "The public does not understand industry, largely because industry itself has made no real effort to tell its story; to show the people of this country that our high living standards have risen almost altogether from the civilization which industrial activity has set up," argued one of the NAM leaders. The only reason people could be duped by the New Deal was that the unions and the federal government dominated public debate. The NAM hired a public relations director, and by 1937 the organization was spending over half its income of nearly $1.5 million on radio programs, motion pictures, billboards, direct mail, a speakers' bureau, paid political advertisements, and other PR efforts. One representative newspaper advertisement depicted a construction worker atop a steel beam, waving at a man below in a limousine. "I knew him when he pushed a wheelbarrow," the caption read—giving a sense of America as a country of cross-class solidarity, in which the man with a chauffeur had risen from the same ranks as the laborer.[25]

But there was also another side to the NAM—one concerned more with the knock-down, no-holds-barred fight against labor unions by every possible means than with winning people over via public relations. It was as though the leadership of the group secretly doubted that simply telling people the "story" of industry actually would produce the desired effect. The 1935 Wagner Act (also known as the National Labor Relations Act) granted workers formal protections against retaliation for being involved in union activity, prohibited certain employer actions like spying on and threatening workers during a union drive, and created a federal agency to oversee union elections and enforce the law. The NAM was at the forefront of the fight against this law. NAM members testified against it before Congress, and after it was passed, the NAM legal department (as well as the Liberty League) argued that it violated the Constitution. The NAM lawyers went so far as to urge industrialists to resist the law, challenge it in court, and wait for it to be overturned. When an upstate New York company developed a strikebreaking strategy, the NAM publicized the "Mohawk Valley Formula" (as it became known) as a "real contribution to civic dignity." In certain labor conflicts the NAM hired speakers to present employers' viewpoints without making it clear that the business group was footing the bill, while companies like General Motors and Goodyear and Chrysler and Republic Steel stockpiled tear gas and (in some cases) machine guns in their factories, arming themselves for the conflagration with their workers that they feared might someday erupt.[26]

Unlike the Liberty League, the NAM made no pretense of building a cross-class organization. It did not claim to be speaking for the silent masses of farmers, workers, and consumers. Instead it openly sought to organize businessmen to articulate a forceful defense of capitalism, to rally a national network of executives to oppose the rise of labor unions, and to defend the rights of management, both practically and ideologically. It tried to use the power of employers as a counter to the power of the state, with the assumption that if business "told its story" publicly and vocally, the rest of the nation would have to pay attention. By the early 1940s, the NAM claimed that its efforts to "sell free enterprise" were triumphing—that it had recruited thousands of "sentinels" committed to proselytizing for business.[27]

But the problem with the organization's diffuse propaganda campaigns was that it was virtually impossible to measure their success. How did one know if the message was getting out there—how could one know what the workers (or anyone else) thought about it? Business could tell its story over and over again, but what if no one cared to listen?

Even though it might have been hard to tell whether the corporate advocates were having any real effect in the short run, for some the personal contacts made during the 1930s provided the foundation for a lifetime of activism against New Deal liberalism. One such partnership was that of Leonard Read and William Clinton Mullendore. Read, the gregarious manager of the Western Division of the United States Chamber of Commerce in the early 1930s, became acquainted with Mullendore, the executive vice president (and later president) of Southern California Edison Company, during the depths of the Great Depression. Read was a relatively recent migrant to California from the Midwest. The child of a poor farming family, he had grown up in a small town in Michigan and had started a wholesale produce company after a stint in the army during World War I, in the hopes of earning enough money to finance his college education. When the business floundered in the mid-1920s, as it encountered fierce competition from chain stores, Read and his family picked up and moved west. He went to work as a real estate salesman in Palo Alto.

But Read's real genius was networking. Despite his financial travails, he soon became involved in the nearby Burlingame Chamber of Commerce. There he was a whirlwind of activity, arranging luncheons at which local businessmen would hear speeches given by leading executives and scientists. He published a brochure enumerating the charms of doing business in the "Sunshine Suburbs." When he arranged a pilgrimage of seven hundred California businessmen to attend the inauguration of Herbert Hoover in 1928, leaders of the national Chamber of Commerce noticed his work, and Read was promoted to become the assistant manager of the Western Division of the Chamber of Commerce.[28]

In the early 1930s, the U.S. Chamber of Commerce, like the rest of the country, was overwhelmed by the Depression. The business group was not particularly interested in advocating on behalf of the free market; it supported Roosevelt's National Recovery Administration, which seemed to be trying to help in ways that did not overtly challenge business power. From his post at the Chamber, Read heard about a Southern California utilities man who was disparaging the National Recovery Administration. Mullendore was no retiring executive but rather a vigorous public speaker, addressing such audiences as the Rotary Club (where in 1931 he thundered against the "apostles of hatred" who were stirring up bad feeling in the country) and the American Bankers Association (where in the fall of 1932 he warned that the electrical industry might be made a political target of hostility toward business overall). Curious about what could be driving this important figure in the Southern California business community to criticize the NRA, Read set up a meeting at Mullendore's office to try to win him over.[29]

But the opposite happened—after a strenuous hour-long conversation in which the utility executive carefully rebutted every Chamber of Commerce position with a detailed discussion of liberty, freedom, and private property, Mullendore had persuaded Read instead. For the rest of his life, Read would think of the conversation as something of a conversion experience; in the words of one sympathetic biographer, Read felt that the meeting had been "ordered by fate, or divinity," which was "shaping his destiny." He left the meeting as a "student of liberty," and the two began to strategize about how to organize businessmen to defend what Read would call the "freedom philosophy," the principles of capitalism.[30]

Read, with his farming background, had little advanced education, in contrast to Mullendore, who, despite growing up as a "Kansas farm boy" during the depression of the 1890s—in one biographical statement, he described his early years living "under conditions which today would be considered on the borderline of poverty"—went on to attend college and law school at the University of Michigan. After World War I, he worked in the U.S. Food Administration and then served as an executive assistant to Herbert Hoover for two years while Hoover was the secretary of commerce. The utilities executive was an opinionated, well-read man, and he introduced Read to other Southern California free-market intellectuals and gave him lists of books to study, by authors ranging from Adam Smith to William Graham Sumner. It was a complete education in the philosophy of the free market. Read looked up to his mentor and absorbed his lessons thoroughly. In later years, he wrote a short meditation on the role Mullendore played in his life: "What a comfort it is, with instinct and reason waging their war within one, the decision as to which will be served hanging in a meaningful balance, to simply ask, 'What would Bill have me do?'"[31]

Despite Read's admiration of Mullendore, the two men had starkly opposing political temperaments. Read was charming, sunny, the consummate optimist. Mullendore, on the other hand, was a sullen critic given to stark absolutism; he never felt that what other people in the movement were doing was good enough. He saw the New Deal as an irremediable disaster for the nation, but believed that it was already too late and nothing could be done to stop it. Mullendore insisted that businessmen had betrayed the free market. He saw the efforts of the NAM and the Liberty League as mere window dressing, hiding a deeper capitulation. "The old military strategy of 'divide and conquer' is still being effectively employed by the New Dealers," he complained to Read. He found it unforgivable that businessmen accepted the price-fixing arrangements of the National Recovery Administration, that they tolerated the new labor unions and Keynesian ideas. There could be no compromise between the old American capitalism and the new socialistic economy of the New Deal: "We cannot have both systems—that is, both the governmentally-controlled and directed and the free enterprise system. We must have one or the other."[32]

Mullendore began to dream of creating an organization of businessmen who would be, in contrast, wholly devoted to the fight against the New Deal. As he put it in a letter to another business friend, "I want to mobilize a group of business leaders in this country who will start shouting from the house-tops and the cellars and any other place where they can obtain a hearing, publicly and privately, that we are approaching disaster and that we must insist that the government's policies with reference to currency, with reference to labor, with reference to competition with business, with reference to pump-priming and using taxation as a weapon of reform, and so on, and so on, must be changed." He imagined a network of a thousand executives who would act as "militant alarmists," each one speaking and acting in his community to resist the changes coming to the country. Read arranged for him to meet with businessmen at the Los Angeles Chamber of Commerce, but Mullendore found the experience dispiriting: "I believe that about 12 out of the 20 agreed with me and to some extent stayed with the point and said that we should make a statement about how bad the situation was and spread the alarm.

In summary, the result of the meeting was quite discouraging so far as leaving much hope that there is any chance of a solidity of viewpoint among so-called business leaders themselves."[33]

Still, Read's mood remained energetic and upbeat—he was incapable of despair. In 1939 he became the head of the same L.A. Chamber of Commerce where Mullendore had been so frustrated just the year before. It was a large chapter of the group, with ten thousand dues-paying members and a staff of over a hundred, and once in charge, Read invited Mullendore and other free-market advocates to speak there and to publish their talks in a journal, the *Economic Sentinel*, that he began for the organization. It was the start of a new kind of ideological mobilization, using the money and the organizational connections of businessmen not so much to attack Roosevelt or the New Deal as to espouse the vision of the free market.[34]

Mullendore and Read in the 1930s were more isolated and less organized than the members of the Liberty League or even the NAM. Their dream of an organization of "militant alarmists" did not come to fruition in the Depression decade. But their vision of recruiting business money and organizing business to support the free market would serve as inspiration in the years after World War II—especially for Read, who would build on the ideas that he and Mullendore had talked about in Southern California during the Depression to start the first free-market think tank of the postwar period, the Foundation for Economic Education.

THE BACKERS of the Liberty League first tried to break into electoral politics in 1936, when they supported Alf Landon, the oil executive and governor of Kansas, in his challenge to Roosevelt for the presidency. There were few bright spots in Landon's dismal race. One of the only ones was illusory: the magazine *Literary Digest* predicted that Landon would win the election by a two-to-one margin, based on 2 million voluntary responses to postcards mailed out to people whose names appeared in telephone directories and on lists of automobile owners. In the end the Landon campaign revealed the political bankruptcy of business conservatism (as well as that of the polling techniques practiced by the *Literary Digest*), for the support of wealthy businessmen became its downfall.[35]

Roosevelt's reelection campaign turned into a relentless assault on the American Liberty League, which one Democrat after another attacked with glee. "Just who are the people to whom [Landon] is willing to be obligated in the unlikely event of his election? Can they be other than the group of which the Du Pont Liberty League is characteristic?" asked the governor of Indiana. In the words of John L. Lewis, the president of the Congress of Industrial Organizations (CIO), Landon was a mere "puppet" of the "Morgans, the Rockefellers and the du Pont dynasties." A Mississippi Democrat excoriated the "American Lobby League" as "apostles of greed." Roosevelt's campaign manager accused the league of being "the ally of the Republican National Committee," which would "squeeze the worker dry in his old age and cast him like an orange rind into the refuse pail." In an effort to deflect such criticism, the Republican Party went so far as to ask the Liberty League to refrain from openly endorsing Landon, even though its members were bankrolling much of his campaign.[36]

The Republican Party desperately tried to get employers to organize their workers to vote against the New Deal. Sterling Morton, an executive at Morton Salt, led the Industrial Division of the Republican National Committee. The mission of the division, he wrote in a memo after Landon lost, had been to "create a feeling of solidarity among the owners, managers and executives, to make them feel that they are not alone in a fight against the New Deal and to give them an opportunity to make their opposition effective by working with a political organization." Morton firmly believed that businessmen should try to influence the votes of their employees, and he urged them to distribute pamphlets and give speeches on company time to their workers about the election. Another memo articulated the thinking behind the plan: "The government and administration of these United States has been placed by a dumb, unthinking populace in the hands of notorious incompetents," and it was the duty of the "industrious, thinking, saving and honest citizens" to "devote their time, energy and fortunes to the sole objective of taking control of the United States out of the hands of those who have betrayed it."[37]

The Industrial Division seized on fears about Social Security to make its case to vote for Landon. Shortly before the election, the division began to distribute special pay envelopes to midwestern employers. Printed on the front was a warning that under the new Social Security Act, employees would lose a proportion of their wages to the federal government—there was "no guarantee" that the money would ever be returned as pension payments. (The envelopes made no mention of employer contributions to Social Security.) Workers collecting their paychecks would have an immediate reminder of how much they would lose under the new social insurance plan. Later in his life, Morton described the central role that opposing Social Security played in the 1936 campaign: "We attacked the Social Security plan, saying that it was a gigantic fraud; that it was not insurance; that any insurance company which offered like benefits for like payments would be closed overnight by any State insurance commission; that it was merely a method of painless taxation of the working man to get money for current extravagance in exchange for Utopian promises. I have had no reason to feel that we in any way misrepresented the situation."[38]

But none of it worked, and despite the best efforts of the Republican Party, Landon lost the election in one of the true landslides of American history. After running a fairly lackluster campaign, he failed even to carry his solidly Republican home state of Kansas, winning only in Maine and Vermont (prompting Roosevelt's campaign manager to revise the political maxim "As goes Maine, so goes the nation" to the immortal quip: "As goes Maine, so goes Vermont").[39]

A congressional investigation that followed the election did still more to demolish the legitimacy of the league and other anti-Roosevelt organizations, especially the role they played in the 1936 election. For example, a group named the Farmers' Independence Council, which shared office space with the Liberty League, did not actually number a single family farmer among its members, instead receiving almost all its support from Chicago meatpackers. Still more ludicrous, Lammot du Pont contributed $5,000, insisting that owning a 4,000-acre estate qualified him as a farmer. The investigation made clear that no matter how hard the Republican Party tried to distance itself from the Liberty League publicly, it had not been able to resist the temptation of du Pont funds—thousands of dollars had flowed to the party over the summer of 1936.[40]

In the end the Landon campaign demonstrated the sheer incoherence of the business conservatives and their opposition to the New Deal. Their conservatism seemed politically meaningless, little more than the desperate attempt of a few rich men to shore up their declining position in society. Although the league's leaders insisted that it would soldier on, it could not survive the campaign of 1936; its activities dropped off markedly, and on September 24, 1940, the *New York Times* reported in a short article that the offices of the American Liberty League had closed. Industry's "story" never caught on. The executives did not create an enormous popular crusade in the 1930s. Alf Landon became a footnote in history. Instead, the New Deal and the unions won.

This does not mean that criticism of the New Deal stopped after 1936. In many ways it accelerated. Southern conservatives feared the centralization of power in the New Deal, seeing that it could someday be used to attack the prerogatives of segregation (though FDR steered clear of doing so during the 1930s). Anti-Communist critics such as Democratic Representative Martin Dies of Texas began to investigate Communists in New Deal agencies like the Federal Theater Project and the National Labor Relations Board, providing a foretaste of McCarthyism. Aggressive new union tactics like the sit-down strike met with condemnation; in the midst of the United Automobile Workers sit-down at General Motors, the *New York Times* editorialized, "If an arbitrary minority is permitted to override the wishes of a majority of workers, and forcibly take control of shops out of the hands of their owners, there is obviously no safety for our industrial system." And FDR's "Court-packing plan" to appoint new justices to the Supreme Court who might be friendlier to the New Deal (one for every justice over seventy who had served for ten or more years; had the plan passed, the president could have appointed six new judges immediately) raised doubts among many who felt that it was a dictatorial power grab that overrode constitutional principles.[41]

But these criticisms of the New Deal did little to rehabilitate the idea of the free market. As the historian James MacGregor Burns has written, in the early 1930s, "a coherent body of conservative thought hardly existed, except to the extent business philosophers had shaped absolutist ideas of laissez-faire to advance the interests of private enterprise." Social Darwinism provided little in the way of a guide to meet the crisis of the Depression. Free markets, laissez-faire policies, private enterprise—all these appeared little more than the "folklore of capitalism" (in New Dealer Thurman Arnold's phrase), fantasies promulgated on behalf of the very rich. By the late 1930s, many economists (such as Gardiner Means, Adolf Berle, and John Kenneth Galbraith) took it for granted that big businesses controlled the economy through administered pricing, that the key determinant of economic health was purchasing power, and that the old nostrums about the market no longer held true in a world of gigantic corporations. Others (such as Harvard's Alvin Hansen) even opined that capitalism had ground to a halt—growth had permanently stagnated, and in the future the dynamic engine of the economy would be the public sector, the state.[42]

Even those intellectuals who did criticize the New Deal during the 1930s took care to distinguish themselves from apologists simply advocating business interests. Among professional economists, two of the most forceful critics of the New Deal were Henry Simons and Frank Knight of the University of Chicago, but both men also took a skeptical approach to business, believing that the excessive concentration of private economic power in the form of monopoly limited freedom nearly as much as the state. "We may recognize, in the almost unlimited grants of powers to corporate bodies, one of the greatest sins of government against the free-enterprise system," Simons wrote. Knight commented that he felt "a certain ethical repugnance attached to having the livelihood of the masses of people made a pawn in . . . a sport, however fascinating the sport may be to its leaders," and cautioned against absolutism in economics: "It would go a long way toward clarifying discussion if it were generally recognized on both sides that there are no one hundred percent individualists and no one hundred percent socialists; that the issue is one of degree and proportion." The social critic Walter Lippmann, who wrote an influential philosophical critique of economic planning, did not feel that the rights of corporations were by any means absolute. And Albert Jay Nock, an eccentric libertarian journalist, whose books describing the idea that a fragile "remnant" was all that remained to counter the power of the state became cult classics among postwar conservatives, rebuffed the Liberty League, denouncing "the whole structure of American business" as "thoroughly rotten" and insisting that "American business never followed a policy of laissez-faire, never wished to follow it, never wished the State to let it alone."[43]

THE DU PONTS, lacking many political or even intellectual allies in the wake of the failure of the Liberty League, remained resolute and irascible opponents of liberalism, even after World War II. In the midst of the upheaval of the 1930s, they had kept their plants under control by establishing a network of company-dominated unions. And their company earned phenomenal profits during World War II: they produced 55 percent of all American gunpowder used to fight the war, not to mention paints, dyes, antifreeze, DDT, rubber, and rayon yarn used by the military. But the du Ponts still felt deeply pessimistic about the future of their country, believing that the old values of respect for property and business were lost forever. Irénée du Pont feared that the opposition had "woven too complete a web," and that "we cannot get the New Deal out of power." Pierre du Pont, too, was largely despondent, writing in 1940, "I belong to a past generation that is accorded small attention in these days." He was infuriated by the fair employment practices statutes that were starting to be passed after World War II. Despite his efforts on behalf of black education, he insisted that "no opinion or law could convince me that negroes, as a race, are equal to the whites." No incremental changes could convince Pierre that the country's politics were improving, not "until the New Deal is thrown out lock, stock and barrel by a free vote of the American people."[44]

A few years after the end of World War II, at the age of eighty, Pierre sadly wrote to a Liberty League colleague, "Looking back over the years, it seems that my activities did not contribute very much to the fundamental problems of our country." He was, he commented, grateful if nothing else to have lived in the "golden age" of the early twentieth century, the years before the blight of the thirties.

Yet although the business opponents of the New Deal were defeated at the time, their ideas—and their money—would prove critical to the creation of a new conservative movement. Even Pierre du Pont's musings on the tragedy of being born into a world that had been lost contained the tentative hope that maybe one day it could change again—the "present difficulties" straightened out by a later generation, even if the du Ponts could not join in the struggle. "Perhaps," he wrote, "we were born too soon."[45]

2 Down from the Mountaintop

IDEAS HAD CHANGED the life of Leonard Read, and he felt sure that he could bring that same flash of illumination to others. In 1937 he published a book called *The Romance of Reality*, setting out his ideas about politics and the economy, arguing that he had looked "in vain" through party politics "for an enunciation of principles" that he could truly support. During the war years, he started a small organization called Pamphleteers, Inc., sending the great works of thinkers like the French laissez-faire theorist Frédéric Bastiat and the nineteenth-century social Darwinist William Graham Sumner to his mailing list of three thousand subscribers.[1]

And then, in the spring of 1945, as World War II was drawing to a close, Read moved to New York for a job with the National Industrial Conference Board (NICB), an organization that since 1916 had sought to provide analysis of the economy to businessmen and a broader public. The president of the NICB hired Read along with another conservative writer in what seemed to Read to be a move to make the organization more aggressively political. But he quickly found the work frustrating—especially the insistence that speakers at luncheons or public meetings needed to represent both sides of an issue. Although he was impervious to the gloom that afflicted du Pont and Mullendore, Read nonetheless had grown tired of working for business organizations that seemed to demand such compromise. He wanted to promote ideological education. After resigning from the NICB, Read visited with David Goodrich, the president of the B. F. Goodrich Company. The executive promised to assist him in starting a new organization—one that would live up to Read's ideals. Read named his new group the Foundation for Economic Education (FEE). Goodrich helped Read reach out to businessmen who could serve on the board of trustees of the new organization; in addition, the social networks Read had created through more than a dozen years of work with the Chamber of Commerce proved invaluable to his cause.[2]

FEE, as it became known, was different from the Liberty League and the National Association of Manufacturers. Although the new group received financial support from companies, it did not seek to represent "business" at all, but instead advocated a stringent, crystalline vision of the free market. FEE sought, in countless venues and arenas, through innumerable leaflets and pamphlets and LP recordings, to disseminate the basic principles of laissez-faire. The real problem, Read believed, was that the executives who lived and breathed the ways of commerce "cannot, *for the most part*, make the case for the philosophy and the way of life for which they allegedly stand." FEE's mission was to teach with "ever-improving clarity" the "private enterprise or freedom philosophy," or the vision behind the free market. The triumph over socialism would result not from a direct refutation of its principles and arguments but from having the courage to "uphold" the "voluntary society, private property, limited government concept." As Read wrote in one of FEE's reports, "Let us give the haven of liberty an intellectual lighthouse that persons may be attracted from the sea of socialistic error."[3]

One of FEE's first trustees was the wealthy and energetic Jasper Crane, who had retired that same year from his position as executive vice president of DuPont Chemical, the company he had served for most of his career. He was in no mood to sit back and enjoy his sunset years. Crane, a tall, mild-mannered, fair-haired man with a high, round forehead, saw himself as committed to the cause of freedom in America, which he feared was in great peril. "We must recognize that we are revolutionaries, that the great mission of America is to be world revolutionaries for liberty," he wrote to a friend. "Our task was well begun and made great progress for 150 years or more; but it is far from being completed. We have latterly met with serious setbacks, which should not discourage us but only intensify our determination to win the fight for freedom in the various areas of life."[4]

Crane was an unlikely revolutionary. He had been an executive at DuPont for decades. The son of a prosperous Newark, New Jersey, manufacturer, he had grown up in privilege and had attended Princeton, where he studied science. He entered the business world by working at his father's company, moving to DuPont in 1915. There he worked his way up the executive ladder, becoming a vice president and a member of the company's executive committee in 1929. He developed hobbies befitting a gentleman: in his spare time, he bred roses.[5]

But in the 1930s, Crane had grown interested in politics. He attended a dinner of the Liberty League and gave public speeches about matters such as the ethical obligations of churches during the Depression. Following a mid-decade visit to Germany, he lectured on Nazism, which he likened to slavery for its socialism (he did not mention the regime's treatment of Jews). Even in the darkest days of the Depression, he defended capitalism vigorously, attacking anyone who thought economic planning was the answer: "We cannot make progress by the planning of a few. We want planning by the many, by a million planners, self-reliant, ambitious, operating in a free economy." The Depression, Crane believed, was moral punishment for the sins and excesses of the 1920s, reflecting the "character breakdown" of the American people. But by burdening business with higher taxes and new regulations, the Roosevelt administration was destroying the economic and political future of the country.[6]

World War II did not change Crane's feelings about the New Deal. The year of his retirement from DuPont, 1946, was also the year of one of the largest strike waves in American history. More than 3 million workers struck between November 1945 and June 1946. Workers in industries across the American economy participated in the strikes—workers in oil, automobiles, steel, electrical products; coal miners and bus drivers and janitors; even the coffin makers in New York City. In cities such as Rochester, Houston, Pittsburgh, Oakland, and Stamford, Connecticut—hardly towns known as centers of radical politics—strikes that began at individual companies rapidly escalated into near-general work stoppages, with strikers congregating in mass rallies and demonstrations, attracting not only the support of their neighbors but that of the local police. Workers struck to protect the unions they had won during the war and to protest the sudden increase of unemployment and decline in wages that had come as soon as the war had ended. They wanted to make sure that they would not be shut out of the prosperity all hoped for in the postwar period—to stake their claim on the American future.[7]

To Crane, this wave of upheaval must have symbolized the magnitude of the struggle that confronted the United States at the end of the war. He seemed largely unaware of the ways in which the New Deal had transformed the lives of his fellow citizens. He had little sense of himself as privileged by dint of his position as a successful and wealthy businessman. Crane simply believed that the country he had grown up in was gone forever. He hoped to devote his retirement to reestablishing it. Despite his gentle demeanor and his careful, precise habits of thought, he rejected a quiet, restrained style of conservatism. The old organizations that had fought the New Deal, he thought, were simply not adequate to the new challenges of the postwar period. "I do not believe," he wrote to a friend, "that N.A.M. [the National Association of Manufacturers] can be the torch bearer in this particular fight." Instead, Crane felt increasingly certain that he needed to organize a cadre of intellectuals and businessmen that would be absolutely committed to the market: "I have been wondering whether we ought to attempt to mobilize a few men who are absolutely sound in the faith and will not compromise, who are earnest in thinking, talking and writing for freedom, and who are resolved to uphold it at any personal sacrifice."[8]

Crane met Leonard Read through Isabel Paterson, a conservative writer with whom they were both friendly. ("He struck me as a man with a conscience, who does feel a responsibility, and is profoundly concerned about the future," Paterson wrote of Crane to Read.) Read gave Crane one of his pamphlets; after reading it, Crane responded, "I agreed with every word of it and was thrilled by it." Crane told Read of his dream of bringing together a small "group of men throughout the country" committed to the fundamental principles of freedom: "I don't have in mind a movement, but rather a search for leadership of perhaps the relatively few men who know the truth and won't compromise with evil." When Read asked if he would be willing to serve as a trustee of FEE, he responded with alacrity that he would do "what I can to help." In FEE, Crane found the committed, principled approach for which he had been yearning; by the late 1950s, he would be donating $15,000 a year to the organization, and he described it in a letter to Irénée du Pont as "Number One in the institutions for the maintenance of freedom."[9]

But while Crane agreed with Read that it was essential to advocate for free-market ideas, he believed that the ideas themselves needed to be clarified and sharpened. It was not enough simply to repeat the same old clichés. He wrote to Read that the time was not ripe for the free-market movement to publish "emotional appeals" in the style of "*Uncle Tom's Cabin*"; first "the intellectual foundation" needed to be laid. People no longer understood what mattered in the world of political economy. They no longer had confidence in capitalism. The crisis that America faced was intellectual, even spiritual in nature (Crane liked to list Bible passages that he felt offered convincing definitions of liberty). "What is needed today is first to lay the intellectual basis for the belief in human liberty, and then to follow that up with an emotional presentation of the blessings and advantages of our system," he wrote to his friend Loren "Red" Miller, the director of the Detroit-based Bureau of Governmental Research.[10]

Crane, quoting another friend, told Miller that "Christianity made little progress until in the Second Century it had the writings of the New Testament; Communism got nowhere until Marx wrote *Das Kapital* (read by very few people at first but gradually gaining enormous influence); National Socialism needed *Mein Kampf* to be effective." The American people, in short, needed a Book. Crane was eagerly looking, as he put it, for the "New Testament of capitalism," the "'bible' of free enterprise."[11]

. . .

For Crane to dream of a new bible for market economics in the years after World War II must have seemed, to most of those around him, at once hubristic and naive. It was not a propitious time to start a revolution; the postwar world seemed ripe for peace between business and government. The flexible hybrid of capitalism and the welfare state pioneered in the United States had proved capable of military triumph over Germany, Italy, and Japan. Despite widespread fears and dark prophecies that the Depression would return once the war was over, the economy weathered the transition away from the controlled economy of wartime with relative ease.

The politics of World War II transformed the attitude in the business community toward Keynesian economics and New Deal liberalism by giving business a chance to lead the nation once again. In 1942, the president of the Advertising Federation of America gave a speech in which he called for the conflict to become known as "the War that Business Helped to Win." Business could save itself politically through its good conduct during the war—it would impress itself upon the minds of the "common man," and in turn, "that common man and his wife, and their boy home from the wars, will register that verdict at the ballot box." New organizations like the Committee for Economic Development, led by businessmen committed to developing a moderate, flexible Keynesianism, grew in prominence in the wake of the war. The president of the U.S. Chamber of Commerce took a restrained tone, telling the Chamber in 1943, "Only the willfully blind can fail to see that the old-style capitalism of a primitive, free-shooting period is gone forever."[12]

This optimistic approach seemed ratified when businessmen won a series of political victories directly after the war. The price controls that had governed the country during the conflict—an anti-inflation measure—were lifted quickly at the war's end, in the wake of business campaigns to roll them back (despite widespread popular fears that price rises would rapidly follow). In June 1947, over President Truman's veto, Congress passed the Taft-Hartley Act, which imposed a host of new restrictions on the labor movement: it prevented sympathy strikes (when one group of workers strikes on behalf of another), banned secondary boycotts (when a union refuses to handle goods made by another, striking union), barred supervisory workers or foremen from joining unions, permitted states to pass right-to-work laws that prohibited contracts with provisions stating that union membership was a mandatory condition of employment, and required all union officers to sign affidavits swearing that they were not Communists. *Business Week* deemed the bill "a New Deal for America's employers." But more important than any one of these provisions may have been the simple fact of its passage: unions had fought the bill bitterly, and their defeat showed that labor's forward momentum of the 1930s was starting to slow. The labor movement stalled, unable to make significant headway in organizing the South or in expanding its blue-collar base to include white-collar workers. Three years later, the "treaty of Detroit" between the United Auto Workers and General Motors enshrined regular cost-of-living increases in the auto workers' contract, an implicit recognition on the unions' part of the legitimacy of profits as long as workers got some share of the growing pie.[13]

The passage of the Taft-Hartley Act and the rollback of price controls were mirrored by a new mood among liberals. During the war, the critical attitude toward business that had dominated politics during the Depression began to be replaced with greater sympathy, as businessmen took up their places in the administration of wartime agencies. Liberals started to argue that the Depression had been the result of a shortage of consumption rather than any fundamental problem of capitalism itself. Labor unions, government spending, and Social Security all supported consumer demand, and they therefore helped business as well as workers. As the historian Alan Brinkley has written, the goal of "full employment" came to replace that of structural economic reform. The onset of the cold war also shifted the ground for liberals, as intellectuals such as Arthur M. Schlesinger, Jr., and Sidney Hook argued that the domestic problem of economic inequality had been solved and that the greater danger in the postwar world was that of Soviet totalitarianism. The repression of the American left in the late 1940s and 1950s was a project of liberals as well as conservatives like Senator Joseph McCarthy. The Truman administration pioneered loyalty-security screening programs and fired about 2,700 federal employees for the slightest suspicion that they might be Reds.[14]

In this new context, many managers and stockholders, executives and owners, did in fact seem to make their peace with the liberal order that had emerged. They began to bargain regularly with the labor unions at their companies. They advocated the use of fiscal policy and government action to help the nation cope with economic downturns. They accepted the idea that the state might have some role to play in guiding economic life.

But at the same time, despite all these changes, it remained difficult for the men who had fought the New Deal in the 1930s to let go of the battle. All they could see in the postwar order was a landscape of defeat. After all, from their perspective, the war had created a newly gargantuan federal government. In the late 1940s, top marginal income tax rates were about 90 percent, and corporate tax rates remained high as well. The government had steady revenue sources that it had never possessed before. Nor were they comforted by the new ideology of Keynesian consumerism, for it implied that the disposable income of workers, not the patient saving and canny investment of entrepreneurs and owners, mattered most for economic health. What was more, no matter how angry labor leaders might be about the Taft-Hartley Act, and no matter how much *Business Week* might crow about its passage, unions in postwar America were a force that could no longer be ignored or crushed, as at the end of World War I. The strike wave of 1946 had made that clear. Socialism and the welfare state appeared to be on the march around the globe. The eastern bloc lay under Stalin's dominion, and in the summer of 1945, Britain—the birthplace of capitalism, the ancestral home of the great liberal thinkers—had elected a Labour government. From the point of view of the opponents of the New Deal, it seemed as though the war had only consolidated the new political order.[15]

Jasper Crane was one of a small core of businessmen (some retired, others still in industry) who had survived the political struggles of the 1930s and remained committed in the postwar era to rehabilitating the idea of the free market. He did not capitulate. Rather, in his search for a new "bible" of free enterprise, he encountered a pair of economic thinkers, refugees from the European catastrophes, who provided a broad intellectual justification for keeping up a bitter opposition to the new economic order.

Friedrich von Hayek and Ludwig von Mises met in Vienna in the years following World War I, after Hayek finished his undergraduate degree at the University of Vienna. In contrast to the classical economics of Great Britain, which focused on the discovery and explication of universal economic laws, the dominant intellectual tradition in Germany and Austria at the time emphasized the historical uniqueness and sociological specificity of industrial development. When Hayek entered the University of Vienna in 1918, fresh from the army, he could easily have become a devotee of this historical school (he flirted with socialism in his college years). But instead his intellectual life took shape under the instruction of the thorny, iconoclastic Mises. Even in the 1920s, Mises embraced the price mechanism—the interaction of supply and demand as reflected in prices—as the perfect way to achieve social order without coercion. He fiercely rejected any form of government intervention in the economy. This made him unpopular with most other economists in Austria at the time, and he never held a full-time salaried post at the University of Vienna. But his convivial private seminar for colleagues and advanced students only, in which the formal papers were followed by lengthy dinners at an Italian restaurant and even longer conversations afterward at a café, provided an intellectual home for many, including his student and protégé, the young Hayek.[16]

Hayek's early research focused on the causes of the business cycle, challenging the underconsumption theories that were starting to become popular in the interwar period. He suggested that stimulating investment in an indiscriminate way—for example, by artificially lowering interest rates—might not spark investment or economic growth.

Economists at the London School of Economics (LSE) recognized in Hayek's thought a potential challenge to the work of a rising star at Cambridge—John Maynard Keynes. The protean Keynes was a hard person to compete with for the limelight. He was effortlessly brilliant, able in the 1920s to make a fortune on the European exchanges during a morning half-hour, then write economics all afternoon. He was a member of the Bloomsbury circle of literary modernists, given to artistic and sexual experimentation, and his economics reflected his willingness to jettison age-old intellectual conventions.

The more conservative economists at LSE brought Hayek to their department in 1931 after the onset of the economic crisis, hoping that he would become an prodigy capable of counterbalancing Keynes. But as the Great Depression deepened, Keynes's reputation flourished while Hayek's declined. Keynes's work proposed solutions to the worldwide economic crisis. His *General Theory*, published in 1936, argued that an economy could settle in equilibrium with high levels of unemployment and that government spending might be necessary to stimulate consumption. In the context of the Depression, no one wanted to hear Hayek's warnings about the dangers and inadequacies of government intervention. Instead, Great Britain—like the United States—began to experiment with deficit financing and building a welfare state.[17]

Although Hayek remained interested in economic theory, the tumult of the 1930s drew him into politics. In 1933 he wrote a short memo describing Nazism as a socialist movement rather than a reaction against communism, as many at the time believed, and gave it to Sir William Beveridge, the director of the LSE (whom he failed to persuade about the free market—Beveridge later authored a proposal for a full-fledged British welfare state). In 1938 he participated in a conference in Paris on the "crisis of liberalism," dedicated to Walter Lippmann's *The Good Society*, a book critical of the New Deal, and that same year he published an extended version of his 1933 memorandum as an article entitled "Freedom and the Economic System." But it was World War II that afforded Hayek the time to write the work that would make his name. Anticipating the onset of the war, the London School of Economics moved to Cambridge in 1939. There Hayek had light teaching duties. He volunteered to help in the intelligence effort, but his Austrian background rendered him suspect. Rattling around the giant old farmhouse where he and his family had been set up, he began to explore the ideas he had started to develop in the 1930s and to write the book that vaulted him to fame: *The Road to Serfdom*, a sweeping critique of the "collectivism" and economic planning that Hayek believed had been ascendant in Western intellectual circles ever since the late nineteenth century, finally triumphing during the Depression.[18]

Over the wartime years, Hayek stayed in touch with his old teacher Mises, who had emigrated first to Geneva and then, in 1940, to the United States. In the middle of the economic and political collapse sweeping the globe, the two men never wavered from their powerful sense that the free market—even more than political democracy—was absolutely central to a free political order. For Hayek and Mises, the market meant something more than private property, dispersed ownership, or free competition. As Mises argued in his 1949 book *Human Action*, "The market is not a place, a thing, or a collective entity." The market created a space of freedom, a world in which individual actions could revolutionize society. People in the free market served each other's ends without themselves being turned into nothing but means. Market prices brought individual actions and decisions into harmony with each other, with no guidance from any higher source. The Austrian thinkers romanticized the individual as a creative hero, the agent of all society. In their philosophy, individuals trading in a free market took on the world-creating power that Marxists assigned to the working class.[19]

Yet while the market offered the greatest possible space for individual freedom, it proved strangely brittle in another regard: it could not tolerate collective decisions or actions. Hayek and Mises criticized the "fashionable concentration on democracy," as Hayek put it—economic planning always constrained freedom, even if people chose it. This was because of the very nature of economic decisions. The marketplace was so complex, the network of transactions composing it so intricate and labyrinthine, that the state could not manage or replicate it. This was a problem at once technical—the information collected by the market was too subtle and elaborate to be mirrored by the state—and political: the market allowed for an immensely wide range of choices, which government planning would not. Because consensus was ultimately impossible in economic affairs, a government given the power to plan the economy would inevitably resort to coercion and propaganda. Hayek admitted that at times modern man would feel subordinated to the market and would chafe against economic forces that he could not control. But he argued that submission to the marketplace was infinitely preferable to deference to a ruler. "Unless this complex society is to be destroyed, the only alternative to submission to the impersonal and seemingly irrational forces of the market is submission to an equally uncontrollable and therefore arbitrary power of other men."[20]

The Austrians admired the spontaneity of the economy, a complex system that came into existence without forethought or planning. Yet they also feared the ease with which the free market could be distorted or even destroyed through clumsy efforts to regulate and plan. The market was at once the robust force that generated all of life and human production and a terribly fragile entity, threatened on all sides. On the one hand, it was in desperate need of protection; on the other, its power was such that any effort to contravene its bidding must end in despair.

Hayek saw himself working in the intellectual tradition of John Locke, Bernard Mandeville, and Adam Smith, but also that of Edmund Burke and Alexis de Tocqueville. Like Burke, the late-eighteenth-century philosopher of counterrevolution, he mistrusted the arrogance of rationalism, the idea that people could understand and shape the world; and like Tocqueville, he was suspicious of the will of the majority. But where Burke asked his readers to recall tradition, the endless, infinite wisdom of the ages embodied in every customary relationship, the Austrian thinkers looked to the marketplace. The ebb and flow of the market brought together all the bits of information in society, more innumerable and complex than any single human mind could ever hope to assimilate. The market, in Hayek's words, took into account the "constitutional limitation of man's knowledge and interests, the fact that he *cannot* know more than a tiny part of the whole of society and that therefore all that can enter into his motives are the immediate effects which his actions will have in the sphere he knows."[21]

But despite their affinities with an older conservative intellectual tradition, Hayek and Mises espoused an idea of the world quite different from the classically conservative one. They admired the entrepreneur's capacity for innovation, and they believed in a vision of a society always in flux. *The Road to Serfdom* said little on the topic, but in Hayek's later writings he sharply condemned traditionalist conservatives, saying that they "cannot offer an alternative to the direction in which we are moving." Conservatives were possessed by a "fear of change, a timid distrust of the new as such." They lacked "faith in the spontaneous forces of adjustment." In contrast, Hayek preferred to define himself as a liberal, in the classic, nineteenth-century sense of the word, even though he admitted that it might be confusing and pointlessly obscurantist to call himself a liberal in mid-twentieth-century America, since the word had largely been taken over by "radicals and socialists." But the distinction was important to him, because unlike conservatives, he "want[ed] to go elsewhere, not to stand still." On the contrary, he believed in "a thorough sweeping-away of the obstacles to free growth." He could "accept changes without apprehension," confident that the "self-regulating forces of the market will somehow bring about the required adjustments to new conditions, although no-one can foretell how they will do this in a particular instance."[22]

There was nothing new about the idea of the market in and of itself. In the late eighteenth century, an era of revolutions against monarchy and aristocracy, Adam Smith had written about society as a self-regulating organism, organized through harmonious processes of trade and exchange. The "invisible hand" transmuted individual self-interest, previously denigrated in Christian thought as selfish and socially destructive, into a social bond that was stronger than prescribed morality. Smith's vision of the market was intimately linked to the revolutionary ferment that surrounded him. He insisted that common people—not the Crown, the nobles, with their elaborate codes of comportment, or the church, with its rituals of devotion—produced all social wealth. The market freed people from the traditional authority of kings. In the United States, the idea of the free market developed against the stark backdrop of plantation slavery, as opponents of slavery argued that contractual relationships were the building blocks of a larger system of economic possibility and material wealth. But after the Civil War, the rhetoric of market liberty became increasingly associated with rigid refusals to permit the government to take any actions to regulate the harsh tempo of industrialization. Social Darwinist thinkers such as William Graham Sumner argued that "the millionaires are a product of natural selection": those who survived the rigors of the market were those best fitted for wealth and power, and those who failed should be left to the gutters. Radicals who organized unions, went on strikes, or demanded that the government protect the lives of the impoverished therefore seemed to threaten the very moral underpinnings of the social order.[23]

Even as economics became more mathematically rigorous, it continued to provide an intellectual defense for the social inequalities of early twentieth-century America. The "marginalist revolution" of the late nineteenth century (led in Britain by Alfred Marshall, in the United States by economists like John Bates Clark) created a new and more scientific-sounding way of understanding the extreme division of wealth in the late nineteenth and early twentieth centuries: both labor and capital received their "marginal" product, equivalent to what they contributed to production. The state, therefore, had no legitimate basis for intervening in the immutable natural laws of the marketplace.[24]

But the commonplace faiths of social Darwinism and the new mathematical neoclassical economics alike were shattered by the economic disaster of the Great Depression. The language of economic competition and the moral superiority of the rich suddenly sounded hollow and false. The notion that the market was fair or just seemed nearly masochistic; the defense of the market had grown anemic and thin. It was associated with power and privilege, the trappings of social hierarchy. The great innovation of Hayek and Mises was to create a defense of the free market using the language of freedom and revolutionary change. The free market, not the political realm, enabled human beings to realize their liberty. It could transcend social class; it would liberate everyone. Hayek and Mises did not emphasize the efficiency of the free market. They did not promise that it would create material abundance, although they believed it would. They celebrated the market because it made people free.

In a way, Hayek and Mises seemed to borrow from the radicals they so opposed, associating their politics with the struggle against tyranny rather than the values of social order or consistency. The Austrian thinkers always framed their defense of the market as an attack on Nazism (short for National *Socialism*, Hayek never tired of reminding his readers), and there too they laid claim to the vision and the language of the left, arguing that the free market, not the welfare state, was the true basis of meaningful opposition to fascism.

Even as the welfare state and the mixed economy were coming into existence, Hayek and Mises set as their political imperative tearing them down. The two Austrian economists saw the whole history of the twentieth century as one of fierce ideological struggle. They believed that Nazism had emerged naturally out of the long tradition of skepticism toward the free market, and the frontline of political conflict, for them, was not the postwar strike wave or the election of 1948 but the battle of ideas. As Mises wrote in a 1942 letter to Leonard Read, "The arena in which the fate of the West will be decided is neither the conference rooms of the diplomats, nor the offices of the bureaucrats, nor the capitol in Washington, nor the election campaigns." Instead, "the only thing which really matters is the outcome of the intellectual combat between the supporters of socialism and those of capitalism." (Read admired Mises and had invited him to speak at the Los Angeles Chamber of Commerce.) This acute sense of the political significance of ideas infused their academic endeavors with the greatest possible urgency—they believed that without their meetings, seminars, papers, articles, and books, the capitalist world they sought to defend would be destroyed from within.[25]

Hayek and Mises did not write specifically for an audience of businessmen. And, of course, their work was far too abstract and wordy for many readers. (William F. Buckley, Jr., the founder and editor of the *National Review*, complained, perhaps a little too harshly, to a businessman friend in 1962 about Hayek's "execrable" writing style: "The first thing I intend to ask the Lord, if a meeting can ever be contrived, is Why does their side get economists who write like Keynes, and our side get them who write like Hayek?") But the ideals that they outlined would inspire resistance to the federal government, labor unions, and the regulatory state throughout the rest of the twentieth century.[26]

NO ONE expected *The Road to Serfdom* to be a success. Three American publishers turned it down before the University of Chicago Press grudgingly accepted the manuscript (in Britain, Routledge was the publisher). The editor at Chicago had minimal hopes for the slim volume, thinking that if someone sufficiently famous could be persuaded to write an introduction, the best that could be hoped for was that it might perhaps sell a couple of thousand copies.[27]

The book thoroughly defied such low expectations. Henry Hazlitt wrote a glowing review in the *New York Times*, pronouncing *The Road to Serfdom* "one of the most important books of our generation," a work on liberty equal to that of John Stuart Mill. (Hazlitt, a journalist who was himself a free-market conservative and a founding member of FEE, had positively reviewed Mises' book *Socialism* in 1938 and had befriended the Austrian when he came to America in 1940, introducing him to businessmen and journalists—as well as Leonard Read—and helping him gain a foothold in the new country.) *Reader's Digest*, edited at the time by the ex-leftist Max Eastman, published a condensed version of the manuscript, sending it into the homes of a million *Digest* subscribers. Hayek came to the United States to do a book tour: "Imagine my surprise when they drove me [to New York's Town Hall] . . . and there were 3,000 people in the hall, plus a few score more in adjourning rooms with loudspeakers. There I was, with this battery of microphones and a veritable sea of expectant faces."[28]

Hayek was on his speaking tour across the United States when he met the man who would help bring him to the University of Chicago: neither a professor nor a dean but a Baptist businessman from Kansas City by the name of Harold Luhnow. Luhnow was no intellectual. He held an agricultural degree and had worked on a ranch herding cattle in his youth;

his interest in politics began with his involvement in trying to shake the stronghold of the infamous Democratic Pendergast machine on Kansas City. Later in life he ran William Volker & Company, a wholesale furniture distribution concern founded by his uncle. From that position he headed the company's philanthropic trust, and over time he shifted the Volker Fund's focus from local charities to free-market ideas. Luhnow was captivated by a speech he heard Hayek give at the Economic Club of Detroit. He met with the economist and pleaded with him to do a "free market study" of the United States, offering to give Hayek money to pay research assistants at the London School of Economics. The product he hoped for resembled Crane's idea of the free-market bible: "We are hopeful that you could bring together a group that would spell out in considerable detail but in language simple enough for the common man to understand, a complete plan for a workable society of free enterprise."[29]

Luhnow was so eager to get the Austrian to America that he offered to underwrite Hayek's salary at an American university. Luhnow and Hayek investigated a couple of different possible academic homes, and in October 1948 the Committee on Social Thought at the University of Chicago agreed to hire the Austrian economist, with his salary of $15,000 a year for ten years to be fully covered by the Volker Fund.[30]

Jasper Crane was an acquaintance of Luhnow's, and he shared his friend's fascination with Hayek's work, as well as Mises', immediately. As he wrote to his friend Loren Miller of the Economic Club of Detroit, "They are both so sound. It ought almost to shame us to have two foreign economists taking the lead in setting us right on the fundamentals." He told Miller that he wished American congressmen would read their work. In May 1946, at Miller's urging, Crane met Hayek for the first time; Hayek was already talking to other businessmen like Luhnow about money for his projects, and Miller may have thought that Crane might be a good donor to the economist as well. The two men shared a lunch that lasted several hours, discussing, among other things, Hayek's plans for a *Road to Serfdom*–style study of the United States, and his hope of starting an international society devoted to free-market ideas. "I was much delighted with him," Crane wrote to Miller afterward, "not only on account of the soundness of his mind and force of his character, but he seemed to me to be a very fine and likeable chap."[31]

Still, in the following weeks Crane seemed plagued with doubts about the projects that Hayek was trying to organize. Shortly after meeting Hayek, he quizzed Miller on whether or not Hayek was Jewish (he wasn't), fearing that he (and the group he would form at the University of Chicago) might be "tinged with the collectivist thought that is characteristic of reformed Jewry." After all, in *The Road to Serfdom*, Hayek had possibly seemed willing to compromise with government on certain things—for example, a minimum wage. Crane felt that this was a disappointingly lax approach, and even though he approved of Hayek's work, he would still have preferred a more consistently antistate stance. Like many businessmen, he ultimately preferred Mises.[32]

But while the businessman differed with the free-market economist on various fine points of theory, the two became linked by a political project. Although he was initially reluctant to get too deeply involved, Crane would ultimately become the American businessman most active in helping Hayek to build the Mont Pelerin Society—the international society that the economist had described to him at their first luncheon—which was an elite intellectual organization devoted to the development of an economics and a worldview critical of the welfare state and economic planning. With founding members from Germany, Switzerland, France, England, Norway, Italy, and the United States, the Mont Pelerin Society provided an international intellectual home for defenders of the free market. Many of those involved were scholars and economists, but conservative journalists (such as Henry Hazlitt, whose 1946 *Economics in One Lesson* would become one of the classic works of popular free-market economics in the period) also participated. In the 1950s, writers from *Reader's Digest*, *National Review*, the *Indianapolis Star*, and *Barron's* joined the group, as did representatives of the Volker Fund and conservative think tanks; even Arthur Burns, the chairman of the Council of Economic Advisers under Eisenhower from 1953 to 1956, became a member. Although it was always primarily an intellectual group, the Mont Pelerin Society created a space where businessmen could work with scholars in a common political and ideological struggle, defending the market against the incursions of New Deal liberalism.[33]

Hayek had dreamed of starting such an organization ever since he participated in the 1938 conference in Paris in honor of Walter Lippmann about the need to rescue and reinvent classical liberalism for the modern age. After the war was over, he talked to Mises and other old friends, like the economist Lionel Robbins and the philosopher Karl Popper, all of whom were enthusiastic about the idea. The group decided to hold its first meeting in Switzerland, at a resort on top of a mountain. The European location meant that Hayek faced the challenge of expensive transportation for all the American guests he wanted to invite, including Henry Hazlitt and the economists Milton Friedman and Frank Knight. He immediately asked Luhnow, his friend and supporter, for assistance. Luhnow was a little reluctant to open his purse. As he wrote to Hayek, "it is almost impossible to keep control of organizations of this sort." But he came around, agreeing to fund transportation from America to Switzerland for several eminent guests (including Friedman and Hazlitt as well as Leonard Read, along with several other FEE staffers).[34]

At Luhnow's suggestion, Hayek invited Jasper Crane to the meeting, though only as an observer whose name would not appear on the official list of participants. Hayek felt it was important that membership for the time being be limited to intellectuals and academics, because if businessmen were present, unsympathetic journalists might be skeptical about the new organization's connections: "I think you will agree that experience has shown that any effort in the sphere of ideas, if it is to be effective, must avoid even the appearance of being dependent on any material interests, and that for that reason we have been careful not to include in the list of persons originally invited, anyone, however sympathetic with our aims, who might be thought by the public to represent specific interests."[35]

Crane declined the invitation to travel to Switzerland. But he expressed great enthusiasm for the meeting's aims. In particular, he agreed that it was important that membership be limited to established scholars, since "the conclusions reached, the philosophy developed, the suggestions made, and the points raised for further inquiry will have, coming from men of the highest scholarship, profound influence in the realm of ideas." And he felt strongly that Hayek's new intellectual society should avoid overt political involvement: "To attempt wide propaganda would in my opinion be quite unwise and would indeed weaken the potential usefulness of the society. That, as the need for it becomes manifest, can be carried on by other instruments created for that very purpose." Tentatively, slowly, he began to become involved with the Mont Pelerin Society. As he would write a few years later, "What the highbrows upstairs talk about today has such a decisive influence on the public opinion of tomorrow."[36]

The first meeting of the new society took place on April 1, 1947, at a small chateau atop Mont Pelerin, near Vevey, Switzerland. For the thirty-nine scholars from ten countries gathered at Hayek's invitation, the past twenty years had been traumatic ones of exile and defeat. They met in the wake of cataclysms both personal and historic to discuss the coming ruin of the world, and their assemblage on the mountaintop marked, for them, at once a new beginning and a last chance to fight back. But what should they call themselves? Hayek had hoped to name his group after the two great nineteenth-century opponents of revolution, Lord Acton and Alexis de Tocqueville. His friends, however, observed that it might seem peculiar to name an organization of classical liberals—defenders of the market system against the forces of socialism—after two Catholic noblemen. In the end, the intellectuals agreed simply to adopt the title of the location of their first meeting—a testament to their sense of the world-historic nature of the undertaking.[37]

There was little publicity for the conference, only one brief story in the *Chicago Tribune* under the headline "Seven Nations Map Freedom Fight in Secret Talk." The press statement Hayek distributed was carefully framed to reveal as little information as possible. After all, the project of the society depended in part on secrecy.[38]

When all were gathered at Mont Pelerin, Hayek gave the keynote address. He thanked everyone present for indulging his "wild experiment."

He believed that it was of the greatest importance that this esteemed group of writers, thinkers, and scholars had come together on the mountain. To stop the drift to socialism, they needed to take a hard look at classical, free-market liberalism, to engage in self-criticism and prevent their ideas from becoming "stationary" or "rigid." They needed to question the "intolerant and fierce rationalism" and "intellectual hubris" that was the legacy of the French Revolution, and to learn to treat with respect those "spontaneous social forces through which the individual creates things far greater than he knows." The members of the society had to be men who had fought with their liberalism, whose beliefs had been honed away from exhausted homilies. Yet at the same time, Hayek believed that a new and deeper commitment could be born out of those inner struggles.[39]

In short, Hayek called, for a rebirth of the defense of the market—one that was more honest, newly subtle, but without compromise. The intellectuals who were there thrilled to his sentiments. "The central values of civilization are in danger," read a statement approved by the members of the new society. As Milton Friedman, who visited Europe for the first time to attend the 1947 conference, said years later, "The importance of that meeting was that it showed us that we were not alone."[40]

CRANE FOLLOWED the developments of the first meeting with great interest, and a few months later he became a member of the society. He continued to believe that ideas could change the course of American history. "Intellectual leadership is in the long run decisive," he insisted in a letter to H. B. Earhart of the Earhart Foundation, a small conservative foundation funded by the money Earhart had made in the oil industry. "Every successful revolution in history has been carried through by a relatively small group of thoughtful people, not by the great mass of people, the latter always looking to the intellectuals for leadership." But at the same time he continued to be wary of the European thinkers. Crane wrote to his friend J. Howard Pew, an executive at Sun Oil: "We will get some things of value from the foreigners, even though they cannot understand our American idea of liberty."[41]

Crane was especially worried that the scholars of Mont Pelerin might be too intellectually peripatetic, that they might not share his own steadfast commitment to free-market ideas. After the first meeting, based on reports from his friends, Crane wrote Hayek a concerned letter about the possibility that ideological deviants might have been in attendance. When Hayek responded with a warning against the "tendency to create an unreasoning orthodoxy which treats traditional liberal principles as a faith rather than a problem on which reasonable people may differ," Crane was not at all impressed. He pointed out that the list of members already included people with a range of views, including "some who are definitely willing to compromise with principle," and argued that this was "unwise," for "the membership should be as far as possible composed of people who are sincerely devoted to the principle of human liberty." He complained to Loren Miller that it seemed the "spiritual note" had been absent from the first meeting of Mont Pelerin. A couple of years later, he wrote Hayek an enraged letter after reading a piece by a society member that suggested, among other things, that wealth was becoming more concentrated in the United States—an idea, Crane seethed, "which stems from Karl Marx."[42]

Despite Crane's occasional displays of ambivalence toward the society, Hayek sought to cultivate him as a potential donor to the group, sometimes through hints, at other times through more direct pleas. In the early years of the society, funds were a constant problem. Efforts to raise money to pay for travel to conferences frequently failed. At first even Crane remained reluctant to give large sums of money or to get more deeply involved as a fund-raiser himself. When Hayek asked him directly for money in 1952, he declined to give, saying that he found the requested sum of $5,000 simply too extravagant.[43]

But in 1956, Crane's attitude suddenly changed. He wanted, he wrote to Hayek, to help organize an American meeting of the Mont Pelerin Society. All the previous meetings had been in Europe. Through a gathering at an American university, "the American public, and particularly the thinking people, would learn . . . of the widespread advocacy of the liberal philosophy and its strong intellectual foundations." Hayek had long been interested in such a meeting but told Crane that he thought that bringing the European intellectuals to America would be prohibitively expensive. "I will be ready to make an active effort to secure the necessary financial aid for such a meeting," Crane responded.[44]

Crane recommended that Hayek recruit men like Sun Oil's J. Howard Pew and the Chicago salt magnate Sterling Morton (who had headed the Industrial Division of the Republican Party during the 1936 campaign and who in the 1950s still gleefully referred to himself as a "Bourbon" or a member of the "old guard"). Pew and Morton might want to join the society—and, more important, might give money to the cause; perhaps the society, Crane suggested, might no longer feel the need to eschew business and businessmen quite as firmly as it once had. "While the membership of the Mont Pelerin Society is and should be predominantly academic, I believe a small admixture of dedicated businessmen is desirable. As the European members get to know them, or I suppose I should say us, they may lose some of their distrust of capitalists." Hayek took Crane's advice. Pew and Morton both became members of Mont Pelerin, as did a few other businessmen: the conservative Indianapolis lawyer and businessman Pierre Goodrich (who, though not related to the Goodrich tire company executive who had helped FEE get off the ground, was an enthusiastic member of FEE's board of trustees for many years; he would call Leonard Read at all hours of the night to talk about politics and economics); William Grede, a midwestern manufacturer who was at the founding meeting of the John Birch Society; and George Koether of U.S. Steel.[45]

Over the subsequent year and a half, Crane raised money for the American meeting, sending letters to dozens of businessmen and small right-wing foundations. His initial pitch described the reasons that men of practical affairs should take an interest in an obscure intellectual society like Mont Pelerin: "While freedom in economic affairs still seems to be losing ground politically throughout most of the world, there is at least one encouraging sign. Among educators there is more awareness of the concept of freedom and increased interest in it. Some of them even evidence a retreat from collectivist philosophy, which has so long dominated academic thinking, and a groping toward a better understanding of liberty." While many potential donors turned Crane down, he persuaded thirty-five wealthy individuals and foundations to help fund the American meeting (he himself contributed $5,000, the very amount that he had deemed too much only a few years earlier). The total amount collected for the meeting was a little over $40,000.[46]

Crane's enthusiastic fund-raising gave him a certain sense of entitlement regarding the program of the conference, and he consulted with Read and others at FEE about it. Commenting on a draft, he wrote, "I only hope there is no slip-up by which any compromisers with basic principles would get on the program." He urged Hayek to think about how to have the "maximum degree of prevention of attacks on genuine free enterprise in the American meeting." Still, a sense of decorum prevented him from interfering in the program too much, except on one point in particular: Crane and the other businessmen donors wanted Ludwig von Mises to play a more central role in the conference than Hayek had originally envisioned. Pierre Goodrich wrote to Crane to tell him that he believed Mises was a critically important thinker and that he should play a prominent role in the conference: "This is Hayek's society, of course, in the sense that he has been president of it for a long time but there is also in this First American Meeting a top place for Von Mises." Crane relayed the message to Hayek. Hayek responded by telling Crane that he would permit Mises to give a keynote address—and that Goodrich (who had donated money to the conference) could even offer a comment or a paper of his own following Mises if he was so inclined.[47]

Crane's attempts to determine the program irritated and alienated some of the other intellectuals. Fritz Machlup, a Johns Hopkins professor who was the treasurer of the society, wrote to Hayek after a meeting of the financial committee, complaining that Crane had tried to discuss the program at the meeting, saying that he had a "great interest" in it because of assurances he had given to the donors. Hayek responded, "Crane is sometimes a little bit of a nuisance but on the whole I have been fairly successful at disregarding suggestions from him I did not like."[48]

Crane also sought to find ways to involve businessmen more deeply in the Mont Pelerin Society, as part of his project of showing intellectuals and "capitalists" that they had little to fear from each other. In early June he sent Hayek a long list of people to invite to the conference, a virtual Who's Who of the business right. He recommended General Robert E. Wood, the president of Sears, Roebuck, who had been an early supporter of America First, the isolationist organization committed to keeping the United States out of World War II; Roger Milliken, a fiercely anti-union textile manufacturer and family friend of William F. Buckley, who donated money to the conference; B E. Hutchinson, the retired finance chair of Chrysler; and the president and chair, respectively, of Beech Aircraft and United Fruit Company, both of whom contributed money to the conference as well. And of course Crane hoped that Hayek would issue an invitation to Walter Carpenter, the chairman of the board at DuPont, as well as Lammot du Pont Copeland (a DuPont executive and a member of the clan—nephew to Pierre, Irénée, and Lammot), both of whom Crane had imposed upon for donations.[49]

Crane tried to shape the American meeting in one final way. He had a vision of taking the European visitors from Princeton, where the meeting was to be held, to view the wonders of American industry in the West. "I am exceedingly anxious that they see something of America beside the Atlantic Seaboard, for one of the great values of the meeting of the Mont Pelerin Society is that these foreign economists, political scientists, historians, and other educators, who know nothing of America, should receive on this visit to the United States some idea of the American way of life, cultural values, and philosophy," he wrote to John Holmes, an executive of the Chicago meatpacking firm Swift & Company. He dreamed of taking the foreign visitors on a trip to the great historic sites of American capitalism—"the stock yards, one of the big banks." In the end, Crane's vision of taking the scholars to Chicago, Cleveland, and Detroit and beyond proved neither financially nor logistically feasible. Instead, on breaks from their conference, the leading free-market intellectuals of Europe took tours of a shopping mall, Tidewater Oil Company, U.S. Steel's Fairless Works, and, of course, DuPont.[50]

The American meeting finally took place in September 1958. It was the largest meeting in the brief history of the Mont Pelerin Society. Ludwig von Mises delivered a keynote address on "Liberty and Property," and the Indianapolis businessman and donor Pierre Goodrich gave a speech entitled "Why Liberty?" The program featured panels on inflation (including papers by Milton Friedman and Henry Hazlitt) and the welfare state (William Grede gave a paper on the "Moral Effects of the Welfare State"). But despite these successes, the conference failed to garner as much attention and publicity as Crane had hoped, and he was a bit disappointed. The experience of the meeting was also marred for him by the erratic behavior of one of the society's European donors, who got into screaming fights with various people at Princeton, did not arrange promised publicity, criticized the United States from the podium, and, worst of all, espoused economics that (in the words of one anonymous observer) "seemed at variance with that professed in the aims of the Mont Pelerin Society." Although Crane remained convinced of the society's importance and ability to provide "international cooperation on behalf of the ideas that we cherish so much of human liberty and the free market place," he never attempted anything as dramatic as the Princeton fund-raising effort again.[51]

But he still continued to participate in the society. He tried to take some of his business friends to Oxford for the 1959 gathering, and he corresponded with British leaders in the world of free-market intellectual life, writing to Ralph Harris (the founder of the Institute for Economic Affairs, the first laissez-faire think tank in England) that he thought—quoting a friend—it would be a good idea to "'invade'" India with "sound economic teaching." Crane's ultimate faith in the power of ideas remained undimmed.[52]

THE VOLKER FUND paid Hayek's salary for ten years, as promised, after which Hayek left the University of Chicago. The fund closed up shop in 1964. Its final president, Ivan Bierley, wrote to Hayek that he planned to go into real estate sales in California instead: "The change from selling ideas to serving the participants in the real estate market is a natural one."[53]

It is not clear that the romantic, political free-market approach of the Mont Pelerin Society would have survived without the support of businessmen like Crane. It was an oddity in intellectual circles in 1950s America. In economics departments, mathematical economics was the rage, focused primarily on inventing new and improved statistical forecasting techniques. Its practitioners, while operating in a generally Keynesian framework, did not concern themselves overmuch with political or theoretical questions. They cared more about methods than about theories, and were more interested in finding ways to measure the significance of particular economic variables than in the nature of freedom or the right relationship between state and society. By contrast, Hayek and Mises—whose work was never heavily mathematical—stood out for their insistence that freedom was at the heart of economic life. Instead of equations, they wrote political texts. Their politics helped them gain support and admirers in the business world. Their vision of the marketplace helped to inspire a deep suspicion of any expansion of the state, which was adopted by many conservative businessmen and activists. Whether or not they read Hayek or Mises in the original, they became familiar with their core ideas through endless repetition and reiteration by think tanks like Leonard Read's Foundation for Economic Education. The work of these two thinkers became, as Jasper Crane had hoped, a bible for those who wanted to turn back the New Deal.

3 Changing the Climate

W. C. Mullendore, who had initially inspired Leonard Read with the power of big ideas, remained skeptical that lofty goals could have any impact on practical realities. From the beginning, he was pessimistic about the likelihood of FEE's success: "You have imagined a project on a grand scale which cannot be sustained on the scale which you are planning, once the project hits the cold reality of the humdrum world in which it will be floundering after you have launched it in one of your high bursts of enthusiasm," he warned his friend. He believed that the confusion and political timidity of other businessmen made any effort like FEE largely irrelevant. He insisted that "unless and until we can get some concerted and consistent effort on the part of business leadership in the country in telling their stockholders, their employees and all of their friends the truth about conditions," the efforts of FEE would be "wasted."[1]

At the same time, however, Mullendore began to use his own position at Southern California Edison Company to spread his views. One of the few moments of political optimism he experienced came when he broke a two-month-long strike at the company in 1953 (the *L.A. Times* wrote that it was "one of the very few strikes in the last 20 years which was won by an employing company"). He told Read that fighting the union—"men licensed by government to use fraud, violence and intimidation to the point of threatening civil disorder sufficient to ruin a community"—was "a great experience, in which I have come more closely to grips with the basic human conflict in the world today than I have come at any previous time in my life." He used the company's quarterly reports to send out political messages—warning, for example, that "our free enterprise system has been replaced by a Government-guided economy (the welfare state), and all free enterprise is basically weakened and endangered." Ayn Rand, a fresh star in the free-market world, wrote to Mullendore to praise these messages to stockholders: "I was glad to see a business leader telling people the truth, and telling it as well and clearly as you did." Mullendore saw himself as a Cassandra figure—if he could not stop the cataclysm, at least he had done what he could to sound the alarm, and he hoped that perhaps his efforts would inspire other businessmen to stand up. "The next life I live will be as a hermit philosopher—not as a corporation executive in a disintegrating world anyway I hope," he wrote to Read. "What a life!"[2]

The indefatigable Read, however, forged ahead despite Mullendore's pessimism, collecting ample donations for FEE from corporate supporters large and small. In 1948 and 1949, for example, companies like Consolidated Edison, U.S. Steel, General Motors, and Chrysler gave FEE $10,000 each, while firms like Honolulu Oil gave smaller donations. The new group purchased and moved into a dilapidated but spacious old mansion in Irvington, New York, a little more than twenty miles north of Manhattan. Over the fireplace, Read installed a plaque with the motto "If to please the people, we offer what we ourselves disapprove, how can we afterward defend our work. Let us raise a standard to which the wise and honest can repair. The rest is in the hands of GOD."[3]

Although Read worked to raise money from business contacts, he never used anything like direct mail to solicit donations. He professed confidence that FEE would succeed or fail in a purely free market, simply taking contributions that came voluntarily from those who read the group's material and were moved to give. "*The Foundation has no source of revenue except voluntary donations*," the group's flyers reminded readers. When people asked him how the group fared financially, Read liked to reply cheerfully that everything was perfect—the donations FEE received were exactly as much as people had been persuaded to give, the implication being that if the organization went bankrupt, that would simply be in keeping with the precepts of the marketplace.[4]

Read hired Ludwig von Mises as a staff member at FEE and helped to finance a part-time position for him at the Stern School of Business at New York University. He wrote Hayek admiring letters, telling the Austrian how much he had learned from his work. Read relished this personal connection, at times asking Hayek for special favors—for example, to bring some Maldon salt back from Europe after a trip. "This seems like a silly request to make of a great economist, doesn't it?" (A bit of a gourmand, Read also corresponded with the chef and cookbook author James Beard about restaurants and gourmet coffee.) When Jasper Crane wrote to Irénée du Pont to raise money for the 1958 Mont Pelerin Society meeting at Princeton, he described Mont Pelerin as "largely influenced by FEE," although he also said that it was necessary to downplay the connection "as we don't want the foreigners to think we are trying to run the show." (Just as he bristled at Crane's attempts to guide the Mont Pelerin Society, Hayek found Read and his broad, propagandistic efforts somewhat annoying. In the early years of Mont Pelerin, he complained that the American contingent at meetings was dominated by people from FEE.)[5]

But while Read learned much from the Mont Pelerin economists, his own organization was relentlessly populist. He was a proselytizer, trying to sell businessmen on the one true faith. The organization made no pretext of influencing important people, nor did it really make much of an effort to shape legislation or policy. Read believed that this would be impossible until the consciousness of the corporate world had changed and that therefore the important task was only to educate. He claimed to believe that no audience was too small—the future needed to be won by persuading one individual at a time. A chance encounter with a businessman on a train or at a meeting might be as important as getting an analysis of a bill into the hands of a noted senator—who knew what the outcomes of any action might be, no matter how seemingly insignificant? The main thing was convincing businessmen to give up their complacent attitudes and take the struggle seriously. The greatest contribution that anyone could make in the campaign for freedom was simply developing his or her own ability to expound upon the virtues of the free market. "The nation cannot be saved," he explained in a 1947 speech to the Commercial Club of Chicago. "Only individuals can be saved from error. Now, whose thinking can I save? Only my own!"[6]

OVER THE COURSE of the 1950s, dozens of new organizations devoted to the defense of free enterprise and the struggle against labor unions and the welfare state sprang into existence, with the support of business-oriented conservatives like Mullendore, Read, Crane, and Luhnow. These groups avoided the harsh glare of electoral politics. Money could, after all, support ideas, print legislative analyses, and hire scholars far more easily than it could create a mass following in support of conservative economic policies.

The economic conservatives of the 1950s positioned themselves in opposition to the politics they saw embodied by the presidency of General Dwight D. Eisenhower. Ike, as he was known, went to the White House after a career in the military and a brief stint as president of Columbia University; a genial, friendly man, he was often mocked by liberals for his love of golf, poker, bridge, and western novels. The first Republican president since Herbert Hoover, Eisenhower sought to reorient his party. He described himself as a "modern Republican," by which he meant a Republican who would not seek to undo the New Deal. As he wrote to his brother Edgar (who tried to push him to adopt more doctrinaire conservative views), "Should any political party attempt to abolish social security, unemployment insurance, and eliminate labor laws and farm programs, you would not hear of that party again in our political history." But his insistence that the United States needed to move in a new political direction also reflected his sincere hope that twentieth-century capitalism could be reformed so that America was no longer divided by class or economic conflict. The Eisenhower administration did not simply tolerate the New Deal. It actively embraced the idea that government could play a positive role in society by transcending the narrow self-interest of economic classes and mediating conflicts between social groups.[7]

Eisenhower believed that the old Republican faith in laissez-faire needed to be updated to reflect the realities of modern capitalism. Government should, he thought, "prevent or correct abuses springing from the unregulated practice of a private economy." He wrote to a business leader in 1952 that he believed that economic inequality was the greatest danger facing America. While he welcomed businessmen into his administration—critics referred to his cabinet as consisting of "eight millionaires and a plumber" (although the plumber, the secretary of labor, was soon replaced by a labor relations manager from Macy's)—he mistrusted the shortsighted or selfish demands of business nearly as much as those of labor unions. His undersecretary of labor, Arthur Larson, wrote a poetic credo of modern Republicanism entitled *A Republican Looks at His Party*, which Eisenhower endorsed with enthusiasm. Modern Republicans, Larson argued, were "in favor of trade unionism," which raised wages and helped to generate the social solidarity that was needed in the fight against communism. Eisenhower and Larson wanted Republicanism to become a "political movement for the mid-century."[8]

The businessmen of the National Association of Manufacturers, those who contributed to the Mont Pelerin Society, the small manufacturers and retired executives and management men who resented the power of unions—all reacted to Eisenhower's endorsement of the basic principles and framework of the New Deal with shocked dismay. Few went as far as Robert Welch, the candy manufacturer from Massachusetts and founder of the John Birch Society, who suggested that Eisenhower was literally a Communist agent, but the sentiment that Ike was a "collectivist" was widely shared. Believing that the growing power of organized labor and the limits on business endangered the entire country, they thought that there was no point in starting with the Republican Party, which no longer represented their views. The intellectual and political culture of the United States needed to be completely transformed. At a time when leading liberal intellectuals like Daniel Bell and Arthur M. Schlesinger, Jr., argued that the rise of fascism and Soviet communism had shattered the capacity for faith in ideology in the West, insisting that most conservatives and liberals alike agreed on the welfare state and the limits of government power, these free-market activists understood, in a way that the liberal thinkers did not, the importance of ideas and the need to shape the terms of debate.[9]

This early mobilization of conservative businessmen helped give life to the cultural and intellectual institutions of the conservative movement. Although the donations they gave were small in comparison to the total profits of their corporations, they were of great importance in building the movement. And the role that the businessmen played in these institutions—whether by donating money to think tanks or by reading the studies those think tanks produced—helped to shape their political awareness as part of a network of business activists.[10]

THE FREE-MARKET movement that had started in the 1930s grew and gained momentum against the backdrop of McCarthyism and the broader climate of anti-Communist politics. All of the institutions of American society—not just the far right—joined in the anti-Communist purge of the early 1950s. But business conservatives helped to drive some of the most extreme parts of the reaction. Although by 1954 many executives were becoming critical of Senator Joseph McCarthy, a *Fortune* survey of businessmen found that even some of his critics were reluctant to reject him completely; as the president of Quaker Oats said, "He's kind of careless with the facts; his arithmetic doesn't always add up; and he goes off the deep end every now and then. Even so, the net overall job is to the good." Robert E. Wood of Sears, Roebuck was less ambivalent: "McCarthy is doing a job that had to be done to put traitors and spies out of our government. You can't be soft with these people." And companies also supported groups like the American Security Council, which claimed to keep private files on more than 1 million people who were said to be possible members of the Communist Party or at least supporters of "statist" policies, and then disseminated the information to member corporations (which included companies such as Motorola, Sears, and Marshall Field) as well as the FBI. Fred Schwarz's Christian Anti-Communism Crusade, which ran open-air meetings to warn of the Soviet menace, attended by thousands in California's sunny Southland, received the enthusiastic backing of Walter Knott (of Knott's Berry Farm fame), Sun Oil executive J. Howard Pew's foundation, Richfield Oil, and the Rotary Club of Los Angeles. In front of rapt crowds, Schwarz, an Australian doctor and evangelical lay minister, described the terrorizing methods that the Communists would use against any owners of common stock when they took over the United States, an event he predicted would come to pass in 1973: "When they come for you . . . on a dark night, in a dank cellar, and they take a wide bore revolver with a soft nose bullet, and they place it at the nape of your neck . . ."[11]

In the fall of 1958, Robert Welch, who had served as a vice president of the National Association of Manufacturers, gathered eleven like-minded industrialists in an Indianapolis home to start a disciplined, secretive organization committed to protecting American institutions against the Communist threat. The John Birch Society, named for an American missionary who had been killed by Chinese Communists right after the end of World War II, advocated working outside the political system to strengthen American patriotism ("Join your local PTA at the beginning of the school year, and go to work and take it over!"). Its adherents lived in a strange world of conspiracy and fantasy, seeing communism and its agents lurking everywhere; as Welch said in one speech, "We are living in fantastic times and a fantastic situation . . . We are in circumstances where it is *realistic* to be *fantastic*." In addition to being a successful manufacturer, Welch had been a theorist of salesmanship before he became a conservative activist (he wrote a book on the subject, *The Road to Salesmanship*, published in 1941), and the John Birch Society employed more than twenty full-time staffers, who went door-to-door recruiting members. Tens of thousands of people eventually joined the organization, many of them solid members of the professional middle class.[12]

Individual corporations such as the defense giant Lockheed Martin also started their own education programs to combat communism in the ranks of their employees. "Wherever Communists have gained power, there have followed bloody purges, slave labor, concentration camps, and ruthless control over every phase of human life," read a circular distributed to all Lockheed's employees. (The National Association of Manufacturers commended the program and suggested that other employers follow Lockheed's example.)[13]

The free-market conservatives took the nightmarish fears inspired by anticommunism and turned them against the entire liberal state, making it seem as though the minimum wage and labor unions were about to usher in a new era of political enslavement. No spies were needed, no conscious treachery—the logic of liberalism itself was the threat. They used the shadow of the Communist danger to bolster their case that dismantling the welfare state was a crusade for freedom. Years after McCar thy had been repudiated, they continued to fight for the market using the tropes they had developed when anticommunism was at its zenith.

The American Enterprise Association (AEA) did not attack communism or try to ferret out internal subversion. Nor did it seek to persuade random people of the beauty of the market, as did Leonard Read and his Foundation for Economic Education. Rather, the association wanted to appear objective, respectable, and neutral, to issue insightful formal reports by people with impeccable academic credentials, and to get its analyses and studies into the hands of the political elite—politicians, journalists, and editors. It sought to advance a critique of modern Republicanism and the contemporary political scene of the 1950s without being accused of being a mere pawn of business (as had been the fate of the Liberty League). And it wanted to do all this while raising money from the business world and building a board of trustees filled with executives from companies such as Coca-Cola, Socony Mobil Oil Company, U.S. Steel, and Eli Lilly. Companies like U.S. Steel bargained with their labor unions; these major industrial companies might not be willing to break openly with the Eisenhower administration or the principles of postwar liberalism. But they also sought to finance the intellectual opposition where they could.[14]

AEA had been founded in 1943 by one of the businessmen who had struggled to protect the public image of business during the New Deal. Lewis H. Brown was an up-and-coming entrepreneurial star in the late 1920s, and in 1929, at the age of thirty-five, he became the president of the Johns-Manville Corporation, a prominent roofing and insulation company. Brown had been distraught about the Depression. "The profit incentive is . . . under general attack," he told an audience of two thousand businessmen in the spring of 1936. "It is denounced as something reprehensible, something to be held in leash by administrative regulation and penalized by statute." Public relations, he decided, was the answer. Brown started an educational program at Johns-Manville, distributing pamphlets and company reports to workers (he referred to them as "jobholders' reports") in an effort to give his employees the sense that they were in capable hands. In towns where the company had plants, he handed out booklets on such topics as its policy on the closed shop, and he hired a cartoonist to do advertisements for local newspapers. But during World War II, Brown determined to go further. It was no longer enough to proselytize only to his workers. He wanted a broader platform. Along with several friends and allies in the business community, he decided to found the American Enterprise Association, to provide congressmen with legislative analyses that he promised would be free of a left-wing bias.[15]

Despite a handful of sharp young staffers (including Phyllis Schlafly, who worked at the group after earning her master's at Radcliffe, decades before she would become well known for her crusade against the passage of the Equal Rights Amendment in the 1970s), a high-profile board of trustees, and some good political connections, AEA floundered in its early years. The group received much less attention and publicity than the Committee for Economic Development—the major business organization devoted to fostering Keynesian perspectives among businessmen. And it nearly fell apart altogether when Congress conducted an investigation into its structure and financing, part of a larger look into who paid the bills for conservative groups. The investigation revealed that nearly all AEA's money came from major corporations, including General Motors ($7,500 in 1949), Ford ($5,000), Chrysler ($3,750), and Con Edison

($3,400); the du Pont family made generous contributions as well, with Lammot du Pont giving $5,000. The congressmen leading the investigation argued that AEA could not possibly serve the disinterested research function to which it aspired. "Can we, for example, assume that the Nation's largest industries would continue to support AEA if it were sponsoring views with which these industries were in basic disagreement?" asked the congressional committee in its final report, arguing that AEA was trying to hide behind a "self-serving façade of objectivity" while "claiming more than human immunity from the pressures of self-interest."[16]

The investigation marked a major crisis for AEA, even though Congress did not take away its tax-exempt status. After Lewis Brown died, in 1951, it looked for a little while as if AEA might disappear. But in 1954, Allen Marshall, then an executive at General Electric, took over as its president. Marshall, who would soon become a vice president at General Dynamics, one of the largest weapons manufacturers in the United States, in turn hired a new full-time staffer, William J. Baroody. Baroody built the flailing organization into a thriving think tank by creating a network of support among businessmen. Carefully, methodically, he talked to one executive after another, following up with invitations to meetings, personal letters, and requests for the businessman to talk to others in his industry. In building this web of financial contributors, Baroody not only sought to strengthen his organization. Raising money was an organizing strategy, a way of deepening and expanding political support.[17]

Baroody was the son of a Lebanese stonecutter. When his father emigrated from Lebanon to the United States, he barely spoke English, and he learned the language from his Irish neighbors in New Hampshire (in fact, Baroody's father had a brogue throughout his life). Baroody grew up an outsider, as an Arab in an Irish-Catholic community (the Baroodys were Melkite Catholics). As a high school senior, he won an open competition for the privilege of giving a public oration on St. Patrick's Day. But his priest barred him from actually giving the speech, whispering that there would surely be a riot if "a Baroody" gave the address. Such episodes of discrimination only made Baroody all the more committed to outsmarting the competition. He became valedictorian of his class, attended graduate school at American University, and then worked at the Veterans Administration (one political rival dismissed him for this as a "former New Dealer") before taking a post at the Committee on Economic Security of the U.S. Chamber of Commerce in 1950. Baroody never sought public office. Nor did he care much about conspicuous consumption; he sometimes wore the same shirt and tie to the office several days in a row. A behind-the-scenes operator, he liked to keep himself out of the public eye, once telling a reporter that "in the Arab tribes, in the ancient times, the Baroodys were known as the tribal conciliators."[18]

Yet despite his modest appearance, Baroody was a driven man with profound ambitions for his new think tank. In a letter he wrote to one potential donor a few years after his arrival at AEA, he argued that liberals had surreptitiously managed to gain control over the public debate. "I, for one, have long been convinced that the climate of a particular society is, to a substantial degree, the product of ideas emanating from its thought leaders—and ideas are the most powerful of forces," he wrote. The problem was that "the leftist movement derives a substantial portion of its strength from its virtual monopoly of the so-called intellectual segment of American society." This position of power was not the result of coincidence or unhappy accident; it had come about "through systematic employment of techniques and devices designed to establish what might loosely be referred to as an intellectual reservoir of leftist ideology." The left controlled academia, and as a result leftists had an "aura of respectability" that could not be "matched by existing resources on the conservative side of the fence." The answer was to create an alternative "intellectual reservoir," one committed to conservatism, a new network outside the university system. "This is no overnight miracle-passing operation," Baroody warned. "It will take time, financial resources, and the exercise of good brain power."[19]

Marshalling those financial resources was the center of Baroody's mission at AEA. He hoped that corporate executives could fill the role envisioned a decade earlier by the conservative intellectual Albert Jay Nock: that of the Remnant, the small group of committed believers who would shepherd conservatism through the dark days of powerlessness, keeping the ideal alive until a more propitious time. As he wrote to William McGrath of the Williamson Heater Company, "It strikes me that there must be literally scores of other companies who share your interest in the preservation of the competitive enterprise system and our form of government . . . It is up to us 'remnants' to pull together in the common effort." Once he went to AEA, Baroody wrote letters to everyone who had ever donated money to the organization, asking them to give; he called companies whose subscriptions had lapsed "revivals," while those who had actively resigned were dubbed "resurrections." After reaching out to all former donors, he made a lengthy list of companies linked by their common interest in "social legislation" and then proceeded to solicit contributions. The organization adopted a new slogan as part of the drive: "A Business Investment in Good Legislation."[20]

But he didn't do it alone. Turning basic fund-raising principles to a new purpose, Baroody sought to motivate other businessmen to contact their friends, business associates, and industry acquaintances to urge them to donate to AEA. With a personal touch, idle apathy could be transformed into a rich source of funds. Baroody carefully picked the trustees for AEA with an eye to winning donations. Adding "top-notch men to the Board of Trustees," he argued, would impress the titans of the corporate world. He would send the executives on the board lists of companies to target and ask them to take responsibility for making the initial contact: "All we are asking is that 'the door be opened' and we will follow up." Businessmen needed to speak to other businessmen, setting up meetings to which AEA staff members could go to make the pitch. "There appears to be no satisfactory substitute for a person to person contact," he wrote to a trustee disappointed by the difficulties of fund-raising; Baroody urged him to try again through personal channels. When businessmen succeeded in winning donations from their friends, he would write them enthusiastic little notes; for example, he wrote to B. E. Hutchinson, a retired finance chairman at Chrysler: "You certainly drew blood fast on Woodall Industries."[21]

Baroody tried to make sure that the organization's research would get to people who could help raise money. When AEA decided to do a study of transportation regulation in the late 1950s, he wrote straightaway to the chairman of the American Car and Foundry Company, telling him of the project and asking if he could help raise money from a small foundation in order to make it happen. The executive happily obliged, and when the study was published, the company ordered five hundred copies.[22]

By 1958, AEA was receiving contributions from twenty-six of the fifty largest industrial corporations in the country. "More and more people in the business community are becoming aware of AEA's work," Baroody wrote in a note to Marshall, describing the "steady though not spectacular" progress of the group. A few years later, in 1962, the group received donations of $10,000 or more from companies such as Allen-Bradley, Ford, General Motors, General Electric, Socony Mobil, and U.S. Steel (as well as from corporate foundations like the Kresge Foundation and the Lilly Endowment), along with smaller donations from companies like Procter & Gamble, Armstrong Cork, and Youngstown Sheet & Tube. And the organization's reach in Washington was increasing. By the end of the 1950s, Baroody could claim that 75 percent of representatives and 84 percent of senators received AEA's bill analyses and studies.[23]

Although AEA did "spot analyses," brief reports that summarized the arguments for and against pending legislation, Baroody had greater intellectual ambitions. He felt confident that broader and more sophisticated ideas would be needed to bring about the sea change in American political culture he dreamed of. To that end, AEA also published longer reports critical of unions and the welfare state, which took a more openly political stance, even though they eschewed overtly partisan politics and generally refrained from direct criticism of Eisenhower. In the late 1950s, the organization embarked on an ambitious interdisciplinary project on the American labor movement. The underlying assumption was that unions were abridging the freedoms of the nation. The reports sought to encourage the American public to identify labor unions with monopolies, knowing that "the anti-monopoly tradition is one of the most powerful influences in American life." One 1957 report found that unions did not really raise wages. Another argued that unions received legal privileges comparable only to those exercised by kings. A third insisted that "autocracy" was rising within labor unions. Other AEA-commissioned studies condemned the Tennessee Valley Authority as "neo-feudalism," rejected federal aid to education, and argued in favor of giving Congress veto power over foreign treaties (this last was a favorite preoccupation of the right during the 1950s, limiting the power of the executive branch to determine foreign policy).[24]

The long-range studies were just the beginning for Baroody—his ultimate vision was of a network of conservative think tanks that could rival the university system. In addition to his work at AEA, he was involved in founding several other conservative intellectual organizations, including the Center for Strategic Studies at Georgetown (which provided a foreign policy counterpart to the domestic focus of AEA) and the Hoover Institution at Stanford. Nor did Baroody's ambitions stop with the United States; like that of the men of Mont Pelerin, his vision was international. Through his contacts in the foundation world, he became acquainted with the leaders of the first conservative think tanks in Europe—men like Ralph Harris, the founder of the Institute for Economic Affairs, the counterpart of AEA in Britain.[25]

At the heart of Baroody's vision remained a network of businessmen, mobilized and poised to deploy their money strategically to uphold the free-market order. In a way, Baroody's analysis was deeply materialist, rooted in a sense of the links between money and power. Yet at the same time, perhaps remembering the scandal in 1950 when Congress threatened to strip AEA of its tax-exempt status, Baroody was acutely aware of the need to disguise the roots of his organization, to keep it from being dismissed as a businessman's group. In 1962 the executive committee of the board of trustees recommended that AEA change its name to the American Enterprise Institute for Public Policy Research, so that it would no longer be confused with a "trade association" lobbying on behalf of business; the new name would "more accurately describe the nature and legal status of the organization." An "association" sounded like the Chamber of Commerce or the National Association of Manufacturers—an institute, on the other hand, was austere, noble, and pure.[26]

During the 1950s, when their views were not represented by the leadership of either of the two political parties, activists such as William J.

Baroody and Leonard Read sought and won support from leading corporations to nurture free-market politics. They had different approaches—Read wanted FEE to be devoted above all to the pursuit of market ideals, while Baroody tried to create an organization that would subtly advance the cause while being perceived as engaged in serious research—but they pursued the same ultimate goal of undermining and challenging the intellectual defenses of liberalism. While they labored to create their think tanks, however, another group of activists was more interested in winning support from business to fund media outlets and organizations that could bring the ideas of the free-market movement to a broader public, out from the sanctum of the intellectual, political, and economic elite into the literal marketplace of ideas.

4 Cultural Politics: Churches, Radio Stations, and Magazines

AMONG LEONARD READ'S friends and FEE's early supporters was Ayn Rand, the novelist whose books—*The Fountainhead*, published in 1943, an international phenomenon made into a Hollywood movie starring Gary Cooper, and *Atlas Shrugged*, published in 1957—were polemical paeans to the idea that there was no morality higher than pursuing one's own self-interest. "I consider you the only man in my acquaintance who has the capacity to translate abstract ideas into practical action and to become a great executor of great principles," she wrote to Read early in 1946. However, Rand thought that FEE should do more to take aim at the underlying moral system that, she was persuaded, supported collectivism—the idea that people should be devoted to an idea of the "common good," that they were obligated to aid the poor and those less fortunate, that "everybody is responsible for everybody's welfare." This moral code, more than mistaken ideas about economics, was, she believed, the real danger to capitalism. But although she wished that FEE would set its sights higher than mere "economic education," she still offered the group her tentative support in its early days.[1]

It did not take long for the volatile Rand to break with FEE, and by the end of its first year she was alienated from the new organization. The conflict came over her sharp criticism of *Roofs or Ceilings?*, a pamphlet written by the economists Milton Friedman and George Stigler that criticized the inefficiencies of rent control (the National Association of Real Estate Boards purchased half a million copies). Friedman and Stigler argued that rent controls were counterproductive because they reduced the incentive for the construction of new housing while encouraging the rise of a black market in rental apartments. For Rand, although she shared their antipathy to controls, this kind of economic argument seemed akin to compromise, as she believed that the defense of the market had always to go back to first principles: that people (including landlords) had an inalienable right to do as they wished with their property, and that social obligations were only a myth used by the weak to hamper the strong. Enraged by what she saw as the economists' deviation, she wrote to Read, "I presume that you do not know what your booklet actually advocates. So I had better tell you: It advocates the nationalization of private homes." Rand became even more infuriated when she learned that Read had circulated a document she had written to offer intellectual guidance to FEE for the criticism of other members of the organization. She had little desire to hear what others had to say—in fact, she had initially offered to review all the documents published by the new organization to make sure that they would live up to free-market principles, or, in her words, "to protect your publications from internal treachery." She wrote Read another outraged missive, saying that she would have nothing more to do with FEE.[2]

Rand's forceful repudiation of any claim to ethics outside of self-interest horrified traditionalist conservatives like William F. Buckley of the *National Review* as well as the anti-Communist writer Whittaker Chambers, who argued that Rand's work was shrill and dogmatic and that a revival of religious values needed to be at the heart of any true conservatism. Rand, for her part, called herself a "radical for capitalism" (explicitly distinguishing herself from the conservatives) and rejected any association with "altruism" or Christian ethics. She was tremendously popular among businessmen.[3]

Still, as much as business conservatives were fans of Rand's work, not all of them were happy with her rejection of Christianity. Some of them were religious themselves and wanted to find a way to reconcile their spiritual beliefs with their market enthusiasms. Others simply believed it was politically important to demonstrate that capitalist principles did not in fact contradict Christian ethics. One of the former was J. Howard Pew.

PEW SERVED as president of Sun Oil, the company that his father had started in the late nineteenth century, for thirty-five years. Even after stepping down from the corporate presidency in 1947, he remained involved with the company, first as a member of the board of trustees and then as the chairman of the executive committee. But like his good friend Jasper Crane, Pew felt that he had another calling.

Pew was a devout Presbyterian, and in the years that followed World War II, his most abiding preoccupation was rescuing the Protestant church in America from what he saw as the dangerous influence of liberal ministers. A small but influential religious left had emerged in the 1930s, led by the theologian Reinhold Niebuhr. In the words of the religious historian Ronald Wuthnow, these religious liberals advocated "a 'third way' between capitalism and Communism—something resembling democratic socialism but legitimated by Christian theology." This socially liberal Christianity was not the only or even the dominant force within the churches in the 1930s, 1940s, and 1950s, years that also saw the spread of the fundamentalist movement, with the creation of organizations such as the National Association of Evangelicals and Youth for Christ. But the growing strength of fundamentalism within Protestant circles did not allay the fears of business conservatives like Pew. In 1951, he wrote to a friend, "We can never hope to stop this Country's plunge toward totalitarianism until we have gotten the ministers' thinking straight."[4]

Near the end of World War II, Pew began to work with James Fifield, a minister in Los Angeles, on an organization named Spiritual Mobilization, which sought (in Pew's words) to foster the "development among the clergymen of this country, of a proper conception of just what constitutes our American way of life and how this ties in with sound religious principles." Fifield had started Spiritual Mobilization during the 1930s, but he wanted Pew's help to build the group. Pew, in return, viewed Fifield as a needed ally. "The New Deal is in a much stronger position than it has been for the last several years," he wrote to the minister in 1944. Part of the reason was that businessmen (like Pew himself) were vulnerable to "character assassination" for their political efforts—which meant that the job of fighting the New Deal could be "much better done by others." (At the same time, Pew maintained that he himself was motivated solely by idealism: "My attack on the New Deal has not been prompted by materialistic considerations, but rather a desire to preserve in America an opportunity for coming generations.") Together, Fifield and Pew planned to send out a hundred copies of Hayek's *Road to Serfdom* to ministers in order to "ascertain what their reactions are," and if they were positive, Pew wanted to "raise the money to send every minister in the United States such a book." Pew put himself to work raising money among businessmen for Spiritual Mobilization. While the group might not be perfect, he wrote in one solicitation letter, it was "worth to business and industry many, many times what it has cost." (Pew was also a supporter of FEE, which he described in religious terms; he wrote to his friend Jasper Crane that the organization was "evangelical, spreading the truth by pamphlets, books, and the use of other media.")[5]

The business conservatives of the 1950s were not the only people seeking to bring together religion and capitalism. The decade saw the rise of anti-Communist preachers such as Carl McIntire and Billy James Hargis, and also the growth of Christian Business Men's Committees, organizations of evangelical businessmen that were more concerned with religious revivalism than with politics (business leaders often featured prominently at the large-scale revival meetings of the 1940s). The fervor of the cold war was already dividing the globe into the God-fearing and the godless, which helped to spur the career of evangelicals such as Billy Graham. Organizations like the Family (otherwise known as the Fellowship Foundation), a network of businessmen and politicians that had been founded in Seattle in the 1930s by the anti–New Deal preacher Abraham Vereide, who tried to involve elite political officials in building a "worldwide spiritual offensive" (to quote one senator involved in the group) to combat communism. (Like the Mont Pelerin Society, the Family was not interested in populist uprisings; as Vereide wrote, "There has always been one man or a small core who have caught the vision for their country and become aware of what a 'leadership led by God' could mean spiritually to the nation and to the world.") But while they were only one small part of the broader attempt to integrate Christianity and anti-Communist politics during the decade, the efforts of men like Pew to enlist religion explicitly in the defense of laissez-faire suggests the desire of the business conservatives to find ways to show that market principles were compatible with divine truths.[6]

The result of this political impulse was Spiritual Mobilization, which took as its mission the invention of a theological justification for capitalism. As doctrinally liberal as it was politically conservative, Spiritual Mobilization never cared about literal, fundamentalist interpretations of scripture. Nor was it particularly concerned with evangelizing in the traditional sense. The organization proselytized not to save souls but rather to save American capitalism.

James Fifield was the minister of the First Congregational Church in downtown Los Angeles, a building with an ornate, cathedral-like façade, complete with an enormous round stained glass window. A dramatic preacher and consummate organization builder, he had left Grand Rapids, Michigan, in the middle of the Depression to go to Southern California. Despite its large physical plant, which included a stage, a gymnasium, fifty-six classrooms, three auditoriums, and a wedding chapel, the First Congregational was on the brink of collapse. Fifield managed to turn the church around financially, eliminating a debt of $750,000 within seven years of his arrival. By the late 1940s, the First Congregational was "the largest, best-known, the most talked-about Congregational church in the United States," in the words of one journalist. The church hosted five Sunday services (including a Golfers' Service at 8 A.M.), a daily radio program, classes in everything from world affairs to rumba dancing, and a

Church of Youth for the younger members of the congregation. Leonard Read was a member and trustee while he was at the Los Angeles Chamber of Commerce. All of the church's activities were tinged with Fifield's conservative politics. Fifield claimed that he had believed in the "social gospel" in his youth, until time and experience convinced him of the divine providence of capitalism. "The blessings of capitalism come from God," he wrote in his 1957 book, *The Single Path*. "A system that provides so much for the common good and happiness must flourish under the force of the Almighty."[7]

Spiritual Mobilization had a twofold mission: strengthening conservative economic ideas among Protestant leaders and bringing politically active businessmen into church leadership. Fifield said that when he first spoke to ministers about Spiritual Mobilization, not many were interested. But then a businessman came to talk to him about the "future of free enterprise," and he realized that if he could not work with pastors, then he could work with executives. His own ideas about capitalism were touched with social Darwinism. "Much of the energy of our so-called 'most civilized' people has been quite unconsciously spent in trying to thwart the laws of nature, which would make the fittest survive, and in supporting and upbuilding the weak, whom nature would destroy and who, if not allowed to pass off the scene as nature has decreed, rapidly multiply and numerically overpower those very people and nations who have sacrificed for their continued existence," he wrote. He was especially hostile to the idea of using the state to help end racial discrimination. In a 1946 sermon on Christian race relations, he criticized the "efforts of minorities to push in where they are not wanted," described the protests that followed the exclusion of the opera singer Marian Anderson from Washington, D.C.'s Constitution Hall as "an abomination unto the Lord," and denounced a proposed Fair Employment Practices Commission for California by saying that he had seen hundreds of official reports but had never "found a single instance of discrimination."[8]

Just as AEA believed that leftists had a "monopoly" on universities, Spiritual Mobilization argued that left-leaning clergymen exercised disproportionate power. "A tightly knit bureaucracy has fastened itself upon institutional religion, and has arrogated to itself the right to speak for the constituency which pays their salaries," wrote one supporter of the group to the conservative columnist and Mont Pelerin Society member Henry Hazlitt. The only way to limit the power of the "pink" seminarians was to urge business leaders to get involved in religious politics. As one proposal to bring together clergy and businessmen put it, "We must restore to the churches an asset which they badly need and do not have today—the wholehearted interest and dedication of top-flight leaders from the fields of education, science, business and the professions."[9]

No single author crystallized the group's beliefs; they emerged in a variety of places all at once. The basic argument was that Christianity had too long been associated with altruism, selflessness, and a devotion to helping the poor—principles that might lead good Christians to advocate government intervention in the economy. To counter this idea, Spiritual Mobilization insisted that Christianity was rightly associated with shrinking the welfare state. "All we can do, consonant with our Christian political responsibility, is to minimize the power and size of our government," read one article in the organization's magazine, *Faith and Freedom.* Far from rejecting self-interest, the members claimed, Christ actively employed it by telling doubters that only by following him could they attain eternal life. "We know that Jesus appealed to many motives, but at no time did He appeal to disinterested altruism," wrote one minister. "Instead, He constantly invoked the profit motive that social dreamers consider the root of all evil." (The head of the National Association of Manufacturers made a similar argument during the 1950s: "The Christian faith itself offers a tremendous incentive to its followers—the profit which they can hope to attain—of eternal salvation in the world to come.")[10]

Spiritual Mobilization engaged in a wide range of educational and propagandizing activities. In addition to publishing articles by conservative clergymen, *Faith and Freedom* provided a regular venue for major free-market thinkers such as Henry Hazlitt, Leonard Read, and Ludwig von Mises. The group ran a radio program called *The Freedom Story*. At one point the organization hoped to found a nondenominational Christian college to teach conservative economic and moral principles. This idea never came to fruition, but in the late 1950s the group did set up a ranch in San Jacinto, California, to serve as a spiritual headquarters. It held conferences, bringing together conservative clergy, and hosted various spiritual retreats for laymen and clergy. Spiritual Mobilization also sought to encourage ministers to get their congregations to vote. "How many members of your church are registered and vote regularly?" one pamphlet asked.[11]

The money to fund these various programs was donated by corporations, ranging from small firms to leading industrial companies. In the mid-1950s, major corporate contributors (donating more than $2,500) included the Chrysler Corporation, Colgate-Palmolive-Peet Company, General Motors, Gulf Oil Corporation, Sears, Roebuck, and U.S. Steel. Even in 1960, when Spiritual Mobilization was running into financial and organizational trouble, it could still attract donations from a blue-chip lineup of major industrial corporations.[12]

When crafting its corporate fund-raising appeals, Spiritual Mobilization pitched its message in pragmatic rhetoric aimed at the bottom line. All manner of economic ills—conflicts between labor and management, decreases in productivity, even "credit positions of major industries"—had their real roots in "the general impairment of spiritual relationships." Donating to Spiritual Mobilization meant making an investment in the country's "rapidly wasting spiritual capital." Improving the spiritual health of the country would lessen workplace conflict and generate economic growth—a kind of religious Keynesianism.[13]

But Spiritual Mobilization experienced increasing difficulty attracting support in the late 1950s. Its claim that the true Christian faith could be summarized in libertarian principles had always been somewhat incoherent. James Ingebretsen, its president in the 1950s, later confessed that he privately believed that religion was "balderdash" and that he had gone to Spiritual Mobilization as a lawyer and libertarian, not a minister: "Fighting the forces that wanted to abolish the free enterprise system was my mission, not promoting Christ!"[14]

The group took a bizarre turn in its declining years. Drawn to a British guru named Gerald Heard, its leaders became more interested in psychotropic drugs and inner spiritual exploration than political change. In ways that anticipated the psychedelic experiments of the 1960s counterculture, they began to test the boundaries of reality, dabbling in LSD. (W. C. Mullendore, Leonard Read's old teacher, was among those drawn to the new psychedelics. As he wrote to a friend in 1962, "LSD steps up our voltage and frequency. To use the new vision thus made available one must be able to 'plug in,' 'get in tune'—to 'harmonize' with this new environment which LSD opens for us to 'correspond with.'") In 1961, Ingebretsen decided to shut Spiritual Mobilization down. "I hope to devote my life and energies . . . to the search for a contemporary and creative spiritual response to the overwhelming problems which now face western man," he told Pew in a farewell letter. "It is only that I believe my temperament is best suited for, and that our present world situation calls for, much more personal, intimate, and revolutionary approaches than proved feasible within the framework of Spiritual Mobilization."[15]

Pew was disappointed to see Spiritual Mobilization go under. "Our fellowship over the years has been quite close," he wrote to Ingebretsen. "It has always been difficult for me to understand why money has been so difficult to obtain for projects like that of Spiritual Mobilization, for the philosophical concepts of that organization deal with the very root of America's problems." But Pew was already on to new projects. In the 1950s he had donated money to help start a group called the Christian Freedom Foundation, which published a magazine called *Christian Economics* containing articles with titles like "What Did Jesus Believe about Wealth?" ("Not only did Jesus believe in this right to property, He also believed that wealth is dynamic, not something that must be redistributed in the interest of justice.") And a few years before Spiritual Mobilization sank, in 1955, a young and rising minister named Billy Graham had written to Pew, asking for his help in starting a new magazine for ministers. "Instead of being liberal . . . it will be conservative, evangelical, and anti-Communist," Graham wrote. "I sincerely believe it is the greatest possible investment an American businessman can make in the Kingdom of God at this moment." Pew readily agreed to participate in the new endeavor, contributing $150,000 to help *Christianity Today* get off the ground. Unlike Spiritual Mobilization, *Christianity Today* was a project genuinely rooted in the network of revivalism and evangelicalism, and it was far more successful than the fringe group that had wanted to bring capitalism to Christianity and businessmen into the church. But its very independence—its determination to be a "forum" rather than an "organ"—at times frustrated the oilman, and in 1964 he offered his resignation from the board of the magazine.[16]

When Ayn Rand met the young William F. Buckley, in the first flush of his success as the author of *God and Man at Yale* (published in 1951, a year after his graduation from Yale), she told him that he was too intelligent to believe in God. In return, Buckley published several sharp critiques of Rand in *National Review*, the literate, worldly magazine he founded in 1955, "consciously aiming at thoughtful people, at opinion-makers." Buckley sought above all to avoid the pitfall of the "popular and cliché-ridden appeal to the 'grass roots,'" the kind of broad campaigns undertaken by groups like FEE. He also thought it critical to distance conservatism from its links to the business world—the very connections that Spiritual Mobilization tried to forge. To rescue conservatism, it was of the utmost importance to "engage the attention of people who have for a long time felt that the conservative position is moribund, that it is shorn up only by the frantic exertions of a dying bourgeoisie."[17]

Historians have argued that in the early years of the conservative movement there were deep tensions between true believers in the free market and intellectuals who saw the decline of religious tradition as the key to the fall of the Western world—men such as Russell Kirk, the Burkean author of *The Conservative Mind*, and Richard Weaver, an English professor at the University of Chicago who admired the romantic nostalgia of the southern Agrarians. *National Review* is rightly known for pioneering what the historian George Nash has described as the "fusion" of conservative ideas, joining the Hayekian faith in the market and critique of the New Deal to the larger moral and political concerns of these writers.

But there was also much in the early years of *National Review* to appeal to conservative businessmen: its credo included special mention of the need to protect the "competitive price system," which it argued was threatened by "the pressure of monopolies—including labor union monopolies" as well as the Big Brother state. In addition to articles on the "atomic disarmament trap," essays on the South that extolled white southerners as the "advanced race" (Isabel Paterson argued that Reconstruction had given the vote to an "ignorant, irresponsible, unpropertied populace"), and cultural critiques of such institutions as *The New Yorker*, the magazine in its early years published articles on the labor movement, detailing scandals and malfeasance in the world of organized labor as well as the politically dangerous plans of the unions.[18]

Buckley's early education had been in the tradition of counterrevolution. His father had been living in Mexico City, investing in real estate and oil, at the time of the Mexican revolution. An ardent Catholic, he hid and protected priests who feared for their lives as anticlerical sentiments rose. In 1921 the revolutionary government expropriated his properties and expelled him from the country. To the elder Buckley, the Mexican and Bolshevik revolutions seemed one and the same. It was a lesson he imparted to his ten children, of whom William F. Buckley, Jr., was the sixth. The young Buckleys grew up far from the oilfields, on a forty-seven-acre estate in Sharon, Connecticut. The children were taught French and Spanish; their father sometimes hired private tutors rather than sending them to the local schools. It was the ideal training for a young conservative raised in the shadow of revolution: serious, confident, faintly aristocratic, and sharply critical of mere "materialism."[19]

The younger Buckley became a cultural and literary icon when he published *God and Man at Yale*. It was a blistering attack on the university and on modern higher education in general, for its teaching of collectivism and Keynesianism and its withdrawal from religion. The book caused a sensation. So did Buckley's second book, a vigorous defense of Joe McCarthy which argued that the opponents of the Wisconsin senator failed to fully apprehend the severity of the Red threat. The books gave Buckley the credibility that he needed to start a new magazine—a magazine that he hoped would be able to "revitalize the conservative position," showing that "the conservative alternative to socialism at home and appeasement of the Soviet Union abroad is both plausible and profound, politically realistic and morally imperative."[20]

Buckley needed not only literary panache but money, and he was lucky to have a friend in the textile manufacturer Roger Milliken, also a graduate of Yale ('37). In certain ways Roger Milliken had a great deal in common with Buckley. He was the son of a wealthy family that had distanced itself from the southern origins of its wealth; his family's textile company, Deering-Milliken, was located in South Carolina, but Milliken was raised and educated in the North, attending Groton and then Yale. After Milliken took the helm of the family's company, in 1947, he moved to South Carolina. Eager to break the image of textiles as a backward industry, he helped to found the Institute of Textile Technology, which did research into matters of interest to textile manufacturers (Could cotton be cleaned more effectively? Were air-conditioned mills more productive?).[21]

Milliken was not a man to take challenges to his authority lightly. When an organizing drive broke out at one of his South Carolina mills in 1956, he campaigned hard against the union. His managers spoke to workers to persuade them to vote against unionization, telling them that Milliken would close the plant rather than bargain. The union drive was fought by the entire local elite: the town newspaper condemned the union, and a committee composed of businessmen (as well as the mayor) offered to bargain for the workers at the mill, provided their demands were "reasonable." Still, the workers voted for the union. Milliken then held a meeting of the other stockholders of his privately owned company, and then, proving that his managers had not issued empty threats, promptly shut the factory down, despite the pleas of the workers and their sudden eagerness to sign petitions decrying the union. "Union Wins and Loses at Mill," read the brief story in the *New York Times*. One loyal worker who had campaigned against the union said that he had been told by company officials that if he opposed the union, the mill would be safe, but "we fought the union. We lost the election. Now we are losing our jobs." A loom fixer who had been at the company since 1919 wryly said, "I had faith in Roger, but if I had to do it over again I'd vote for the union." (The union charged Milliken with unfair labor practices; twenty-four years later, the case was settled in the union's favor.)[22]

Before Buckley founded *National Review*, he helped Milliken contribute money to sponsor a study of whether the bestseller lists of the *New York Times Book Review* and other major newspapers were demonstrably biased against conservative authors. The results were published in the *American Mercury*; the author complained that because "entrenched leftist book reviewers" ignored conservative books, readers didn't know to ask for them, and therefore they could not make the bestseller lists. Milliken also volunteered to organize a dinner of New York businessmen who wanted to support the conservative cause actively, although he admitted that "there is not a lot that those of us who are active in business can do except give financial support."[23]

But financial support was precisely what the movement needed most. When Buckley asked Milliken to help finance a new conservative magazine, the textile magnate was one of a few businessmen to step up to the plate. He bought year-long subscriptions to the *National Review* and gave them as presents to more than one thousand businessmen and friends throughout the South, and he also regularly purchased advertising in the magazine. When the *National Review* faced a severe financial shortfall that almost put it out of business in the late 1950s, Milliken upped the number of ads from thirteen to thirty-nine. At a time when Buckley was relying primarily on his personal fortune and gifts from his father to keep the magazine alive, Milliken's contributions—which Buckley suggested could be valued at about $20,000 in the first year—were invaluable. "The incomparable Roger Milliken," as Buckley described him in a letter to a friend, was the magazine's "most important asset."[24]

Buckley advised Milliken on recruiting conservative speakers for business events like Chamber of Commerce meetings in the South, and at one point relayed to him the news that a hotel executive in California planned to refurbish the hotel's curtains using Milliken's products, "on the grounds that they advertise in *National Review*." The contract, Buckley wrote, would likely be in excess of $50,000. "Who says it doesn't pay to advertise in *National Review*?" Writing to Milliken's brother after he sponsored subscriptions for three hundred college students, Buckley expressed his gratitude: "What would American conservatism do without the Millikens! Horrible thought."[25]

Milliken was not the only businessman to support *National Review*, though few were equally generous. Buckley raised money from Lemuel Boulware, the General Electric vice president. Sterling Morton, the old Republican Party organizer, contributed a few thousand dollars to the new venture. (Milliken, like Morton, also contributed to the Mont Pelerin Society.) Jeremiah Milbank, a New York financier, donated to the magazine, giving $10,000 in the late 1950s, and tried to raise money. Companies purchased advertising in the magazine as a way of helping out.[26]

Still, some old business opponents of the New Deal could not recognize the possibilities of the new magazine, and the editors were perennially frustrated by the difficulties they confronted in raising funds as the magazine struggled to survive throughout its early years. Buckley entreated Mullendore to contribute, telling him that he was "the most intelligent and instructed man" Buckley had met on the West Coast. But Mullendore, wary as always of big new ideas in the years before his experiments with LSD, could not be persuaded to donate money to a cause he perceived as largely futile. "I hate to be so pessimistic about it, but as I hear and observe the orgy of optimism in which American business leadership is now indulging at the hour of our greatest danger, I am terribly discouraged," he wrote to a friend who had contacted him on behalf of *National Review*, as he politely declined to give a dime.[27]

PUBLISHING WAS not the only arena in which business donations were important in supporting the fledgling conservative movement. Clarence Manion's radio show, *The Manion Forum of Opinion*, was broadcast weekly on Sunday nights starting in October 1954. Like Buckley, Manion was a Catholic; he had been born in Kentucky and was a loyal if frustrated Democrat (he never forgave Woodrow Wilson for breaking his peace pledge and joining World War I) until the late 1930s. A law professor at Notre Dame during the Depression years, he abandoned the

Roosevelt administration when the drums began to roll for World War II, joining the isolationist organization America First. After World War II, Manion—though still a registered Democrat—became an ardent supporter of Robert Taft. Taft, the son of a former president, was an Ohio senator who had been elected in 1938 on a platform that denounced the New Deal as "largely revolutionary," accusing it of "deliberately stirring up prejudice against the rich" and enforcing a "redistribution of wealth which would soon lead to a socialistic control of all property and income." He became a leader of the isolationist forces in Congress, seeing the new military power of the United States as another threat to the domestic producers and small entrepreneurs who guaranteed the country's freedom. Manion was drawn to Taft's militant opposition to the New Deal as well as his embrace of small business and his claim to stand for the populist entrepreneur (even though Taft himself hailed from the same elite background as the members of Roosevelt's brain trust, having been educated at Yale and Harvard Law).[28]

When Eisenhower defeated Taft at the 1952 Republican convention, Manion helped to organize Democrats for Eisenhower. But he was as fed up with the Republicans as he was with the Democrats. Taft urged Eisenhower to consider Manion for attorney general, in reward for his political service. But instead Eisenhower tucked him away as the chairman of a blue-ribbon commission looking into the relationship between the federal government and the states. It didn't matter to Manion at that point—he had become consumed with the cause of the Bricker amendment, a constitutional amendment sharply limiting the president's power to negotiate and sign treaties (it was sponsored by John Bricker, another senator from Ohio, who in 1946 had referred to the New Deal as the "most reactionary force in history"). Manion wanted to see a referendum in all forty-eight states before any treaty could be signed. He went on the national circuit speaking on behalf of the Bricker amendment. No one was very surprised when Eisenhower quietly let him go.[29]

Manion retreated to his home in South Bend, Indiana, where he and his wife lived on a forty-five-acre estate. Along with the president of Sears, Roebuck, General Robert E. Wood—who never abandoned the military honorific he'd earned fighting in the Philippines and in World War I and building the Panama Canal—he founded the group For America. One of the last Old Right isolationist organizations, For America espoused "enlightened nationalism" against "our costly, imperialistic foreign policy of tragic super-interventionism and policing the world single-handed with American blood and treasure." Within one month of founding the group, the organizers claimed to have received more than five thousand phone calls, telegrams, and letters pledging support and membership. But the organization went nowhere, in part because it took as its central mission passing the Bricker amendment, which was voted down in Congress in February 1954. Wood began to look into other places to invest his activist dollars—for example, the Soviet Union. If ten American executives would put $40,000 each into building a resistance movement, he thought, they could instigate an internal revolution.[30]

Manion chose to work closer to home: he started the *Manion Forum of Opinion*, a weekly radio program, out of his office in the St. Joseph Bank Building in South Bend. The program painted a dystopian picture of 1950s America as a nation teetering on the brink of totalitarianism. In one prospectus, the *Forum* expressed its opposition to "the murderously oppressive Marxist Federal Income Tax; gigantic and unnecessary subsidies of tax money for fantastic highway and housing projects; Federal aid to education which would inevitably be followed by Federal Socialist control; tyrannical control of American workers by politically and ruthlessly ambitious union czars; appeasing and fraternizing with Communist mass murderers, thugs and slave masters." Manion sought to terrify his audience into supporting local control of the schools, right-to-work laws, states' rights, and a rebirth of patriotism. As he put it, "Fear is essential to the salvation of the American republic."[31]

Where AEA drew its donations from blue-chip companies, the *Manion Forum* culled the fortunes of the country's local manufacturing elites, small and midsized concerns such as Sunshine Biscuits, Inc., of Long Island City, the Tool Steel Gear & Pinion Co. of Cincinnati, and the P. H. Hanes Knitting Company of North Carolina. Manion's favored way to raise money, like Baroody's, was to use the interpersonal connections between businessmen to win contributions. Local manufacturers who supported the *Manion Forum* would write to their suppliers and urge them to donate to the radio program. "Only industrialists and businessmen are able, as a group, to shore up the defenses of the United States against the tides of Socialism," read a letter written by the head of the Milwaukee-based Acme Galvanizing, Inc., which went to the sixty-three firms that sold products to the company.[32]

Businessmen urged each other to contribute to the *Manion Forum* as a matter of principle as well as business sense. Luther Griffith, of the West Virginia–based Griffith Lumber Company, wrote an urgent plea: "I am sure you agree with me that our headlong plunge into Socialism must be stopped. If it is, it will be up to us industrialists and businessmen to do the job. We are the Americans who have the most to lose by the descent of the Nation into the Marxist Welfare state." (In private correspondence with Manion, Griffith revealed a different set of concerns, complaining that a small group of "international financiers" were behind the push to communism and insisting that "I do not believe that we have the right to impose Negro children on white children in schools. Propinquity leads to intimacies and all history proves the Negro race to be an inferior race and one which when mixed with white blood produces mongrelization.") A Lawrence, Massachusetts, manufacturer echoed the argument that businessmen had a special responsibility to support Manion's program: "Industrialists and businessmen in all the states have maintained this very necessary program. So they should. I am glad to say my company and I have been among them. We consider this both a matter of American patriotism and good business." The *Manion Forum,* wrote its longtime contributor William Grede (who was also a supporter of the Mont Pelerin Society), was "the businessman's friend and the socialist's foe."[33]

Manion kept careful lists indicating how many workers different supporters employed, along with the amount of money they contributed (both personally and through their businesses) and whether they were willing to act as sponsors for the radio program. If their business had been hurt by foreign imports, someone at the station made sure to write it down. No donor was too small to be carefully courted. For example, Norman

Gould of Goulds Pumps in Seneca Falls, New York, donated only $25 to $50 a year, but Manion deemed him a "very influential man in his area"—he also wrote fund-raising letters on behalf of the *Manion Forum*. If an executive had written letters to politicians, any future correspondence from the station would be sure to compliment him on his letter-writing efforts. Executives at companies such as the Henderson Cotton Mills in North Carolina that were facing labor trouble got small stars next to their names in the lists, along with a note: "Do not write without mentioning his courageous stand against the union." Manion's painstaking observations helped him raise money for the radio program. But they also served another function: they were a way of tracking and encouraging business activism. Raising money—again, as for Baroody—was also a tactic for deepening political support.[34]

The *Manion Forum* won accolades from its supporters and listeners, midsized businessmen who sent Manion glowing letters—"You are doing a wonderful job, and I only wish there were more like you in our country"—along with checks. The show had special appeal among the old-timers, the longtime opponents of the New Deal. Sterling Morton sent $500 in 1956, along with his enthusiastic declaration of support for the "repeal or limitation" of the Sixteenth Amendment, which established the progressive income tax (he forecast that perhaps it would go the way of Prohibition).[35]

Manion's open recruitment of business supporters might have seemed at odds with William F. Buckley's elevated style. But Manion's radio program was sufficiently successful that he was an obvious choice for Buckley to invite to join the founding board of directors of *National Review*. The relationship went both ways; Buckley donated money to the *Manion Forum*, and Manion tried to bring Buckley into the world of business activism. At one point in 1956 a businessman supporter of the *Manion Forum* wrote to Manion asking if he could help bring Buckley to speak to an audience of executives interested in limiting the size of the government and in the "importance" of individual rights ("this is more than just another manufacturers' association seeking a speaker"). Manion sent the request on to Buckley, along with a note encouraging the magazine editor to take time out to go address the businessmen and reminding him that not only was it a "good outfit," the request came from a "paying customer." The *Manion Forum* survived for decades through building and cultivating just such connections.[36]

The think tanks, radio stations, magazines, and intellectual organizations that were funded by business contributions during the 1950s helped to form the infrastructure for the rise of the conservative movement. From the Mont Pelerin Society to the *National Review*, from Spiritual Mobilization to the American Enterprise Association, from the Foundation for Economic Education to the *Manion Forum*, they produced the ideas, popularized the language, and built the support for conservative economic politics at the very height of postwar liberalism. Some did better than others—*National Review* thrived while Spiritual Mobilization fell apart; the American Enterprise Association became a conservative institution, while the Foundation for Economic Education (although it never went out of existence) seemed to recede in importance as its ideas caught on with a wider audience. All of these organizations relied on the contributions of businessmen, and all of them sought to encourage businessmen to do what they could to fight the power of the welfare state—and, more immediately, the threat of unions. It was only a matter of time before the cultural and intellectual push began to spill over into a world far removed from its abstractions: that of the factory floor.

5 How to Break a Union

"SIX BILLION DOLLARS by 1963": General Electric published the goal in *Fortune* magazine in 1955, when its annual sales grossed just under half that amount. The fourth largest publicly held industrial company in the United States, GE was the third largest employer in the nation, with 136 factories in 28 states.[1]

Out of those plants flowed the consumer bounty of the postwar era, the new appliances that decked out the suburban homes springing up across the nation: washing machines, refrigerators, television sets. The generators and turbines that energized the factories where the residents of the freshly minted subdivisions worked rolled off the GE production lines. So did many of the weapons that made up the country's arsenal, tucked away in underground silos scattered through the deserts and the Great Plains.

But the company produced more than the material components of the affluent society. During the 1950s, GE also undertook an extensive campaign of political reeducation for the more than 190,000 people who worked for the company, seeking to win their political loyalties back from New Deal liberalism—and especially from the labor unions.

At the time, about one third of the country's workforce belonged to a labor union, more than ever before in American history. Having finally achieved collective bargaining rights after decades of struggle, the leaders of the labor movement no longer sought a radical transformation of

American society. They portrayed themselves as common soldiers with management in a war against communism. Many (although not all) distanced themselves from the burgeoning political movement for racial equality. They hoped that by acknowledging their fundamental allegiance to the social order, they could maintain the stable bargaining relationships with employers that they had won at last, safeguarding the unions that had been built out of the strikes of the 1930s and 1940s, helping their members to win ever-stronger contracts and ever-improved conditions of life.

Yet the new power of organized labor fundamentally transformed the country. The strength of unions in postwar America had a profound impact on all people who worked for a living, even those who did not belong to a union themselves. When union members won higher wages or better benefits, those gains were often adopted by non-union companies as well. Unions helped to ensure that the productivity gains of the postwar period were more equitably shared between owners and workers. Despite occasional recessions (as at the beginning and end of the 1950s), real median family incomes climbed steadily between 1947 and 1973. Fringe benefits that had once been rare expanded greatly; the number of workers covered by private pension plans rose from 3.8 million in 1940 to 15.2 million in 1956. The number of people with hospital insurance climbed from 6 million in 1939 to 91 million by 1952. Vacations became more common, so that by 1960 it was not unusual for workers to have four weeks of paid leave a year. "The labor movement," said Walter Reuther of the United Auto Workers, "is developing a whole new middle class."[2]

What is more, although the decade is not often remembered this way, the 1950s were also years of intense industrial conflict. Workers engaged in an average of 352 major authorized strikes a year during the 1950s, a record for the postwar period. In addition to the authorized strikes at large companies, there were wildcat work stoppages; in the steel industry alone, according to trade association records, there were 788 unauthorized strikes in the period 1956–1958. Because of this, many working-class people did not view the steady improvement in their material lives as the inevitable result of better technology or increasing productivity.

They knew the intimate and detailed political history behind each wage increase, every pension benefit. Many believed that their higher wages had been won by the strike threat a few years back; they were convinced that attending the union meeting or paying union dues had helped win the health insurance.[3]

This shift in loyalties that began with the victories of the labor movement in the 1930s, as much as the pressure that an organized workforce could put on the bottom line, made business conservatives see unions as a threat to their power and prestige. The deeper threat of organized labor went far beyond dollars and cents. If workers believed that they owed their benefits to the time they spent on the picket line, why would they respect the authority of the boss? Business conservatives also worried about the political mobilization of their workers which seemed implicit in the model of industrial unionism. They feared that unions would turn workers out to the polls to press for higher Social Security benefits, more public spending, and an expanded welfare state. These meant higher taxes for business, of course, but they were also dangerous for a different reason: they implied the potential economic independence of the worker from his job. In all these different ways, unions seemed to business conservatives to be the embodiment of the most social-democratic tendencies within liberalism. Defeating them was therefore the key to undoing the New Deal order.

The struggle against unions during the 1950s took many forms. When workers tried to organize, they at times had to cope with a barrage of propaganda, such as employer-led meetings at which the company president would alternately threaten to shut the factory if the union won and promise to make all kinds of improvements if only the workers would vote against joining the union. Despite federal restrictions on "unfair labor practices," sometimes the strongest organizing committee activists would be fired, as an example to all the others. Corporations in northern cities frequently pursued a less direct anti-union strategy: instead of fighting the union, they would simply shutter their plants and move south, seeking rural workers who were not yet savvy to the rhythms of industrial employment, people they could count on to be docile, at least for a while.

The southern United States, where labor unions had never been able to organize during the 1930s and 1940s, became a reservoir of low-wage non-union labor, a Mexico inside the United States at a time when tariffs made Mexico itself too expensive. In time, of course, those tariffs came down, and the companies that had once moved to Tennessee closed up once again to move to Ciudad Juárez.[4]

But not all companies had the option of shuttering their northern factories to make the move south and evade unionization. Those that couldn't were faced with a difficult choice. They could bargain with the unions, trumpeting a new golden age of labor relations; the strength of the United Auto Workers compelled General Motors to adopt this program (even as the auto giant began to shift production out of Detroit). Or they could resist. And that was what GE chose to do. The top executives at GE believed that the New Deal and the labor movement had seduced workers with a false, misleading vision of how the economy worked, and they were convinced that the company had the job of setting the record straight and winning back the loyalty of its employees. GE became known throughout the business world for its staunch resistance to union power, and, on a deeper level, to the entire liberal political economy of the New Deal. As the company publicist Edward Langley put it, GE was "so obsessed with conservatism that it was not unlike the John Birch Society."[5]

General Electric was not the corporation one might have expected to emerge as a bastion of free-market ideology, for its top leadership had long adopted a progressive management style. The company had been formed in the late nineteenth century, when J. P. Morgan oversaw a merger intended to lessen the cutthroat competition in the industry. Two young executives, Gerard Swope and Owen Young, the liberal darlings of their age, brought the sprawling company into the modern era. This remarkable pair of men entered their professions (they were trained as an engineer and a lawyer, respectively) during the Progressive era, between the last years of the nineteenth century and the country's entrance into

World War I. The lessons they learned in that time of political upheaval—when state legislatures passed the first laws protecting the health and welfare of workers and consumers alike—stayed with them throughout their careers. Gerard Swope met his wife while he was teaching math in the evenings in a settlement house in Chicago after his days of work as an engineer at Western Electric; they were married in 1901 by the legendary social reformer Jane Addams. He went to GE from Western Electric, where he had built a successful executive career, to head the company's international operations.[6]

Owen Young did not have as activist a past, but during the early years of the twentieth century he had learned to be sensitive to public opinion. When he took over the company's legal department in 1913, GE had been charged with violating federal antitrust law. The company settled with a consent decree, but Young followed up the work in the courtroom by sending "a group out into the highways and byways to find out what the plain citizen thought of General Electric." The news was not good: most people saw GE as an impersonal, power-hungry corporation, one that would break the law in order to earn higher profits. Young begged the company president, Charles Coffin, to try to reach out to the public; Coffin absolutely refused, declaring that a company's only job was to "make goods and sell them." Young remembered his experiment, though, and when he was promoted to become chairman of the board in 1922, he set out to transform GE's image in the public mind. He wanted consumers to have a new opinion of GE—to see GE products as synonymous with a gentle and sophisticated modernity, not the harsh competition of the industrial world. One of the first things he did was to choose Swope as the company's president.[7]

Together the two trailblazing executives pioneered a program for what Young described as a "new generation" in the life of big business. They rejected the savage techniques of the corporate titans of the late nineteenth century—the "robber barons," as they were called, men such as J. P. Morgan, John D. Rockefeller and Andrew Carnegie. The new executives did not denounce their predecessors too harshly; they suggested that the armed battles with workers, the price wars, the chicanery, and the blood of the industrial past had all been necessary, albeit tragic, components of the rise of the United States as a world economic power. But they believed that the 1920s marked a new age. The obligations of modern industry were no longer only to stockholders but to society as a whole. "Today, when the corporation has become an institution, the duty of management is no longer solely to the investor," Young said in a 1922 interview with a business journalist. "Corporate management has become a trusteeship for the entire institution as distinguished from being the representative of any single part."[8]

The company hired an advertising firm to portray it as the bearer of "electrical consciousness," liberating men and women from meaningless drudgery, brightening the path to a better, freer world. "Woman suffrage made the American woman the political equal of her man," read one advertisement of the early 1920s. "The little switch which commands the great servant Electricity is making her workshop the equal of her man's." When people saw the GE logo, Swope and Young wanted them to be reminded of "the initials of a friend."[9]

Under Swope and Young, the company sought good relations with its employees. It provided them with welfare programs, stock-purchase plans, and pensions. In 1937, during the Depression, while other companies fought the electrical workers' union, GE signed a nationwide contract with the United Electrical Workers (UE) without a strike. Swope strongly supported Roosevelt and the New Deal, even devising a plan to end unemployment that bore a close resemblance to FDR's National Recovery Administration.[10]

The company prided itself on engendering a deep public spirit in its executives, teaching them to see themselves as stewards of the economy. Members of the upper echelon of corporate management were expected to play an active role in civic life, serving on the boards of hospitals and local charities; they were supposed to embody the ideal of the executive as responsible for the well-being of the whole community. Top-ranking executives and promising underlings went for annual jaunts to summer camps on a small island in Lake Ontario owned by GE, where the company would ply them with food and liquor while they listened to presentations and participated in skits and sports competitions. These company meetings often turned into raucous pep rallies. The company's president in the 1940s, Charles E. Wilson ("Electric Charlie"), a blustering former boxer whose craggy face bore the traces of punches thrown long before, whipped up the crowd with pugilistic challenges to competitors who boasted that one day they would overtake GE in sales and earnings: "They should live so long! Their grandchildren should live so long!" After Wilson's speech was done and the crowd of junior executives had been worked into a frenzy, a company band would march in to lead the best and brightest at GE in a spirited parade around the campgrounds, singing "Onward Christian Soldiers."[11]

The electrical workers' strike in 1946—part of the strike wave that one journalist described as bringing the country to the brink of a "catastrophic civil war"—transformed GE's attitude toward its unions. The new generation of postwar leaders had come of age in a different time from Swope and Young. Wilson and his successor, Ralph Cordiner, who served as company president from 1950 to 1958 and chairman and CEO from 1958 to 1963, did not grow up in an era of settlement houses and socialism. They had entered business during the "roaring" 1920s, when unfettered capitalism seemed in the public interest and public relations and advertising were growth industries. Compared to the earlier generation, they held far more conservative political visions, and their sense of how management had been besieged by the New Deal order was more acute.[12]

Still, Wilson and Cordiner had different personalities and political orientations. Cordiner was withdrawn and meticulous (one of his nicknames was "the Undertaker," and another was "Razor Ralph"), whereas Wilson was theatrical, hyperbolic. Wilson had a close relationship with the Democratic administration of the late 1940s and chaired President Truman's 1947 Committee on Civil Rights (which recommended the desegregation of the armed forces). Cordiner, who was a GE vice president in 1946, was by contrast a true market ideologue. When Wilson left GE, he did so to head the Office of Defense Mobilization during the Korean War; in contrast, Cordiner served as finance chair for the Republican National Finance Committee during Barry Goldwater's 1964 presidential bid after leaving GE. But despite their many differences, both men were shocked by the events of 1946.[13]

The national strike wave began in September 1945, only one month after V-J Day. The oil workers were the first to strike, 43,000 in 20 states. Then 200,000 coal miners struck to demand collective-bargaining rights for their foremen. Forty-four thousand lumber workers in the Northwest, 70,000 midwestern truckers, and 40,000 machinists in Oakland and San Francisco walked off the job in the fall of 1945. At General Motors, the United Auto Workers asked for a 30 percent wage increase, without an increase in prices, in order to prevent erosion of incomes through rapid price hikes as controls were lifted at war's end. When the company refused, the union asked it to "open the books" and share information about pricing decisions, claiming that the public was entitled to know why inflation was necessary and essentially asking the company to continue to allow in peacetime the influence that public and labor representatives had exercised on prices during the war. One hundred and seventy-five thousand General Motors workers went on strike in November 1945. The wave of strikes crested in January 1946, when the Bureau of Labor Statistics called the strike wave "the most concentrated period of labor-management strife in the country's history." Strikes swept through coal mining, the meatpacking industry, steel production. Milk workers struck in Detroit, bus drivers and newspaper printers struck in Seattle, school maintenance workers struck in Flint, Michigan, phone operators and telegraph workers struck in cities across the country.[14]

At the same time, General Electric was beginning its negotiations with the United Electrical Workers. The union had grown dramatically during the war, winning more than eight hundred union elections (held on a plant-by-plant basis) to become the third largest labor union in the Congress of Industrial Organizations. At its peak, the UE represented 600,000 workers. It was no longer the fragile organization that Swope had agreed to recognize but a powerful national union representing electrical workers not only at GE but at the company's main competitors, Westinghouse and General Motors. The union was demanding a two-dollar-a-day raise for all workers, a goal that its leaders had determined in industry-wide meetings would help to make up for the wage restraint of the war years. On a frigid December day shortly before Christmas, union leaders met in New York with Charles Wilson to discuss the company's counteroffer. As the company president basked in the glow of a sunlamp on the forty-fifth floor of GE's executive offices on the corner of Fifty-first and Lexington, he told them that the final offer was a 10 percent raise for workers making over a dollar an hour and ten cents an hour for those making under a dollar (in other words, a raise of eighty cents a day)—no negotiations. Hundreds of thousands of workers walked out of GE (and GM and Westinghouse) the following month.[15]

The company was unprepared for what followed. In some of the striking communities, for much of the strike, the workers essentially controlled access to the plants. Hundreds of workers encircled the factories in long picket lines, refusing access to white-collar and management employees and allowing only limited numbers of maintenance men through the lines. In Schenectady a local court issued an injunction against the pickets, but the union blatantly ignored it, vowing to bring out still longer picket lines and posting ads in the papers saying that picketing would begin early in the morning. In Bloomfield, New Jersey, workers built a picket line of four thousand workers, including supporters from other companies in the area, to picket in heavy snow.[16]

One of the most dramatic confrontations of the strike occurred in Philadelphia, where eight hundred strikers defied a court order limiting the number of pickets. They were greeted at 6 A.M. at the plant gates by "the largest concentration of policemen seen in the city in a score of years," according to the *New York Times*. The police granted them permission to march past the plant once; about six hundred did so, marching four abreast, and their ranks swelled as they marched. Two hundred war veterans led the picket, and in the front was a wounded veteran carrying an American flag. Right in front of the factory, a sound truck played the national anthem and strikers removed their hats. When the marchers began to move again, the policemen followed them. As they passed the plant, a mounted patrolman rode to the front and seized the flag while other police rode into the marchers, swinging their batons. The chief of police read the crowd the riot act. Fifty mounted policemen moved into the strikers, followed by platoons on motorcycles and hundreds of foot patrolmen. Mounted police chased strikers through the streets. Seven picketers were arrested, and there were cries of "Cossacks" from the crowds. "If an America citizen wants to see Gestapo methods, it would pay them to visit the picket lines and see the action of the city police," one union leader told the press. Even more picketers showed up the next day.[17]

People in the communities where GE plants were located did not rally around the company; many openly supported the strikers. Restaurants delivered hot lunches to the strikers. College students arrived to walk the picket lines. City governments in Ohio, Massachusetts, Connecticut, New Jersey, New York, Indiana, West Virginia, California, and Pennsylvania endorsed the aims of the strikers, and fifty-five U.S. senators and congressmen signed a public statement supporting the strike. In Bloomfield, New Jersey, where there were both Westinghouse and GE plants, five thousand picketers marched to the center of the town carrying signs saying "Our Fight Is Your Fight," "GI versus GE," and "We're not dumb clucks—we want two bucks." The rally was led by seven supportive policemen and by picketers on horseback. The local American Legion post supported the strikers, and its band joined in the parade. The mayor opened the rally with a prayer: "Help us so that when we pray each day, 'Give us this day our daily bread,' the 'us' will include all people." One policeman told the *New York Times*, "I can't talk officially, but any working man would be for the strike." The children of strikers marched on the picket lines, bearing signs reading, "I'm backing my Daddy" and "More Money Buys More Shoes."[18]

Wilson, a proud, autocratic man, was shocked and horrified by the strike. "These bitter conditions . . . have never been obvious in our own relationship with our people before they were unionized, or after they were unionized. I mean we haven't had bitter and bad controversies between the management and the unions," he testified before Congress. Wilson couldn't believe that he would not be allowed to enter his own company's premises. "To me it is the height of stupidity that we, as a corporation, should not be allowed to get into our plants, people who are not members of the union," he complained. But as terrifying as the sudden rebellion of the workers was the sensation of isolation for the GE officials. Local mayors, policemen, children, restaurant owners, college students, the American Legion, teachers, ministers—all seemed to be on the union's side, all seemed to believe that GE had committed grievous sins.[19]

GE had no choice but to settle. The employees won an eighteen-and-a-half cent hourly wage increase—about $1.50 a day. GE managers experienced it as a crushing defeat. This was in part a matter of hard economics: employee compensation had amounted to 36 percent of sales in 1944, but in 1946 it jumped to 50 percent. But the sense of indignation went beyond what could be captured by accountants. Management had been shut out of its own plants; it had been ostracized by the community. How could this have happened? How could so many people believe that GE was in the wrong?[20]

The top executives at GE hired a man by the name of Lemuel Ricketts Boulware to solve their labor crisis. Boulware had met Wilson and Cordiner during World War II, when all three worked at the War Production Board. After the war the GE leaders hired him as a "marketing assistant" but also gave him the responsibility of overseeing labor relations at GE's seven "affiliated" companies. It was impossible not to notice that during the strike, the workers at the factories that Boulware managed stayed on the job. The 1946 strike affected Boulware deeply. Reflecting back on it a few years later, he said that it brought home that "we had a worsening situation which had already grown to such dangerous and wholly intolerable proportions as could no longer be disregarded." The job that Boulware was offered after the strike, as vice president of employee and community relations, was a plum post for someone with little experience in the field. Boulware's background was in the white-collar public relations specialties of sales and marketing, which had burst onto the corporate scene in the 1920s, and before going to GE he had done little in labor relations. Still, he agreed to take it on.[21]

Boulware had grown up in Kentucky, and although by the time he went to GE decades had passed since he had left his home state, his voice retained just the slightest touch of a southern twang. More than six feet tall and powerfully built, he had attended college at the University of Wisconsin, where he served as a loyal member of his fraternity and a captain of the baseball team. Boulware was gracious, charming, and well known for his debonair style and loquacity, especially with people he liked. His employers recognized his talents early. Before going to GE, he had worked as a sales manager for the Syracuse Washing Machine Company, where he trained sales staff. He helped to found the Marketing Executives Society, writing articles on sales and advertising as solutions to the bitter price competition companies faced during the Depression. He was confident in the potential of his craft to mend social ills. Boulware represented a new breed in industry: the college-educated man who came in at the upper levels, never having been soiled by the shop floor. In the middle of the Depression, he and his wife embarked on a world cruise.[22]

During his GE career, Boulware peddled probusiness ideology with the same robust zeal and entrepreneurial fervor he had once used (as a *Fortune* magazine article put it) to sell washing machines. He became a one-man advertising campaign for the free market. Boulware made fighting the unions come to seem *moral*, a righteous cause, forward-looking, necessary to make a better America. In his silvery phrases, anti-unionism was no longer the retrograde evil of Pinkertons and machine guns that the New Deal had vanquished in the 1930s. He spoke of the political obligations of business to protect the free market with such seductive conviction that he transformed a politics that had seemed to have vanished into a dark industrial past into a commercial for the bright new days that lay in the future.[23]

Boulware was an unusual corporate vice president, for his frame of vision and reference extended far beyond his own company. He believed that all across the country, unions and management were engaged in a titanic struggle over the future of the United States. GE was merely one terrain on which the larger battle would be fought. American management needed literally to sell its policies to the American people. As he wrote in a 1945 memo, shortly after arriving at GE, "Management is in a *sales* campaign to determine *who* will run business and the country,—and to determine if business and the country will be run *right* . . . Who has been winning this sales competition for 13 years, and who still is, is all too evident in elections, labor laws, the attitude of all public servants, and the convictions held by workmen and the public about management." The memo went on to detail all the ways the company should aim to counter negative publicity, including "leadership in all heart-warming local activities," like helping "crippled children" and "injured veterans." For Boulware, unions represented "the most familiar symbol of the socialist opposition to maximizing the free market." The fight with GE's unions was "not only over current profits" but "our whole right to run the business in the balanced best interests of all, and our ability to have GE grow, serve, prosper and even survive."[24]

Boulware overhauled GE's contract negotiation strategy, rejecting the standard pattern of negotiations. Both sides typically went in asking for more than they thought they would get, and when the company gave way and allowed a wage increase or a new benefit, the union could take credit for "winning" the improvement. Boulware decided to attack the perception that unions were able to improve conditions for their workers. Under his leadership, the company essentially stopped engaging in genuine give-and-take bargaining sessions with the union. Management met with union representatives, sat and listened, and took some notes. But then it would unveil its own contract to the workers and the community, often with great media fanfare. Regardless of what the union said or did, the company insisted, the final offer was the final offer. All that the union could do was accept the contract as offered. Threats of strikes—even strikes themselves—would not move the company, as they had in 1946. After all, as Boulware told the *Wall Street Journal*, a strike "obviously should not be any factor at all in determining whether an offer or settlement is to represent more or less than what's right." The union should never be able to claim a victory for the workers. The company determined wages, benefits, and work rules according to its knowledge of the market, and it gave these to workers, almost as a gift. The union was only a destructive interloper, distorting the information given by the free market.[25]

The union, furious, dubbed the new negotiation strategy "Boulwarism." Boulware himself always rejected the term, preferring to describe his tactics as nothing but good common sense—acting in the "balanced best interests" of all. "The term was coined by some bad people who have been desperately trying the emotional diversion of putting what they hoped would be the worst possible name on the very fine thing which is our GE relations program of striving all year long to do right voluntarily and be known to do so," he told a student who contacted him about a course project in 1960.[26]

Boulwarism was not only about contract negotiations. The other side of labor relations at GE was a ceaseless education campaign in the ideology of the free market. Boulware tried to use the company as a gigantic school, handing out readings, organizing classes, setting up book groups. No interaction was too small to teach a lesson about the market. Boulware was especially interested in using supervisors to teach workers. Starting in 1947, all of GE's supervisors—whom Boulware referred to as "job salesmen"—were given manuals containing suggested answers to workers' tough questions. They were supposed to respond by reciting the catechism of the marketplace. For example, workers might gripe that big business was "greedy and unprincipled" and that its growth came at the expense of workers and small business. The supervisor was supposed to respond, "The size of a business is determined by the amount of goods it sells. In the absence of monopoly, the amount of goods it sells is determined all over again every day by the votes of individuals in that most free and democratic of processes, the 'plebiscite of the marketplace.'" One worker who wrote to the company newspaper to complain about not getting a Christmas bonus received this comforting response: "We feel that every time the state, an employer, or anyone else takes over one of our individual responsibilities completely, we are one step farther along the road to socialism and a halt to progress."[27]

Supervisors and managers, Boulware believed, were "thought-leaders" who would exercise influence over others in their social circles. All of society was composed of hierarchical little social groupings, in which some people were leaders, others followers. The divisions were in the end natural ones of character, although they might be reinforced by social position. Boulware feared that labor leaders—and supporters of the union who were willing to argue on its behalf—had been able to secure positions as "thought-leaders" and that they were therefore able to exercise a disproportionate influence over what workers believed. He saw this informal cultural power as the secret of labor's success.

For GE to win good contracts, supervisors, managers, and executives needed to hold intellectual sway over their employees, which they could achieve only by becoming "thought-leaders" themselves. To this end, Boulware distributed reading lists to GE managers and supervisors, including works by economic thinkers associated with the Mont Pelerin Society (which was at the time still waiting for Jasper Crane's support to hold the American meeting) and the Foundation for Economic Education (the perfect realization of Leonard Read's hope of getting his educational materials into the hands of executives). Boulware urged GE's managers to regularly read the editorial page of the *Wall Street Journal*, the columns of William F. Buckley in the *National Review*, and *The Freeman*, a conservative journal published by FEE. Every supervisor received a copy of John Flynn's *The Road Ahead*, a short book that portrayed the New Deal as the first nightmarish step toward totalitarianism and slavery. The company distributed a specially commissioned economics textbook written by the economcs columnist Lewis Haney to workers and managers. Deluged with reading material, GE's supervisors were then encouraged to hold reading groups and study sessions at their homes in their off hours. In addition, the company published newsletters for workers, and all of GE's employees were expected to attend a course—on company time—about free-market economics. While think tanks like the American Enterprise Association (where William Baroody was at the time seeking to build a base of support in the business community) still had to beg for donations to print their studies, companies like GE could swamp their managers and workers with printed material without having to go hat in hand to anyone else to foot the bill.[28]

Boulware also tried to do outreach in the broader community through "Planned Community Advertising" programs, which used "all the techniques of modern two-way communication" to broadcast the company's goodwill to the towns in which its plants were located. He helped to establish plant tours for clergymen in the hopes of organizing their support for the company. (Later in his life, he would remember: "The clergymen were the worst. They were always against us.")[29]

Boulware believed that GE's problems were shared by all corporations in modern America. He longed to build a political movement of businessmen, one that had the zeal, the savvy, and the organization to challenge the power of unions, and he spoke frequently to business audiences, admonishing them that "the really critical public relations problem is now almost purely a political one." He warned business against complacency, finding it ironic that the United States spent billions around the globe to contain communism while "too many of us in and out of government and unions and business are joyously, if not hysterically, embracing one after another of the very ideas, influences, features or ingredients of this same collectivism—this socialism that can surely lead us off the deep end into the exact type of police state we so fear." He hated the ideas of using federal dollars to educate "'poor' people in Alabama, Mississippi and Arkansas," spending government money on airports and downtown business sections, and giving aid to "'distressed areas.'" To stop such depredations, there was no choice but for business to bear the burden of politics: "No one else seems to be willing to go through the agony of trying to put what we think is right and what we instinctively know is right into language that is intelligible and convincing to the great mass of citizens who at the moment are being lied to by their government and by their unions." He ended his speeches with an exhortation for "inner regeneration," reminding businessmen that they must "literally be born again" in the fight for the free market.[30]

At first many of the GE supervisors whom Boulware wanted to turn into proud job salesmen dismissed his ideas about the struggle-to-the-death between the union and the company as melodramatic and overly ideological. Many came from working-class backgrounds and had worked their way up from the factory floor, and they were far from confident about unfettered free markets. But many in this generation of managers quit the company or were fired, as Ralph Cordiner introduced a wave of policies designed to restructure the corporation in the 1950s. Cordiner sought to introduce a new market culture into GE's daily life. He asked many longtime managers to relocate to new plants being built outside the old centers of GE's strength. He introduced new structures of bonuses indexed to profitability into pay scales. He took away old perks such as personal assistants. To replace the generation of managers alienated by these changes, the company began to recruit on college campuses, so much so that soon a BA seemed a prerequisite for a management job. The newly hired managers, like Boulware, had never worked on the shop floor; they received special training at a school for managers that GE began to operate in the 1950s, providing a professional education for executives that replaced GE's sociable retreats.[31]

The company also made some hires based largely on political compatibility. For example, early in 1957 another executive recommended that Boulware pick up a man by the name of Peter Steele, then the director of education for the Associated Industries of Missouri. Steele's main claim to fame was his authorship of a pamphlet entitled *Blueprint for World Revolt*. At GE his job would be to try to win over the leaders of national liberal groups to the GE program: "Just like in war, someone has to go in and individually contact the enemy." Steele wrote to his brother that Boulware was "without a peer among businessmen who speak up for what they believe and the General Electric Company is way out ahead of others in the realization of what needs to be done and its willingness to take up the lead in doing it." From his new post, Steele urged the company to donate financial support to conservative think tanks such as the American Enterprise Association. After leaving GE, he, like Cordiner, devoted himself to the presidential campaign of Barry Goldwater.[32]

But while GE was able to build a managerial staff committed to its ideological aims, the company could never count on its line workers to share the same degree of sympathy. It therefore sought to use its economic power—its control over the livelihoods of the men and women who worked there—to make the case for the free market. Throughout the 1950s, GE, like many other corporations, was shuttering plants in the North and moving production to new facilities in the South. Privately, Boulware thought about plant closures in terms of finding ways to discipline the workforce. He wanted to remove jobs from northern cities like Schenectady, where "the pay is too high for the value of the work done" and where "employees are unresponsive to guidance and in the matters of co-operation." Publicly, however, GE justified its decision to transfer jobs out of the northern industrial cities in terms of the company's need to compete with other firms employing low-wage southern workers. One article in the company paper asked workers to imagine themselves in the place of stockholders: "Put yourself in the investor's shoes. Where would you invest your money if you had reason to believe American production costs were headed higher, and American profits lower?" Boulware warned workers before contract negotiations that low-cost foreign competition was forcing prices down, leaving companies to face "the customer strike, or sit-down," as "empty factories with broken windows across the older industrial areas shout loud and clear." In this fiercely competitive context, who could blame GE for closing the factory if there was trouble? The *Works News*, one of the company's publications targeted at employees, queried: "If there is a strike, how long would it take the company to regain its market position once it has settled? How many jobs will be lost before the company could regain the business it would lose during a strike? Would my job be one of those that would be lost? Would the loss be temporary or permanent?"[33]

The lesson was clear: get with the program or pay the consequences.

FEW OTHER Fortune 500 corporations during the 1950s fought unions with the same publicity and intensity as GE, and few developed such a highly politicized internal corporate culture. Nonetheless, Boulware's labor relations techniques began to spread through the business community. One conservative activist tried to sum up his role: "You have exerted an influence far beyond GE, stiffening the backs of business men across the country. You probably do not realize how far-reaching [is] the influence of your insight and example."[34]

In 1957 and 1958 the country was hit by the most severe recession the postwar period had seen. In the newly austere economic climate, corporations were more eager than they had been to find ways to cut their costs. *Business Week* argued that "labor costs—indirect and direct—are universally cited as the chief cause of the profits decline." The ideas of intellectuals associated with think tanks like AEA and magazines like *National Review* helped to legitimate and justify opposition to labor. Ludwig von Mises described unions as exerting economic violence, writing that collective bargaining was "bargaining at the point of a gun." Friedrich von Hayek saw unions as inherently coercive: "It can hardly be denied that raising wages by the use of coercion is today the main aim of unions." In October 1961 the academic journal *Industrial Relations* devoted several articles to employer alliances and the new "hard line" emerging in management.[35]

With Eisenhower in office, the National Labor Relations Board also moved to the right. Several decisions by the board opened up new opportunities for companies to resist unionization, providing employers with new leeway to persuade their workers not to organize. For example, in one case (*Livingston Shirt Corporation*), the board ruled that employers had the right to hold "captive audience" meetings during working hours, at which managers could try to persuade workers not to vote for a union; in the past, employers had been obliged to provide union organizers with equal time to speak to employees. In subsequent cases, the board determined that an employer had the right to tell workers that he would tie up an election decision for several years through appeals, or that foreign-born workers risked deportation if the "Communist" union won. And in *Blue Flash Express*, the board ruled that a manager had the right to interrogate workers one-on-one about whether or not they had signed union cards.[36]

Employers began to look for ways to exploit these new possibilities for opposing unions. In the late 1950s, the National Association of Manufacturers began to hold management training sessions, instructing employers in strategies that they could use to fight union drives. NAM distributed mimeographed packages of letters and leaflets that employers could hand out if they faced a unionization campaign. Some invoked the specter of strikes: "Don't believe the union organizers when they say a strike couldn't happen here in our plant. It could happen here! It could happen if a union comes in to represent your employees, especially if that union is the _____ [here the NAM pamphlet indicated that the employer could fill in the name of the union in question]. They have called many strikes—some of them long and brutal and bloody." Others claimed that the union would be unable to win settlements for workers that were more generous than those the company was willing to extend anyway: "If the company is forced to do something by a union it isn't likely to be as liberal as it is when it gives something of its own free will." One sample letter from 1961 captured the strange combination of intimacy and anonymity in these anti-union communications: when sending an anti-union letter to an employee, the manual warned, the proper mode of address should be "Dear Mr. And Mrs. Employee (make it personal)."[37]

The first anti-union consultants appeared during the 1950s as well, anticipating the rise of the union-busting consultants who would flourish during the 1970s. Men like Nathaniel Shefferman, who had been a labor relations consultant at Sears, Roebuck during the 1930s, taught companies how to stave off organizing drives. As a result of this newly concerted fight, the number of unfair labor practices—illegal acts such as threatening, bribing, spying on, or firing workers during an organizing drive—rose sharply in the late 1950s, nearly doubling between 1955 and 1960. The proportion of union victories in representation elections—in which workers vote on whether or not they want to be represented by a union—began to fall.[38]

The push against labor was not limited to the shop floor. Businessmen started to become more politically active in the antilabor cause as well. In the fall of 1958, *Fortune* announced in a headline that "the American corporation has rediscovered politics." The story detailed the surge in political interest and organizing that had swept through many major corporations as they prepared for the fall elections and started to ready themselves for the presidential campaign of 1960. "Whether we want to be there or not, Gulf and every other American corporation is up to its ears in politics, and we must either start swimming or drown," said the vice president of Gulf Oil.[39]

In 1959, GE manager of public affairs J. J. Wuerthner published *The Businessman's Guide to Practical Politics,* which called for businessmen to get involved in fighting "a tightly organized and highly centralized group of organized-labor leaders whose basic objective of collective bargaining has now become a secondary function, replaced by a new objective of seizing both political power and, ultimately, control of government." Companies began to organize workshops and seminar series instructing their managers in how to run for political office, how to do door-to-door campaigning, and how to organize a precinct. Gulf Oil started distributing scorecards for Congress to its shareholders, showing how various senators and representatives voted on issues of concern to the oil business. Union Carbide, New Jersey Bell Telephone, Chase Manhattan Bank, and Prudential Insurance Company all began to use their company publications to tout political issues and to report on the political activities of employees (Chase even gave citations to staff members for exemplary political and civic work). "Right-to-work" initiative campaigns, which sought to make it illegal for contracts to require union membership as a condition of employment, swept through western states in the late 1950s and were often spearheaded by politically active business leaders, and although most of them failed, the connections that were forged during the campaigns often lasted. Boulware was at the front of the effort to get businessmen to be more active in politics. In one speech, for example, he told an audience of executives at the Phoenix Chamber of Commerce that politics was their "biggest job" in 1958, arguing that the state's right-to-work law had provided a significant incentive to the company in its decision to build a factory there.[40]

But the significance of GE's experiments in politics and in labor relations during the 1950s lies not only in the part that it played in this groundswell of open opposition to labor. Boulwarism represented a new way of thinking about workers, as a kind of captive political audience, a group of people who could be organized to oppose the New Deal and liberalism through lectures, reading groups, and political messages. Boulware never believed that the working class was inherently liberal or Democratic. The union organized workers in one way; his program sought to organize them in another. Instead of being radicalized on the job, they could be instructed in the ways of the marketplace. Corporate culture could be used to reinforce a set of conservative political beliefs, and middle managers could be turned into organizers. Yet this dream revealed the tension inherent in the entire vision of free-market utopianism taught and transmitted through the corporate structure. The idea of the market was supposed to be one of freedom and individuality, yet in the workplace it was taught in rigidly top-down fashion, with the managers and supervisors playing the role of teachers to a subordinate audience. Few other companies during the 1950s made such a radical attempt to shape a political corporate culture (although other companies, such as Wal-Mart, would do so later on).

THE ELECTRICAL workers' union had been weakened by internal conflicts in the late 1940s, which left it a far less formidable opponent for GE than the autoworkers' or steelworkers' unions were for the lead companies in those industries. The union had split in two in 1949, when UE had left the CIO after its lead officers refused to sign affidavits testifying that they were not members of the Communist Party. The union federation then granted another charter to a newly formed, staunchly anti-Communist group, the International Union of Electrical Workers (IUE), which succeeded in wooing many GE workers away from the UE. The result was a divided labor force—an ideal testing ground for Boulware's propaganda campaigns. Employment security for workers at GE lagged behind that in other unionized mass-production industries; especially notable was the absence of a union shop clause in the GE contract, mandating that all workers had to join the union, a standard provision in most other mass-production industries at the time.[41]

The success of Boulwarism became clear when the IUE, which represented more GE workers than any other union, decided to try to stand up to GE management in 1960. The conflict began when GE announced that it needed to take back certain benefits it had granted in the previous contract in order to compete in the recession of the late 1950s. The IUE, led by its president, James Carey, chose to fight, and called for a strike in the early autumn of 1960, despite some evidence that its ranks were split and there was little support for a labor action. The company immediately responded that neither threats nor strikes would make it revisit its position. In the buildup to the strike, the company was adamant that it would keep its plants open no matter what; there would be no recap of the events of 1946. Boulware had retired by that time, although he remained very active at the company and was central in planning the 1960 strike strategy. His successor told meetings of management employees, "The Company will take a long strike rather than accede to demands that are detrimental to the future of the business or that infringe on the basic individual rights of employees." For Boulware, the 1960 strike marked a turning point in twentieth-century American history. As he wrote, "GE is the first major US employer in twenty years to be willing to take the financial and political risks of serving its employees' interests and their communities' interests by trying to keep its plants legally open when some dictatorial top union officials have decreed those plants be illegally shut down."[42]

Despite the conflicts within the union, the strike started stronger than anyone might have expected. Many plants were not able to maintain production, and in some cities thousands of workers turned out to picket. Boulware was enraged. The pickets always seemed to him implicitly violent. One draft of a pamphlet that he wrote asked, "Are you now in the grip of a SUPER-GOVERNMENT of LAW-BREAKERS? Can or do this super-dictatorship's imported or local goons damage at will your person, your family, your car, your neighbor's savings, your city's property and future?"[43]

The company met the picket lines with a sophisticated series of direct appeals to the workers, asking them in letters, phone calls, and personal visits to reconsider and come back to work. The company directed supervisors to keep close records of their contacts with workers. They were reminded to target those workers whom they deemed well respected by other employees. GE took out full-page ads in the *New York Times*, the *Wall Street Journal*, and local publications, advertising its point of view, attacking the union, and denouncing the picketers. The company sent letters and pamphlets to shareholders, reminding them that in addition to having a direct interest in GE, they were consumers and businessmen who were "adversely affected" by inflation and high wages and by the "union's restriction of output and insistence on destroying property and otherwise breaking the law when they call a strike." GE even encouraged secretaries and other female employees to pose as the wives of strikers and call in to radio talk shows to express anger at the union and beg for the strike to end.[44]

All these efforts greatly weakened community support for the strike, which crumbled within two weeks. The *New York Times* labor reporter A. H. Raskin pronounced it "the worst setback any union has received in a nationwide strike since World War II." Businessmen across the country wrote to Boulware to congratulate him on his victory. "I think the GE approach is going to be emulated by many companies," an oil industrialist told the *Wall Street Journal*. "The time has come to put the facts on the barrel head, and [the corporations] intend to do it." Another admirer wrote Boulware a letter brimming with enthusiasm about his victory over the union president: "Your crowning glory—Carey bites the dust! The recognition being given you is grand and you must love Carey now that he stuck his neck out and gave you the chance to prove your policy. Now perfect it for politics and USA will be saved."[45]

But the sweetness of victory was soured somewhat when three GE executives were sentenced to short prison terms the following February for their role in a price-fixing conspiracy. Cordiner had given a speech chastising those morally weak executives who had condoned price-fixing, insisting that no "wishful thinking" could evade the "free buyer's relentless embracing of the upper band of excelling performers and rejecting the lower band of performers." Later there were accusations that Cordiner probably had been privy to the conspiracy. The company's celebration of the glories of the free market extended only so far. And even though the company won the strike, the union immediately brought a lawsuit against GE through the National Labor Relations Board, charging the company with failing to bargain in good faith. In 1964 the board—its politics having changed somewhat since the 1950s, with Kennedy's appointments—ruled in favor of the union, citing not only the company's contract negotiating strategy but its entire program of corporate relations as evidence of its bad-faith bargaining.[46]

No matter how successful the company might be in winning strikes, agencies like the NLRB were not always controlled by people sympathetic to the company. The next step for Boulware was to find ways to take his organizing within the company into the political world. The idea of a populist base for free-market politics, the vision of persuading working-class men and women to cheer for the boss, the faith that libertarian economic ideas were not only the province of the elite but could actually become the faith of the people as well, lived on outside the company through the influence it had on its most famous employee: Ronald Reagan.

REAGAN WENT to General Electric as a failed movie actor tired of working the Las Vegas circuit. He left poised to begin his political career.

By the time Reagan arrived at GE, his life and his political vision were in some ways fully formed. He had already cultivated his trademark charm, combining the patina of stardom with the approachable folksiness he had learned in his midwestern youth. Reagan's experiences with Hollywood radicals before and during his stint as president of the Screen Actors Guild had given him a firsthand dislike of the Communist Party. He testified before the House Committee on Un-American Activities, speaking against the organizing tactics of the Communist Party, which he denounced as undemocratic, sneaky, and symbolic of an overall contempt for freedom in radical circles.

But despite his deepening anticommunism in the early 1950s, Reagan had not altogether left behind his old appreciation for the New Deal or the Democratic Party when he went to GE. During his childhood in Dixon, Illinois, his father (an alcoholic) had been an often-struggling shoe salesman, his mother an amateur actress and ardent member of the Disciples of Christ. The Works Progress Administration had rescued Reagan's father during the Great Depression, and the entire family voted loyally for the Democratic Party for years afterward. In 1948, Reagan delivered a stirring radio address (sponsored by the International Ladies Garment Workers Union) on behalf of President Truman. In 1950 he again campaigned for Democrats. He had not yet developed his faith in the free market. But over his time at General Electric, he would become an ardent free-market conservative. In later years he would describe his time at GE as a "postgraduate course in political science" and an "apprenticeship" for public life.[47]

GE hired Reagan in 1954—the peak of Boulware's time at the company—to host a new weekly television series sponsored by the company, *GE Theater*. These were hour-long dramas starring well-known actors of the day (one, a western retelling of *Christmas Carol*, featured Jimmy Stewart), and in the late 1950s *GE Theater* topped the ratings for Sunday nights. The company edited the program carefully to make sure that all the episodes conformed to its idea of "taste," occasionally removing segments such as one in which the instruments of an airplane lost in fog began to malfunction (GE made such instruments.) Although Reagan was skeptical initially about the new job—because he thought television was killing the movies—he agreed to do it, won over by the salary of $125,000.[48]

In addition to hosting the television show, appearing in company advertisements, and generally being the public face of the company, Reagan was expected to travel around the country visiting GE factories and making speeches to the workers. The idea was to give workers a sense of connection and identification with the company by allowing them to meet one of its chief spokesmen. He would stop for short informal chats, meeting with salaried employees and hourly workers in separate groups. At first there was little political content to the speeches; Reagan talked up company products and made small talk with workers, and sometimes even stopped by workers' homes to continue the conversation, as when one woman asked him for advice for a depressed young son and Reagan went over on a Saturday morning to talk to the boy. He described the house that he and his wife, Nancy, lived in, furnished with all manner of electric gadgets paid for by the company—as he put it, "everything electric except the chair."[49]

Reagan's plant tour was a smash hit as a public relations program. GE's managers believed (with some condescension) that their employees would be easily overwhelmed by the glamour of meeting a real celebrity. Earl Dunckel, a GE manager who traveled with Reagan on the plant tour, claimed that women in the factories were especially titillated by meeting a movie star, although sometimes Reagan tried to dissuade them from their own Hollywood stardust dreams (Dunckel remembered him saying, "I'd do almost anything to keep another one of these little girls from going out there and adding to the list of whores out in Hollywood"). The men in the plants, Dunckel insisted, were jealous of the adulation of the women workers and hence more skeptical of Reagan at first. They would stand in small circles making fun of the Hollywood actor. But Dunckel also thought that Reagan knew what to do to warm them up. "He would carry on a conversation with the girls just so long. He knew what was going on. Then he would leave them and walk over to these fellows and start talking to them. When he left them ten minutes later, they were all slapping him on the back saying, 'That's the way, Ron.'"[50]

On these national speaking tours, Reagan was immersed in the world of economic ideas. Since he was afraid of flying, he would take long train trips across the country to the far-flung factories with other GE executives, talking politics all the way. Dunckel remembered their discussions: "Whenever he would try to defend New Dealism, or what was passing for it at the time, we would have some rather spirited arguments. I think this helped him to realize, as he put it later, that he didn't desert the Democratic Party; the Democratic Party deserted him." Reagan always insisted that no one ever told him what to say. As he wrote years later to a friend who had worked with him at the company, "My speeches were totally my own." Yet he must have been exposed to the reading lists of Henry Hazlitt and John Flynn, the Lewis Haney book and the subscriptions to *National Review*, not to mention the company's own ceaseless barrage of publications. The heated ideological atmosphere within the company surely shaped Reagan's developing political views—about taxes, about the welfare state, about unions, and about economic freedom.[51]

As his speeches grew more deeply political, Reagan's appeal as a speaker increased as well. Soon he was talking not only to workers at the plants but to audiences of local businessmen at the Rotary Club and the Chamber of Commerce, at gatherings of the Elks Club and meetings of groups like the California Fertilizer Association, the National Electrical Contractors Association, and the National Association of Manufacturers. Soviet communism, he told them, was not the only threat facing the United States. The slow accretion of social legislation—the Veterans Administration, Social Security, federal education spending, and farm subsidies were examples he liked to mention—would bring totalitarianism before anyone even noticed. "We can lose our freedom all at once by succumbing to Russia or we can lose it gradually by installments—the end result is slavery." As for the taxes that funded it all, Reagan told audiences, "There can be no moral justification of the progressive tax"—it was the brainchild of Karl Marx. He described the tactics and rationale of the "statists" in Washington: "Get any part of a proposed program accepted, then with the principle of government participation in the field established, work for expansion, always aiming at the ultimate goal—a government that will someday be a big brother to us all."[52]

Lemuel Boulware admired Reagan immensely and spoke about him glowingly to colleagues and friends. Whether or not Boulware was fully aware of it at the time, this was someone able to take his approach and "perfect it for politics." Reagan, like Boulware, was able to turn the idea of government as the servant and spokesman of the worker on its head, creating a universe in which the corporation was the liberator and the state the real oppressor of the working class.[53]

6 Suburban Cowboy

J. William Middendorf, a successful Wall Street investment banker, was among the people who responded to the call for businessmen to fight labor and liberalism by getting involved in politics. In the late 1950s, he and his business partner, Austen Colgate (a member of the family known for its toothpaste company), had purchased a seat on the New York Stock Exchange. Only a few years later their firm had offices in Boston, Baltimore, and San Francisco as well as New York. Middendorf, still a young man in his late thirties, had a fine house in Greenwich, Connecticut, right next door to the home of Prescott Bush, the senator and father of George H. W. Bush; in the evenings he could sometimes hear the "Whiffenpoof Song" of Yale floating across the backyard. But Middendorf, a Harvard man, always had ambitions that went beyond the financial world. His political inspiration came straight from Hayek, Mises, and Leonard Read, and he was an avid reader of the publications of the Foundation for Economic Education (he told Read that he considered *The Freeman*, the magazine the group published, among his personal "bibles for the economic re-education" he'd had to give himself after graduating from Harvard.)[1]

In November 1962, Middendorf received a mysterious invitation from the political consultant F. Clifton White to a critical meeting—"this is *the* important one"—to be held at the Essex Inn Motel on South Michigan Avenue in Chicago in December. Clif White made his living organizing businessmen to be political activists. He had little interest in seeking political office himself. "I learned that the Almighty selects all of us for different roles in life," he wrote in his memoirs, and "mine was not to be the star but rather the man behind the scenes who gets things done." He worked with the Effective Citizens Organization, a group founded by a New Jersey life insurance executive after Eisenhower's first presidential victory. "One of my main concerns at the time was that businessmen, for the most part, did not understand politics and the mechanics of the political system, while the unions did," he wrote. "The lack of political activity in the business community created an imbalance in favor of the unions, and I decided to do something about it." White heard about Middendorf through these networks. The investment banker had served as the treasurer for a losing congressional race in Connecticut; he was, in other words, the model businessman taking political action.[2]

Years later Middendorf would remember the December meeting in Chicago as a "watershed," the moment when "a practical modern conservative political movement" was born. "It was our symbolic St. Crispin's Day," he later wrote. At that meeting F. Clifton White explained how the fifty-five men gathered in a small conference room—many of them contacts from White's work in organizing businessmen—could win the 655 delegate votes they needed to obtain the Republican nomination for the presidency for Arizona senator Barry Goldwater. By that time White had already spent a year working to put together the backbone of a Goldwater campaign for the nomination in 1964, gathering contacts and supporters, and as improbable as it seemed that a small band of conservative activists outside the normal mechanisms of the party could take control and get their candidate in place, the men in that room committed to the plan. Middendorf became one of the trustees of the campaign's finance committee. Electing Barry Goldwater would consume his imagination until it was all over in November nearly two years later. As he wrote to Leonard Read in the summer of 1964, he believed that the "Goldwater movement" was nothing less than a "libertarian movement incorporating the ideals of

The du Pont brothers—Irénée, Lammot, and Pierre—started the American Liberty League in 1934 in order to fight the New Deal. (Better Living, *1950 / Courtesy of Hagley Museum and Library)*

Opponents of the New Deal were often mocked during the 1930s as being patently self-interested and out of touch with the realities of the Depression. *(William Hudson,* Columbus Citizen *1935 / Library of Congress)*

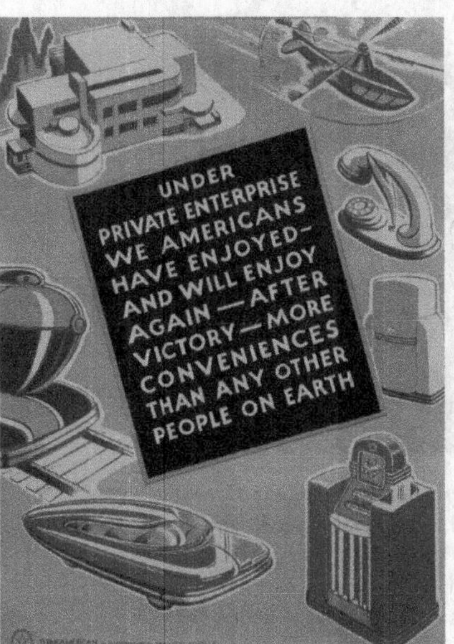

World War II helped to rehabilitate the image of business, which had been damaged during the Depression, as companies and the government alike presented the conflict as necessary in order to safeguard freedom of consumption, among other goals. *(Kelly-Read & Co., Inc., Rochester, New York, 1943 / Library of Congress)*

The National Association of Manufacturers sought to shape public opinion through radio programs, editorials, and billboards like this one in Dubuque, Iowa. *(John Vachon, April 1940 / Courtesy of Ann Vachon)*

Economists at the 1958 meeting of the Mont Pelerin Society toured the Tidewater Oil Company's Delaware Refinery after visiting the DuPont Company in Wilmington, Delaware. From left to right: Louis Boudin, of the University of Paris; L. Augustin Navarro, director, Institute of Economics, Mexico; Harold Brayman, director, public relations, DuPont Company; Frank Knight, University of Chicago. *(Courtesy of Hagley Museum and Library)*

Ludwig von Mises was Friedrich von Hayek's mentor, and he became one of the most popular conservative economists among business opponents of New Deal liberalism; Leonard Read hired him at the Foundation for Economic Education. *(Courtesy of the Ludwig von Mises Institute, Auburn, Alabama)*

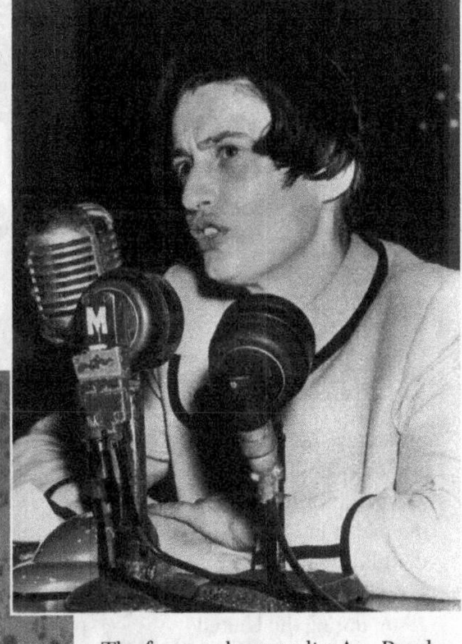

The free-market novelist Ayn Rand testified before the House Committee on Un-American Activities in Hollywood in September 1947. Rand was friendly with Leonard Read and W. C. Mullendore and briefly helped the Foundation for Economic Education, until she and Read had a falling-out. *(Bettmann/Corbis)*

William F. Buckley's first book, *God and Man at Yale* (1951), chronicled his experiences as a Yale undergraduate. He started the *National Review* in 1955, with financial help from the textile magnate and fellow Yale graduate Roger Milliken. *(Bettmann/Corbis)*

Striking workers carrying an American flag fought with police officers on the picket line outside the Philadelphia General Electric plant in February 1946, during the United Electrical Workers' nationwide strike of the industry. (*Bettmann/Corbis*)

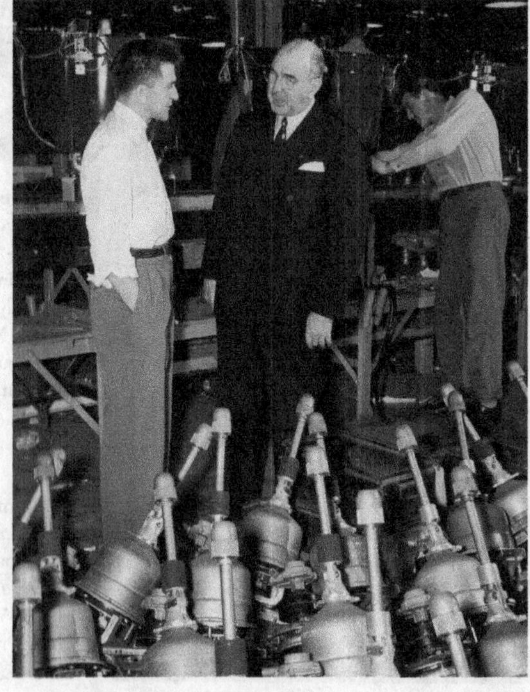

Lemuel Ricketts Boulware visited this General Electric factory in Chicago in 1945. Boulware helped pioneer an elaborate corporate communications strategy for fighting the unions at the company after the 1946 strike. (*Courtesy of University of Pennsylvania Libraries*)

Ronald Reagan spoke to workers at a General Electric plant in Danville, Illinois, in October 1955. *(Courtesy of the Ronald Reagan Library)*

As the United Auto Workers strike at the Kohler Company stretched on, the union organized a national boycott of Kohler products. *(Courtesy of Walter P. Reuther Library, Wayne State University)*

BUSINESS
Politician: "If you don't make politics your business you may soon have no business."

During the recession of the late 1950s, companies began to do more to become politically active. (C. D Batchelor / *Courtesy of Daily News Archives)*

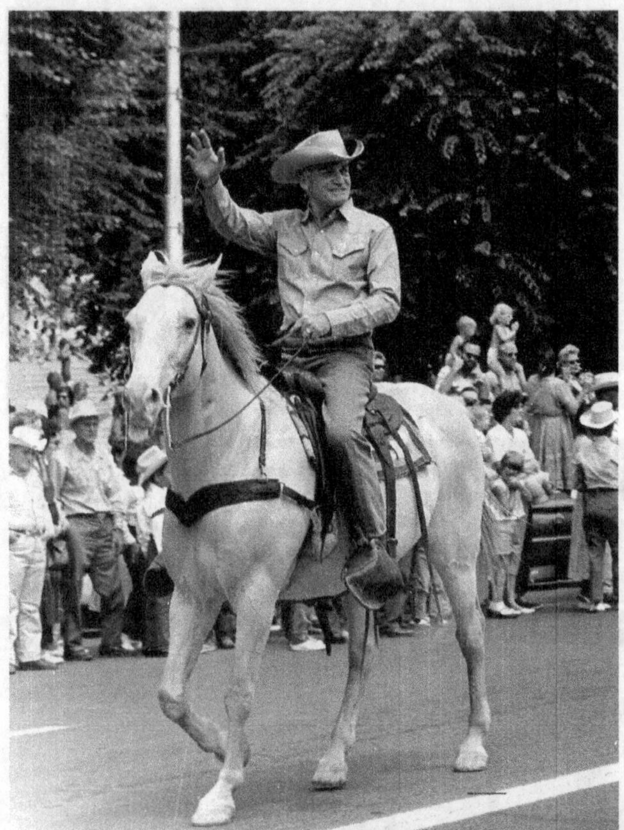

Arizona senator Barry Goldwater riding a horse, July 4, 1963. Although he was a department store owner, he embraced the image of the cowboy. *(Courtesy of Arizona Historical Foundation)*

In the 1964 election campaign, Goldwater supporters manufactured this carbonated beverage named after their candidate. *(Courtesy of Arizona Historical Foundation)*

Student protesters burned down the Bank of America branch in Isla Vista, Santa Barbara, in 1970, an event commemorated by this "Bank of Amerika" poster, which summed up the "attack on the free enterprise system" that Lewis Powell, Jr., feared. *(Library of Congress)*

Richard Viguerie used reels of computer tape to store the names and addresses of conservatives. *(Wally McNamee, 1980 / Corbis)*

North Carolina senator Jesse Helms endorsed Ronald Reagan for president at the Republican convention in Detroit in the summer of 1980. *(Bettmann/Corbis)*

Jerry Falwell, the founder of Moral Majority, spoke with Ronald Reagan before the candidate's address to the National Religious Broadcasters in October 1980. *(Ron Edmonds / Corbis)*

Ronald Reagan visited the New York Stock Exchange in March 1985, reprising his campaign trip from March 1980. *(Harry Hamburg / Courtesy of Daily News Archive)*

Ludwig von Mises" and Friedrich von Hayek, among other thinkers. It was more than a political gambit; for businessmen like Middendorf, it was a cause.[3]

DURING THE YEARS that Barry Goldwater occupied the national spotlight, journalists loved to take photographs of the Arizonan wearing his broad-brimmed cowboy hat. They portrayed him as an honest, rugged southwesterner, tanned and handsome, as befitted the clichés. Even his character flaws—his rigid, simplistic division of the world into good and evil, his tendency to speak straight regardless of the circumstances or the feelings of others—seemed the natural result of his frontier upbringing. His foibles possessed a certain rustic charm.

But this image of Goldwater was not really accurate. Despite his embrace of the cowboy mystique, Goldwater was never a nostalgic man. He loved technology and gadgets of every sort. He was an ardent and talented nature photographer; when he journeyed down the Colorado River in a flimsy vessel, he went to great lengths to capture the entire journey on film (and then showed the movie all over the state). He was passionate about ham radio. As a child, he wrote Thomas Edison a fan letter: "I have studied electricity since I was a little kid and am going to keep it up until I am an old one." For Goldwater, it was never enough simply to experience the grandeur of the southwestern vista. He had the modernist's need to capture nature. Even his Phoenix house was filled with Monticello-like contraptions: a movie screen that lowered automatically from the living room ceiling, a flagpole that raised the Stars and Stripes at sunrise and lowered it at sunset.[4]

Far from being a frontiersman, Barry Goldwater was a member of the Phoenix upper crust. He was not an entrepreneur but the son of the boss. In the last years of the nineteenth century, his father had founded Goldwater's, which grew into the largest and fanciest department store in the desert city of Phoenix. When his father died in March 1929 at age sixty-two, Barry inherited the business, securing his spot in the city elite. As he wrote in 1938, "I was one of the lucky few who was born with a silver spoon in my mouth, and I am doing my best to keep it there."[5]

Goldwater practiced civic participation. He was president of the Chamber of Commerce and the Community Chest. He even joined the Smoki Clan, an organization of Arizona businessmen who dressed in Native American garb and performed traditional dances to celebrate and promote doing business in Arizona. He prided himself on being a model employer: employees at Goldwater's worked a five-day, forty-hour week even before the passage of the Fair Labor Standards Act. The store paid wages well above the national average for retail employees, and provided pensions and health and life insurance long before these were typical fringe benefits. The store ran a farm eight miles from Phoenix governed by an elected committee of Goldwater's workers, where the store's employees could tend their own vegetable plots. They could take vacations in the company cabin. They could even learn to fly using the company plane. One newspaper reported that after a new store opened its doors, Goldwater took fourteen of its employees out to a restaurant for chicken and champagne. But such beneficence had as its flip side a fierce hostility to organized labor; in their very existence, unions seemed to suggest that workers needed to speak for themselves, that no employer, however generous, could entirely subsume their interests.[6]

The Great Depression and the New Deal drew Goldwater into politics. He voted for Herbert Hoover in 1932. "I think the foundations of my political philosophy were rooted in my resentment against the New Deal," he later wrote. He disliked the wage and price codes that the National Industrial Recovery Act tried to push into Goldwater's. At first he obediently hung the blue eagle that symbolized participation in the National Recovery Administration in the windows of his store. But he took the eagle down early in the spring of 1934.[7]

Later in the 1930s, Goldwater began to portray himself as a champion of frail and frightened businessmen beleaguered by power-hungry workers and the rapacious federal government. In a guest editorial for the *Phoenix Gazette* entitled "A Fireside Chat with Mr. Roosevelt," he accused the president of supporting corrupt labor unions: "Witness the chaos they are creating in eastern cities." In another guest editorial, this one called "Scared-e-cat," in honor of the cowering businessmen, he lambasted business for being too timid to challenge the president: "There isn't a businessman in this country today that does not fear the future status of our rising tax figure, yet he confines his suggestions for correcting the situation to his intimates who will agree with him."[8]

Once he was in the Senate, looking back, he insisted that his desire to stand up for business against the force of government and the New Deal had driven him into the public sphere. "I got into politics because I was disgusted with the way business associations in my community failed in upholding their city government," he told an audience in the late 1950s. "The only reason I ran for the United States Senate was the fact that businessmen were complaining their heads off, but doing nothing about it." His first public campaigns targeted the growing union presence in Arizona; to counter unions' rapid expansion during World War II, Goldwater helped to organize retailer support for a right-to-work campaign in 1946, preventing workers at a unionized workplace from being required to join the union. A few years later he ran for the Phoenix City Council. Then, in 1952, he ran for the Senate. "Do you agree with the Truman New Deal?" he asked his constituents. "Do you believe in expanding federal government? Are you willing to surrender more of your liberty? Do you want federal bureaus and federal agencies to take over an ever increasing portion of your life?"[9]

In his first Senate race, Goldwater reassured voters that he would not try to dismantle all the social programs of the New Deal; he did not seek to turn back the clock to 1932. By the time he ran for reelection in 1958, his tone had sharpened. His campaign that year directly took on the "labor bosses," and his victory—by a larger margin than in 1952—seemed to demonstrate that an antilabor politics could at times attract votes even from working-class people. By 1960, when he denounced Eisenhower's "dime store New Deal" from the floor of the Senate, his break with "modern Republicanism" was complete. For a generation, he insisted, Republicans had criticized the "welfare state, centralized government and federal control" while quietly passing legislation to extend all three:

"We are against federal aid to schools, but we have suggested a little of it; we are against federal aid to depressed areas, but we have offered a plan for a little of it; we recognize that to increase the minimum wage would be inflationary and would result in unemployment but we suggest a little increase; we have constantly held that the federal government should not provide socialized medicine, but now a spokesman offers a plan for a little of it . . . When we have completely taken care of everyone from the cradle to the grave, where amongst us will be the strength to make our decisions, to lead our economy, to lead our people, or to defend us in time of war?" Like Hayek and the men of the Mont Pelerin Society, Goldwater denounced the welfare state as a covert step to socialism: "[The collectivists] have learned that socialism can be achieved through welfarism quite as well as through nationalization."[10]

Still, Goldwater himself was not a purist when it came to the market. How could he be? Arizona had flourished thanks to generous gifts from the federal government for the development of infrastructure and the expansion of defense. Goldwater pushed for tariffs to protect copper mining, one of Arizona's leading industries, from low-wage overseas competition. In his first term, he even supported the Eisenhower administration's proposals to extend Social Security and raise the minimum wage. But he rarely mentioned such deviations from the strict rules of the market in his public pronouncements.[11]

More than any other, the event that brought Goldwater to the attention of business conservatives across the nation, while also marking a turning point in antilabor political activism, was the Kohler strike. Nestled in the small town of Sheboygan, Wisconsin, the Kohler Company hardly seemed a place where history would happen. A manufacturer employing several thousand workers, mostly descended from German and Slavic immigrants, the Kohler Company resembled the mills of the South, in which the employer controlled virtually all aspects of social life in the town. The company leased homes to workers and ran a dormitory, named the American Club, where single workers could rent rooms and enjoy recreational facilities. In the early decades of the twentieth century, it provided health insurance and a softball diamond and horseshoe grounds for relaxation; at Christmas, it gave family men a goose and single men a watch or a pocket knife.

Such perks disappeared during the Great Depression, at Kohler as at many other companies. Workers tried to organize a union to protect their dwindling wages and their jobs. But their strike quickly turned violent when Kohler deputies fired tear gas and then shot into a crowd that was throwing rocks at factory windows. Forty-seven strikers were wounded, and two young men were killed. The strike quickly unraveled, and Kohler workers did not try to organize again for twenty years. But in the early 1950s they voted to join the United Auto Workers, after growing frustrated by the company's reluctance to deal with complaints expressed through their employee association.[12]

At first Kohler agreed to negotiate, but the meetings quickly broke down when the management team refused to accept provisions that were standard parts of contracts in the 1950s: a union shop clause, an agreement for binding arbitration (specifying that disagreements about the interpretation of the contract would be settled by a neutral third party). The Kohler workers went on strike in April 1954—a strike that would not end until the early 1960s.

The strike pitted Kohler's owners against the UAW, one of the most powerful unions in the country. Its leader, the scrupulous, idealistic, and militant Walter Reuther, personified the victories of the labor movement in the 1930s and 1940s. He had organized an early sit-down strike on the West Side of Detroit, he was assaulted by Ford-hired thugs in 1937, and he led the UAW through the 1946 strike against General Motors. Reuther believed that workers would be strong in the workplace only if they were able to exercise political power as well. After all, before the Wagner Act and the creation of the National Labor Relations Board in the 1930s, the labor movement had been perennially vulnerable, unable to build lasting institutions, and strikes were bloody, drawn-out affairs; only the legal rights secured by the act made it possible for workers to make the democratic choice to join unions without risking their lives and livelihoods. Reuther also believed that the expansion of the public sector would help workers, and he tried to push the Democratic Party in the postwar period toward a more social-democratic politics. A *Saturday Evening Post* article from 1948 described him as "the most potent symbol and spokesman" for union workers, because he "views the labor movement primarily as a militant political force." All of this made Reuther especially frightening to businessmen. Frederick Crawford of Thompson Products, a strongly anti-union manufacturer of auto parts, wrote to the National Association of Manufacturers that Reuther was "a socialist at heart; [he] can see no place for the stockholder in American industry, and [he] is a ruthless, ambitious, unprincipled labor leader who expects to be the first labor president of the United States."[13]

Herbert Kohler, on the other side, was a stout, jovial man with white hair, bushy eyebrows, and a resonant, booming voice. Kohler's entire life was centered on the family company. Although he had attended Yale, he had returned home to work in the manufacturing plant during the summers, sometimes even on the assembly line, so as to be able to sympathize better with the men whose working lives he would someday control. He was deeply committed to a vision of himself as an ethical employer, and he experienced the strike as a personal betrayal. He slept on a cot inside the factory every night for the first few months of the 1954 strike. Strikers told stories of Kohler approaching the plant, waving a club and bellowing, "I am the law!"[14]

His chief adviser, Lyman Conger, the head of Kohler's legal department, was skinny and frail, physically the opposite of his boss. He had not been born into the local elite but had painstakingly worked his way up the ladder at Kohler over the course of twenty-six years, beginning in the enamel shop as a common laborer and attending law school at night. More than one observer described Conger as humorless and intense, the quintessential political ideologue. One UAW supporter who attended a Conger speech wrote afterward, "If I were writing a novel on industrial relations and presented a character as Mr. Conger appeared, I would expect the critics to complain I was exaggerating and had presented an implausible picture. You have to hear such a fanatic to believe there is such an animal in real life."[15]

During the first days of the Kohler strike, in the spring of 1954, the picket lines outside the Kohler plants were at once festive and angry, a fierce carnival. Thousands of workers gathered every day outside the factory gates, marching "belly-to-back" to prevent strikebreakers from entering the plants. The bloodshed of 1934 remained a living memory. Workers carried signs reading "'34 was Before the War, We'll Be Free in '54" and posed for photographs wearing gas masks. They packed halls for meetings, hanging banners proclaiming that the two sides of the strike were "Tear Gas, Guns and Clubs or Democratic Collective Bargaining." Local merchants donated cigarettes, groceries, and cigars to the strikers. Stories circulated in the union's daily strike update: a picnic where strikers "boycotted" sausages cooked by a scab; a pro-union bartender who, hearing that two beers had been sold to a worker crossing the picket line, walked to the house of the customer late at night and returned the money paid for the drinks.[16]

But two months into the strike, the company got an injunction to prohibit the union from having more than twenty-five pickets at a gate at a time. Kohler began to hire strikebreakers to operate the plant—boys from the farmland around Sheboygan eager to get a chance on the assembly line, workers who had gone on strike in April but who wanted to return to their jobs as the chill of autumn approached. The hiring of strikebreakers sent tremors through the town, as the strikers viewed those who crossed the line as "traitors" to the community. Churches canceled their summer picnics after fights broke out between strikers and those working at Kohler. Strikers began to hold angry "home demonstrations" at the houses of workers known to be crossing the picket line. "He is no more my son," said one striking father of his son who kept going to work.[17]

Violence started to ripple through Sheboygan. Nighttime visitors slashed tire wheels, put sugar into gas tanks, threw paint remover onto cars, and tore shrubs from the ground. Houses were paint-bombed and fistfights erupted at bars. The local union's president was hung in effigy, a knife stuck in his back. One elderly man, the father of a strikebreaker, fractured his vertebrae when he was knocked to the ground by an out-of-town UAW employee. When he died, a year and a half later, even though doctors ruled that the immediate cause of death was a heart attack, his family blamed the union.[18]

The strike began to leap beyond the boundaries of the city. The union, blocked from picketing, tried to organize a national boycott. T-shirts and caps with the slogan "Don't Buy Kohler" were sold across the country. Construction workers sometimes refused to install Kohler sinks and bathtubs. The city of Boston passed a resolution urging municipal contractors to boycott Kohler.[19]

Kohler, in turn, became the hero of small manufacturers across the country. Company executives spoke before a staggering array of business audiences—the Economic Club of Detroit, the National Association of Manufacturers, the Executives Club of Chicago, the Associated Industries of Alabama, Vermont and Georgia, the Alabama Cotton Manufacturers Association, and the National Association of Accountants, just to name a few. They gave virtually the same speech everywhere they went. Herbert Kohler would come before the podium. "Who runs this country?" he would ask his audience. "That is the basic issue at Kohler. That is the potential question for ALL industry. We must meet this issue fighting." (Peter Steele, the public relations manager at GE, wrote to the Kohler PR chief that his wife thought Kohler "a doll—a living doll.") The company became a regular advertiser in *National Review*, and Herbert Kohler spoke at meetings organized by Leonard Read to raise funds for the Foundation for Economic Education. Company leaders met with politicians and businessmen interested in passing state laws prohibiting union shops.[20]

In 1956, Kohler announced that his company was building a new plant in Spartanburg, South Carolina. "You here in the South, and this will include us also as we become established here, are facing a new influx of carpetbaggers," Kohler warned the Spartanburg Chamber of Commerce. "And if they get the foothold and obtain the power they are after, the result will be as fraught with evil as the experience of ninety years ago, which you recall with such horror and indignation and most of us in the North with such shame."[21]

Clarence Manion became a special champion of Kohler's cause. In October 1957 the radio host planned an interview with the company president on the "longest and most violent strike in American history." Kohler denounced the "goons from Detroit" and the "mobs" surrounding strikebreakers' homes and "terrorizing their wives and children." One of the networks that usually ran the Manion program refused to broadcast the interview unless the UAW was permitted to respond, saying that Kohler's speech was "derogatory and inflammatory." Manion then used the episode to raise money for the radio station: "We can only conclude that anti-American forces, which are now grasping out to get control of all media of communication in the United States, took it upon themselves to prevent the great pro-American address of Mr. Kohler from being heard by the American people."[22]

In 1957, Barry Goldwater was serving on the Senate Select Committee on Improper Activities in the Labor or Management Field (known as the McClellan Committee), which had been formed to investigate charges of abuse and corruption within the labor movement. The committee uncovered sensational cases of theft grand and petty, sweetheart deals between unions and corporations, as well as connections between labor unions and the Mafia. But Goldwater was not content with investigating the Laborers and the Teamsters. These unions might be corrupt, but they were not politically dangerous. He insisted that the committee investigate Walter Reuther and the violence at Kohler, and when Democrats on the committee protested that there was no reason to do so, he accused them of protecting a political ally. Goldwater had support for bringing Reuther to testify in Washington. One Texas businessman sent Goldwater a letter asking that he make sure that Reuther (whom he called "the most powerful and dangerous man in America today") appear before the committee: "If this is not done, I feel the committee is not doing its duty." Enclosed with the letter was a check for $1,000. At a fund-raising dinner early in January 1958, Goldwater told his audience that Reuther was "a more dangerous menace than the sputniks or anything Russia might do."[23]

There was no evidence that the union leadership was responsible for the violence at Kohler. Nor was there any suggestion of financial wrongdoing. But Goldwater nonetheless succeeded in pressuring the Democrats on the committee to bring Reuther and the Kohler strike before the Senate. The hearings themselves were anticlimactic, and Reuther's impassioned three-day-long performance on the stand wound up making Goldwater look foolish ("You substitute your prejudice for the facts," he told the senator, adding that Goldwater and the other conservative senators on the committee had "kind of antiquated" viewpoints). Everyone already knew that the Kohler strike had been long and bitter, and the McClellan Committee did not uncover any proof of a conspiracy of violence, much less any financial malfeasance. Even the *National Review* conceded that the hearings "may be judged a considerable propaganda victory for Walter Reuther."[24]

Still, for diehard Goldwater supporters, the hearings only helped to shore up his image as a man brave enough to stare down the most powerful union in America and to stand up for businesses like Kohler. The national organizing around the Kohler strike had helped create an audience among businessmen for a politician like Goldwater. His reelection campaign in the fall of 1958 took on the union leaders who he claimed were sending organizers and loads of cash to help finance the opposition in Arizona. He did not mention the thousands of dollars that flowed to him from businessmen across the country grateful for the position he had taken against the power of labor. "As Vice-President and Manager of a Division of Dravo Corporation, I participate in a great many negotiations with Unions. I feel the work of men such as yourself is essential to keep labor relations in this country on an even keel," read a representative letter from a Pittsburgh executive, whose company collected $1,000 in management donations to send to the Goldwater campaign.[25]

By being one of the only national politicians willing to criticize the politics of the welfare state openly and vigorously, by taking on the labor leader who more than any other stood for the rise of powerful industrial unions and the politicization of the union movement, Goldwater had moved far beyond the parochial world of Phoenix. He seemed poised to become the standard-bearer for business conservatism against the liberals in the Republican Party.

. . .

EARLY IN 1959, Clarence Manion began to talk to his friends about finding someone who could take up the conservative cause within the Republican Party—a candidate capable of challenging Eisenhower's "modern Republicanism." They thought at first that a southerner might be best, someone who could bring together northern businessmen with southerners disaffected by the early victories of the civil rights movement. Then Goldwater gave a speech in South Carolina arguing that *Brown v. Board of Education* violated the Constitution. The fledgling South Carolina Republican Party was euphoric. Manion and his friends knew that they had their man.[26]

Manion approached Goldwater about writing a book, which he hoped would spell out a full program for the conservative movement. (He already knew the senator, who had appeared on the radio program in 1957, in a broadcast entitled "Senator's Personal Integrity Tops 'Modern Republicanism.'") Goldwater was initially reluctant. After he accepted, he wrote to Stephen Shadegg, his campaign adviser: "My complete incapacity to be an author is well known to everybody, so before I even attempt a thing like this, I would like to have your suggestions." But Manion, full of ideas, also provided Goldwater with a ghostwriter, L. Brent Bozell, a brother-in-law of William F. Buckley who worked at *National Review.* Bozell and Goldwater met in August 1959 to hash out the book; after the meeting, Bozell wrote to Manion that Goldwater seemed "a little poetic and corny" in the way he wanted to state his views but that most likely they could work out a manuscript. The initial title that Manion proposed was "What Americanism Means to Me," and one of Manion's friends urged "Revolutionary Conservatism," but Goldwater settled on *The Conscience of a Conservative.*[27]

At the same time Manion wrote to the companies that subscribed to his radio program, inviting them to participate in a special committee for "conservative political action." The plan was to finance publication of the book (Manion would set up his own publishing company), sell it "to corporate businesses and to others at a profit," and use the proceeds to fund Goldwater's challenge to Richard Nixon for the Republican nomination for the presidency in 1960. As Manion wrote to Roger Milliken, who was a donor to the *Manion Forum* as well as one of the leading figures in South Carolina's Republican Party, "We could sell thousands of these to corporations with the dual purpose of raising money and spreading the Goldwater gospel."[28]

As the publication date for the book approached, Manion began to contact businessmen to arrange for their advance purchases. "We have sent out 100 telegrams to selected heads of corporations and the responses are very encouraging," he wrote to Goldwater. He sent out circulars to businessmen letting them know that they could deduct the expense of their bulk copies of *Conscience* from their taxes as a business write-off and then distribute the "wonderful gospel so courageously preached" for free to "stockholders, employees, libraries, school teachers, etc." He wrote to the Hollywood star Adolphe Menjou in early April, "If a million of these books could be spread throughout the country and appropriately publicized, the world would be changed—I really mean it."[29]

The book that resulted sought to reinvent conservatism and rescue it from the stain that had been on it ever since the days of the Liberty League: the charge of being the staid, self-interested philosophy of the elite. Goldwater (or Brent Bozell, whose ardent Catholic faith may have helped to give *Conscience* its distinctly antimaterialist slant) opened the book by telling his readers that conservatism was not, as they might have been told, a "narrow, mechanistic *economic* theory." Nor was it a selfish campaign for "the preservation of economic privilege and status." On the contrary, real conservatism was a philosophy that "puts material things in their proper place." Far from being the ideology of a handful of wealthy businessmen, conservative philosophy was the embodiment of timeless truths about the nature of human society, reflecting the divine order of the world, the laws of God. It treated the individual, not the mass; it saw economic and political freedom as "inextricably entwined"; it embodied the perfect balance between liberty and social order. The liberals of the New Deal (and of Harry Truman's Fair Deal) had sought to contravene these ancient precepts. In their blind hubris, their foolish confidence in their own power, they had created an overreaching federal government and permitted the spread of labor unions, both of which threatened to swallow up, dominate, and destroy the free individual. The welfare state, Goldwater insisted, transformed "the individual from a dignified, industrious, self-reliant *spiritual* being into a dependent animal creature without his knowing it." Labor unions and the welfare state oppressed the very people they were supposed to free.

But what made *Conscience* even more potent as a political document was that it did not restrict its analysis to economic matters. Goldwater took aim not only at the labor movement and the New Deal but at the emerging civil rights movement, and specifically at the Supreme Court's 1954 decision in *Brown v. Board of Education.* He sought to use the same language that the business conservatives had used to protest the New Deal—portraying themselves as outnumbered, outmanned, but engaged in principled resistance against mob-like mass movements and a tyrannical state—to appeal to the white opponents of the civil rights movement. Nothing in the Constitution, he insisted, mandated that black children in the South attend the same schools as white children. Indeed, the Constitution was not "intended to, and therefore it did not, authorize *any* federal intervention in the field of education." Personally, he reassured readers, he supported the racial integration of schools. But the sovereign rights of the states embodied in the Constitution made it impossible to support using the federal government to say anything at all about how they should educate their children. The racial hierarchy of the South was merely a private question of local preferences: "The problem of race relations, like all social and cultural problems, is best handled by the people directly concerned."

Despite such prim optimism about the market, the tone of *Conscience* grew dark when it came to the Soviet Union. Goldwater tried to rally his followers to be prepared to fight a literal war. The fear of nuclear holocaust must not be permitted to dispel the martial spirit; the "cornerstone" of American foreign policy should be "that we would rather die than lose our freedom." Individual freedom could only be protected in the end if citizens were persuaded to sacrifice their lives.[30]

Short, graceful and easy to read, *The Conscience of a Conservative* tried to give laissez-faire boilerplate the moral rigor of social philosophy.

It translated the ideas of Hayek and Mises into a compressed, elegant credo, accessible to virtually anyone who might pick it up. No longer could conservatism be made to seem only the worldview of a wealthy class of conformists; conservatives would present themselves instead as rebels, individualists, true believers in first principles. The book reversed the old drama of the rich against the poor, the privileged against the powerless, by spelling out a faith for people who saw themselves on the brink of being overpowered by ideological foes but who were determined nonetheless to fight on. As the *Wall Street Journal* put it, Goldwater "boasts conservative principles, yet he confounds his enemies by defending them on strictly humanitarian grounds."[31]

The Conscience of a Conservative did better than anyone, even Manion, could have imagined. Published in early April 1960, it reached number ten on *Time* magazine's bestseller list and number fourteen on the *New York Times* list by the end of June. By the end of the year it had sold half a million copies. Businessmen did their part to buy copies: Fred Koch of Wichita bought 2,500 for circulation through the Kansas Republican Party; Anaconda Copper ordered 500. In the end, however, the book's success was a genuine phenomenon. It sold especially well on college campuses, tapping into a market for conservative ideas that no one had really known to exist. It was the first truly popular conservative classic of the postwar period.[32]

Goldwater did not challenge Nixon for the party's nomination in 1960, as Manion had hoped. On the contrary, at the Republican convention he admonished his supporters to "grow up" and work to elect the Republican candidate. But Stephen Shadegg, the senator's old campaign manager, had other ideas. As he wrote to a resolute Goldwater supporter a few weeks after the convention, "We're with you—just beginning for '64."[33]

He wasn't the only one thinking about the possibility. In the summer of 1961, over lunch in a New York City hotel, F. Clifton White, the political consultant who specialized in organizing businessmen to be activists, talked with William Rusher, the publisher of *National Review*, about trying to obtain the Republican nomination for 1964 for a real conservative. The two had been friends in the Young Republicans, and later in the summer they met with a third YR comrade, John Ashbrook, by 1961 a freshman congressman from Ohio. The three made a list of their most trusted acquaintances—White picked men he'd known through his business-in-politics program—and planned to gather in Chicago at the end of October. At the October meeting, White laid out a plan to (as he put it in later years) "make the Republican Party the effective conservative instrument in American politics." He would carefully build an organization of conservative Republicans who would elect delegates loyal to the cause—who could be absolutely counted on to support a conservative candidate at the 1964 Republican convention.[34]

Even though Goldwater didn't know too much about White's group—they met with him to let him know they were organizing a conservative bloc within the Republican Party but said they wouldn't make any decisions about a candidate until after the 1962 midterm elections—he kept trying to expand his contacts in the corporate world. In May 1961 he gathered New York executives—the president of the New York Stock Exchange, the chairmen of Merrill Lynch, Morgan Guaranty, and Chase Manhattan Bank, and representatives of Goldman, Sachs and Morgan Stanley, among others—for a special luncheon at the Wall Street Club. "To know that American business finally recognizes the threats to their very existence is encouraging," he told the attendees afterward. He kept detailed lists of the names and addresses of businessmen who went to receptions hosted by the United Republican Finance Committee, while his campaign manager collected the names of conservative young public relations men who might be loyal Goldwater supporters. In the spring of 1963, Goldwater asked a business friend to survey executives to gather opinions about his possible run for the presidency and received positive responses from a variety of corporate leaders. J. William Middendorf wrote to the candidate at that time, insisting that support was growing stronger even in Manhattan: "It is simply amazing the enthusiasm that is now spreading through the country for you and we sense it everywhere—surprisingly enough I see a great deal of it growing right here in New York City."[35]

Goldwater knew that if he ran for president against John F. Kennedy, he would be challenging a popular and wealthy incumbent. He was well aware that he would probably confront the phenomenally rich Nelson Rockefeller in the struggle for the Republican nomination. He knew that he could appeal to the midwestern manufacturers and textile men who had backed him in 1960 and who had underwritten *Conscience of a Conservative*. But he likely also believed that he could pick up support from Wall Street and perhaps from larger companies too. Businessmen had always helped Goldwater's political career.

THE GOLDWATER campaign gained momentum even before Goldwater formally announced his candidacy, during the summer and early fall of 1963. The men and women who had listened to Manion's radio program, who had signed on to the right-to-work campaigns, who had attended Fred Schwarz's Christian Anti-Communism Schools, who subscribed to *National Review* or the evangelical *Faith and Freedom*—at last they had someone who might be a presidential candidate. And as the jails of Birmingham filled with civil rights protesters in the spring of 1963, Republican strategists saw an opportunity to build the base of the party beyond the network of conservative activists and business supporters by wooing white voters in the North and the South.

In a June 1963 memorandum, Peter Clayton, the former executive director of Citizens for Eisenhower-Nixon, spelled out his argument for how Goldwater could win. Until the middle of March, Clayton wrote, he had believed that the moderate Nelson Rockefeller was the obvious choice for the Republican nominee. But he had changed his mind, because of "the so-called 'civil rights rebellion' of the Negro race and the encouragement, or seeming encouragement, this 'rebellion' receives from the President, Attorney General and official Washington." Black protesters, Clayton argued, had abandoned their "peaceful, hopeful striving for social justice" in favor of "strident, militant actions seemingly undeterred by the antagonisms which these actions create." As a result, hostility to the civil rights movement had "spread like wildfire" through the country.

White Americans, Clayton believed, were looking for an alternative to President John F. Kennedy, and that alternative, as long as Goldwater continued to stick by his position that "local problems must somehow be solved locally and that private property must remain inviolate," was clearly Barry Goldwater.[36]

Goldwater was in some ways an odd choice for the candidate of racial backlash. He prided himself on his personal opposition to segregation and discrimination. During his years on the Phoenix city council he had encouraged the integration of the city's high schools. In the 1950s he was a member of the NAACP (he quit when they "began calling me an s.o.b."). But his critique of *Brown v. Board of Education* and his argument that he supported "all efforts by the states," exclusive of violence, "to preserve their rightful powers over education" made clear that he could appeal to the defenders of Jim Crow. And in 1964, he voted against the Civil Rights Act. In a speech on the Senate floor in which he explained his decision, Goldwater conjured a terrifying totalitarian vision inspired by the cold war nightmare of "a federal police force of mammoth proportions," breeding an "informer" psychology of "neighbors spying on neighbors, workers spying on workers, businessmen spying on businessmen" if the bill should pass.[37]

Not long after Clayton wrote his memo, Clif White, in the thick of his efforts for Goldwater, commissioned a polling agency to study the impact of the civil rights movement on the electorate, especially in northern cities. Shortly following the famous March on Washington in August 1963, White's pollsters asked voters in New York, "Do you think the Kennedy administration is really interested in helping Negroes gain equal rights, or are they just trying to use the racial issue to gain political advantage? What is your view on the Civil Rights March on Washington which took place a week or so ago? Do you think this helped advance the cause of equal rights for Negroes or did it do more harm than good?" The results for a similar survey on civil rights done in Boston came back in the fall. "When the civil rights controversy poses a close-to-home threat," the report from the Opinion Research Corporation read, "people do get aroused and disturbed, even if they are not directly involved, and this ire can be an influence in voting behavior in the forthcoming Presidential campaign." What was more, anxiety about civil rights "appears to cut across party lines. It is not just a Republican issue, but one that bothers voter types who are traditionally Democrat." Antagonism to the civil rights movement had the potential to unify white voters across the country, across the lines of class and party.[38]

By the early fall of 1963, Goldwater looked as if he might be the front-runner for the Republican nomination. A *Saturday Evening Post* profile late in the summer pronounced him the most likely to win the campaign because "white votes for Goldwater might at this time of racial crisis vastly outnumber black votes for Kennedy, in the North as well as in the South." J. William Middendorf wrote glowing letters to the businessmen who contributed to the National Draft Goldwater Committee. "When Barry becomes president it will in no small measure have been accomplished through the superb efforts of the Millikens," he wrote to Gerrish Milliken, expressing gratitude to the two Milliken brothers. In September 1963, the Goldwater campaign held a rally at Dodger Stadium in Los Angeles. Even though Goldwater had not officially declared himself a presidential candidate, more than 40,000 people paid a dollar each to attend. A select group of four hundred went to a $100-a-plate dinner before the event (in the morning, Goldwater breakfasted with Billy Graham and then met with a group of black voters to try to explain how he was for both civil rights *and* states' rights). A drum-and-bugle corps of girls in bright uniforms marched in front of the candidate, who rode in a white convertible, while the eager crowds chanted, "We Want Barry!" In the words of the *New York Times*, it was "the gaudy, frenetic sort of scene that could be expected at the peak of an election campaign"—only it was more than a year before the election, and there was no official campaign. There was talk about Goldwater as the Republican frontrunner. Pundits made gleeful comparisons with Kennedy in 1959.[39]

Less than two months later, Lee Harvey Oswald shot the president. The assassination rocked the Goldwater campaign. Almost everyone assumed initially that a deranged right-winger had killed Kennedy. Although the Draft Goldwater Committee pulled in its typical $25,000 the week after the assassination, donations fell sharply in December 1963 (partly because of a fund-raising moratorium). Goldwater had been looking forward to campaigning against Kennedy, whom he saw as a decent and respectable opponent. But he was frightened of Lyndon Baines Johnson. He also knew that as a native son, Johnson would have an advantage in the South. He tried to back out of the race, but too much money, time, and hope had already been invested for the candidate to extricate himself, and the campaign went forward.[40]

While White researched ways for the Goldwater campaign to win the support of white voters in the North and South, many of the longtime business activists in conservative circles donated money to the campaign. More than $25,000 came from the du Pont family and their circle (including $3,000 from Jasper Crane, who was still doing what he could to support the conservative cause). The Eli Lilly family donated, as did Walt Disney and Walter Knott; Horace Stoneham, the president of the San Francisco (formerly New York) Giants; the president of Gimbels; and Charles Edison, the former governor of New Jersey and owner of the Waldorf-Astoria. The chairman of the board of the Libbey-Owens-Ford Glass Company contributed; so did the director of Aetna. Dan Gainey, the former chairman of Josten's, Inc., which made class rings, served as the finance director for much of the campaign. Late in the year, Ralph Cordiner of General Electric took over fund-raising for the Republican National Finance Committee. Lemuel Boulware, also retired from General Electric, personally contributed about $10,000 to the campaign. (He and Goldwater formed a mutual admiration society; in later years, Goldwater would write to Boulware: "I can remember very well the great inspiration that you provided for me as you so stubbornly, rightly, and forcefully fought with the union that was trying to take over your company. I wish we had more like you around. The woods are full of softies today, not many tough ones left.")[41]

Even more support for Goldwater would come from small businessmen. Funeral directors, for example, were frightened by the possibility of congressional hearings to investigate the funeral industry in the wake of the publication of Jessica Mitford's 1963 exposé, *The American Way of Death*. The owner of an Arizona funeral home sent letters to his colleagues reminding them of the "increased socialistic attacks upon our profession." Funeral directors wrote back expressing their enthusiastic support for Goldwater as "the only hope we have to keep the Federal Government out of our business." The increasing level of political activism among business was also evident in congressional races. "The U.S. corporation's flirtation with politics that began shyly enough in the late 1950s has blossomed into a warm romance," read one 1964 *Wall Street Journal* piece, reporting on the increase in political activity.[42]

Finally, free-market intellectuals helped the Goldwater campaign. The University of Chicago economist and Mont Pelerin Society member Milton Friedman had published his classic tract *Capitalism and Freedom* just two years earlier. The book, which was based on a 1956 series of lectures that had been sponsored by the Volker Fund, provided a positive program for the free-market movement, translating the broad principles that Hayek and Mises had outlined into clever and straightforward prescriptions for economic policy. Friedman's style was audacious: he cited the Hollywood blacklist of Communist writers during the McCarthy years as evidence of the superiority of a free-market economy; after all, the blacklist had eventually ended, and even while it was in effect the blacklisted writers had sometimes been able to find work under pen names. Inequality of income was a positive good, because it helped spur intellectual diversity: "In a capitalist society, it is only necessary to convince a few wealthy people to get funds to launch any idea, however strange." And he opposed fair employment practices legislation that prohibited racial discrimination in hiring, describing such prejudice as a "taste": "Is there any difference in principle between the taste that leads a householder to prefer an attractive servant to an ugly one and the taste that leads another to prefer a Negro to a white or a white to a Negro, except that we sympathize and agree with the one taste and may not with the other?" In 1964, Friedman took the framework of *Capitalism and Freedom* and applied it as an informal economic adviser for the Goldwater campaign, writing an essay for the *New York Times Magazine* on "the Goldwater view of economics," which he defined as a coherent economic philosophy committed to "freedom of the individual to pursue his own interests so long as he does not interfere with the freedom of others to do likewise; opportunity for the ordinary man to use his resources as effectively as possible to advance the well-being of himself and his family." Nor was Friedman the only free-market intellectual to get involved with Goldwater; William Baroody took a leave of absence from AEI and threw himself into consulting and writing speeches for the campaign.[43]

Goldwater's campaign reached a crescendo at the Republican convention at the Cow Palace—a mammoth structure in a suburb of San Francisco that had been built in the 1930s by the Works Progress Administration—in the summer of 1964. There, the activists whom Clif White had patiently mobilized in his cause gathered for a raucous display of their affection and power. Goldwater delegates made up a two-thirds majority at the convention; most of them were under fifty, white, male, and at least middle-class if not wealthier. They were anything but obedient foot soldiers for the Republican Party. They had gone to Goldwater rallies and pored over *The Conscience of a Conservative*, and they were at the Cow Palace for one reason only: to nominate their man. These were the people who plastered their cars with bumper stickers reading AuH_2O (pro-Goldwater decals were available in languages from Spanish to Finnish) or "This Car Is Solid Goldwater," or featuring pictures of Goldwater's trademark clunky black glasses. They drank Gold Water, a specially produced carbonated beverage. Four teenagers from Nashville started a band dubbed the Goldwaters; their first LP was entitled *The Goldwaters Sing Folk Songs to Bug the Liberals.* One Goldwater loyalist took her German shepherd, named Rebel, to rallies wearing a sign: "Goldwater wouldn't pull a dog's ears OR your leg." Flocks of Goldwater Girls greeted the candidate at his campaign stops. The chairman of a Tennessee bank raised more than $10,000 for the Goldwater campaign with his line of Goldwater "droplet" jewelry—flecks of twenty-three-carat gold suspended within clear plastic drops of "water," which could be worn as pendants, earrings, lapel pins, or bracelets.[44]

At the Republican convention, White organized his delegates with care, setting up a buddy system so they could keep tabs on each other. But his best efforts could not contain their indecorous glee at their sudden sense of themselves as a popular political force. Goldwater supporters from the spectator galleries (though not the delegates—White was monitoring them too closely for that) booed the speeches of the moderate Republicans, drowning out their pleas to repudiate the John Birch Society. They reveled in the golden balloons and glittering bits of confetti that cascaded from the ceiling of the Cow Palace when their candidate's name was officially placed in nomination. And they adored the lines in Goldwater's speech accepting the Republican Party nomination: "I would remind you that extremism in the defense of liberty is no vice! And let me remind you also that moderation in the pursuit of justice is no virtue!" Delivered in the midst of a bitter platform fight within the Republican Party, in which Goldwater's opponents had wanted to pass a resolution condemning "extremist" groups, the lines were intended to reaffirm Goldwater's image as a man who held principle above all else.[45]

But if the creation of a passionate, mobilized group of activists kept the Goldwater campaign careening forward, the entire subculture of the rallies and the meetings and the trinkets managed to alienate the "modern" Republicans. They weren't welcome in the campaign; in fact, they were the enemy, just as much as the Democrats. This open hostility to the elder statesmen of the party met with a harsh response. The New York Republican senator Jacob Javits described it as "the beginnings of an American totalitarianism." Nelson Rockefeller issued a press release: "The extremism of the Communists, of the Ku Klux Klan, and of the John Birch Society—like that of most terrorists—has always been claimed by such groups to be in the defense of liberty." The *New York Times* editorial page announced that Goldwater had diminished "a once great party to the status of an ugly, angry, frustrated faction." Senator J. William Fulbright likened Goldwater's style of conservatism to Stalinism.[46]

After the Republican convention, both the mainstream press and the Johnson campaign portrayed Goldwater as a man teetering on the edge of complete psychological breakdown. In September 1964, *Fact* magazine published an article titled "The Unconscious of a Conservative" which proclaimed that 1,189 psychiatrists had pronounced Barry Goldwater mentally unfit to be president. (More than 650 said he was perfectly sane, as far as they could tell.) "Goldwater's speeches are waves of verbiage which have no clear-cut meaning and which resemble the written productions of schizophrenics," wrote one doctor. Another psychiatrist opined, "Mr. Goldwater and many of his followers belong to that unfortunate group of neurotic persons who would like to be dead in order to 'get it over with' because of their enormous pathological need to find an *answer* for everything . . . He resembles Mao Tse-Tung." Goldwater was "authoritarian, megalomaniac, grandiose, basically narcissistic," with an "infantile, magical manner of thinking and feeling." One director of a community clinic closed his missive by saying: "In allowing you to quote me, which I do, I rely on the protection of Goldwater's defeat at the polls in November; for if Goldwater wins the presidency, both you and I will be among the first into the concentration camps."[47]

The psychiatrists' letters, no matter how unscientific the poll, crystallized the liberal vision of Goldwater as psychically fragile and mentally imbalanced. This kind of coverage led the Columbia University historian Richard Hofstadter to describe Goldwater as a "pseudo-conservative" seeking to play upon "paranoid suspicions . . . impossible demands . . . [and] millennial dreams of total victory." When Lyndon Johnson's campaign ran the famous daisy commercial, depicting a young girl pulling the petals off a flower while an ominous voice counted down toward nuclear catastrophe, it rammed home the central message, repeated in Democratic campaign posters featuring pictures of mushroom clouds: in the time of the cold war, the summer of the Gulf of Tonkin incident in Vietnam, no one could trust Goldwater's finger on the nuclear trigger to be steady.[48]

AS THE GOLDWATER campaign began to fall apart, the candidate's underlying weaknesses began to emerge clearly. One of the deepest problems he faced was his difficulty in winning lasting support from business, especially from larger corporations. While he had been able to attract some followers, business was by no means unified around the conservative Republican.

By the early 1960s, the Democrats were trying to distance themselves from their antibusiness image. Early in 1963 the Kennedy administration had introduced legislation calling for major cuts in individual and corporate income taxes. The bill was a Keynesian proposal intended to stimulate demand by letting the government run a deficit; it did not cut government expenditures by the amount it cut taxes. But to win business support, Kennedy administration officials began to defend the bill by arguing that high taxes diminished the incentive to save and to invest. Executives from large corporations organized to support the tax reductions, while asking that government expenditures be cut back to prevent ballooning budget deficits. "No administration that is 'antibusiness' would have pushed through these two measures," said the executive vice president of the American Bankers Association, referring to the adoption of a new depreciation timetable and an investment tax credit. More than three thousand executives joined a Business Committee for Tax Reduction. Four days before his death in Dallas, Kennedy spoke at the Florida Chamber of Commerce, reminding those in attendance that his administration had passed investment tax credits, liberalized depreciation guidelines, lowered transportation taxes, and was proposing major personal and corporate tax cuts. "Many are still convinced," the Democratic president told the assembled Florida businessmen, "that a Democratic Administration is out to soak the rich, increase controls for the sake of controls, and extend at all costs the scope of federal bureaucracy. The hard facts contradict these doubts."[49]

Johnson proved even more adept than Kennedy at wooing executives. Less than two weeks after Kennedy's assassination, Johnson summoned eighty-nine of the country's leading CEOs to the White House for a special meeting. "We have much work to do together," he told them. He made sure that the White House photographer snapped a portrait of the president with each guest and then sent them copies. He invited them all back for dinner at the White House in January, to give them a special advance briefing on his upcoming State of the Union address and to enumerate for them all the budget items he planned to cut—responding to their criticism of the deficit spending. The next day the CEO of Merck sent an appreciative telegram: "In spite of the difficulties ahead you will certainly receive strong support for your program in the business community." In June 1964, the president of Hill & Knowlton, a public relations firm, told an audience of public relations executives that "President Johnson, like his predecessor, has gone out of his way to speak encouragingly to top business groups." And the proof of Johnson's sympathy to business (and Kennedy's before him) was his endorsement of the tax cuts.[50]

The Johnson campaign raised much of its cash through special appeals to wealthy businessmen, such as the President's Club, which numbered four thousand members across the country, each contributing at least $1,000. As the campaign season heated up, corporate support for Johnson accelerated. The former president and general counsel of Ford pronounced that he was "willing to work in every possible way for the election of President Johnson," while Henry Ford II was one of the most prominent contributors to the Democratic candidate. Campaign aides helped to encourage the creation of an organization which they dubbed Republican Businessmen for Johnson; announced in September, the National Independent Committee for President Johnson and Senator Humphrey organized more than three thousand CEOs for the president. Among the members of the Business Council, a relatively apolitical organization of CEOs from large corporations, thirty-six contributed to Republican candidates for office and thirty-three to Democrats—a sharp shift from 1960, when seventy-three had donated to Republicans and seven to Democrats.[51]

Goldwater's aides were angry at what they saw as the lack of spine among executives, even before the backlash that followed the Republican convention. "Six months ago most of these businessmen in Oregon were saying if only we could get somebody like Goldwater to run for president, we might save the nation. Now they have him and the bastards are sitting on their hands," wrote Stephen Shadegg in March 1964. Business leaders who had once proclaimed their ardent support were suddenly "colder than last week's mashed potatoes." Because "we're not in the lead, the fat cats are holding back. If we can make enough forward progress politically, the fat cats will climb on the wagon." But Goldwater never did surge forward, and the businessmen went with Johnson in the end. Goldwater's support from business ebbed so low that even Dan Gainey, one of his top fund-raisers, was rumored to have confessed after the election that he hadn't actually pulled the lever for the candidate: "I just couldn't bring myself to vote for him."[52]

Failing to get support from businessmen in the months leading up to the election, the Goldwater campaign decided to try a new tactic: finding ways to translate the conservative message into rhetoric that could mobilize working-class voters. Even though Goldwater's low-tax, non-union vision for economic growth won the support of some union members in Arizona, Clif White thought that his surveys about reactions to the civil rights movement indicated the potential for success with a different strategy—one that focused on fears of racial integration and on a broad call for morality in politics.

As the election approached, the New York City offices of Citizens for Goldwater-Miller (the group for Goldwater and his vice-presidential candidate, New York congressman William Miller, that White was tapped to lead after the Republican convention, much to his frustration; he'd hoped for a higher post) saved a survey of forty white ethnic voters in Queens—mostly first- and second-generation Americans, some recent immigrants, mostly lower middle class—that a supporter sent into the office. About half were for Goldwater and half either for Johnson or still undecided. The issues the Goldwater supporters felt most strongly about were "rising crime" and "fear of integration"; even Johnson supporters were agitated about these problems. Nearly everyone opposed busing children from one neighborhood to another to integrate the public schools. "Most of those voting for Johnson thought Goldwater was right with respect to the 'racial issue,' but thought he was anti-union or would weaken social security," according to the survey. The most striking aspect of the poll was the finding that the economic elements of the conservative program—"'right-to-work' and voluntary social security"—made an "almost universal negative impression" on the Queens voters. But these could be trumped if the Republicans changed their platform to capitalize on racial fears. And that's exactly what the Goldwater supporter suggested: "Signs should not simply read 'Vote Goldwater' but rather 'Make our neighborhood safe again. Vote Goldwater.' Or 'Streets must be made safe again. Vote Goldwater' or 'Don't experiment with our children. Keep neighborhood schools. Vote Goldwater' or 'Our children want education—not transportation. Vote Goldwater.'"[53]

The letters coming into the Goldwater campaign offices from political allies and supporters made similar suggestions. In September one political consultant wrote that on Long Island the busing program was known as the LBJ program, for "Let's Bus Juveniles," and suggested that "race riots" might sway New York City voters. Another Goldwater supporter, a Wall Streeter who wrote to the campaign while on a business flight, argued that "much more must be done to exploit the white backlash," saying that whites feared that "Negroes will move into their neighborhoods." The white backlash, he declared, was "the biggest single reservoir of votes that Goldwater can tap into but you will have to get more to the point, if you are going to get these votes."[54]

White wrote a memo to campaign headquarters laying out a new strategy for Goldwater. To have any chance of winning the election, Goldwater needed to "utilize (and build) fully the one key issue which is working for us—the moral crisis (law and order vs. crime and violence)." Instead of talking about taxes, unions, Social Security, the welfare state, or the labor bosses—all the issues of the business conservatives that had been Goldwater's political staples throughout his life—he should focus on something new and different: the "moral crisis in America today," a diffuse sense of alienation about "crime, violence, riots (the backlash), juvenile delinquency, the breakdown of law and order, immorality and corruption in high places, the lack of moral leadership in general, narcotics, pornography." Morality, White was convinced, could be in 1964 what "the missile gap" had been in 1960. The Goldwater campaign should make sure that the sense of moral crisis would be "sharpened, heightened, and used to dramatically focus the anxieties and animosities of the voting public against the opposition."

White suggested organizing a "Mothers' March for Morality" in mid-October, which would be a "precinct-drive for spiritual regeneration." He thought that Goldwater needed to reach out to Christian groups, such as Youth for Christ and the Campus Crusades. The campaign should no longer be about the welfare state and the power of labor but about the moral life of the United States. The issues of race and culture, White believed, could easily be joined to the politics of the free market. The welfare state, after all, was the product of just the same unrestrained collective yearnings that produced moral chaos.[55]

With Goldwater's blessing, White decided to make a documentary that would help reorient the Goldwater campaign around the themes of moral decay. To do so, he joined forces with Rus Walton, a Republican activist. Walton was one of the leaders of the United Republicans of California, an organization founded to unify California conservatives, and he had been the head publicist for the National Association of Manufacturers throughout the 1950s. There he had experimented with various propaganda techniques. One of his proudest creations (as described by historian Rick Perlstein) was a little booklet about the Kohler strike designed for women's clubs. The cover featured a picture of a woman ducking for cover as if she were desperately scrambling to escape a menacing assailant. The copy told readers to beware the "uncontrollable power, wealth and political influence of unions and union bosses."[56]

Choice, the film that Walton and White collaborated to create, was no more subtle about the political dangers confronting the United States. The movie opened with shots of a black sedan racing down a mountain-lined road veering from side to side. It then shifted to a rapid montage of teenagers dancing wildly, news footage of police arresting black demonstrators, and a topless dancer swaying at a nightclub. This "nightmare" America of reckless desire stood opposed to the old ideal of decency and freedom, the dream for which men had sacrificed and died way back at Valley Forge. In a tone at once outraged and salacious, the movie connected scandals brewing in the Johnson White House to rising crime, pornography, gambling, political demonstrations, and drug use, a world in which everything was permitted. The growing wealth of the United States—the "false promise of the fast deal"—had destroyed the moral toughness of the nation: "Paychecks are fat. Everybody seems to be getting his. I'll get mine, the people say." With a staccato rhythm thrumming in the background, the camera lingered over the titles of pornographic novels—*Call Me Nympho*, *Hotrod Sinners*, *Jazz Me Baby*, and *Male for Sale*. The "new America," a nation on the brink of "mobocracy," had lost sight of the ancient moral truths: "Nation under God. Who's he?" Illegitimate births clogged the relief rolls, narcotics traffic set a "new depraved record," and policemen were no longer permitted to enforce the law: "No longer is a uniform a symbol of authority." All of it led to an atmosphere of pervasive danger and criminality, implicitly endorsed by the highest-ranking leaders in the land: "Beating. Rape. Murder. Some other country? No [with a low, rueful laugh]! Here. Now."

The movie's denouement featured John Wayne, rifle hanging prominently on the wall behind his head, telling the audience that the future of America lay in their hands. The scene shifted to Goldwater at the Republican convention, showered by balloons pouring down from the rafters. "CHOICE," blared the final title. As Walton told one reporter, the film was intended to rouse "raw, naked emotions." The campaign, he said, was "catering to the Midwest. This film will obviously and frankly just play on their prejudices."[57]

White sent the movie to Citizens for Goldwater groups across the country, accompanied by a press release claiming that the film had been produced by a group called Mothers for a Moral America, led by thirty "prominent American mothers," with 250,000 members nationwide. In reality, the mothers' group was simply a concoction of the campaign. Initially the movie was supposed to air on 150 NBC television stations. But the network refused to show *Choice*, objecting to the shots of seminudity and topless women and asking that the campaign edit out the revealing frames. But it was too late—the movie had already been distributed to activists, and it quickly fell into the hands of the Democratic National

Committee. Journalists denounced the film's racial stereotypes of black people as looters and rioters. Goldwater finally viewed the movie, which he previously hadn't seen. "I'm not going to be made out as a racist," he told White. "You can't show it." White and Walton never edited *Choice*, and they canceled its mass showings.[58]

Although the movie was not used in the official campaign, Goldwater did adopt its themes of moral crisis. His campaign took on a gothic tone in its late months. He denounced the "seven big-city riots" of the year, the rising drug abuse, the $500 million-a-year pornography business, the increase in violent crime. The candidate trumpeted his opposition to busing: "I am firmly opposed to the transfer of children from their home neighborhoods to achieve racial balance without consent of their parents." Just as the labor unions and the welfare state represented the will of workers run amok, trampling on the laws of God and nature, so too the actions of the federal government to desegregate the schools embodied an illegitimate infringement of sacred individual liberties. The moral decay creeping through the nation was almost a secondary by-product of the New Deal and Fair Deal liberals' lack of respect for tradition and hierarchy and the old social order.[59]

Goldwater diehards rallied to the new message with enthusiasm. In a September campaign trip to Montgomery, Alabama, campaign workers planned to gather 250 girls in long white dresses to greet their candidate. So many young women insisted on participating that they wound up with 565. "When that man entered, it was one of the most emotional moments that I have ever seen," said the organizer of the event. In a visit to Atlanta, young business students showed up at rallies with their arms in slings, embodying the slogan "We'd Give Our Right Arm for Barry." Junior high school students screamed out his name: "Barry, Barry!" And in South Carolina, Goldwater had to leave a campaign stop early as an enthusiastic crowd became uncontrollable; Roger Milliken and his wife, waiting to greet the candidate, had to run out of the way when an eager mob overwhelmed them. Forty-five people at the speech wound up receiving first aid—thirty-five had fainted, two had had heart attacks, and one child had developed hives.[60]

Nowhere was this connection between the old economic rhetoric and the new emphasis on social and moral decay more clearly drawn than by Ronald Reagan. By 1964, Reagan had left General Electric. He was making a full-time career out of stumping for the conservative movement, speaking at Chambers of Commerce and Rotary Clubs across the country. In the fall of 1964, Reagan had been asked to fill in for Goldwater at a $1,000-a-plate fund-raising dinner in Southern California organized by the oil magnate Henry Salvatori. Along with a few other Southern California entrepreneurs—men like Walter Knott and Cy Rubel of Union Oil—Salvatori had raised large sums for the Goldwater campaign. The speech was such a success that Salvatori and the others decided to press for Reagan to appear on national television in a half-hour political advertisement the campaign had purchased on NBC. One week before the election, Reagan was on the air. In contrast to Goldwater's strident, frenetic style, his speech was smooth, gentle, and principled, his tone calm and his manner suave.[61]

The speech he gave that night in late October posed the decision facing the nation in stark terms. Reagan made sure to say right away that as a former Democrat, he understood well that "the issues confronting us cross party lines." He explained how Social Security wasn't really an insurance program at all (even though the liberals called it that) and how a young man could earn more if he invested his Social Security dollars in the stock market. He discussed the promise of health insurance for the elderly and the failures of such programs in Europe. Most of the speech was about economics and the moral necessity of opposing government regulations and the advance of socialism, of refusing to "trade our freedom for the soup kitchen of the welfare state." But he also spoke about welfare mothers—about the young woman (whether a composite figure or a real person is difficult to say) with seven children in California who wanted to divorce her husband, a laborer, to make a little more money under Aid for Families with Dependent Children: "She got the idea from two women in her neighborhood who'd already done that very thing." At the end of the speech, Reagan returned to the language of Roosevelt, echoing the words of the man who had brought him into politics years before, speaking of the nation's "rendezvous with destiny"—to "preserve for our children this, the last best hope of man on earth" or to "sentence them to take the last step into a thousand years of darkness." Just as FDR had united the country against the "economic royalists," Reagan—an easy identification figure for former Democrats, thanks to his own change in political loyalties—implicitly promised to join the American people together in a fight against the new aristocracy: the government bureaucrats steadily expanding the state.[62]

The speech was a fund-raising triumph. Money poured in as conservatives across the country seized on Reagan's amalgam of economics and moral fervor as the definitive distillation of all that they believed, all that they held dear. And it helped to propel Reagan toward the governorship of California two years later, when the same businessmen who had organized the speech asked him to run for the office and put together the money to finance an exploratory trip up and down the state. When Reagan won, they would serve as a kitchen cabinet of informal advisers for the former GE spokesman throughout his time in Sacramento.[63]

But although Reagan's speech helped launch his political career, it could not rescue Goldwater. The Arizonan lost the general election by a margin of 16 million votes. He won the five states of the Deep South—Mississippi, Alabama, South Carolina, Georgia, and Louisiana—as well as his home state of Arizona. And that was it.

The mainstream press treated the defeat as the final, crushing blow to the narrow remnant of conservatism that had lingered in American politics ever since the New Deal. "Barry Goldwater not only lost the Presidential election yesterday but the conservative cause as well," James Reston wrote in the *New York Times*. "He has wrecked his party for a long time to come and is not even likely to control the wreckage . . . His belief that the American people would turn against the principles of social security at home and collective security abroad was rejected." Madame Tussauds Wax Museum in London put its sculpture of Goldwater on ice (although a museum spokesman noted that it would not be melted down: "We will put him to one side in case he comes in use later on").[64]

The political movement that Lemuel Boulware and Jasper Crane, J. William Middendorf and F. Clifton White, the NAM and FEE, William Baroody and Roger Milliken had all tried to build seemed to have reached its limits in the wake of Goldwater's defeat. It had failed to prove capable of winning the allegiance of middle- and working-class voters who still felt that they were doing well within the liberal order. And it was not even able to attract and hold the loyalty of businessmen. Even if companies wanted to strengthen free-market politics through donations to groups like the American Enterprise Association and the Foundation for Economic Education, they were not willing to break with a Democratic regime that was still able to deliver economic growth—especially when it looked like a sure deal to be returned to power.

7 The Attack on the Free Enterprise System

IN NOVEMBER 1968, Goldwater won his Senate post back and wrote to his old friend Denison Kitchel, "It's rather strange and ironic isn't it; here is Lyndon Johnson sitting at his ranch a total disgrace and here am I having just won the biggest election of my life four years after he clobbered me. Fate is a fickle thing as it dangles."[1]

Indeed, much would change in America in the years that followed the defeat of Barry Goldwater's attempt to take the White House. The liberals who had seemed so confident in November 1964 suffered a dramatic turnabout, faltering as the turmoil surrounding the Vietnam War mounted. Just four years after Johnson's decisive victory, after the Tet Offensive demolished the idea that the United States was cruising toward military victory, the president could not garner enough support within his own party to run for reelection. In April that same year, riots swept through the cities of the nation after the assassination of Martin Luther King, Jr., in Memphis; thousands of National Guardsmen were sent into the streets to quell the uprisings. That fall Richard Nixon, the former vice president who had lost to John F. Kennedy in 1960, ascended at long last to the Oval Office, after running a campaign that explicitly rejected Johnson's Great Society antipoverty programs with appeals to "law and order." But his election, far from restoring order, only deepened the divisions splitting the country.

Even though businessmen were not the literal architects of the war in Vietnam, the antiwar movement seemed to hold them morally responsible for its devastation. The war, after all, meant military contracts for the companies that built napalm bombs and the airplanes that strafed the jungles of North Vietnam. It was a crusade for capitalism, devoted to protecting American institutions by stopping the spread of communism through the East. Many young people radicalized by the antiwar movement had actually turned against all the mainstream institutions of American society, including labor unions and the government, not only corporations. But the counterculture targeted business with special fury. As the radical historian and New Left activist Staughton Lynd wrote in the *Guardian* in November 1969, "Why . . . do we continue to demonstrate in Washington as if the core of the problem lay there? . . . We need to find ways to lay siege to corporations."[2]

In the early 1970s, antiwar activists pioneered a new kind of protest, one that hinged on exposing the corporate role in the war. More than a thousand dissident shareholders and proxies attended the Honeywell Corporation's spring 1970 annual meeting in Minneapolis to protest the company's manufacture of fragmentation bombs. Hundreds of young activists crowded into the conference room and jeered at the company president, who was forced to adjourn the meeting after only fourteen minutes while Honeywell security guards used mace to force the protesters across the street. Meanwhile, Dow Chemical became the target of more than two hundred demonstrations for its role in producing napalm. Whenever Dow tried to recruit college seniors, activists would show up to protest; one Dow public relations officer was prompted to observe, "In frequency and consistency of attack this is a record unmatched over the past two years even by recruiters for the U.S. armed forces."[3]

Perhaps the company targeted most dramatically by the counterculture was the Bank of America. The spate of attacks on the banking chain began in the winter of 1970 at Isla Vista, near the University of California at Santa Barbara, when protesters burned down one of the bank's branches. The Bank of America, one young demonstrator argued, was "the representative here of the establishment." The bank insisted on immediately rebuilding its Isla Vista branch, taking out full-page advertisements in newspapers across the country to publicize its commitment to doing so: "We believe that at some time and in some place Americans must decide whether they intend to have their decisions, and indeed their lives, ruled by a violent minority." The company met with student activists and expanded the mortgage loans it made to minorities, seeking to demonstrate noblesse oblige. ("We don't deny that we're part of the Establishment," insisted one company vice president. "We don't think there's anything wrong with being part of it.") But soon after the Isla Vista branch reopened, protesters attacked it again. This time a university student—actually a moderate desperately trying to prevent violence—was fatally wounded by a police officer at the demonstration. Over the next few years, branches of the Bank of America across the country were hit by firebombs and pipe bombs dozens of times. Small bombs were also set off at the corporate headquarters of companies like Mobil Oil and IBM, and in March 1971 an explosion tore a hole through the men's bathroom in the Capitol building. Yet the crowds of hundreds of thousands that formed in Washington in April that year to demonstrate against the war and the mounting disaffection of the army itself were as threatening as any dynamite could be.[4]

In the new radical critique of the corporate world, more was at stake than the war alone. The environmental movement charged industry with poisoning the land, air, and water of the country, while the consumer movement accused business of manipulating consumers into buying dangerous products. Cars, plastics, chemicals, the factory system itself—the entire infrastructure of consumer society seemed predicated on the hidden, deadly violence of pollution. Books such as Rachel Carson's *Silent Spring* introduced an environmentalist analysis of corporate policies to a broad audience. In *The Greening of America* (first published as a *New Yorker* article), Yale professor Charles Reich described the "revolution of the new generation" taking shape among hippie youth and challenging the power structure of a country that was "dealing death, not only to people in other lands, but to its own people." Meanwhile, in 1965 a young consumer advocate named Ralph Nader had published a book about the "designed-in dangers" of automobiles, *Unsafe at Any Speed,* arguing that the absence of legislated safety standards and regulatory oversight for the production of cars meant unnecessary death and injuries to drivers (the first line: "For over half a century the automobile has brought death, injury and the most inestimable sorrow and deprivation to millions of people"). When Congress called Nader to testify about changing automotive safety standards the subsequent year, General Motors hired private detectives to tail him and dig up dirt. The plan backfired, ultimately discrediting GM instead of Nader, who went on to found the Center for Responsive Law in 1969 and to advocate for consumer protection from corporate managements bent on profit above all else. When Nixon signed the Environmental Protection Agency and the Occupational Safety and Health Administration into existence in 1970, the new government agencies, with their broad regulatory powers, seemed a legislative outgrowth of these direct actions and lobbying campaigns against business.[5]

The student radicalism of the era was not restricted to a narrow fringe. On college campuses, the same students who might have seemed headed toward respectable positions in junior management instead took over buildings (as at Columbia University in 1968) and led demonstrations. College students at all kinds of schools protested the war, sometimes (as at Kent State and Jackson State) meeting with deadly violence for doing so. A study done by Oklahoma Christian University in 1973 found that undergraduates gave businessmen the lowest rankings for ethical standards (Ralph Nader was at the top); half of all seniors identified themselves as leftists, compared to one third of all freshmen.[6]

The turbulent politics of the era also shook up relationships between workers and their employers, as the largest strike wave since the immediate postwar years swept the nation. Between 1967 and 1976 the average number of workers on strike per year rose by 30 percent. In 1970 alone there were 34 work stoppages that involved more than 10,000 workers each, including a 197-day construction worker strike in Kansas City, a two-month national strike at General Motors, a December strike of

360,000 railroad workers, a strike of the nation's postal workers (in direct violation of federal law), and a strike at General Electric of 133,000 workers (the first since the 1960 disaster; the labor movement hailed it as a sign that Boulwarism was on the wane). Economic issues were at stake in many of the work stoppages; workers wanted wage increases to make up for inflation. But the strikes were also seen as a sign of the "blue-collar blues," rebellions against the discipline and hierarchy of the workplace. When the postal workers struck in March 1970, the *New York Times* noted that the action seemed to encourage "the lawlessness already so rampant in many sectors of society that it is beginning to undermine national stability."[7]

The student demonstrations at Columbia University, the University of Chicago, and Kent State, the bombs at the Bank of America, the accusations of Ralph Nader, the new government regulations, the sudden new working-class militancy, the activists invading corporate offices—all of it seemed a single continuum, one discordant challenge rising against American businessmen. In 1972, *Business Week* reported on "America's growing antibusiness mood"; one polling company announced that its surveys found that the 1970s would be "the worst attitude climate in a decade" for big corporations. Only 20 percent of the public described itself as having a great deal of confidence in business leaders. Some executives, mostly from small and midsized companies, began to organize their own groups to protest American policy in Vietnam, citing the war's political repercussions as well as its impact on inflation. "A lot of young people are disoriented and have lost confidence in the economic and political system and don't draw the distinction between the two," Henry Niles, the former chairman of the Baltimore Life Insurance Company and a member of Business Executives Move for Vietnam Peace, said to the *New York Times*. Other businessmen were less sympathetic to the demonstrators. David Rockefeller, the chairman of Chase Manhattan Bank, told *Newsweek* in 1971—one year after his company's annual meeting had been disrupted by activists demanding that the bank divest from South Africa and take a stance against the Vietnam War—"Some people are blaming business and the enterprise system for all the problems of our society."[8]

What was worse, the challenge came at the very moment when the prosperity that had buoyed the economy throughout the postwar period suddenly seemed to evaporate, as inflation and unemployment began their slow, baffling, tandem climb. Rising food prices, especially for meat, triggered special frustration. In the spring of 1973, amid reports of an increase in deer-poaching and of butchers' plans to start selling horsemeat, consumer activists and unions organized a national boycott of meat in the hopes that it would force companies to stop hoarding meat and lower their prices. "Milk up, meat up, bread up, we're fed up," chanted demonstrators outside supermarkets in New York City, carrying banners that read "Devalue Pot Roast, Not Dollars." Early the following year independent truckers went on strike to protest the high price of gasoline. Although the OPEC oil embargo, in which oil-producing nations refused to sell to countries that had supported Israel in the 1973 war, was the immediate reason for the price spike, many blamed the energy companies for the shortage, arguing that they were intentionally keeping gas off the market to raise their profits. As one trucker insisted to the *Chicago Tribune,* "I think the fuel crisis is a hoax and the federal government is in the middle of it." A New Jersey man told the *Wall Street Journal*, "The fuel companies, they've got the fuel; they just want to jack the price up." Another man, whose car bore a sticker for George Wallace, the pro-segregation governor of Alabama who ran populist law-and-order campaigns for president in 1968 and 1972, appealing to "beauticians" and "construction workers" against the liberal elites and civil rights activists, displayed a remarkable political flexibility when he explained to the paper, "I'm for either him or the Communists, I don't care, just anybody who wouldn't be afraid of the big companies."[9]

Many businessmen at the time interpreted the nation's mounting macroeconomic ills—especially inflation, which accelerated from 2 percent a year for most of the postwar period to 6.7 percent a year between 1967 and 1979—primarily as the result of labor flexing its muscles (although they also blamed loose money and the expansion of the government budget). "The gravest economic problem facing the Western world in the early 1970's is cost-push inflation powered by excessive wage increases," reported *Fortune*. "What is happening, throughout the Western world, is that organized labor is overreaching." Unions were making demands on employers that could no longer be met through increased economic productivity; business therefore passed the costs on to consumers through higher prices, which in turn sparked new demands for higher wages. "The U.S. can't afford what labor wants," read one *Business Week* headline from April 1970. "In a nation where the government is formally committed to maintain full employment, what forces will restrain the perfectly human demand of labor for more money and more power?" The demands of construction workers' unions, a *Fortune* article argued, were "shaping up as the most important obstacle in the way of subduing inflation." While in the old days unions might have helped to humanize American industry, another contributor wrote, in the modern day "organized labor has now become a destabilizing and dislocating force—made more unmanageable by large political influence."[10]

Politicians and businessmen, journalists and academics argued throughout the decade about how to jolt the nation out of the economic doldrums. Could the problems plaguing the American economy—stagnating profits, rising unemployment, inflation, the inability to compete in the international economy—be resolved by letting the free market work? Or did the market only exacerbate the problems? Just as American businessmen felt themselves the subject of political animosity at home, their corporations were no longer able to dominate the international market with the old easy and casual confidence. The "American Century" seemed to be nearing its close.

THROUGHOUT THE spring of 1971, the sixty-four-year-old lawyer Lewis Powell and his longtime friend and neighbor Eugene B. Sydnor, Jr., worried about the crisis confronting American business. The two were among the most prominent citizens of Richmond, Virginia. Powell was a former president of the American Bar Association and a named partner in a leading Richmond law firm. He sat on the board of directors of several large corporations, including Philip Morris. Sydnor was the president of the Southern Department Stores chain; he was also a director for the U.S. Chamber of Commerce, the same organization that Leonard Read was working for when he met W. C. Mullendore in the 1930s. From his vantage point in Richmond, Lewis Powell watched the rise of the militant demonstrations against the war in Vietnam with great concern. The previous year, in June 1970, he had written a memorandum to President Nixon expressing his fears that the antiwar movement had been successful in tarring the perception of the United States around the world, convincing people that "it is America—not the Communist superpowers—which is repressive, militaristic, and imperialistic." To have any chance of winning in Southeast Asia, the United States needed to do more than exercise its awesome military force; it needed to win the moral victories, to fight on the shadowy terrain of images and impressions.[11]

But Powell's deeper preoccupation in the spring of 1971 was with the weakening political position of American business in a country turning against the war. He saved newspaper and magazine articles all through the summer months that year. He kept a *Fortune* profile of Ralph Nader, which described the advocate as a "passionate man" who was "aimed at smashing utterly the target of his hatred, which is corporate power . . . There seems something of the desert in him still, the ghost of some harsh prophet from his ancestral Lebanon." Powell read a *New York* magazine article about the "new populism" targeting concentrated wealth and power. In *Barron's* he saw described an ominous new organization meeting in New York City called the Socialist Scholars Conference. Sydnor sent him *Wall Street Journal* editorials urging General Motors to take a stand and defend itself against Nader's allegations, and he clipped op-ed pieces from the *Richmond Times-Dispatch* reporting that almost half of the students polled on twelve representative college campuses favored the "socialization of basic U.S. industries."[12]

Powell and Sydnor were not men who were used to being passive spectators of history. They wanted to do something to fight back. Sydnor thought that he had the answer: he wanted to transform the U.S. Chamber of Commerce, which had settled into being a quiet business organization, into a powerful force capable of defending business in the new and uncertain political world.

Sometime in the summer of 1971, Sydnor asked his eminent friend to craft a special memorandum for the Chamber of Commerce, outlining a thoroughgoing political strategy that the business community could use to confront the new threats it faced. Powell agreed, and in August he delivered it to Sydnor for distribution to the high-ranking leaders of the Chamber. It was a confidential memorandum bearing a bold title: "The Attack on the Free Enterprise System." Although Powell was not connected to the Watergate scandals that would soon rock the Nixon administration, the depiction of American politics in "The Attack on the Free Enterprise System" echoes the fevered paranoia of Nixon and his top advisers, suggesting the widespread sense of crisis among elite figures in politics and business alike as the 1970s began. Powell opened his memo by warning American businessmen that they faced unprecedented political danger. "No thoughtful person," he began, "can question that the American economic system is under broad attack." He conceded that previously (for example, in the late nineteenth century and during the Great Depression) a radical fringe of anarchists and Communists had dreamed of fomenting armed revolution. But the present crisis was different. "What concerns us now is quite new in the history of America," he wrote. "We are not dealing with episodic or isolated attacks from a relatively few extremists or even from the minority socialist cadre. Rather, the assault on the enterprise system is broadly based and consistently pursued. It is gaining momentum and converts." The attacks on business came not only from the "extremists of the left" but also from "perfectly respectable elements of society: from the college campus, the pulpit, the media, the intellectual and literary journals, the arts and sciences, and from politicians."

Powell believed that the young radicals of the New Left had declared war on business. He catalogued the explosions at military recruiting stations, munitions manufacturers, and the Bank of America branches. But such open acts of violence were less dangerous in the long run, he argued, than the speeches of Ralph Nader and the writings of Charles

Reich. These intellectual denunciations of capitalism sought to justify government regulation—or even nationalization. Institutions such as universities had nurtured enemies of business throughout the postwar period, quietly paying the salaries of academics who wrote books critical of businessmen and teaching students to hate the economic engine of America. Now this fifth column was starting to come out into the open. "This setting of the 'rich' against the 'poor,' of business against the people, is the cheapest and most dangerous kind of politics," wrote Powell.

Yet American businessmen seemed incapable of thoroughly recognizing the challenge they faced, let alone resisting it. They were too apathetic, anxious, and passive to use their power to quell the assault on capitalism. Why, Powell asked, should businessmen patiently tolerate their critics? After all, they were the trustees of universities like Yale. They owned the media stations that reported on Nader. They had resources, money, and social prestige. And yet they seemed frozen and incompetent. Powell acknowledged that managers and executives were not exactly trained to conduct "guerrilla warfare" against the propagandists of the left. But he was nonetheless disappointed at the fact that they had shown "little stomach for hard-nosed contest with their critics," and "little skill in effective intellectual and philosophical debate."

To meet the challenge, businessmen needed first of all to acknowledge that it was real. "The overriding first need is for businessmen to recognize that the ultimate issue may be *survival*—survival of what we call the free enterprise system, and all that this means for the strength and prosperity of America and the freedom of our people." They then should marshal their power to influence the universities, the media, and the courts. They had to strive consciously to shape the political debate on college campuses by organizing speakers' bureaus, evaluating textbooks, and ensuring "balance" in faculty hiring through their roles as donors and trustees. They should keep television programs under "constant surveillance" for excessive criticism of the profit system, while seeking to fund special programs espousing views in favor of the free market. Finally, they needed to follow the example of the civil rights movement and try to use the courts and the judicial system to win rights for business and to protect the marketplace: "The judiciary may be the most important instrument for social, economic and political change."

Most of all, businessmen needed to recognize that "political power is necessary; that such power must be assiduously cultivated; and that when necessary, it must be used aggressively and with determination—without embarrassment and without the reluctance which has been so characteristic of American business." Rather than timidly try to disguise the power of industry, businessmen should use their financial muscle to shape the politics of the country. "There should not be the slightest hesitation to press vigorously in all political arenas for support of the enterprise system. Nor should there be reluctance to penalize politically those who oppose it." They should form programs to mobilize stockholders—"*twenty million voters*"—for political action. They should throw themselves into political conflict.

Individual corporations did not have the resources to conduct this multisided campaign alone. Businessmen needed to work together through organizations like the Chamber of Commerce. "Strength lies in organization, in careful long-range planning and implementation, in consistency of action over an indefinite period of years, in the scale of financing available only through joint effort, and in the political power available only through united action and national organizations." Echoing the faith of men such as Leonard Read, Jasper Crane, William F. Baroody, and Lemuel Boulware, all of whom thought that businessmen should try to rise above their short-term interests to take part in a philosophical and political crusade, Powell argued that businessmen were morally obligated to abandon their quiescent bipartisanship and take up ideological politics, for the fight for free enterprise was not in the end about profits but about "individual freedom" itself.[13]

Eugene Sydnor was delighted by Powell's memorandum. In a note thanking Powell, he described it as an "excellent presentation of the vitally important case for American Business to go on the offensive after such a long period of inaction and indecision in telling the American people the facts of life as they unhappily exist today." Powell circulated his handiwork to a few of his friends, including the general counsel of General Motors, whom he urged to speak to the "top management of GM" to involve them in the program of pressuring the Chamber to "become a vital force to defend the enterprise system and the freedoms which it sustains." Together Powell and Sydnor went to Washington, D.C., to share the memorandum with a vice president at the Chamber, who promised to take its ideas under serious consideration.[14]

Two months after Powell wrote his report for the Chamber, President Nixon nominated him to serve on the Supreme Court. Powell sailed through the confirmation hearings without his essay on the dangers confronting American business ever coming to light. When the news of the nomination broke, Sydnor wrote to his friend with enthusiastic congratulations. He reiterated that he was "particularly pleased" that Powell had been able to "draft the excellent and comprehensive memorandum for an action program for American business" before getting tapped for the Court, and he assured Powell that the Chamber would meet soon to take up the challenge. Sydnor said that he would be delighted for Powell to remain involved with the effort, if he deemed it "ethical." But once in office, Powell declined Sydnor's requests for continued meetings with the Chamber of Commerce (although he did get together with his old Richmond friend in May 1973, at which point the Supreme Court justice asked for some extra copies of his memorandum).[15]

Powell's reticence may have stemmed at least in part from the revelation of his confidential memorandum in September 1972, when the journalist Jack Anderson obtained a copy and wrote about it in his *Washington Post* column. Anderson was indignant that Powell had dared to present himself as "the model of a moderate, reasonable, judicious legalist" in his Senate confirmation hearings—the opposite of the seething counterrevolutionary of the memorandum. Powell's views in the memo, Anderson wrote, were "so militant that it raises a question about his fitness to decide any case involving business interests." After Anderson published excerpts from the memo in his column, the Chamber of Commerce released it publicly. Sydnor seemed "disturbed" that the journalist had gotten his hands on it, but Powell declined to comment.[16]

Anderson had intended his column to embarrass Powell and the Chamber. But some businessmen felt that by breaking the story of the memo and broadcasting its message to the public, Anderson had unwittingly done a great public service. One delighted reader wrote a letter published in the *Washington Post*: "If Mr. Anderson, through his usual sewer line connections, had not gotten his hands on this confidential document, it would probably still have been gathering dust in U.S. Chamber files. But now the Chamber has distributed the Powell memorandum to its wide membership revealing the shocking situation we are facing in this country today, plus Mr. Powell's excellent suggestions for combating these insidious attacks. Thank you, Mr. Anderson!"[17]

THE POWELL memorandum crystallized a set of concerns shared by business conservatives in the early 1970s. Many who read the memorandum (following the publicity Anderson gave it) cited it afterward as inspiration for their political choices. John M. Olin, the chemical tycoon who founded the conservative Olin Foundation (which helped to fund the law-and-economics movement), wrote to William Baroody at the American Enterprise Institute: "The Powell Memorandum gives a reason for a well organized effort to re-establish the validity and importance of the American free enterprise system." The Pacific Legal Foundation, a California organization formed to counter public-interest law firms and represent the interests of business and private property holders, quoted the Powell memorandum at length in its prospectus. Executives passed the memo to one another; someone in the DuPont legal department, for example, gave a copy to the company's CEO, along with a note saying that he might find it useful.[18]

Other businessmen gave speeches expressing similar ideas. David Packard, the CEO of Hewlett-Packard, spoke at a 1973 meeting of the Committee for Corporate Support of American Universities, calling for businessmen to stop giving unrestricted donations, because a "militant minority" of the faculty had taken control of most campuses. Instead, executives should specifically fund programs that "contribute in some specific way to our individual companies, or to the general welfare of our free enterprise system." In a 1972 commencement address at Western Kentucky University, Donald Kendall, the chairman and CEO of PepsiCo, accused young Americans of "economic illiteracy," which he believed fueled hostility to business and ultimately posed the "gravest threat to free enterprise and the democratic standards that have brought us the highest standard of living on earth." Alan Boyd, the president of Illinois Central Gulf Railroad, warned in 1974 that "free enterprise" might soon become "the biggest victim of our social idealism, shot down by well-meaning people and groups who aimed at poverty, injustice, racial prejudice, or consumer protection."[19]

The corporate reports of companies like GE and H. J. Heinz and Standard Oil sometimes echoed the Powell memorandum, including political statements along with analyses of their earnings. Black & Decker warned its stockholders in 1975, "The hour is getting late. It is time for the voices of those individuals favoring fiscal responsibility in government and a free business system to be heard." The electronics company Gould, Inc. included a special message in its annual report that same year entitled "The Perils to the Free Enterprise System," cautioning readers that "today, not only leftists but also responsible conservative and liberal economists are projecting pessimism about the survival of the free enterprise system as we know it."[20]

Powell's ideas were also shared by intellectuals such as the law professor Robert Bork, who told the American Enterprise Institute board of trustees: "Business leaders will have to decide whether they are really willing to let the corporate system slide and perhaps expire without putting up a determined fight." Irving Kristol, a leader of the "neoconservatives," an informal group of former liberals and leftists who declared their growing affection for conservative politics in the 1970s, took up the mission of calling business to arms with special vigor. Kristol had actually been a Trotskyist during his Depression-era days at City College in New

York. But by the early 1970s he had become a columnist for the militantly conservative editorial page of the *Wall Street Journal,* where he began to write columns aimed at raising the consciousness of the corporate class; by the end of the decade he had become a fellow at AEI.[21]

As the journalist Sidney Blumenthal has written, Kristol analyzed business with the intensity of a former Marxist. He argued that in order to resist the challenge of the New Left, executives had to give up their old habits of "thinking economically" and start to think "politically." They had to learn to forgo short-term profits in favor of "securing the trust and confidence and good will of the public." The oil companies, for example, which reaped windfall profits during the energy crisis of the early 1970s, should have confronted the image problem those profits were sure to cause rather than simply insisting that they had the right to them. If the oil executives had been thinking politically, they might have refused to collect the profits, or even lowered the price of gasoline; at the very least, they could have announced that there would be no increase in dividends or executive salaries. They would sacrifice a little cash, but they would gain greater standing in the eyes of the public.[22]

A dialectician long after his departure from the Young People's Socialist League, Kristol believed that businessmen had such difficulty acting politically because the system of capitalism itself gave them nothing transcendent to defend. "Who on earth wants to live in a society in which all—or even a majority—of one's fellow citizens are fully engaged in the hot pursuit of money, the single-minded pursuit of self-interest?" he asked. "Who wants to live in a society in which selfishness and self-seeking are celebrated as primary virtues?" To secure their economic position, businessmen needed to give their support to other social institutions—the family, the church—that could preserve moral and social values and that had the emotional weight to command true allegiance. The survival of capitalism depended on the capitalists themselves rejecting "selfishness," Kristol argued—a line that might have seemed likely to alienate businessmen. But at least some listened. For example, in the autumn of 1976 Kennecott Copper invited Kristol to talk to its executives about "what corporations should be doing to facilitate their survival in today's society—particularly, what mining companies should be doing."[23]

Strident, melodramatic, and alarmist, Powell's memorandum and Kristol's columns struck a nerve in the tense political world of the early 1970s, giving voice to sentiments that, no matter how extreme they might have seemed, were coming to sound like common sense in the business world during those anxious years. Not all businessmen shared Powell's passions. But those who did began to act as a vanguard, organizing the giants of American industry.

8 Turning the Tide

IN OCTOBER 1972, William J. Baroody, the president of the American Enterprise Institute, spoke at a Business Council meeting in Hot Springs, Virginia. The Business Council was an august group of executives who met periodically to discuss the economy but generally remained aloof from political engagement. Baroody was there to inspire them to get involved.

The free-market economy, Baroody told his audience, was in danger of being destroyed by environmentalists and other radical activists who he thought were hostile to the very "institutional framework of a free society." To fight back, businessmen could not rely only on behind-the-scenes lobbying. After all, politicians were constrained by their constituencies. More important was finding ways to influence "public attitude formation"—the ideas and beliefs of the general public. Baroody ended, as he always did, by reminding the crowd that to break the "virtual monopoly in public policy idea formation" held by liberals and the left, American business had to step up its contributions to public policy research centers that shared "a belief in the fundamental values of a free society"—in other words, although he did not make the pitch quite so baldly, to organizations like AEI. The "abdication of the corporate class" had permitted this dismal state of affairs; only its engagement could reverse the tide. As Baroody wrote in another context, AEI and its donors were engaged in nothing less than a "war for the minds of men."[1]

Baroody had delivered this message countless times in various formats ever since he went to AEI in the early 1950s. In the early 1970s, though, more people were starting to listen. The men of the Mont Pelerin Society and the Foundation for Economic Education had had the misfortune to spin their theories at a time when the economy was stable and growing. But the intellectual activists of the 1970s worked in an era when liberalism seemed no longer able to deliver on its promises, even from the standpoint of economics. The Keynesian economists who still dominated policy-making circles—and who had claimed only a few years earlier to have mastered the business cycle—were stymied by the simultaneous inflation and unemployment that began to afflict the economy during the decade. If they used deficit financing to invest in the public sector and lower unemployment rates, they would add to the problem of inflation; if the Federal Reserve tried to halt inflation by tightening interest rates, the result would be more people out of work. At the same time economists began to argue in favor of deregulating industries such as the airlines, saying that businesses had been able to "capture" regulatory agencies and that the market could serve consumers better than the state; legal scholars began to advance the idea that lawyers and judges should be trained in economic analysis (at times winning support from business funders to start new centers devoted to law and economics). And as this broad skepticism about the appropriate relationship between the market and the state began to spread through academic and policy-making circles, a new space opened up in political life for men like Baroody, who had been trying for decades to build an intellectual opposition to liberalism.[2]

OVER THE years since Barry Goldwater's defeat, AEI had fallen on difficult times. Baroody had given his all to the Goldwater campaign. He had taken a paid leave from AEI to travel around the country with the candidate, working eighteen-hour days formulating strategy and writing speeches. Other AEI staffers, such as the young libertarian Karl Hess, also joined the Goldwater campaign. Goldwater wrote his speech accepting the Republican nomination in Baroody's hotel room, with his little group of advisers gathered around. Baroody's role in the campaign was so important that after it was all over, F. Clifton White, bitter about the defeat, blamed Baroody's and the AEI crowd's lack of practical political expertise for Goldwater's loss. After November 1964, Baroody wrote Goldwater an emotional note thanking the candidate for having allowed him to participate in the "difficult, frustrating," yet deeply important campaign: "You have symbolized for me (as well as for millions of other Americans) and will continue to personify the sensible and reasonable philosophy of American government."[3]

Baroody's commitment to the Goldwater campaign had not escaped the attention of journalists and Democratic politicians, who wondered whether AEI might once again be testing the limits of its tax-exempt status to engage in partisan political activity. Even within AEI there was some concern about how Baroody and the other staff members could help the Goldwater campaign while remaining on the right side of the law. The chair of the board of trustees wrote a letter to Baroody in the summer of 1964 saying that he was well aware of Baroody's "long personal friendship" with Goldwater and that he would not expect Baroody to "turn your back on a friend simply because he has become a candidate for the Presidency." (He was probably referring primarily to Goldwater's support in the late 1950s, when the senator wrote fund-raising letters for the organization.) But the letter also carefully spelled out that since he and Baroody agreed that AEI could not devote its own resources to the political effort, Baroody would be granted leave to cover his time working for the campaign.[4]

It didn't matter, and neither did the portraits of liberal congressmen that Baroody hung on the walls of his office to confuse visiting journalists. Early in 1965, a reporter at the *St. Louis Post-Dispatch* broke the story that Baroody had in fact remained on AEI's payroll, even earning a raise of $4,000 for the year he'd been working on the Goldwater campaign. The organization became the subject of a congressional investigation, followed by an IRS inquiry into whether it was violating its tax-exempt status. (AEI's ideological opponents cheered on the investigation: in October 1965, a researcher from the labor-supported Group Research

Institute wrote to the office of Congressman Wright Patman, who was conducting an investigation into tax-exempt foundations, pointing out that Stephen Shadegg's memoir of the Goldwater campaign contained detailed descriptions of the work done by Baroody and other AEI staffers and that this seemed to make a case "of staggering proportions" for the "revocation of the tax-exempt status" of the group.) Neither investigation had especially serious consequences for AEI; the IRS found that it was in fact a nonpartisan research institute. But although it kept its tax exemption, the investigations still seemed to prompt AEI to modify its style. In 1965 the organization inaugurated a new event: its "Rational Debate" series, which featured well-known liberals publicly debating conservative thinkers. The first event in the series featured the leading liberal historian Arthur Schlesinger, Jr.—a choice that must have infuriated the purists in the conservative movement.[5]

When Baroody spoke at the Business Council meeting, other free-market think tanks were starting to appear in Washington, D.C., for the first time in many years. Baroody was not only campaigning to urge his executive audience to contribute to the conservative intellectual cause; he was actively competing against other organizations, most formidably the Heritage Foundation.

The Heritage Foundation began with an executive who had been deeply moved by Lewis Powell's memorandum. Joseph Coors, tall, thin, and sincere, the youngest of the Coors brothers who owned the Colorado brewery, would always remember the document. Many years later he told one interviewer that the memo had "stirred" him, and that after reading it he had wondered why businessmen were "ignoring" what seemed to be impending political disaster.[6]

But in truth Coors had been interested in politics long before he read Powell's memorandum. He had supported Barry Goldwater in 1964. Especially impressed by Ronald Reagan's speech before the election, he attended the Republican convention four years later as a pledged delegate of the California governor. Friends described him as a true believer, with intense, deeply held convictions. He responded to political developments that he disapproved of with the angry petulance of a child, as though the passage of a law or the wrongheadedness of a demonstrator were a personal insult.[7]

During his tenure as a regent of the University of Colorado (his only elected post), Coors fought an ongoing struggle against campus radicals and the New Left. At one point he urged that tenure be denied to a professor who had been the campus adviser to the New Left group Students for a Democratic Society (SDS); at another he argued that SDS should not be permitted to hold its national convention at the school. When the president of the university expressed support for hosting the SDS meeting, Coors did not back down but instead called for him to resign. He financed a conservative campus newspaper to compete with the official college paper (which had published cartoons mocking him). He brought Reagan to speak on campus. He even irritated his fellow regents by circulating articles from the John Birch Society magazine.[8]

Although the campus was a focal point for Coors's early activities, he was no stranger to politics within the workplace. His beer company had long been fiercely hostile to its union. Even the local union president admitted that Coors workers had a "pretty lousy contract," under which they could be fired for saying negative things about Coors or doing anything that might be perceived as damaging sales of Coors beer. The Colorado Civil Rights Commission twice found the company guilty of discriminating against black employees in the early 1970s. Coors administered lie-detector tests to all job applicants, asking them questions to ascertain whether they would make trouble if hired. By the late 1960s, civil rights activists across the country were organizing boycotts of Coors beer. (A few years later, Coors hired the former GE manager John T. McCarty to head its public affairs program; Lemuel Boulware described his protégé's results at the beer company in glowing terms, as the "only complete relations program I know which is carried successfully all the way in and out of a business by every responsible employee at every level.")[9]

In the summer of 1970, Coors wrote a letter to Colorado's Republican senator, Gordon Allott, asking for suggestions of things he could do to help reshape American politics. His assistant subsequently traveled to Washington to do research on conservative organizations in which Coors could invest his money. Through Senator Allott's office, Coors became connected with Paul Weyrich, a conservative young staffer from a working-class Catholic background. Weyrich enlisted Coors to solicit donations from his executives for a new organization, the Committee for the Survival of a Free Congress, which was trying to raise $2 million in 1974 to defeat "100 of the most liberal, anti-business and pro-welfare congressmen on Capitol Hill," as one fund-raising letter put it. Coors also founded a television production company to produce news footage intended to counter liberal bias in the media (its president, who had been Coors's personal assistant, described Martin Luther King, Jr., as an "avowed Communist revolutionary").[10]

But Paul Weyrich was not only interested in fund-raising. He cared about ideas. And he wanted to convince Coors that it was time to begin a new intellectual organization devoted to the conservative movement. Weyrich felt that the American Enterprise Institute had become mainstream, hackneyed, tired—that it was so concerned about appearing respectable that it was no longer willing to take a stand for conservative principles. AEI had grown timid—all it wanted was to stay out of the political fray. After Richard Nixon was reelected in 1972, Patrick Buchanan (then a Nixon staffer) wrote a memo arguing that conservatives needed to build an institute outside the government that could be the "repository of their political beliefs." It needed to be partisan, aggressive, and openly political, all of which meant that "the AEI is not the answer."[11]

Weyrich and Coors took a little while to get their organization off the ground. But after a couple of false starts, they established the Heritage Foundation, in 1973. (Weyrich had come up with the name under pressure from Coors; the morning the name was due, he went for a walk with his wife and glimpsed a sign signaling new construction: COMING SOON: HERITAGE TOWN HOUSES.) While AEI focused on economics and foreign policy, Heritage in its first years also sought out the front lines of the culture wars. The foundation gave legal advice to the parents of Kanawha County, West Virginia, who in 1974 organized community-wide school boycotts (joined, at one point, by a strike of the local coal miners) to prevent the use of textbooks containing passages from the work of black authors such as James Baldwin and Gwendolyn Brooks and poets like e. e. cummings. It published an early pamphlet attacking "Secular Humanism and the Schools," criticizing progressive educators in the tradition of John Dewey for their disregard for "the Judeo-Christian moral order." The group brought the same intensity to its promotion of the free market, running essays in its *Policy Review* (an academic-style journal) on such topics as the economic damage done to African Americans by the minimum wage and labor unions; Jay Van Andel and Richard M. DeVos, the cofounders of Amway, contributed a piece about "The Government Versus the Entrepreneur." In an interview with the *Washington Post,* Weyrich sniped at the older conservative organizations: "I don't understand why people who are free-market-oriented stop being free-market-oriented when there's competition that encroaches on their activities."[12]

But for all the ways in which the Heritage Foundation sought to distinguish itself from AEI, the new organization drew its ideas and its personnel from similar sources. The board of trustees in the 1970s was dominated by longtime business conservatives such as the California construction magnate J. Robert Fluor and Frederic Rench of Racine Industries—not exactly leading members of the national business community—and it won contributions from companies including Dow Chemical, General Motors, Mobil, Pfizer, and Sears, Roebuck, as well as banks like Chase Manhattan and individual businessmen such as Richard Mellon Scaife and Roger Milliken. Edwin Feulner, the second president of Heritage (who contributed a great deal to building the organization), was a lifelong economic conservative who had discovered the creed while an undergraduate at Regis College in Colorado, where he had read Barry Goldwater and William F. Buckley. He had been elected to the Mont Pelerin Society at the youthful age of thirty-two. Before he went to Heritage, he had been a congressional staffer for ten years, and he took with him to the think tank men like Hugh C. Newton, the public relations director for the National Right to Work Committee. In short, although the New Right of the 1970s might have a new style, it still drew its money and its personnel from the old cadres of the business right.[13]

WILLIAM BAROODY responded to the arrival on the conservative scene of the Heritage Foundation with disdain. When one longtime supporter wrote to him to ask a few questions about Heritage, Baroody responded dismissively that the new think tank was only "reinventing the wheel" and that it was not doing anything that was not "already receiving the attention of AEI."[14]

Perhaps Baroody's aloofness hid a deeper anxiety about competing with the upstart organizations. But despite the myriad challenges AEI faced in the early 1970s, Baroody did not have any real reason to worry. The same fears that propelled businessmen to contribute to Heritage also spurred their donations to AEI. The organization did not suffer the same setback following the 1965 investigations that it had after the 1950 congressional inquiry. On the contrary, between 1970 and 1980, the think tank's annual budget swelled from about $1 million to more than $10 million.[15]

Baroody proved a master of transforming the political disasters of the 1970s into opportunities for growth. As one internal memo explained, "There is a groundswell of public opinion against big business in general . . . The CEOs can now see some ominous handwriting on the wall." The investigations into the Watergate scandal, for example, had uncovered financial donations from corporations to Nixon's campaign that violated federal campaign laws—and that seemed at times to be payments for political favors (more generous price supports for milk, or a favorable antitrust settlement). The Nixon campaign had used these illegal corporate gifts—sometimes laundered through overseas subsidiaries—to pay for many of its capers, like the bugging of the office of Daniel Ellsberg's psychiatrist (Ellsberg was the military analyst who leaked the Pentagon Papers to the press in 1971). Twenty-one companies pled guilty to breaking the law. It might not have looked like the ideal moment for AEI to raise money from corporations.[16]

But rather than retreat, as soon as the scandal broke, Baroody met with a small group of his trustees to undertake a major new fund-raising drive. They agreed that the controversy made fund-raising for AEI all the more crucial, for it threatened to scare contributors away at the very moment when Democrats had obtained control of Congress and when the activism of AEI was therefore most acutely in demand. The trustees sent letters to hundreds of executives to urge them to increase their funding to the group. As always, Baroody persuaded individual businessmen on the board of trustees to take a significant personal role in raising money. "AEI has the program, we have the contacts," read one letter from Herman Schmidt, the general counsel of Mobil Oil.[17]

Baroody targeted specific groups of executives for particular initiatives. He got John Swearingen, an executive at Standard Oil, to pitch a research project on energy at the American Petroleum Institute at just the moment when OPEC's boycott of the United States began to cause energy shortages. After rising meat prices in 1973 prompted public demonstrations and boycotts of meat, Baroody decided that it was exactly the right time to start a new Center for the Study of Government Regulation—with the support of executives in the food industry, despite the fact that the interested businessmen knew that if they were to succeed in changing the intellectual culture, it would only be because they were able to maintain a critical distance from the organizations they founded. And John M. Olin of the Olin Foundation donated thousands of dollars to AEI so the organization would campaign against raising the estate tax, which he deemed "socialism out and out," fearing that if it were to be increased, "my estate would be practically liquidated upon my death."[18]

Not only Baroody but his children—especially his three sons—prospered as the organization grew. William J. Baroody, Jr., Baroody's eldest son, took the reins as president of AEI in July 1978; he had had a career in conservative politics, working for the Republican congressman Melvin Laird, with whom he eventually went to the Pentagon, and then as an assistant to Presidents Nixon and Ford. Joseph Baroody ran the company that handled public relations for AEI. Michael Baroody did not work for the organization, but he too was a loyal activist in the conservative movement, as a special assistant to the Kansas senator Robert Dole. All the sons benefited from the connections of their father. As Bill, Jr., told an interviewer, "I can't claim I got to where I am totally on my own. It's clear we had a built-in opportunity." One 1975 magazine profile described Baroody as "the ruling patriarch of Washington's First Family of Political Conservatism."[19]

For nearly twenty years Baroody had been readying himself in the wings; at last it seemed as if the organization to which he had devoted his life might be ready to take center stage. The emergence of new think tanks like the Heritage Foundation—as well as the libertarian Cato Institute and the Manhattan Institute, concerned with urban policy—actually helped AEI to define a new image for itself: the home of respectable conservatism, as compared with the far right at Heritage. AEI could garner the support of moderates and more conservative donors at the same time. For example, the Ford Foundation, often scoffed at by conservatives, gave AEI a $300,000 grant in 1972, while the Lilly Endowment donated $500,000 at about the same time. The organization gained prominent and respectable political sponsors. President Gerald Ford attended a meeting of the board of trustees in 1975, along with Alan Greenspan, the chair of the Council of Economic Advisers, and promised his support ("I would like to do anything I can to help"). Two years later, out of office, Ford became a distinguished fellow at AEI. The organization began new initiatives, such as a series of seminars for corporate executives on topics like health policy, regulatory reform, campaign finance, and "capitalism and its critics," modeled on a similar program directed at businessmen run by the more liberal Brookings Institution. And as the think tank won new support in a broader intellectual and political climate shifting toward the right, the intellectuals whose careers it helped to build were able to exercise new influence in turn.[20]

• • •

Murray Weidenbaum was one of the thinkers whose work blossomed with AEI. Weidenbaum, an academic economist who had served in the Nixon administration, founded the Center for the Study of American Business at Washington University in St. Louis in 1975. The center received gifts from General Electric, the chairman of the aircraft manufacturer McDonnell Douglas, the Olin Foundation, and the J. Howard Pew Freedom Trust, among others. The American Enterprise Institute published some of Weidenbaum's research studies, and he was also one of the two editors of the journal of AEI's Center for the Study of Government Regulation (the other was a rising legal scholar named Antonin Scalia).[21]

Weidenbaum made his name analyzing the economic impact of government regulation. He argued that the United States was undergoing a "second managerial revolution," in which government bureaucrats were indirectly expanding their power over the economy through regulation. "A massive expansion of government controls over private industry is under way in the United States," he wrote in 1977. The Occupational Safety and Health Administration and the Environmental Protection Agency might have laudable goals, but in reality they only produced "waste, bias, stupidity, concentration on trivia, conflicts among the regulators, and, worse of all, arbitrary and uncontrolled power," he argued in a 1975 piece. He loved to make fun of the agencies' bureaucratic quirks: the orders that companies build precisely the same style of restroom for men and women, the toy safety buttons that were found to contain lead paint, the debates over how spittoons should be cleaned or how thick toilet partitions should be or what defined the size of a hole. He derided the notion that $3 billion a year was spent paying the salaries of "enforcers" to make such determinations. The true economic cost, he believed, was far higher, for it included the "millions and millions" of hours that corporations spent trying to comply with government regulations. In one especially dramatic study, Weidenbaum estimated that the burden of government oversight on the private sector was a staggering $100 billion a year, passed on to consumers in price increases. If regulations were dismantled, the American economy would be freed from a tremendous burden; economic growth could be restored.[22]

Weidenbaum's work was widely distributed and cited in the business press. He received coverage in the *Wall Street Journal* and *Nation's Business.* Executives repeated his estimate that regulations cost the economy $100 billion a year and emulated his work, conducting their own analyses of the cost of regulation.[23]

Weidenbaum focused closely on regulation and economic policy. George Gilder, by contrast, wrote passionate jeremiads against modern liberalism's effect not only on the economy but on culture, sexual relationships, and morality. Gilder had once been a liberal Republican, a member of the Ripon Society, a group formed to rebuild the Republican Party after the Goldwater crisis. (The Rockefeller family—the consummate example of liberal Republicanism—actually helped to raise Gilder after his father died when Gilder was young; Gilder's father had roomed with David Rockefeller at Harvard.) But the feminist movement and the counterculture pushed Gilder to the right. His first book, *Sexual Suicide,* was a harsh critique of the women's movement; his second, *Naked Nomads,* catalogued the hazard that single, unattached men posed to social order. His first substantive treatment of economics came in his 1979 *Wealth and Poverty,* which was written with the financial support of the Smith-Richardson Foundation, a conservative foundation funded by the Vicks cough-drop fortune which also donated generously to AEI.[24]

Gilder's aim in *Wealth and Poverty* was ambitious: to demonstrate that capitalism was an inherently moral economic order. He started by arguing that businessmen had been badly misunderstood. Far from being motivated by crass commercialism, greed, or even simple self-interest, Gilder argued, capitalists were driven by "a spirit closely akin to altruism, a regard for the needs of others." Businessmen did not strive to amass fortunes out of crude materialism. They wanted merely to have the "freedom and power to consummate their entrepreneurial ideas." The marketplace was not a narrow space for the pursuit of profit, ruled by accountants and sober stock advisers. Rather, it was a dream-space of quasi-artistic exploration, in which entrepreneurs developed their insights in a selfless pursuit committed solely to the betterment of humankind.[25]

Yet the market was not only this bohemian dream. It was a measuring stick for morality that meted out rewards to people who lived virtuous lives while punishing those who violated codes of decency. "Work, family and faith" were the only solutions to poverty. Gilder derided the idea that poverty among black Americans had anything to do with racism; he rejected the notion that poor people had to struggle against significant external obstacles. Instead he viewed material poverty as a window into the soul of the dispossessed; it proved only that the poor person was unable to work or establish a family or maintain the religious faith that Gilder felt was essential to achieving success.

The real danger of the welfare state was that it created a mode of subsistence and survival free of the morality enforced by the market. Aid to Families with Dependent Children created fatherless families. Unemployment insurance subsidized people who no longer cared to work. Social Security lifted the burden of adult children to care for their aging parents and so loosened family ties. Disability insurance created the incentive to magnify small physical ailments. Instead of giving people security, the social safety net put them collectively in danger by eating away at the motivations and relationships needed for true wealth and happiness. The false safety it engendered replaced risk-taking and halted economic growth, and as a result the attempt at social solidarity only made everyone feel more "anxious and insecure."

For Gilder, the decadent features of modern capitalist life (psychedelic drugs, free love, communes) were really only the by-products of these perversions of the market. People in a growing and dynamic economy would find ample outlets to realize their ambitions, and they would live upstanding lives, devoted to their families and to improving the common well-being of the society. Restoring capitalism and fighting the counterculture were for Gilder the same political project. The goal for him was not only material wealth but also moral rejuvenation. As he wrote in the concluding passages of *Wealth and Poverty,* "It is love and faith that infuse ideas with life and fire."[26]

But while Weidenbaum and Gilder helped to shape the developing popular critique of the ineffectiveness of liberal regulatory initiatives, by arguing that they hampered the economy and warped the moral sense of the nation, Jude Wanniski concentrated intensely on the need to cut marginal income tax rates, and he was actually able to affect policy more directly than the other thinkers. Although his focus seemed narrow, he managed to encapsulate in his critique of tax rates an entire political philosophy of opposition to the state, and his career soared in the intellectual climate of declining Keynesianism. Wanniski was anything but a professional economist, but he had been fascinated by economics throughout his life. As a young child, he had listened for hours to his father arguing with his maternal grandfather, a coal-mining Communist, about exploitation and revolution and the historic role of the working class. When Wanniski graduated from high school, his grandfather gave him a copy of Marx's *Capital.* Wanniski did not become a careful student of the intricacies of Marxism—he never finished the book—but he did learn that debates about economic theory could explode with intense political emotion. Economics was not a sterile subject, filled with numbers, formulas, and opaque curves of supply and demand. It was instead the stuff of high drama.[27]

Wanniski worked hard to establish himself as a journalist. But his curiosity—and his family interest in political economy—eventually took him back to the "dismal science." In the early 1970s he came upon the work of two academic economists, Arthur Laffer and Robert Mundell, whose ideas would change the course of his life. The two men were both professional economists whose careers had hit turbulence. Mundell had been a rising star at the University of Chicago until his advocacy of supply-side theory began to marginalize him in the profession. (His personal eccentricities and notorious sloppiness with regard to detail did not help; once, as president of an international economics society, he failed to appear to deliver his own keynote address.) Laffer had gone from being an assistant professor at the University of Chicago to serving under Nixon at the Office of Management and Budget, where other economists criticized his unorthodox economic forecasting techniques. After leaving Washington, Laffer became a professor at the University of Southern California, where both his career and his lifestyle flourished. A *Wall Street Journal* article on Laffer described his home on a hill overlooking the Pacific, where he and his family lived with a menagerie of pets including a weasel, seven turtles, and eight parrots, including one, Molly, who would perch on Laffer's shoulder while he worked by his "kidney-shaped" pool. Laffer told the reporter that he had once lost fifty pounds in forty days simply by immersing himself in cold water for extended periods of time (the lower temperature, he insisted, made his body burn more calories). His approach to economics featured similar iconoclastic enthusiasms.[28]

In the early 1970s, Mundell and Laffer began to meet with Robert Bartley, the editor of the *Wall Street Journal*'s editorial page, and Jude Wanniski, who was writing for the *Journal*, to talk about economics. By 1974 their informal chats had evolved into a regular discussion group, which met at a Wall Street steakhouse. Wanniski learned from his economist friends a dramatic new interpretation of the economic ills that America was encountering in the early 1970s. The supply-siders tried to change the very terms of the debate. The real problem, they argued, was not insufficient demand but a lack of investment (the "supply side" of the economy). The economy had become so burdened by the heavy weight of taxes and regulation that people simply no longer had the incentive to invest their money. If the regulatory apparatus could be lifted, then they would once more be inspired to buy equipment and start new companies. Production would then increase so significantly that growth would resume without inflation. The "Laffer Curve" (also publicized by Wanniski) argued that past a certain point, raising taxes would actually cause government revenues to decline, as taxes sapped the willingness of companies to invest and of individuals to work. Governments could best stimulate the economy, then, by cutting tax rates and thus creating incentives to invest.[29]

Few of these ideas received much serious analysis within academia at the time. Wanniski did not publish in peer-reviewed economics journals, instead synthesizing the economists' arguments for the editorial page of the *Wall Street Journal*. (The doctrine got its name from one of its opponents, Herbert Stein, the chairman of the Council of Economic Advisers under Nixon and Ford, who scornfully referred to "supply-side fiscalists" in an offhanded way at an economics conference; Wanniski adopted the phrase in his essays for the *Journal.*) But when it came to writing a book, he needed more financial support. After he applied to the Smith-Richardson Foundation, which was wary about funding a major treatise on economics by a writer without an economics degree, Smith-Richardson called up AEI to see if they'd take him. AEI made Wanniski their first resident journalist, giving him a yearlong position to write his book.[30]

The result was called *The Way the World Works,* and it leapt from descriptions of Alexander the Great to discussions of the rise of Hitler to critiques of Keynes and the New Deal. But at the heart of the book was an insistence on the universality of microeconomics. Ordinary people, Wanniski argued, possessed an innate, intuitive grasp of economic policy: "In earliest childhood, we discover these concepts, broadening our portfolios to embrace the marginal utility of grandparents, uncles, aunts and playmates. At the same time we are discovering our own marginal utility in the portfolios of others. We do something cute and there is general laughter and approval, do it again and receive diminished attention from mother and father, do it a third time and get blank stares." A newborn baby crying for a diaper change was in fact taking a course in accounting: "The price of one diaper is one scream." Children viewed parents as common stock: "Mother may seem like a sufficient investment for a long while, a solid AT&T yielding a steady 6 percent return day after day. But one day the bottom drops out of AT&T; mother is in ill humor. And Dad, who had been dragging along with almost no yield, suddenly spurts ten points on the market."[31]

Wanniski suggested that the reason for the recession of the 1970s was that people understood that their economic activity was not in fact rewarded at its full price because of excessive taxes and government regulations. Too few economists, he argued, thought about economics in terms of "what makes people want to work and produce." They talked about the economy as though it were something to be controlled and managed by government, where supply-side theory made "the incentives and motivations of the individual producer and consumer and merchant" the center of economic policy. If the Republicans returned to the essential message of cutting taxes, they could rise above their "dismal condition" and regain political power; after all, the party's decline since 1930 primarily reflected "its failure to understand the nature of the Laffer Curve." Wanniski was so focused on the powers of the tax rate that at times he suggested that cutting it would unleash almost utopian outcomes. In one op-ed piece for the *New York Times,* he wrote that cutting taxes and stopping inflation would reduce drug abuse and divorce and also help the country win the cold war: "Instead of a society smothered, crushed by disincentives, with all its tensions, there would be light, air and hope . . . We will once again feel confident about ourselves as a nation, and the Russians would view us in a different light."[32]

Because they believed that cutting income taxes across the board would only exacerbate the inflation plaguing the country—if it didn't simply swell budget deficits—few economists paid much attention to Wanniski's ideas. He found a more receptive audience in the Republican Party, especially in the figure of Jack Kemp, a Republican congressman from upstate New York. Kemp, a former quarterback for the Buffalo Bills whose father had been an entrepreneur in Southern California, became fast friends with Wanniski when the two men met by chance one day on Capitol Hill. Wanniski had been conducting interviews for an article when he stopped in Kemp's office on a whim and was surprised to learn that the congressman was an ardent fan of his *Wall Street Journal* editorials. With Wanniski's guidance, Kemp introduced legislation in Congress for an across-the-board tax cut that would slash the top rate from 70 percent to 50 percent, cutting income tax rates across the spectrum by an average 30 percent. Kemp had no interest in old-fashioned government-slashing; in fact, he argued that simply reducing spending, as fiscal conservatives wished to do, was "inhumane" and "barbaric." The economic logic of Wanniski's broad and sweeping tax cuts might be flawed, but politically it offered a way to oppose the welfare state while embracing an even more populist program: making everyone an entrepreneur. No longer did austerity need to be the language of the day—cutting the government only meant returning incentives to the people.[33]

Kemp modeled himself on JFK (whose initials he fortuitously shared), right down to his hairstyle, and cited the Kennedy tax cuts of 1964 as his political inspiration. On his desk he kept a statuette of Don Quixote, along with a little figure of Lincoln. His plan, he promised, would not "separate labor from capital" but would "bring back the rewards not only for capital but also for labor." It was in the interest of the working class. He brought Arthur Laffer—who was by this time traveling around the country to speak to executives about supply-side theory for $4,000 a speech—to Washington to testify in favor of the tax reduction bill. The Republican National Committee adopted a version of Kemp's proposal as part of its national platform, and chartered two planes to fly "tax squad" speakers around the country in the run-up to the midterm 1978 elections. The victory of Proposition 13, which slashed most property taxes in California, seemed to indicate rising antitax sentiments across the country. In 1978, after a campaign led by the Republicans, the maximum capital gains tax rate was reduced from 35 to 28 percent (the top marginal income tax rate at the time was 70 percent).[34]

At first the Democratic Party scoffed at the Kemp-Roth proposal (introduced in the Senate by William V. Roth of Delaware, a Harvard Business School graduate and conservative Republican who was more concerned than Kemp about the possibility that sharp tax cuts would cause the deficit to balloon). Walter Heller, who had been chairman of the Council of Economic Advisors under Kennedy, jeered at Kemp's attempts to claim the mantle of JFK, saying: "The retrospective Kemp-Roth view of the Kennedy-Johnson tax cut is simply wrong." But before long the Democrats too began to advocate lowering taxes. In 1980 one of Democratic president Jimmy Carter's leading advisers gave a speech declaring that the "economic policy of the 1980s must place *greater emphasis on the supply side of our economy.*" Not everyone agreed that the way to do this was through the sharp tax cuts advanced by Kemp (whose proposal did not pass), but more and more people from both parties began to insist that tax policies should be crafted to encourage business investment rather than consumption.[35]

The ideas carefully honed during the years when conservatives had been excluded from power were taking the place of the old faiths of the New Deal era. The new generation of free-market thinkers—in contrast to Friedrich von Hayek and Ludwig von Mises—wrote far less about communism and the dangers of a planned economy. They were more enamored of specific policies, more ironic about the failures of bureaucracy, in some ways more fixated on particulars and less interested in describing the workings of the whole system. Their rhetoric was one of hope and optimism instead of danger and foreboding. They lacked the gloomy grandeur of their predecessors, perhaps because they sensed that the world was turning in their favor. Hayek even won a Nobel Prize in economics in 1974—a sign of the growing appreciation for his work in the larger intellectual community.

9 Building the "Business Activist Movement"

In the spring of 1978, Justin Dart, the chairman of the board of Dart Industries of Los Angeles, a conglomerate pharmaceutical business that also made Tupperware, spoke at a conference at the Colonnade Hotel in Boston. The meeting was attended by more than a hundred executives of northeastern companies who wanted to learn how to set up political action committees (PACs), lobby legislators, and keep their employees and stockholders informed about politics.

On before Dart was George Herbert Walker Bush, the former director of the Central Intelligence Agency. Bush's speech to the business meeting emphasized the disturbing expansion of the federal government in the 1970s. "Less than fifty years ago, Calvin Coolidge could say that the business of America is business," he noted. "Today, the business of America seems to be the regulation of business." To redress the problem, Bush insisted, businessmen needed to do more to help elect politicians "whose natural inclination is to reduce government." He hoped that in the fall midterm elections, corporations would strive to "change control of the Congress, one or the other of the houses." Nor should they stop there. They needed to move heaven and earth to "change control of the White House in the next election."

Then Justin Dart got up to tell the executives how to make that change happen. The key, he said, was building a corporate PAC. He told his audience, "A company that doesn't have a PAC is either apathetic, unintelligent, or you've got a death wish." He reminded the businessmen not to restrict their gifts to politicians from the populous and liberal states, or the states where their companies were headquartered, for all the states were equally represented in the Senate: "A senator from Idaho is just as valuable in the Senate as a senator from the great states of California and New York." And Dart rejected the notion that corporate PACs were corrupting the political process. "I don't advocate that business buy a legislator," he insisted. "Rhetoric is a very fine thing; a little money to go with the rhetoric is better. They listen better."[1]

The 1978 political action conference was part of a series organized by the U.S. Chamber of Commerce, the National Association of Manufacturers, and the Center for the Study of Free Enterprise at the University of Southern California (where Arthur Laffer taught). Justin Dart often spoke at the meetings. His participation in the workshop series was in many ways the capstone of his lifelong efforts to organize businessmen to give financial support to candidates sympathetic to the business cause.

A former Northwestern football tackle, Dart had been an executive at the Walgreens chain in the 1930s. In 1941 he left to work for other national drugstore lines, and in 1947 he opened the world's biggest drugstore, in Hollywood, with a star-studded party that cost $90,000 and included among the decorations 10,000 orchids. He became known for such lavish events. Although his companies went through some growing pains, by the late 1970s Dart Industries was number 154 on the Fortune 500 list.[2]

Dart had been interested in politics almost as long as he had been in business. He had supported Alf Landon in his 1936 campaign against Roosevelt, raising money for the Kansas governor by selling one-dollar sunflower boutonnieres. "I was for anybody that was against Roosevelt, because if it hadn't been for the Southern Democrats, he'd have given our country away," he told an interviewer. Decades later he still blamed FDR's "socialistic ideology" for inflation.[3]

Dart first put his political skills to use in 1956, when he became one of the star fund-raisers in California for President Eisenhower's reelection campaign. He carefully targeted the state's business leaders, asking them to donate $5,000 each. "You're the shepherd of your flock," he would say, "and it's up to you to collect the money." He made it a test of their power and influence over their management employees: "Look, you've got more influence with the people working for you than I have. Don't ask me to go ask them for a philosophically oriented contribution. You do it. You've got the muscle; I haven't." Businessmen who initially had no intention of donating to the Eisenhower campaign found themselves taking out their checkbooks after hearing Dart's rap. In 1966, Dart raised money for Ronald Reagan in the governor's race so successfully that he won a place in Reagan's "kitchen cabinet" of corporate advisers during Reagan's years in Sacramento.[4]

Dart supported Reagan because the politician rejected the "Rooseveltian socialistic philosophy." For Dart, social issues like "abortion, NAACP, Equal Rights," and even the Watts riots were "trivial" compared to the overriding issues of economic and military strength: "If we're strong financially, economically, we're going to enjoy the respect of all the countries in the world. When we get weak industrially, economically, we lose a big hunk of that respect. When we get weak militarily, we get our nose tweaked by a bunch of little countries."[5]

In the 1970s, following a 1975 decision by the Federal Election Commission that formally permitted companies to use their funds to solicit political contributions from employees, Dart refined his fund-raising strategies still further. (The FEC decision followed a suit filed by Sun Oil against the previous restrictions; the Federal Election Campaign Act of 1971 had permitted companies to create PACs but limited their funding to shareholders and executives, but after the Sun Oil decision, companies were allowed to raise contributions from employees as well as management and to set up multiple PACs.) Every year Dart Industries' corporate headquarters would bombard the company's eight hundred executives with letters, pamphlets, reports, and copies of political speeches delivered by Dart, while also organizing "economic education" meetings to give employees information on political issues. Dart informed his managers and executives that he personally gave the legal maximum of $5,000 a year and recommended that anyone earning over $100,000 contribute at least 1 percent of his salary. If his executives did not take out their checkbooks after receiving the mailings, Dart would follow up with a telephone call. "If they don't give, they get a sell," he told the *Wall Street Journal*, meaning that if they turned down the initial requests, he gave them his personal pitch.[6]

Dart was so passionate, so enthusiastic about the mandate for executives to start PACs, that he became known as the Johnny Appleseed of the corporate PAC movement.

MEN LIKE Lemuel Boulware and F. Clifton White had dreamed for decades of using the combined financial and political strength of business to reshape American politics. In the 1970s, as American businessmen confronted the challenge of the counterculture while facing economic decline, they started to follow the prescriptions of the earlier generation of corporate activists. In 1970 most Fortune 500 companies did not have public affairs offices; ten years later 80 percent did. In 1971 only 175 companies had registered lobbyists, but by the decade's end 650 did, while by 1978 nearly 2,000 corporate trade associations had lobbyists in Washington, D.C. Thanks in part to Justin Dart's speeches and the educational seminars sponsored by the Chamber of Commerce and other business organizations, the number of corporate PACs grew from 89 in 1974—the year before the Sun Oil decision—to 821 in 1978. They became an increasingly important source of funding for political campaigns, while the number of union PACs stalled at 250. Newspapers commented on the increasing prominence of business in the nation's capital. As the *New York Times* put it in 1978, "These are the days of wine and roses—or champagne, even, and orchids—for business interests in Washington."[7]

The executives who asked their managers to donate to PACs and who rallied their shareholders to vote according to their economic interests wanted to make sure that the economic slowdown was blamed primarily on labor unions and excessive government regulation. They were opposed not only to the broad ideological challenges of the radicals of the counterculture and the New Left, but also to the specific policy solutions that liberal Democrats proposed to cope with the recession that gripped the country. During the 1970s, the Democratic Party tried to find ways to recapture its base among blue-collar workers, winning back those who had supported Richard Nixon in 1968 and 1972. Liberals in the party sought to develop a new class-based politics, one that could pull these lost Democrats back into the fold. To that end, they pushed for legislation to strengthen labor unions by expanding workers' rights to organize. They tried to create a federal agency to advocate for consumers, advocated for a full employment bill backed by the AFL-CIO and civil rights groups, and sought legislation to break up giant energy companies. In 1975, two senators—former vice president Hubert Humphrey and liberal New York Republican Jacob Javits—even introduced a bill to create a national planning agency. (Walter Wriston of Citicorp denounced it as a "program designed to destroy the free market system and with it our political liberty.")[8]

This push to reinvigorate the old New Deal electoral coalition by combining class politics with appeals to civil rights activists was not the only strategy within the Democratic Party during the decade, as the party's leaders sought to recover from George McGovern's 1972 defeat. Jimmy Carter in particular, like other centrists in the party, wanted to recast the Democrats' message to draw in white middle-class suburbanites. But the liberal factions in the party still had enough strength and confidence to push their agenda forward, especially in the years after Watergate, when the Democrats held a solid majority in both houses of Congress. All these measures reflected their convictions that the country could recover only if workers and consumers were given the social power to challenge the stranglehold large corporations held on the American economy, and that the Democratic Party could maintain power only if it continued to appeal to voters along class lines. These were the visions that the business leaders mobilized against.[9]

. . .

THE BUSINESS Roundtable was founded on the idea that celebrity executives could become a disciplined phalanx defending the interests of business as a class. The membership of the organization was limited exclusively to the chief executive officers of companies in the Fortune 500—the nation's largest companies, controlling millions of livelihoods and billions of dollars. The guiding idea behind the Business Roundtable was that politicians might shrug off a company's middle management and paid lobbyists, no matter how large and powerful the company was, but they would listen to the CEO. As John Post, the organization's executive director, told the *New York Times* in 1976, "Senators say they won't talk to Washington reps, but they will see a chairman."[10]

The CEO of DuPont in the early 1970s was one of the first executives to become involved in building this elite organization, in keeping with the company's longstanding tradition of political involvement. Charles "Brel" McCoy, a careful, restrained man who had worked at the chemical giant for decades before becoming the CEO, knew well the importance of finding ways for businessmen to defend their companies from public attacks. In 1968 civil rights activists had sharply criticized DuPont when National Guardsmen occupied the black neighborhoods of Wilmington, Delaware, where the company was headquartered, for nine months after riots following the assassination of Martin Luther King, Jr.—one of the longest such deployments justified as necessary to prevent racial violence in the country's history. Although the company was not directly responsible for the actions of the National Guard, community activists and civil rights leaders viewed it as complicit. They handed out leaflets outside the company's New York and Philadelphia offices and denounced "DuPont control."[11]

Then, in the summer of 1970, one of Ralph Nader's public-interest research organizations decided to focus on DuPont for a research study about the relationship between corporations and government. In Delaware, of course, the company's power was closely entwined with state and local government alike. Eight young men and women (part of the group known as Nader's Raiders) moved into a dilapidated Victorian house in

Wilmington and spent the summer interviewing people about DuPont, asking about everything from its policies regarding minority hiring and promotion, to the unusually large number of its employees and former employees holding political office in the state, to its relationship with local newspapers. (The company had been wary about the project; executives had wondered whether DuPont should "resist" the project "because it was a vigilante organization, self-appointed and anti-DuPont," according to one corporate memo written after the fact, but it eventually agreed to cooperate.) The report, released late in 1971, was titled *The Company State*; it alleged that "in Delaware, the mother state has virtually been replaced by the mother company; corporate power is no longer private, but has nearly pre-empted public power." It was a perfect illustration of the kind of antibusiness activism that Powell had written about in his memorandum (which was still confidential) only three months earlier.[12]

McCoy lashed out at the Nader report in the press, telling the *New York Times* that not only was it "negative" and "one-sided" but it espoused "a political philosophy that is alien to the essential directions of American public policy and proposed to alter drastically our economic system, which is based on free enterprise." Local publications just made fun of it: *Delaware Today* published a satirical poem based on Poe's "The Raven" entitled "The Raider," all the stanzas of which concluded with a line that rhymed with "Ralph became a household bore."[13]

Even before the Nader report was released, the DuPont CEO had spoken to a meeting of businessmen on the subject "How Should Business Respond to Its Critics?" "You've heard it all before," he said. "Our plants are unsafe; the jobs we offer are dehumanizing; we are destroying the environment and don't care; technology is out of control; society is in the grips of the military-industrial complex; our cities are collapsing while we hide on our suburban estates. In short, as our most angry critics see it, business is morally bankrupt, and the whole economic system ought to be sent back to the shop for a major overhaul." Some of the skeptics, McCoy acknowledged, were beyond reaching. But it was time to show those who could still be convinced "why the profit system is worth protecting for everybody's sake, not just for the benefit of the stockholders." A year later

McCoy got a letter from John Harper, the chairman of the board at the Aluminum Company of America (ALCOA). "There has been increasing discussion and expression of concern about the decline of business' role in and impact on decisions in the Federal system," Harper wrote. In the summer of 1971, President Nixon had reinstituted wage and price controls for the first time since World War II in an attempt to slow inflation. Harper didn't mention it in his letter to McCoy, but early in 1972 he and Fred Borch, the CEO of General Electric, had shared their ideas about the need for businessmen to make their voices heard in politics so that labor unions and consumer groups would not dominate in the capital, with John Connally, the secretary of the treasury, and Arthur Burns, the chair of the Federal Reserve Bank. Harper's letter to McCoy—which he sent to the chief executives of ten other companies at the same time—asked if the executives would be interested in helping to build an organization that could take "effective action," that could "speak with real authority in the difficult months and years" facing American business.[14]

McCoy joined right up. In March 1972 he went to Washington to attend the first meeting of what would eventually become the Business Roundtable, which was formed when Harper's small group of executives (which became known as the "March Group") merged with two larger organizations, the Labor Law Study Group and the Construction Users Anti-Inflation Roundtable, which sought to unify employers to fight for more business-friendly labor laws and against the power of construction unions. Justin Dart was not at that first meeting, but by the end of the decade he too would be a member of the Roundtable, along with dozens of other CEOs from the nation's largest corporations.[15]

THE BUSINESS Roundtable tried at first to invest in programs that would indirectly influence the public view of business, following the tactics adopted long ago by groups like the National Association of Manufacturers. One early memo read, "Business has very serious problems with the intellectual community, the media and youth . . . the continuing hostility of these groups menaces all business." Claude Wild, a Gulf Oil executive, spoke to the March Group in September 1972 about the public relations problem: "Government, labor, the study groups, public advocates, consumer group cells, and others are already well along in their preparations for next year. Our political friends, who today feel they are entering a hostile arena when they go out to fight for us, are not going to pursue the battles ahead with either zeal or determination, unless they can look around and see us and our companies entering that same arena against the same hostile forces." A report done for the Roundtable by consultants shortly after the group was formed gave a prominent place to the Powell memorandum, even including the memorandum as an appendix. The consultants felt that the Roundtable founders were not yet taking Powell's comments seriously enough and urged the group to be more ambitious and aggressive and put forward a "total attack program."[16]

To combat the negative vision of business, the Roundtable's Public Information Committee suggested finding new ways to educate the public about economics through classes at the high school level, perhaps even "a 'Sesame Street' for young and middle-aged adults (or anyone else likely to vote or write to his Congressman)," in order to "accomplish the kind of re-orientation of attitudes which preservation of the free enterprise system demands." The group spent over a million dollars, raised through a special assessment on members, to place a series of paid advertisements in *Reader's Digest*—ads that seemed to be articles or essays written by the magazine's staffers but were in fact paid for by the Roundtable. One piece in the 1975 series defended the very principle of profit ("Profits are not, as some people seem to think, clutched in the hands of a few cigar-smoking tycoons"); another argued that "the way we earn our 'daily bread' in this country is under attack as never before" and offered responses to criticisms that the "free enterprise system makes us selfish and materialistic" and that "free enterprise concentrates wealth and power in the hands of a few." The idea, as John Harper explained, was that "people who have greater economic knowledge have a much more favorable attitude towards business."[17]

The Business Roundtable also set out to raise money for AEI, inviting William Baroody to speak at their meetings and encouraging Roundtable members to contribute to the conservative think tank. AEI, one Roundtable executive wrote, was "working toward the same objectives the Business Roundtable is except that they have a longer range approach than we do."[18]

Although the Roundtable started out with the idea of investing in broad public relations campaigns, there was much disagreement within the organization about whether such campaigns were really effective. The most ambitious—like the *Sesame Street* of economics—never came to pass. The organization's efforts soon shifted primarily to lobbying, although always within the broad framework of changing the perception of business—and it was here that the Roundtable was able to have the largest impact on the politics of the capital.

The Roundtable transformed the longtime agenda of business conservatism—the old faith of Boulware and Goldwater—by translating it into a pragmatic antirecession program. The group did not argue against labor unions or the welfare state on the ground that they restricted business freedom. Rather, even when making pointed political arguments, the Roundtable reframed the debate in terms of "capital formation," a dry, technical term referring to the capacity of the American economy to generate capital. "Current tax policies have caused a low rate of savings in the US and have acted as a disincentive to investments which would be beneficial to the long term health of the domestic economy," one 1980 statement read. "The Business Roundtable believes that future changes in tax policy should aim at improving the investment or supply side of the economy in order to increase the quality and scope of our productive capacity." The major problem the American economy confronted was a shortage of investment, and the Roundtable merely wanted to make policy changes that would encourage new economic growth. The economic problems confronting the United States during the decade were largely the product of a hostile political climate: cut taxes and regulations and the economy would grow again.[19]

Such rhetoric might not have sounded like a political rallying cry. But that was precisely the point. The Roundtable did not want to be perceived as an anti-union organization. Instead of thundering against the tyrannical power of labor, as Lemuel Boulware might have done, the Roundtable argued that unions bore great responsibility for inflation and that therefore union members should not be allowed to collect food stamps while out on strike (echoing a position that could be found in *Fortune* and elsewhere during the decade). No longer was the issue one of fundamental political principles or the rights of management; it was one merely of cost-benefit analysis.[20]

The Roundtable had the same attitude toward government regulations. The chair of the organization's Environmental Task Force in 1973, Bert Cross of Minnesota Mining and Manufacturing, complained that the environmental movement's "demands for 'pure air' and 'pure water'" in very short time frames were "technically impossible" and "economically and environmentally unsound." John Harper argued that only deregulation could solve the energy crisis: "The best step for this nation would be immediate decontrol of the oil industry." Edgar Speer, the CEO of U.S. Steel and chair of the Roundtable Energy Users Task Force, echoed him: "All must be convinced that it is not a government function, within our free-enterprise system, to regulate supply and demand, i.e., free-market forces must be allowed to establish the energy supply-demand equilibrium. Until better understanding exists there is little hope of progress." And the organization opposed the full employment act backed by the civil rights and labor movements, calling it a "thoroughly bad" piece of legislation; as Lewis Foy of Bethlehem Steel wrote: "If enacted, the bill will inaugurate 'centralized planning' for the whole economy, a cure that will subvert our system of free enterprise and be worse than any disease we now have."[21]

The Roundtable strongly opposed the creation of the Consumer Protection Agency (CPA), a government agency that would have advocated on behalf of consumers and would even have had the power to provide financial assistance for citizens involved in lawsuits against corporations, on the grounds that it was economically dangerous, another "administrative entanglement" to be avoided. To fight the proposed agency, the Roundtable commissioned a $25,000 study on popular support for it; when the results showed low public enthusiasm for the idea, the group publicized them widely, despite criticisms from the Library of Congress about the survey's methodology. And in 1979, in an attempt that seemed influenced by Murray Weidenbaum's analysis, the Roundtable produced a study attempting to show the enormous costs to business of complying with new government regulations concerning occupational safety and environmental pollutants. While acknowledging that "most government regulation originates from genuine concern for the achievement of desirable economic and social goals," the Roundtable study argued that regulations were causing inflation, slowing growth, hampering inventions, hurting small business, making it difficult for American companies to compete in the international market, and "limiting capital formation."[22]

The Roundtable organized its members to lobby Congress directly; they received notifications of policies worked out by the Roundtable's committees as well as upcoming congressional votes and reminders to be in touch with senators and representatives. The headquarters of the organization matched chief executives from companies like Sears, Bristol-Myers, General Foods, and Westinghouse with the perfect politician for each one to contact. Then the congressmen and senators would be visited by one CEO after another, often representing companies with businesses in their districts, each calmly explaining his opposition to labor law reform or the Consumer Protection Agency or the Full Employment Act or antitrust revision—whatever the main issue might be. "Letters, telegrams, personal representations from your employees, shareholders, customers and suppliers to every Senator are urgently needed today," read a letter from Robert Hatfield, the CEO of Continental Can and chair of a Roundtable task force on economic organization, to the Roundtable members, urging them to take action against a law that would have permitted Congress to break up large oil companies. (In another address to the Roundtable, Hatfield reminded the members of what was at stake: "We all know what Mr. Nader has in mind: A federal watchdog in every boardroom.")[23]

Such lobbying continued to have a public relations component. John Post, the Roundtable's executive director in its early years, argued that in order to respond to what he viewed as "a new crisis for capitalism," chief executives needed to be personally willing to "face the fire of adversaries and of the press." As Thomas Murphy, the CEO of General Motors, said in an address to the Roundtable in 1978, "We must involve ourselves in a very personal way . . . Through us, the public must see corporations in the same human terms that they see the president, or George Meany, or Ralph Nader." Executives had to stop being shadowy figures behind the scenes and become visible characters in the daily drama of politics.[24]

The Roundtable's carefully calibrated rhetoric of economic growth enabled the organization to distance itself from more aggressively political conservative groups, such as those associated with the New Right. Its leaders never took public positions on abortion, feminism, or gay rights. (Roundtable executives occasionally criticized the Equal Employment Opportunity Commission; John Harper argued that corporations ought to be left alone to develop their own affirmative action policies and that the EEOC would mean more class action suits.) It rejected the foreign policy positions of the New Right, supporting the Panama Canal treaties that turned the canal over to Panamanian control, which were strongly opposed by conservative activists. When it seemed that the federal government might limit the ability of American corporations to do business with Arab nations in response to the Arab boycott of Israel and companies doing business with Israel, Roundtable executives met with the Anti-Defamation League in an effort to hammer out principles that would circumvent any antiboycott legislation. (Exxon and GE in particular took the lead in opposing such laws, which would have greatly interfered with their business operations as well as impeded energy supplies more broadly; as Clifton C. Garvin, Jr., the chairman of Exxon, wrote, "Continued access by the United States to growing supplies of Arab oil is of major importance as is the task of enhancing the security of these oil supplies.")[25]

Even on economic matters, the Roundtable advocated tax breaks and investment credits carefully targeted at business, which it viewed as more fiscally prudent than the dangerously inflationary across-the-board 30 percent income tax cuts that Jude Wanniski and Jack Kemp were pushing. For some, the Roundtable seemed downright liberal: the *Wall*

Street Journal editorial page lambasted the Roundtable for daring to suggest that corporations might bear some social responsibility for alleviating inner-city poverty.[26]

The organization's genteel and flexible conservatism enabled many of its chief executive participants to develop good relationships even with Democratic president Jimmy Carter after his election in 1976. (Not that the group had encountered much difficulty trying to relate to Democrats earlier; in 1974, its leaders had been invited to meet with congressional Democrats and to give them position papers on topics like inflation, capital formation, productivity, and taxation.) Even though *Business Week* had warned that Carter (who had, after all, been a peanut farmer) was a classic southern populist who would bring "the 1970s version of the New Deal" to Washington, political observers like the journalist and former Nixon staffer Kevin Phillips noted Carter's close relationship to Georgia corporate powerhouses such as Coca-Cola and Lockheed Martin. Once in office, Carter made it clear that his administration represented a new kind of Democratic Party. As he said in the 1978 State of the Union address, "Government cannot solve our problems. It cannot set our goals. It cannot define our vision. Government cannot eliminate poverty or provide a bountiful economy or reduce inflation or save our cities, or cure illiteracy, or provide energy." Irving Shapiro, the CEO of DuPont in the late 1970s, spoke of the positive relationship Carter had with businessmen: "The President started out on the premise that he should not be personally involved. Now he is accessible. He talks. We have no trouble getting ourselves heard." Shapiro was in a good position to know. He and Reginald Jones, the CEO of General Electric and a fellow Roundtable member, would take limousines to the White House to meet with the president. (Later in life, Shapiro would write that "business, or at least big business, generally has done better on narrow issues with the Democrats than with the Republicans.")[27]

The Roundtable's discreet lobbying helped to defeat the liberal legislative agenda for the decade. The organization received a new level of public attention in the summer of 1978, when (despite some initial disagreement about whether or not to get involved in the fight) it raised extra money from its members to help beat a labor reform bill. The proposed legislation would have made it easier for unions to organize workers by expediting the process for organizing and holding National Labor Relations Board elections and by establishing stiffer penalties for employers that fired workers. At first some of the Roundtable companies were reluctant to get involved, fearing conflict with their unions. But they were outvoted, and the Roundtable dug in. In their fight against the labor law reform bill, the large corporations of the Roundtable were part of a coalition with groups representing small businessmen. When one senator from Florida mentioned in a casual way to an aide that he had spoken to plenty of executives from big corporations about the labor law bill but hadn't heard much from small business, "as if by magic" his office was flooded with small Florida entrepreneurs, who were flown to Washington in the Lear jets of their larger corporate brethren. Postcards, mailgrams, telephone calls, and visits from members of business organizations deluged Senate offices. The president of Sears, Roebuck sent a letter to all the suppliers from which the retail giant purchased its products, arguing against the law, expressing his personal fear that it would be a disaster for the nation, and asking them to contact their representatives to stop the bill from passing.[28]

When the bill was returned to committee after nineteen days of filibustering by the Utah Republican Orrin Hatch—who was so personally committed to defeating the bill that he'd warned seminars of McDonald's franchise owners that they were guaranteed to face an onslaught of new union organizing drives if it passed—everyone understood what it meant. "For the first time in twenty years, the business community has vanquished organized labor in a fight over a 'gut' issue for labor," wrote the *New York Times*. The Roundtable—and the rest of the business lobby—had arrived.[29]

THE ROUNDTABLE, with its rhetoric about "capital formation" and its membership of leading CEOs, represented one side of corporate politics during the decade: pragmatic, tough, and powerful. The U.S. Chamber of Commerce embodied another. From the point of view of the leadership of the Chamber of Commerce, the Roundtable wanted to make businessmen into stodgy corporate suits. But the Chamber saw entrepreneurs and executives as the true populists of the nation.

The man most responsible for remaking the Chamber was Richard Lesher, the child of a union plasterer in rural Pennsylvania who had put himself through college and graduate school (he held a Ph.D. in business administration from Indiana University). One local Chamber chapter leader commented that in terms of the Chamber's history, "It's almost like BC and AD—only it's Before Lesher and After Lesher." Six feet tall, Lesher was, in the words of a friend, a "bully boy with a steel-trap mind." His career prior to the chamber was a strange combination of public, private, and nonprofit work; he had gone from a job teaching corporate finance at Ohio State University to NASA, where he worked in "technology utilization," to a brief career as a management consultant and as president of a nonprofit organization that researched ways to dispose of garbage. He became president of the Chamber of Commerce on the recommendation of a headhunting firm in 1975, a couple of years after the board of directors of the organization had decided to adopt a political strategy endorsing most of the points Lewis Powell had made in his memorandum.[30]

The board of the Chamber hired Lesher largely because of his emotional intensity about the job. "He convinced us that he really wanted to do something about preserving the American economic system," said one board member. Lesher was glad to go to the Chamber, for he had a deeply political streak. "I believed that if any organization had the potential to turn the country away from its drift towards socialism, this was the institution," he said in an interview years later. In a speech in the summer of 1975, not long after he arrived at the Chamber, Lesher told an audience of businessmen that given the trends toward greater government regulation of the economy and the expansion of the public sphere, they had to ask themselves whether capitalism could in fact survive. After referencing the dangers of standing idly by in Nazi Germany, Lesher concluded with a flight of rhetorical fancy inspired by John Donne:

So in closing, I ask you, for whom the bell tolls?
It tolls for you and me,
It tolls for capitalism and for the free,
It is struck by thee, and thee, and me,
Oh, how I wish we had an enemy that we could see.[31]

Impassioned and lurid, this was not the kind of speech that the men in charge of the Business Roundtable—men like Charles McCoy and John Harper—were likely to give, no matter how concerned they were about the future of free enterprise. But it did appeal to men such as Jay Van Andel, one of the founders and top officers of the Amway Corporation, who became chairman of the Chamber of Commerce in 1979. Van Andel and his high school friend Richard DeVos, who grew up in Grand Rapids, Michigan, had started Amway (the contraction was short for American Way) in 1959. According to company legend, the two boyhood chums had decided at an early age that they would become tycoons together, and after a brief flirtation with starting a flight school, they became distributors for a California vitamin product known as Nutrilite. When Nutrilite ran into financial difficulties, they decided to start their own direct-marketing firm; their first product was an all-purpose cleanser called Frisk, but before long they had expanded into many different kinds of goods. The company was founded on the principle of direct marketing. People signed up to be Amway distributors and then sold the company's products to their friends, their families, and anyone else they could find. Each distributor also sought to register new Amway salespeople, whose sales they would also have a claim on.[32]

But although Amway distributors did sell products, the company was really sustained by its ability to generate faith in an inspirational ideal of entrepreneurship. Amway was much more than a simple direct-marketing firm. It was an organization devoted with missionary zeal to the very idea of free enterprise. The company sustained tremendous support for its goods and operations through large rallies attended by thousands of distributors, which doubled as celebrations of free enterprise and capitalism. At one such event, held at the Capital Centre in Washington, D.C., in the summer of 1975, Van Andel gave a speech dotted with quotations from Ronald Reagan to a raucous crowd of more than 30,000, in which he called for a new American revolution to "regain freedom" by getting "the government's hands out of our pockets." The last times the arena had seen a crowd so large, one spokesman said, were when the Rolling Stones and Bob Dylan had come to town. The event ended with a series of questions posed by DeVos to the thousands of distributors in attendance, as stardust fell from the ceiling and simulated fireworks exploded on screens: "Which Way Will You Go? Free or Slave? Mediocre or Excellent? Socialism or Capitalism?" The response that roared from the floor, tens of thousands strong, was "Excellence!"[33]

Van Andel had good reason to celebrate economic freedom. By 1979, Amway had made him one of the wealthiest of the "invisible rich," *Fortune*'s phrase for people whose fortunes had been amassed through private companies; the magazine estimated that his net worth was somewhere between $300 and $500 million. Van Andel took his vision of a popular campaign for capitalism with him to the Chamber of Commerce, whose magazine dubbed the new leader "a salesman for free enterprise." He also had ample cause to resent regulations: Amway was under investigation in the late 1970s by the Federal Trade Commission, which was trying to ascertain whether the company was in fact a pyramid scheme. In the charges, the FTC claimed that the company's sales plan contained an "intolerable potential to deceive" and was ultimately "doomed to failure"—but the verdict in the end favored Amway. As he said when he came to the Chamber, he hoped to create an "improved climate for the free enterprise system," because "personal freedom and free enterprise are like Siamese twins—you can't have one without the other."[34]

During the 1970s, under the leadership of Lesher and Van Andel, the Chamber of Commerce tried to transform itself into a social movement for capitalism. The first thing Lesher did after taking charge was craft a new mission statement, declaring that the Chamber's reason for existence was to "advance human progress through an economic, political and social system based on individual freedom, incentive, initiative, opportunity and responsibility." Lesher viewed the adoption of this credo as the critical step that the organization took toward success, for it "gave us a positive purpose to work for and encouraged us to think of ourselves as more than just a lobby."[35]

This politicized and ideological model of organizing business was very different from the quiet influence embodied by the Business Roundtable. The Roundtable sought to exercise power by restricting its membership to the biggest of big companies. The Chamber believed in mobilizing the masses of the business world—any company, no matter how large or small, could join the organization. The Chamber rejected the Roundtable's tendency to seek out politicians from the Democratic Party and try to make common ground. It backed the Kemp-Roth tax cuts long before most other groups. It openly denounced the Carter administration with such intense conviction that the White House stopped inviting the Chamber to its meetings, even as it continued to host Roundtable executives such as Reginald Jones and Irving Shapiro. The Chamber professed not to care. "To be effective," Lesher said in a 1981 interview, "you've got to stand up and be counted. You've got to be willing to take on people in office who can hurt you."[36]

When Lesher took over at the Chamber, the organization had 1,400 Congressional Action Committees. Each one included about twenty businessmen who were charged with responsibility for lobbying their local representative. When the Chamber headquarters put out an alert, the local Congressional Action Committee would send letters and place phone calls to the politicians. Under Lesher's leadership, the number of Congressional Action Committees rapidly grew, to 2,700 by 1981. The Chamber established a new litigation division—perhaps inspired by Powell's mandate to work through the judicial system for the rights of business—which filed dozens of briefs on matters such as the question of whether strikers could legally receive unemployment benefits. And Jay Van Andel took responsibility for creating a grassroots organization called Citizen's Choice, with membership open to anyone, so that ordinary citizens, not only businessmen, could lend their support to the Chamber's crusades. By 1981, three years after its founding, Citizen's Choice claimed 76,000 members, and the organization said that it could generate 12,000 phone calls within twenty-four hours. And despite the grass-roots slant of the Chamber, larger corporations remained well represented; Donald Kendall, the chairman and CEO of PepsiCo, served as a regional vice chairman in 1979, as did the president of Sears, Roebuck.[37]

All of the Chamber's projects resonated with the call to build a strong popular movement to defend capitalism and free enterprise. The organization started with children, selling an education kit entitled "Economics for Young Americans" to its members, who were then supposed to "persuade" teachers, principals, and school boards to get the kits into classes in public schools. The Chamber celebrated businessmen who went into classrooms to teach kids about business, who set up councils to vet textbooks, and who distributed colorful cartoon guides to capitalism along with their corporate reports. Executives who invited students into their businesses were extolled as model corporate citizens. For example, at the height of the energy crisis, Southern California Gas Company executives brought college students from the area to the company to study its operations in depth. After their final projects were completed, students reported dramatically changed perspectives of the business. As one put it, "I had previously taken it for granted that the gas company was selfish . . . This is not true. It is a self-sufficient company that has not lost human concern for its customers." The student went on: "Let me point out that my negative opinions of the gas company have changed because of facts, not because I was brainwashed."[38]

The Chamber experimented with a wide variety of strategies for media outreach and political organization. The group started a television debate show (*It's Your Business*) in 1979. It created a PAC that did not contribute money to political campaigns but rather tried to use its resources to do fund-raising and organizing work, showing businessmen that they could get involved in politics in ways that went well beyond check-writing. The Chamber's publication, *Nation's Business*, praised William Mitchell, the president of Safeway, when he gave a speech to his company's annual meeting that called for a "business activist movement," for which he hoped that Safeway's 60,000 shareholders might provide a "nucleus" of support. After all, politicians might easily dismiss letters from a few companies, but "31 million communications from 31 million stockholders would cause a groundswell that could not be ignored."[39]

Nor did the Chamber of Commerce restrict itself to matters of business in the 1970s. The organization helped to build a bridge between the social backlash against the civil rights, gay rights, feminist, and antiwar movements and the business backlash against regulation and the welfare state. *Nation's Business* ran monthly columns by James J. Kilpatrick, a southern journalist known for his vigorous defense of segregation during the 1960s, on matters such as school prayer, crime, the Equal Rights Amendment, public employee unions, the Panama Canal Treaty, and other staples of conservative political debate. The magazine published surveys of its membership (which were hardly scientific—they were simply reports on reader responses to questions posed in the magazine's pages), finding, for example, that *Nation's Business* readers opposed the ratification of the ERA and supported prayer in the schools. It ran articles celebrating the property tax revolt that exploded in California in 1978, calling for deregulation to solve the energy crisis, and warning that the collapse of Social Security was imminent.[40]

Business organizations had previously sought to keep silent on cultural matters, but under the leadership of men such as Richard Lesher and Jay Van Andel, the Chamber of Commerce wanted to make sure that the "voice of business," as it called itself, was unmistakably conservative from a social as well as an economic standpoint. *Nation's Business* suggested that the crisis of legitimacy that businessmen confronted during the 1970s could partly be met with the enthusiastic celebration of traditional and conservative cultural values—that defeating the counterculture was the key to the rescue of capitalism. As Kilpatrick wrote, the college students who identified themselves as "left of center" on economic matters also held liberal attitudes regarding abortion and premarital sex. In another column, he observed, "Ours is not an atheistic or antireligious society. The rituals and traditions of religious faith are part of the fabric of our national life." The implication was that it was genuinely in the interests of business to support the family and the church and the nation, that shoring up the traditional culture of the country would also create a political climate favorable for business. This was not simply a question of strategic positioning—it reflected a deeply held set of beliefs about the world. The Chamber of Commerce, as one *Fortune* article put it, was less a lobbying group and more a "political party"; Lesher and Van Andel had transformed it from a "stodgy business federation" into the beginnings of a "mass movement."[41]

The Chamber and the Roundtable sought to bring businessmen into politics. But Lemuel Boulware might also have appreciated the efforts of the decade to exercise political influence in the workplace. New anti-union consulting companies with names like Modern Management Methods offered seminars to teach managers and supervisors how to combat union organizing drives. These consulting firms would contact companies where the workers had filed a petition for a union election—information publicly available through the National Labor Relations Board—and paint a frightening portrait of the consequences of unionization for the employer, telling supervisors, "This is no union campaign. This is a war." They would encourage a legal challenge to the way in which the union was defining the bargaining unit (the people eligible to participate in the union election). The consultant would explain to the boss how to teach the company's supervisors how to spread anti-union messages, and how to threaten them if they were reluctant to participate in the anti-union campaign. Supervisors would be carefully instructed to listen for and report on the union sentiments of employees. The consultants and lawyers prepared special letters and memos for distribution to the workers (a tactic that the National Association of Manufacturers had described in the 1950s), warning of the strikes and disruption sure to result from a union victory. They taught managers to hold captive meetings to preach against the union to small groups of workers. And if it seemed the company might lose nonetheless, the consultants suggested firing the strongest union members, even though this was against the law. "You got to remember you only lose once," one consultant told his audience. "What happens if you violate the law? The probability is you will never get caught." Even the victories that unions won during the decade—like the long strike against textile manufacturer J. P. Stevens that resulted in the company's recognizing the union—became the occasion to rally business against labor.[42]

The intensifying hostility to unions in the private-sector workplace went along with a new antagonism toward strikes of public-sector workers. Sanitation workers who went on strike in Atlanta in 1977, for example, were fired and replacements for them were hired—a move away from the long-standing reluctance to hire permanent replacements to break a strike. The public-sector labor movement had made great gains in strength in the late 1960s and early 1970s; one conservative activist referred to public-sector unionism as a "blight" that was "in essence a product of the 1960s." When the labor movement tried to win a federal law that would have granted collective bargaining rights to all government employees, the conservative movement denounced the effort. As the newsletter of the National Right to Work Committee warned, a "union-run Congressional clique" was seeking "the keys of government through compulsory unionism."[43]

The new visibility of businessmen in Washington was one side of their growing confidence; their willingness to play hardball with unions in their own companies was—as Boulware might have anticipated—the other.

THE BUSINESS Roundtable organized the executives of gigantic corporations to lobby their representatives on behalf of business as a whole; the Chamber of Commerce tried to create a social movement among corporate executives and shareholders. But on the true frontlines of the movement were humbler men like Ferrol G. "Bill" Barlow, a sixty-one-year-old plumbing and electrical contractor in the small town of Pocatello, Idaho.

In 1975, Barlow became a hero to small businessmen around the country when he refused to let representatives of the Occupational Safety and Health Administration (OSHA) into his business to conduct an inspection without a warrant. Barlow insisted during the long legal battle that ensued that his choice was a matter of principle, not self-interest. A copy of the Bill of Rights hung on his wall, and he claimed that his company had a spotless safety record. But the John Birch Society member (who was also a Democrat) was not interested in reforming OSHA; he had a succinct opinion of the agency: "Just like a rabid dog, it needs to be destroyed."[44]

Barlow took his case all the way to the Supreme Court, demanding that OSHA no longer be permitted to search businesses for violations of health and safety laws without first obtaining a warrant. Such a lawsuit cost far more than the small businessman could have paid alone. The American Conservative Union (ACU), one of the political organizations founded in the wake of Goldwater's defeat in 1964, gave Barlow the financial support that he needed to bring the suit. "The support of the ACU has been indispensable, both from the standpoint of money and in getting the word out," wrote Barlow's lawyer.[45]

Fighting OSHA became one of the political causes unifying small businessmen and bringing them into politics in the late 1970s. Even before Barlow won his Supreme Court case in 1978, the ACU began preparing for the next step in what it was calling the Stop OSHA campaign. The organization used the Freedom of Information Act to obtain a list of the 180,000 companies that had received citations for violating federal job-safety regulations since the agency's creation in 1970. The ACU then sent out mailings to all of them (one set began, "Dear Victim of OSHA"), urging them to become involved in putting a halt to the overweening power of OSHA—to "stop OSHA at the door," to not allow the agency's inspectors into their plants and to support the ACU. The ACU staffer in charge of the campaign was jubilant about forcing the agency to hand over the list of names: "Here was OSHA selling us the rope we were going to hang them with!" The ACU distributed guidelines for dealing with OSHA, with titles like "When OSHA Knocks at Your Door," which advised businessmen to demand warrants and prevent the inspectors from entering without them: "It is important to remember that even the smallest victory may provide the key that finally puts an end to the bureaucratic nightmare that OSHA has brought on this country." By encouraging businessmen to demand warrants before allowing OSHA in to conduct a search, the ACU saw itself engaged in an active campaign to undermine the agency. "The more OSHA has to give warrants, the more it slows them down. We want to give them a dose of their own red tape," said one ACU official, who also admitted that his ultimate dream was either "abolishing OSHA or dramatically overhauling it."[46]

Small businessmen around the country wrote checks to the Stop OSHA campaign. Many felt pressed to the wall by the recessions of the decade, by having to compete with larger corporations and with businesses from abroad that used lower-cost labor. The actual penalties that OSHA charged companies that violated its standards were fairly low; during the 1970s, the average penalty was a mere $193. But many owners of small businesses were angry and frustrated at the very idea of someone coming into their company and telling them what to do, and while the penalties for violating the law were low, they may have felt that the costs of reorganizing production to be in compliance with OSHA standards (which varied by industry) were more challenging to bear.[47]

Often the small businessmen who responded to the ACU's campaign were seeking legal help. "Our small 35 employee shop has an excellent safety record but cannot comply with OSHA regulations and stay in business," wrote the representative of one Texas metal company. "If you or your organization can help us since we do not now have qualified legal aid, we will certainly contribute to your fund." Another company head wrote asking for the ACU's help since he could not "undertake the financial burden" of challenging the citation he had received—and he wanted to do so, not only to serve his own self-interest but because an anti-OSHA ruling would be "so significant to industry in general." The ACU did not provide financial assistance to any businessmen after Barlow, but the organization did refer companies to the lawyers who had handled the Barlow case in the hope that they might be able to take on additional clients. Other businessmen wrote seeking support for starting local Stop OSHA chapters using ACU pamphlets and literature. As the president of one Virginia construction company wrote, in a letter that also contained a $250 check, OSHA was "one of the most extravagant and ineffective laws ever passed by Congress."[48]

The overwhelming majority of the companies that contributed to the Stop OSHA campaign were small and midsized manufacturers; the ACU said that it had received no response from Fortune 500 companies, even those that had received OSHA citations. Many of the small businessmen who donated to the drive saw fighting OSHA as just the first step in a broader campaign to challenge the system of government regulations. Some wanted to take on the EPA. "Such requirements as 'zero discharge' into sewers is just impractical," claimed one metals manufacturer. Another small industrialist sent a pointed note: "I would like to know if you have any plans in the near future to initiate action against the Equal Opportunity Employment Commission to curtail the actions of people filing charges against the employer indiscriminately." At times they expressed their frustration with the broader problems they faced in the difficult business world of the 1970s. One North Carolina businessman, a supporter of Senator Jesse Helms who claimed to have spent $1 million to be "allowed to stay in business" under OSHA's rules, was also upset by the "flood of textile imports from very low-wage countries" that had entered the United States since Carter had taken the presidency. "National production has ceased to rise. No wonder," complained a company head from Idaho. "OSHA—Harassment of IRS to us—EPA etc. Get on them. We don't need any more help by NLRB—for unions. We want to grow things and produce. How is it possible with these monkeys on our backs?"[49]

Not all of the ACU's legal advice was worth taking. One Ohio manufacturer got a ninety-day jail sentence when he tried to act on the ACU's suggestions and barred OSHA from conducting an inspection even after the agency presented a warrant. (The ACU had advised that not all warrants were legally valid.) But in some ways the legal fight was less important than the political one. By rallying businessmen to take direct action and literally prevent OSHA from inspecting their companies, the ACU helped to build a political network of small and midsized companies mobilized around their shared opposition to government regulation. Not only did the ACU win the Barlow case; the organization took partial credit for eliminating over a thousand of OSHA's "nitpicking regulations" during the Carter years.[50]

By the end of the 1970s, a new lineup of business organizations had come into existence to campaign on behalf of weakening regulations, limiting labor unions, and rolling back taxes in order to respond to the economic stagnation of the decade. Business leaders were taking a harder line with labor unions in the workplace as well as in the public sphere. The think tanks had grown dramatically. The Heritage Foundation produced one hundred studies and books in 1979 and expanded its Washington real estate holdings the next year. The AEI catalogue was crammed with eighty pages of studies on topics ranging from Social Security to Saudi Arabia, and the specialized initiatives for which the organization had canvassed businessmen took off as well: the group unveiled its National Energy Project in the winter of 1973, and the Center for the Study of Government Regulation opened in March 1976, with an advisory board of executives such as Robert Hatfield of Continental Can and George Shultz of Bechtel. By 1980 the AEI development committee included corporate stars like Walter Wriston of Citibank—an outspoken defender of the market and critic of regulation—Reginald Jones of General Electric, and Thomas Murphy of IBM.[51]

The business conservatives insisted that they had the solutions to the recession: deregulate, cut taxes in one way or another, restrain wage-led inflation. Their confident insistence that they had the answers at a time when no one else knew what to do to resolve the economic slowdown—especially as the Democrats were also beginning to distance themselves from labor unions and the old politics of the New Deal era—made it seem as though the political culture of Washington was starting to swing in their direction at last.

Barry Goldwater wrote in his journal, "Today as I sit in the Senate in the year 1979 it is interesting to me to watch liberals, moderates and conservatives fighting each other to see who can come out on top the quickest against those matters that I talked so fervently and so much about in 1964 . . . Now that almost every one of the principles I advocated in 1964 have become the gospel of the whole spread of the spectrum of politics, there really isn't a heck of a lot left."[52]

10 Making the Moral Majority

"THE SIMPLE TRUTH is that there is a new majority in America," wrote Richard Viguerie shortly after the 1980 election. "And it's being led by the New Right."[1]

Viguerie wrote these words after spending more than a decade organizing for conservative causes—long years during which he raised money, wrote letters, and published a magazine for the movement. He was the self-made man of conservatism, a direct-mail innovator who made a fortune selling his famous list of names of conservative donors to activists eager to dip into the money well. He exercised so much control over the conservative funding base that some critics dubbed him the "godfather of the right."[2]

Born in a small town on the outskirts of Houston, Viguerie was the son of a midlevel petrochemical executive and a nurse who kept a vegetable garden. From an early age he defined himself politically as a conservative. As a reclusive teenager he adored Joseph McCarthy and Douglas MacArthur, and in college he became active in the Republican Party of Texas. In 1961, at the age of twenty-eight, he took on the role of executive secretary for Young Americans for Freedom. He started to do fund-raising work for the organization and quickly found that he preferred private, anonymous direct-mail solicitations to the slightly craven posture he had to adopt when going to ask wealthy men for cash.

His breakthrough came in 1964. As disappointed as he was by Goldwater's defeat, Viguerie nonetheless had the presence of mind in the days after the loss to go to the office of the clerk of the House of Representatives, where he copied down 12,500 names of Goldwater contributors by hand. These donors formed the foundation for a master list of the most committed conservatives in the nation. By the late 1970s, Viguerie had collected the names and addresses of 15 million supporters of conservative causes, which he carefully stored on 3,000 rolls of magnetic tape and scrupulously guarded in his offices in a Virginia suburb of Washington, D.C.[3]

Despite his firmly conservative politics, Viguerie practiced an ecumenical approach to 1970s culture. He liked health food, ate raw lettuce to keep his acid-alkaline count in balance, and kept a jar of wheat germ handy. Although he and his wife were practicing Catholics, Viguerie dabbled in various other faiths. One of his children attended a Christian fundamentalist school, because the Vigueries believed that the rigorous religious curriculum would teach good moral character. Yet Viguerie was also drawn to Eastern religions, including the doctrine of reincarnation. The promise of rebirth deepened his libertarian convictions. As he told one reporter, "We must experience things for ourselves rather than having the government do for us, because we are constantly preparing ourselves for our future lives—perhaps thousands of them."[4]

In 1975, Viguerie branched out from the business of selling mailing lists to start a magazine: *Conservative Digest*. The publication sought to unify the disparate strands of a conservative movement that seemed all of a sudden to be on the march throughout the country. In 1969, a year after Nixon won the election, his aide Kevin Phillips wrote a book called *The Emerging Republican Majority*, which predicted that Nixon's victory was no fluke but that white voters in the South and in cities in the North and Midwest would soon form a voting coalition that could replace the old New Deal alliance, ushering in an era of conservative power. A series of conflicts in the early 1970s seemed to lend credence to his arguments by showing the breakdown of the liberal order. In May 1970, only a few days after Nixon announced the invasion of Cambodia and National Guardsmen killed student protesters at Kent State, construction workers in New York City beat up student demonstrators protesting the war on

Wall Street. The following year, in Pontiac, Michigan, ten school buses in a depot were dynamited to protest busing programs that were intended to integrate the school districts. In 1972, in Canarsie, Brooklyn, hundreds of white parents blocked the steps to a neighborhood school building and boycotted the local schools to try to keep black children out. In 1974, the parents of Kanawha County, West Virginia, kept their children home from school to protest the introduction of new textbooks incorporating selections from Malcolm X and Norman Mailer (the Heritage Foundation sent legal support). And the passage of *Roe v. Wade* in 1973 was beginning to bring Protestants into an antiabortion movement.[5]

But the question was whether the working-class parents of Boston and Kanawha County could form an alliance with the old antigovernment, anti-union base of the movement. As the *Wall Street Journal* observed in 1976 of the longtime free-market advocates in the Republican Party, "They may be able to make common cause with working class 'social conservatives' against busing or abortion, but what happens when these same blue-collar or white-collar workers want bigger Social Security or unemployment compensation payments, more government spending on health care, or tighter government controls on utility bills?"[6]

Viguerie believed that the real base for the conservative movement needed to be blue-collar white people, the descendants of Irish or Italian or Eastern European immigrants, with "traditional" social values. Such voters could, he thought, be wooed away from their support for social and economic programs and labor unions through an appeal to them as individuals concerned about protecting their families, their neighborhoods, and their homes from the dangers posed by radicals. Viguerie published editorials urging conservatives to court the labor movement and to reach out to individual workers on "domestic social issues," even if the "labor bosses" remained out of reach. In a piece titled "Let's Get Union Members to Support Conservatives," he argued that union members were the ideal constituency for the conservative movement: "The individual union member began to realize that the more social programs his boss forced on the government, the more it was going to cost him." A 1976 article by the former Nixon staffer Patrick Buchanan outlined the future of the

Republican Party as "the party of the working class, not the party of the welfare class." The free-market businessmen and working-class social conservatives could make common cause, wrote M. Stanton Evans, the president of the American Conservative Union: "The important thing . . . is not that some of them reach their political positions by reading Adam Smith while others do so by attending an anti-busing rally, but that all of them belong to a large and growing class of American citizens: those who perceive themselves as victims of the federal welfare state and its attendant costs."[7]

To go with this heavy dose of populism, *Conservative Digest* sometimes affected a tone critical of business. Pat Buchanan wrote in 1977 that conservatives needed to make "an agonizing reappraisal of our heretofore almost uncritical support for American business." They had to fight the perception that conservatives were "lackeys of the National Association of Manufacturers or the U.S. Chamber of Commerce, volunteer caddies ever willing to carry the golf bags of the 'special interests.'" They needed to separate themselves from the business world: "If there is any political future for us, it is forfeit, so long as we let ourselves be perceived as the obedient foot soldiers of the Fortune 500." Viguerie followed up with an editorial arguing that "it is no longer axiomatic that whatever is good for General Motors is good for the country and that whatever is good for big business is good for conservatives." Businessmen had helped to further the cultural decline of the United States in myriad ways, such as advertising their products in pornographic magazines. They weren't capable of defending the free market—airline executives had testified before Congress that they needed regulations to survive. Viguerie even wrote that Ford was planning to build an auto factory in the Soviet Union, although he was only repeating a rumor rampant in conservative circles, and he eventually retracted the claim. He urged conservatives to boycott companies taking positions antithetical to their own: "What better place to confront the big businessman than in the free market place for which he professes such love and devotion?"[8]

But Viguerie also saw himself as a strenuous advocate for the free market. As such, despite drawing distinctions between being probusiness and promarket, he published many articles that sought to appeal to the same businessmen he sometimes criticized, by praising corporate PACs and advising "How Businessmen Can Stop Losing in Politics." *Conservative Digest* reprinted the speeches of Business Roundtable leaders and referred readers to the "excellent" political education courses of the Chamber of Commerce. It eagerly solicited business advertisements by trotting out its antigovernment bona fides. One such appeal read: "Mr. Businessman: Has the FTC gotcha down? Is the IRS holding you up? Are you getting heat from OSHA and gas from EPA? Is the EEOC straightening you out and the SEC slapping you down? You got troubles, friend. But maybe we can help. Our 400,000 readers are card-carrying capitalists. In a good scrap, you'd want them on your side. Just whistle, and we'll put in a good word for you."[9]

Viguerie argued that the blue-collar workers of the nation and their manufacturing bosses were natural allies against media elites, intellectuals, academics, and poor people on welfare. The industrialists and their assembly-line employees embodied the productive forces of the country, while the effete representatives of liberalism formed a coalition of waste and indulgence. Philip Crane, a conservative congressman from Illinois, reported in *Conservative Digest* on a meeting that he'd attended with union workers in Youngstown, Ohio: "Before this century is done we will all clearly see the battle lines that are being drawn: those who work for a living versus those who don't. The union members we spoke to are work-oriented people—eloquent in their condemnation of working on the government payroll instead of the private sector." The magazine printed fulminations against "rich liberals" and poetic denunciations of liberalism:

> *I think that I shall never see*
> *A liberal who appeals to me;*
> *A liberal who beats upon the breast . . .*
> *For all the world, he knows what's best! . . .*
> *"Ban the bomb! Boycott the grapes!"*
> *"Pity the perpetrator when he rapes";*

"Herd commuters onto buses";
"Tax the oilman if he fusses!"
The media adore his ideas murky;
But to me, he's just a liberal turkey;
For livings are earned by fools like we,
But these liberals want it all for free.[10]

Viguerie teamed up with an unlikely ally in 1976 to try to bring his conservative populism into electoral politics: William Rusher, the publisher of *National Review.* Rusher seemed nothing like a populist at first glance. He was a Manhattanite who loved to quote Shaw, Shakespeare, and Voltaire in casual conversation. One journalist described him as the only conservative in America who was a member of not one but two wine societies. But in 1975 Rusher published *The Making of the New Majority Party,* a book that made the case for a conservative alliance between businessmen and the working class. Class divisions between "haves" and "have-nots" no longer mattered in America, Rusher argued. Businessmen, manufacturers, hard-hats, blue-collar workers, and farmers were arrayed against a "new class led by elements" that were "essentially nonproductive," including academics, government workers, and the media. Liberal "verbalists," Rusher charged, such as sociologists and journalists, had invented the social programs of the Great Society and had "consciously promoted the growth" of a new constituency of poor people that "exists simply as a permanent parasite on the body politic—a heavy charge on both its conscience and its purse, carefully tended and forever subtly expanded by the verbalizers as a justification for their own existence and growth." Businessmen and workers should join together as productive Americans opposed to impoverished people on welfare and their bleeding-heart defenders in the world of liberal cultural elites. But neither political party was sufficiently committed to organizing this "new majority"—conservatives needed to start a third party to accomplish the task.[11]

Viguerie was inspired by Rusher's book. Together, the two men decided to try to take over the American Independent Party, which had been George Wallace's political vehicle until he abandoned it in a quest for political legitimacy in 1972. Viguerie wrote an editorial arguing that conservatives should break from the Republicans: "Conservatives have been married to the Republican Party for over 100 years. It is time for conservatives to file for divorce." Rusher wrote to his friend William F. Buckley, "I have been a prisoner in the Republican Party's chain-gang too long, and I intend to try something different this year, even if it only amounts to a change of chain-gangs!" With financial support from the anti-union textile manufacturer Roger Milliken (the former donor to *National Review* and supporter of Goldwater) and the Heritage Foundation donor Joseph Coors, they started the Committee on Conservative Alternatives (COCA) to explore political possibilities for conservatives outside the Republican Party. "The workers in this country are fed up with the shirkers, and they are fed up with the government taking the fruits of their hard work to support those who don't and won't work," Senator Jesse Helms pronounced at COCA's first press conference.[12]

Viguerie hoped that Ronald Reagan, the candidate of the economic right, fresh from his second term as governor of California and starting to look toward national politics, could somehow be persuaded to run for the presidency on the American Independent Party ticket with George Wallace, the candidate of the social right. At the time, Reagan was growing eager to pursue a broader role in national politics. As he wrote to Lemuel Boulware, his old friend from GE, "I promise you I'll be trying to stir up the business world, including the exhortation to fight back against government's increasing lust for power over free enterprise." He even told the aging GE executive that an article Boulware had written for *Human Events* (a conservative magazine) had been the basis for some of his own speeches. Boulware still had great hopes for Reagan. When the politician began a radio program in 1974, Boulware wrote to him, "You are the lone one with the knowledge, facility, zest and credibility needed to make the initially disillusioning facts be both economically understandable and humanly attractive."[13]

Viguerie hoped that together, Reagan and Wallace could mount a challenge to Gerald Ford, the mainstream Republican whose politics seemed weak and tepid to the circle around *Conservative Digest.* But the attempt was more fantasy than realistic strategy: Reagan was intrigued by Rusher's book, but his flirtation with starting a third party was quickly quelled by his backers and advisers, who wanted him to remain a Republican. Instead, Reagan challenged the incumbent Ford for the Republican nomination, choosing the liberal Republican Senator Richard Schweiker of Pennsylvania as his running mate instead of the volatile Wallace.[14]

Rusher and Viguerie went to the American Independent Party convention in Chicago anyway. Viguerie offered to run for president himself on the third-party line. But the party's delegates rejected the outsiders (one quizzed Viguerie about a rumor that he'd attended a convention in a saloon, while another accused him of being an acquaintance of William F. Buckley—part of the Rockefeller elite). "They're not conservative, they're out-and-out kooks," one of Viguerie's friends commented. Instead, the party nominated as its candidate in 1976 the former governor of Georgia Lester Maddox, a notorious segregationist whose main claim to fame before his entrance into politics was his vigorous attempt to prevent the integration of his chicken-shack restaurant in Atlanta. The convention even featured a keynote speaker who denounced "atheistic political Zionism" as the "most insidious, far-reaching force the world has ever known." Realizing that association with the racist and anti-Semitic far right would not help their cause, Rusher and Viguerie immediately resigned from the party. In a postscript to the campaign, Rusher ended up asking Coors to help pay off the debts that had been incurred by the project.[15]

Even though it failed, the COCA experiment was still important as a sign of the ways in which conservative activists were seeking to reframe their movement as an alliance between workers and businessmen. It was not so much that Viguerie, himself an entrepreneur, wanted to reject business conservatism, despite his occasional critiques of the Fortune 500. Rather, he sought to create a movement that would be capable of bringing together employees and executives, blue-collar workers and the men who employed them. At the same time, as a salesman of sorts, Viguerie was also well aware that abortion, busing, pornography, gun rights, and crime were exactly the kinds of morally charged and dramatic issues that were capable of galvanizing public support. "To imagine that the New Right has a fixation on these issues misses the mark," Viguerie wrote. "The New Right is looking for issues that people care about, and social issues, at least for the present, fit the bill." To win elections, Viguerie believed, conservatives needed to develop a program that went beyond the tax cuts and antiregulation politics of the American Enterprise Institute. As the Heritage Foundation leader Paul Weyrich commented in an explicit jab at the Business Roundtable, "We talk about issues that people care about, like gun control, abortion, taxes, and crime. Yes, they're emotional issues, but that's better than talking about capital formation."[16]

Showing how the language of the free market could be used in the fight against racial integration, Senator Jesse Helms brought southern whites, who as a group had been Democrats since the Civil War, into the Republican Party. Over his years in Washington, Helms became known as a strident political leader for the cultural right. But his political career had really begun in the world of business conservatism.[17]

Helms was the child of a police officer in Monroe, North Carolina, a sleepy small town in the vicinity of Charlotte. After a short stint in college and a period working as a staffer for Senator Willis Smith, he became the executive director of the North Carolina Bankers Association in the early 1950s, lobbying on behalf of the state banking industry. In someone else's hands, the position might have been quiet and sedate, a comfortable, undemanding post. Helms took the opposite approach. In addition to his lobbying work (which some colleagues suggested was instrumental in getting finance-friendly legislation passed in North Carolina), Helms transformed the *Tarheel Banker,* the association's regular newsletter, into an outspoken political publication. One year after *Brown v. Board of Education,* he wrote an editorial suggesting that if North Carolina did not want to desegregate its schools, the alternative might be to create a separate private school system (as some southerners were already attempting to do, by pulling their children out of public schools and starting new all-white private schools). But he did not make his argument using the typical tropes of segregation: white supremacy, the religious justification for separating the races, or fear of miscegenation. Instead he questioned the basic principle of public education. "We are far from convinced that public schools are the only way to make education available to our people," he wrote. "There is the private enterprise way which offers the same wide horizon for enlightenment." By accepting public education, whites in North Carolina had conceded on a basic principle that would make it hard to maintain segregated schools. After all, if the government controlled the schools, why *shouldn't* it also mandate who went to which one?[18]

Helms believed that it was more rhetorically effective to argue against public institutions in general and on principle than it was simply to defend segregation. "I prefer to oppose integration by attacking the cause rather than the Negro," he wrote to a reader in 1957. "Socialism caused the Southern problem; it is the club which is now being held over our heads." The South should simply avoid integration by abandoning the public schools. "If the South had been prepared to say in unity that we were ready to close our schools rather than surrender to the Supreme Court, the professional Negro and his liberal friends would have been handed the dilemma." A "white supremacy campaign," Helms argued, would not help the cause of the South. He concluded: "Just as I believe that the Southern white people have their rights, I feel also that the Negro is entitled to his. I cannot attack the Negro as a race, but I can in good conscience attack a socialistic system that lends itself to undue power by any group."[19]

Helms played an active part in various campaigns to advance opposition to the welfare state and labor unions. From 1957 to 1961 he served on the Raleigh City Council, where he organized businessmen to oppose "socialistic" measures. He resisted the construction of a third public swimming pool in Raleigh because the city operated one for each race and a third pool might induce pressure to integrate it: "Government at all levels should stop, insofar as practicable, its expansion into social areas. It is not mandatory that we have public swimming pools or tennis courts or parks." After leaving the city council, he brought conservative activists such as Clarence Manion to speak to North Carolina businessmen. He worked with an organization called Citizens for the Preservation of Constitutional Government, which tried to expand conservative strength in mainstream business clubs like the local Chamber of Commerce. Along with other business friends, he tried to bring the Effective Citizens Organization, F. Clifton White's business-in-politics group, to run luncheon seminars for Raleigh business leaders to teach them the ins and outs of political activism. When it came to economics, the old Austrian Ludwig von Mises was Helms's favorite thinker. "I'm a sort of Von Mises economist, and I don't see any way for us to get out of the swamps until we drain off some of the specious political and economic philosophies which have been controlling the country," he wrote to a friend, complaining about government subsidies for Lockheed Martin. His ideal president, he claimed, would have the "candor of Hoover," the "charm of Kennedy," and the "economic awareness of Von Mises."[20]

After he left the North Carolina Bankers Association, Helms became a television and radio journalist at WRAL in Raleigh, a television station owned by a conservative who hired Helms to give "free-enterprise" editorials on the air. There Helms continued to speak out against the civil rights movement as it grew in strength. As at the *Tarheel Banker*, he transformed his criticism of the movement for black equality from a defense of segregation into an argument about the rights of private property. When lunch-counter sit-ins began in Greensboro, North Carolina, Helms claimed that he was not troubled by the demands of the young black students to sit and be served at the counter like equals. "It is not easy to argue with the Negroes' position that these dime stores encourage trade from all races in other departments but draw the line at serving food for consumption at the counter," he said on his evening opinion program, *Facts of the Matter*. "Frankly, if I were Negro, I would not like it either." But what bothered him was the protesters' assertion of *rights* even as they ignored the property rights of the shopkeepers—which for Helms were virtually sacred. "A dime store, and its lunch counter, is not a socialistic enterprise. It is not operated by the government." And the owner had the right to say whom he would serve. Helms even went so far as to say that he would not object in the least to black people organizing economic boycotts of segregated lunch counters and refusing to eat at them, but that actually sitting down at the lunch counters meant violating the rights of the store owners to run their businesses as they saw fit.[21]

Helms had been a lifelong Democrat, like most southerners in the era of one-party dominance. But his loyalty began to waver with Barry Goldwater's vote against the Civil Rights Act of 1964, and he was so impressed by Nixon's "law and order" campaign in 1968 that he switched his registration a few years later. When he ran for the Senate for the first time, in 1972, wooed by an old friend who was a prominent North Carolina anti-union lawyer, he ran on the Republican ticket. Helms's campaign won large sums of money not only from the mill owners of the Piedmont (including Roger Milliken) but also from national figures in the world of the business right, like the Los Angeles Reagan supporter Henry Salvatori and Pittsburgh's Richard Mellon Scaife (one of the heirs of the Mellon fortune, and, with Joseph Coors, one of the main early donors to the Heritage Foundation). With the support of such businessmen, Helms used the ideas of individualism, free choice, and property rights to attack any policies that promised greater racial equality and integration.[22]

In some ways, Helms's political migration mirrored that of the rest of the white South. Upper-class white southerners had begun to drift away from the Democratic Party in the 1950s, a realignment that accelerated as Democratic support for the civil rights movement increased. But the rise of the Republican Party in the South also reflected the emergence of a newly affluent white suburban population in the region, which embraced ideas of economic growth and low taxes. These suburbanites did not define themselves as segregationists; like Helms, they often tried to distance themselves from the virulence of white supremacy. But at the same time they firmly rejected activist policies to further integration, such as busing and affirmative action, on the grounds that they violated principles of meritocracy and private property rights. Helms was poised halfway between the old southern Democrats, with their open racism, and this new conservative ascendancy. His ability to translate the politics of racism into the rhetoric of the free market helped him to create a new kind of southern conservatism—one that could speak to conservatives not only in the South but across the country.[23]

In the fall of 1979, the televangelist Pat Robertson sent out a special report to Christian leaders across the country under the title "A Christian Action Plan to Heal Our Land in the 1980s." Robertson was no stranger to political debate. He was already the star of the *700 Club*, the Christian talk show distributed to more than a hundred television stations, and he ran the Christian Broadcasting Network, which offered round-the-clock religious programming. Robertson's "electronic church" was transforming the culture of evangelism. But the subject matter of his 1979 Christian Action Plan was not the typical fare of sin, salvation, and the culture wars. Rather, Robertson insisted that the moral illness threatening the United States in the late 1970s had its roots in the nation's political economy.

Robertson had chosen the date of the missive—October 1979—with care: it was the fiftieth anniversary of the stock market crash that had inaugurated the Great Depression. And the Depression, Robertson wrote, did "more to shape the existing framework of U.S. government policy than any other single event in recent history." The legacy of the Great Depression included "a powerful central government . . . an anti-business bias in the country . . . powerful unions," and, most important of all, "the belief in the economic policy of British scholar John Maynard Keynes, to the end that government spending and government 'fine tuning' would guarantee perpetual prosperity." Robertson conceded that such measures might have played a role in ending the Great Depression. But fifty years later they were responsible for the "sickness of the '70s"—the devaluation of the dollar, inflation, the decline in productivity. Robertson called for a "profound moral revival" to combat the economic weaknesses plaguing the United States. "Those who love God must get involved in the election of strong leaders," he insisted, and they should choose men and women who were "pledged to reduce the size of government, eliminate federal deficits, free our productive capacity, ensure sound currency."[24]

Robertson was not the only religious leader to focus on economic policy in this way in the late 1970s. Although the "religious right," as it became known, was always deeply moved by issues having to do with family and sexuality, and had formed in part as a backlash against feminism and gay rights, its spokesmen often framed their political positions in antigovernment language—which made it possible for them to form an alliance with the business conservatives.

Since the collapse of Spiritual Mobilization there had been few serious attempts to encourage Christians to become involved with the political movement against labor unions and the welfare state. During the 1960s, conservative groups would occasionally try to organize Christians for conservative politics. The allure was obvious: churches offered the potential to build a mass movement, a conservative populist network to counter that created by labor unions. The devout oilman J. Howard Pew and the former CEO of GE Charles E. Wilson (described by John Conlan, an organizer who later became a congressman from Arizona, as a "choice fund raiser" who "loves the Lord") attended a couple of meetings of the Freedoms Foundation, which attempted in the early 1960s to build local political machines of Christians devoted to the conservative cause. Men of "prominence and character," as Conlan put it, would "infiltrate and capture the organs of elective machinery in their respective communities." But the effort never really took off. Nor did another attempt in 1962, when a Colorado real estate developer named Gerri von Frellick captured headlines for a few weeks after he started a new group called Christian Citizen, which sought to build "a 'grass roots' movement organizing itself on a national scale to train Christians how to accept leadership responsibilities" in precinct-level politics. This too quickly foundered, despite some early support from the Minnesota congressman Walter Judd, himself a well-known evangelical and conservative leader, and Bill Bright, of Campus Crusades for Christ. The Anti-Defamation League charged Christian Citizen with anti-Semitism, and local Denver newspapers suggested that it might be associated with the John Birch Society. Von Frellick insisted, somewhat unconvincingly, that despite its name, Christian Citizen was tolerant, open to all: "We don't care if he's liberal, conservative, Democrat, Republican, black, white, or Jew—if he is converted."[25]

The real problem with these halfhearted gestures toward mobilizing Christians for conservative politics was that they had no organic basis in any church community. They were largely instrumental—founded by business activists who wanted to show how libertarian and Christian principles coincided, or who simply thought that religious people could provide a mass base that their movement otherwise lacked. But in the 1970s, as the upsurge of religious fervor that has sometimes been described as the Third Great Awakening began to sweep the country, shifting the balance of the country's Christian population toward evangelical and fundamentalist churches and away from the old mainline denominations, religious leaders such as Pat Robertson and the Baptist preacher Jerry Falwell began to attempt once again to bring Christians into politics. To fight the culture wars, they sought to transcend the old divisions of creed and doctrine, to bring conservative Protestants and Catholics together to transform American society. (This was never fully successful—separatist fundamentalists like Bob Jones, Jr., condemned Falwell as "the most dangerous man in America today as far as Biblical Christianity is concerned" because he was willing to work with Roman Catholics, Jews, and Mormons.)[26]

But although their politics centered on the cultural conflicts of the decade, these religious men talked about economics as well. They argued that the growth of the state explicitly threatened the church, because the state was advancing norms and policies that contradicted true Christian values, and they insisted that Christians needed to organize to resist government power. The evangelical leaders of the 1970s sought to connect the idea of the market and opposition to the power of government to the war over American culture. In this respect they sounded remarkably similar to the businessmen who were organizing through the Chamber of Commerce and even the Business Roundtable at the same time—not in their emphasis on social issues (which the Roundtable avoided) but in their mutual insistence on the problem of a too-powerful central government.

Jerry Falwell always told his life story as the classic tale of a self-made man, and from his earliest days he nourished an entrepreneurial commitment to building as large a ministry as he could. In 1971 he wrote about the importance of ministers using the insights of the corporate world to infuse the church with new funds and new members, writing that "business is usually on the cutting edge of innovation and change" and that therefore "the church would be wise to look at business for a prediction of future innovation." (Specifically, Falwell felt that churches should imitate shopping malls and provide a wide range of religious offerings so as best to attract the largest number of members.) And over the years Falwell's church did grow, coming to include not only a congregation of thousands but an elementary school, a high school, a college, and a seminary. The revenue of the *Old-Time Gospel Hour* (his television show) jumped from $1 million a year in 1971 to $1 million a month in 1975.[27]

In his early years as a minister, Falwell had been fiercely critical of preachers who became involved with politics. In his March 1965 sermon "Ministers and Marchers," he lashed out against Martin Luther King, Jr., accusing him of being used by Communists and insisting that the primary goal of any Christian leader had to be preaching the gospel: "Preachers are not called to be politicians, but to be soul winners." (Not that Falwell had entirely eschewed politics himself; early in his career he preached a sermon called "Segregation or Integration?" which argued that integration would destroy the white race; in later years he rejected this position.) But early in the 1970s Falwell changed his mind, deciding that he wanted to use his religious authority to play a role in politics. And although his first forays into political life were in the arena of culture—in 1977 he worked with the former Florida beauty queen and orange juice spokeswoman Anita Bryant in her campaign to overturn a gay rights ordinance in Florida, and in 1978 he went to California to support a state referendum that would have banned gay men and lesbians from teaching in the public schools—he was also interested in preaching the gospel on economics.[28]

In May 1978, Falwell began to publish a newspaper titled the *Journal-Champion* (in 1980 the name of the paper was changed to *Moral Majority Report*). The publication explicitly sought to provide Christian insight on matters beyond the specifically religious. This was no church newsletter but a political magazine. As one January 1979 editorial put it: "We must not be limited to the news of our churches and schools, at a time when politics and governmental processes of our national, state and local governments affect the vitality and very existence of our churches and Christian schools." The ultimate point was political action: "It is tragic when Christians don't vote."[29]

Early issues of the *Journal-Champion* carried numerous articles calling the faithful to the fight to cleanse America of sexual sin: homosexuality, pornography, and abortion. But interwoven with this campaign were descriptions of the economic and political crisis facing the United States. "The greatest threat to the average American's liberty does not come from Communistic aggression, crime in the decaying cities or any other external cause," read an article in the June 1978 issue. "It comes from the growing internal encroachments of government bureaucrats as they limit the freedom of Americans through distribution of rules and regulations, many times called guidelines." The newspaper criticized OSHA's "insulting or silly" regulations, and published an open letter to Congress denouncing the "faceless bureaucrats who sit in strategy meetings and formulate federal guidelines," saying that they "pinch our pocket books, restrict our work privileges, govern our spending habits, determine the 'safety' restrictions of our businesses and influence the type of homes we live in." It ran articles that argued that the welfare state was "corrupting a whole generation of people" and that Christian politicians needed to "roll forward the clock in progress toward individual initiative and individual freedom and family responsibility in our society."[30]

During the property tax revolt in California, when middle-class homeowners angry about their rising bills voted for a proposition essentially repealing their local property taxes, the *Journal-Champion* expressed enthusiasm. In language reminiscent of that which might be used to scold a pregnant teenager, it condemned New York City for asking for federal aid during its financial crisis: "The city should have believed in financial responsibility before it got into trouble." It criticized unions, saying that while the labor movement had accomplished much in the past, modern Americans "see the need to curb the crime and corruption among union leaders," and even supported the Kemp-Roth bill for individual income tax cuts, borrowing rhetoric straight from Jude Wanniski.[31]

At times the *Journal-Champion* tried to ground its economic arguments in religious language. Inflation, the publication suggested, was a form of divine punishment for a nation in thrall to the false idol of the dollar. "Because of sin, God usually spanks His people in the pocket book—farmers get hit in their crops, other Americans get hit in the paycheck," just as those who fell into disfavor with God in the Old Testament were visited by famine, drought, or grasshoppers. "God is bringing the entire nation to its financial knees. If we want to control inflation, we should set our spiritual house in order." But at other times the newspaper carried articles that sounded as if they could have been written by any aggrieved consumer: "We have double-digit inflation, high unemployment, and we cannot get our mail delivered from one city to another." One writer enthusiastically praised free enterprise and the "ability to generate business without fear of government intervention," writing, "I can't imagine living in a society where we could not have a Big Mac, an ice cream cone, an Orange Crush or where the government was advertising an oil treatment for your car, a roll-on deodorant, or that 'little dab'll do ya' business." At such moments the *Journal-Champion* seemed nearly as taken with popular culture as any secular magazine.[32]

Falwell's ideas moved from theory into politics in the spring of 1979, when he founded Moral Majority in Lynchburg, Virginia, with a small group of conservative activists. Richard Viguerie was at the meeting; in 1976 he had observed, "The next real major area of growth for the conservative ideology and [political] philosophy is among evangelical people." Paul Weyrich of the Heritage Foundation was present at the meeting too, and so was Ed McAteer, a former sales representative for Colgate-Palmolive who had left his corporate job to work for the Christian Freedom Foundation, a group that sought to build "a communications network of 'born again' free enterprise–oriented Christians that reaches down into every precinct in the district." Weyrich and Viguerie were not themselves members of the evangelical network (neither one was even a Protestant), but they recognized—as the organizers of Spiritual Mobilization had done long before—the political potential of the conservative church. At the meeting they spoke about the need to organize people who might seem to be separated by geography or by religious denomination around a new set of moral principles—to build a new organization that would speak on behalf of a "moral majority." The goal of the new group would be to mobilize Christians at the grass roots to participate in politics. And while Falwell emphasized the moral imperative of pushing for legislation that would protect the family and fight pornography and homosexuality, he also argued that part of the job of Moral Majority would be "lobbying intensively in Congress to defeat left-wing, social-welfare bills that will further erode our precious freedom." His book *Listen, America!*, published in 1980, included chapters on abortion, pornography, homosexuality, and the evils of television and the music industry—but it also included passages criticizing excessive "government intervention in business," mourning the "sad fact . . . that government is the major source of our economic instability in this country" and praising Milton Friedman's *Capitalism and Freedom.*[33]

The antigovernment and probusiness rhetoric of the *Journal-Champion* was not the only area of overlap that Christian conservatives had with business activists. Evangelical leaders often framed their entrance into politics defensively, arguing that they were resisting the growing power of the state. They claimed to seek power not in order to establish binding moral rules for the broader society but merely to protect their own institutions from the intrusive government. Christians mobilized to fight proposed changes in tax law that they thought would endanger the tax-exempt status of religious organizations. They campaigned against attempts to regulate financial donations sent via the postal service, which could have limited the fund-raising abilities of Christian television and radio programs. "Clearly, the bill is not only a bureaucratic nightmare but a direct attack on America's religious community," wrote the National Religious Broadcasters in a letter mailed to ministers and pastors across the country, imploring them to rally their parishioners to defeat the legislation and the "anti-clerical forces" behind it.[34]

The most dramatic confrontation between evangelical churches and the state in the 1970s was the struggle between the Internal Revenue Service and Christian private schools. The conflict had its roots in the widespread white resistance in the South to the racial integration of public schools after *Brown v. Board of Education.* Many white southerners took Jesse Helms's advice. They pulled their children out of public schools that were starting to admit black students, and they started an alternative network of new, all-white private schools instead. Some of these called themselves Christian schools; as institutions of religious instruction, they could claim tax exemptions. Even more began to call themselves Christian schools after the Supreme Court ruled that private schools could not deny black students admission because of their race, because they assumed that the IRS would never dare to attack the tax exemptions of religious institutions. Not all Christian schools were "segregation academies"—a legitimate Christian school movement had been gaining strength in the years after the Supreme Court banned prayer in the public schools. Nevertheless, during the years of the civil rights movement, their growth was spectacular: in the early 1950s there were fewer than 150 Christian schools in the country; by 1981 there were about 18,000. It was very difficult to tell the Christian schools apart from those that had been founded solely in an attempt to evade racial integration, which actively refused to admit black students.[35]

In August 1978, responding to the pressures of civil rights leaders, the IRS issued a new set of guidelines for Christian private schools. According to the new rules, in order to qualify for tax exemptions the schools needed to demonstrate actively that they were not practicing racial discrimination. If the school had been founded (or if it had dramatically expanded enrollment) at the time of public school desegregation, and if it had an "insignificant" number of minority students, it would be subject to an intensive review process to see whether the low nonwhite student population was the result of active discrimination. If the IRS deemed that the school discriminated in its enrollment process, the school would lose its tax-exempt status.[36]

The new rules touched off a wave of criticism. More than 100,000 letters poured into the IRS after they were announced. Thousands of missives flooded Congress. Hundreds of furious school and church leaders attended public meetings in Washington. "The issue is religious freedom," wrote Jerry Falwell. "We are crusading against abortion-on-demand, pornography and sex and violence on television, and government intervention. But I am especially concerned about the IRS attempt to legislate regulations that will control Christian schools . . . Fundamental pastors are unalterably opposed to intrusion by bureaucracies into our religious freedom." The evangelical minister Tim LaHaye, who had just published an anti-homosexuality screed entitled *The Unhappy Gays* and who would in later years write the *Left Behind* series of popular novels chronicling the aftermath of the Rapture, wrote that church-related schools saved taxpayers billions of dollars, and that the attacks on the Christian schools might prefigure an assault on the church itself: "Doesn't it seem strange that the U.S. government is lenient on communists, criminals, drug pushers, illegal aliens, rapists, lesbians, homosexuals and almost anyone who violates the law, but is increasing its attacks on Christians?" The entire issue demonstrated the necessity for Christians to get active in political life. As Robert Billings, the founder of the National Christian Action Coalition, exclaimed, "The cost of political negligence is slavery! As our government increases its crippling pressure on the Christian home, school and church, the need for Christian action becomes increasingly critical. If Christians do not master politics, we will, most certainly, be mastered by those who do."[37]

The IRS and the Christian schools became a special organizing point for activists outside Christian networks as well. James McKenna, who had been a lawyer at the Heritage Foundation, marshaled a variety of arguments in a special booklet he wrote in defense of the schools. First he claimed that desegregation had "accelerated chaos in public education," making the formation of separate schools necessary. Then he borrowed a page from the civil rights movement and insisted that the private schools reflected the "diversity" of the nation's heritage: "If different is wrong, a part of the richness of our heritage dies with it." Finally he suggested that the entire crisis might be "providential," shining a light on the shadowy machinations of the IRS and showing the nation why the time had come to become "involved in the political process as a Christian." He concluded, "Resistance is a duty." The American Conservative Union gave a special press conference at which its president castigated the IRS for casting itself "in the role of social engineer and policy maker." The new regulations, he insisted, represented "an unwarranted and vast mechanism for the expansion of government power," and libertarians as well as Christians had a deep investment in fighting them. The ACU took credit for helping to generate the overwhelming number of letters to the IRS through one of its "Legislative Alerts," which bore the title "IRS Says: Guilty until Proven Innocent." *Conservative Digest* devoted a cover story to the Christian right, writing that the tax rules were "just one more example of ever-increasing government meddling in religion."[38]

The controversy over the schools had managed to unify the leaders of the Christian conservatives and the broader antigovernment right. Congress prevented the IRS from implementing its guidelines. In 1980 the Republican Party platform contained a plank promising to "halt the unconstitutional regulatory vendetta" against the Christian private schools. In later years, New Right leaders such as Paul Weyrich would say that the fight against the IRS was what had really galvanized evangelical Christians and made them enter politics—not the Equal Rights Amendment, not abortion, but the fight against the tax man. As Robert Billings told *Conservative Digest*, "Jerome Kurtz [the commissioner of the IRS] has done more to bring Christians together than any man since the Apostle Paul."[39]

Even in the 1950s, the businessmen who had wanted to win churches away from the politics of the Social Gospel, according to which Christians had an obligation to take political action to aid the poor, had assumed they would need to struggle against liberal tendencies within Christianity. But by the 1970s this was no longer the case. The churches had become the natural allies of the businessmen. For preachers like Falwell and Robertson, no matter what aspects of religious doctrine might separate them, there was no need to agonize about whether the welfare state or government intervention or labor unions should be defended on the ground that they were pursuing the Christian goal of helping the poor. For these religious entrepreneurs, who had built their ministries with the savvy of marketers and the confidence of executives, it was natural to have faith in the marketplace and to see the state as a challenge to the strength and vibrancy of their churches. Yet at the same time, despite the efforts of *Conservative Digest* to tie a disparate movement together, and regardless of Falwell's theology of the market, there remained a certain dissonance in the religious and social conservatives' advocacy of capitalism, for the communal values of family and tradition they claimed to uphold were inevitably undermined by the logic of laissez-faire and the turbulence of commercial society. The leadership of the movement might speak the language of the market, but for the believers themselves there must have remained a schism. For all the ways in which the businessmen and the churches were able to work together, the alliance between them also required the suppression and avoidance of deep conflicts, even at the moment of its birth.

11 The Market Triumphant

On a chilly day in March 1980, a few days before the New York State Republican primary, Ronald Reagan visited a white-columned building at the corner of Wall and Broad Streets in New York City, its elaborate façade depicting men and women pulling levers and pushing wheels, their efforts overseen by the 22-foot-tall figure of Integrity standing in the center like the angel of the market: the New York Stock Exchange.

Reagan's presence electrified the exchange. A burst of cheers broke out when the candidate appeared on the trading floor. Stockbrokers crowded around him, grabbing his hands and tossing paper into the air like confetti. It was, in the words of one observer, an "unbelievable mob scene." After the day's trading ended, two hundred people paid two hundred dollars each to attend a fund-raiser organized by several specialist brokerages in the Luncheon Club upstairs, where Reagan also met with William Batten, the chairman of the exchange. Eager traders bombarded him with questions, not only about the future of finance. "People asking questions were more concerned with the state of the country, economically and even morally, than with our industry," said one witness to the frenzy, "and he was great."[1]

The leaders of the stock exchange saw in Reagan a candidate whose rhetoric celebrated the power of the entrepreneurial investor as the central motor of the economy, who believed that the inventive genius of the individual businessman created the "industrial might" of the nation as a whole and that the meeting place of buyers and sellers on the corner of Wall and Broad epitomized the genius of the American economy. He handily won the state's Republican primary the next week.

REAGAN HAD been running for the presidency in one way or another ever since he gave his "time for choosing" speech for Barry Goldwater a week before the 1964 election. After he was elected governor of California in 1966, Republicans began to talk about him as a possible presidential candidate for 1968. His California business supporters raised nearly half a million dollars to try to jump-start a run for the nomination. They even hired F. Clifton White, the architect of the Draft Goldwater campaign.[2]

Although Reagan did not make a serious attempt at the nomination that year, he continued to think about the possibility of doing so in the future. His time as governor of California consolidated his approach to conservative politics. While he remained an ardent believer in the free market, he also began to give voice to the moral politics implicit in his economic vision, arguing that public universities (like the University of California system) provided havens for adolescent experimentation with drugs and social rebellion, while the welfare system sanctioned women having children without husbands. Cutting the government would force these people to shape up in the stern arena of the market. During his first term as governor, Reagan used the National Guard to impose martial law on the Berkeley campus following an especially chaotic set of demonstrations; in his second, he introduced an overhaul of the state welfare system. By the time he left the California governorship, in 1975, he had amassed a record that helped to redefine free-market conservatism. Being antigovernment and laissez-faire also meant defending a conservative social vision, as well as making a commitment to expand the military and take a hard stance against the Soviet Union even while shrinking the public sector. Reagan's 1976 bid for the Republican nomination failed, but it nonetheless helped to build a network of support within the party, positioning him to become the candidate to challenge Democratic president Jimmy Carter in 1980.[3]

Yet even in early 1980, when the NYSE rallied for "the Gipper," the support of the business community for Ronald Reagan was far from certain. Few business executives were confident that Reagan had the answers to the economic problems they faced. The stagnation of American manufacturing, the perennial crisis of inflation, and the slowdown of growth all seemed without easy or obvious solutions. Many in the business world thought Reagan's ideas overly simplistic and his promises of tax cuts dangerously inflationary. Some manufacturers hoped that the next president would pursue "reindustrialization," a program of tax cuts and subsidies that would aid American manufacturing and help it to compete against European and Japanese companies; *Business Week* devoted an entire issue to advocating such policies that summer. But Reagan generally rejected such proposals, because in his view they meant interfering excessively with the free market. "Despite his tireless call to get government off their backs, most of the businessmen polled feel lukewarm about him," *Fortune* reported in a May 1980 article.[4]

Executives were not the only people to be doubtful about Reagan in 1980. Many political observers all across the spectrum of opinion saw the Republican Party as a ghost—a once-potent organization that had lost its direction and almost even its reason for being. Three years before the Reagan campaign, in the summer of 1977, *Fortune* had published an article entitled "The Unmaking of the Republican Party." The piece had argued that the party was on the verge of disintegration. It had lost its historic support among professionals, managers, executives, the college-educated, and African Americans, and it was on the edge of losing the support of big business as well. New Deal liberalism was "reeling under the most serious challenge in its history," but it seemed that the Republican Party lacked the ability to "chart a new course." These sentiments endured into the election year. In February 1980 the *New York Times* columnist William Safire repeated the old Hollywood rumor that Ronald Reagan had been slated to star in *Casablanca* before a last-minute casting change brought Humphrey Bogart in instead. Would 1980 repeat that twist of fate? "There is a quality to him now that attached to political figures as dissimilar as William Jennings Bryan and Robert Taft—a general feeling that he may be a man whose cause may triumph but whose own time will never come," Safire mused.[5]

The field early in 1980 was crowded with candidates who seemed to be more appealing to businessmen than Reagan. John Connally, the secretary of the treasury under Richard Nixon, looked like the frontrunner in the corporate world in 1979, with money coming in from executives at companies such as Lockheed Martin, Mobil Oil, Standard Oil, and PepsiCo. That year Connally raised $9.2 million, $2 million more than Reagan. As a Texas corporate lawyer, Connally represented a moneyed roster of clients in the oil and financial industries. He rarely entered the courtroom, preferring to spend his time as a "counselor to businessmen," who felt flattered by his attention and his intelligence. New Right activists, still smarting from Reagan's choice of Richard Schweiker as a running mate in his failed 1976 bid for the Republican nomination, leaned toward giving their support to Connally. Richard Viguerie dedicated a special section of *Conservative Digest* to a dramatic endorsement of him.[6]

But the very quality that made Connally so appealing to businessmen—his obvious comfort in the halls of power—was also his greatest weakness politically. Connally was too much the consummate corporate insider. A grand jury had charged him with accepting an illegal donation of $10,000 from the Associated Milk Producers while urging the expansion of price supports for milk when he was serving in Nixon's cabinet, and although he had been acquitted, the stain lingered. His long history in Texas politics was littered with payments for legal services amortized over decades in order to reduce the tax burden and with other similarly dubious negotiations. Connally was clearly a member of the club, tangled in connections but seeming to lack principles—anything but a populist.

George H. W. Bush, formerly the head of the CIA, also seemed a candidate who would appeal to businessmen. A thin-lipped Yale man and a loyal member of Skull and Bones (like all good Bonesmen, he refused to reveal the secret handshake even when questioned about it on the campaign trail), he received contributions from the oil industry as well as from the Chase Manhattan Bank chairman, David Rockefeller. Bush presented himself as a serious and responsible conservative, in contrast to Reagan the fire-breather—he was thoughtful and reserved, wary about government, a gracious man with a moderate temperament, the antithesis of an ideologue. Even when he tried to dress down and act the populist on the campaign trail, drinking beer and eating hot dogs, his campaign tried to accentuate his differences from Reagan, to set Bush's discriminating intelligence against Reagan's wholehearted and simplistic faith. Unlike the California governor, here was someone who had experience in Washington. Bush dismissed Reagan's talk about shrinking the government as bombastic campaign nonsense: "When he says 'no growth' . . . he should be made to explain it," he insisted. Perhaps, Bush mused before the Florida primary, Reagan intended to shrink the federal budget by cutting Social Security benefits for retirees. Pressing every possible advantage, he sent his second son, Jeb, to speak to Cuban workers at Sweet and Low plants in Miami, repeating the initials CIA like a mantra to stir the longings of homesick anti-Castro refugees.[7]

John Anderson, an Illinois congressman from Rockford, a small city soon to be swallowed up by the Rust Belt, embodied yet another vision of what it meant to be a conservative. Anderson was sharply opposed to social conservatism and moral absolutes. He defined himself as an evangelical Christian, but he supported abortion rights, the busing of children between districts to create integrated schools, and the regulation of handguns. In 1970 he had described the Vietnam War as "the most tragic error in diplomacy and military policy in our nation's history." Anderson opposed tax cuts, arguing that cutting government spending and eliminating the federal deficit had to be the first priorities to end inflation. He fought against subsidies to bail out the bankrupt Chrysler Corporation, even though that company had a plant with hundreds of jobs in his district. He promoted tax cuts for savings accounts to encourage investment, enterprise zones to help businesses in poor urban neighborhoods, and an overhaul of government regulations. Yet despite his fascination with clever ways to use the market to achieve social goals, he rejected Reagan's fervent antistatism. "I must confess to this audience that I am not a younger Ronald Reagan with experience," he told the crowd at an Iowa forum early in 1980. "He takes a view of the economy that I think pretty much goes back to the time of Adam Smith and the invisible hand. He doesn't see a genuine role for the federal government when it comes to advancing the cause of human rights or civil rights in this country." His candidacy won early support from some businessmen, such as Felix Rohatyn of Lazard Freres, David Rockefeller (who also supported Bush), the former president of Neiman Marcus, and media leaders like the chairman of Time, Inc. The liberal philanthropist Stewart Mott was won over by Anderson's unusual political program. Even some Hollywood Democrats, such as Paul Newman, who volunteered to film fund-raising commercials for Anderson, gave their support to the maverick candidate.[8]

Jimmy Carter, as president, had proved himself able to work with businessmen through organizations like the Business Roundtable. Some executives (like DuPont's Irving Shapiro) remained outspoken supporters of Carter right up to election day. But even the Roundtable was turning away from the president during the election year. Carter had canvassed Fortune 500 executives for their support for another voluntary wage-and-price-control program to fight inflation in the fall of 1979, asking them to agree not to raise prices or wages or to significantly boost executive salaries. The Business Roundtable grudgingly encouraged members to do as the president wished. But in the summer of 1980 the Roundtable openly rejected the voluntary program, saying that it meant continuing to blame business for the problem of inflation—a problem that was the fault not of the corporate world but of government regulations and spending. It was a sign that Carter's appeal in the business world was decidedly waning—as it was throughout the country. Carter's foreign policy failures, especially the capture of the American embassy in Iran, highlighted the weakness of the United States in the post-Vietnam world. His response to inflation and to lines at gas stations during the energy crisis (expressed in a July 1979 address that became known as the "malaise speech") was to suggest that Americans look inward and free themselves from their desperate dependency on consumption. None of his proposals seemed capable of rescuing the nation. As one St. Louis executive told the *Wall Street Journal* in April, "I can't imagine anyone doing a worse job than Carter, except maybe Kennedy."[9]

Yet there was no obvious successor. The field looked so open, and support for an openly conservative politician like Ronald Reagan seemed so tentative, that even former President Ford flirted with a presidential bid, coyly letting the GOP know that if he were asked to run, he wouldn't say no. "I hear more and more often that we don't want, can't afford to have a replay of 1964," Ford mused to the *New York Times*. And then he repeated the fateful wisdom learned that painful year: "A very conservative Republican can't win in a national election."[10]

But Reagan's supporters disagreed. The candidate won primary after primary in the winter and spring of 1980. The minor Republican candidates dropped out early. John Connally quit after South Carolina; the more than $12 million he spent on his campaign yielded the vote of a single delegate at the Republican convention. After dangling his hat above the ring, Ford ultimately declined to drop it in, stating that he had lost whatever interest he might have had in seeking the nomination. George Bush put up the most dogged challenge, getting off to a strong start in January, when he carried Iowa, and picking up states throughout the season, but even he eventually had to concede, although his campaign was tenacious enough for Reagan to choose him as vice president. By the time the Republican convention was held in Detroit in mid-July, it was clear that Reagan would be the Republican candidate. Yet his campaign continued to have a complex relationship to business, for its genius was that it managed to court the business world while appearing to stand for principles that had little to do with the immediate interests of business at all.[11]

THE STOCK market had struggled through the recession years of the 1970s, as people confronted with unemployment, inflation, the energy crisis, and defeat in Vietnam lost their confidence in the market along with their bullishness for capitalism and sold their stocks in favor of bonds or plain old cash. Seven million fewer people owned stocks at the end of the decade than at the beginning. *Business Week* ran a cover story grimly proclaiming "The Death of Equities" in August 1979 ("Only the elderly who have not understood the changes in the nation's financial markets, or who are unable to adjust to them, are sticking with stocks," it argued). Yet Reagan had been among the faithful even at the market's nadir, going so far as to propose, during his failed challenge to Gerald Ford in 1976, that Social Security funds should be invested in the stock market—in "the industrial might of America." And early in 1980, some of the leaders of New York's financial community began to reach out to the Reagan campaign.[12]

In January the vice chairman of the financial company E. F. Hutton wrote to Reagan's campaign staff, inviting the candidate to spend half a day with the financial community in mid-March (such a visit, he suggested, would be a profitable use of Reagan's time—he estimated that it could net the campaign at least $250,000 in contributions). Also in January, Reagan's longtime adviser Edwin Meese met with James Fuller, a vice president at the NYSE, for a friendly chat about the direction the campaign was taking. Shortly after, Fuller indicated that the NYSE wanted to help, as best it could, by doing "issue research" for Reagan so his campaign could develop its platform on matters of importance to business.[13]

The correspondence resulted in Reagan's successful March visit to the stock exchange (although there is no record of whether it in fact earned the campaign as much money as the E. F. Hutton chairman had hoped). But the efforts of Fuller and the stock exchange did not stop there.

In June 1980, Fuller organized a meeting in New York City between Reagan, who by that time had nearly secured the Republican nomination, and a small group of businessmen. It was to be the first meeting of a new organization of top-flight executives who would provide advice to Reagan throughout the rest of the campaign. The businessmen met in the Hoover Suite of the Waldorf-Astoria Hotel—the very hotel that Herbert Hoover had fled to after leaving Washington following Roosevelt's inauguration forty-seven years before. One participant in the meeting commented to the *Wall Street Journal* on the irony of the name of their conference room: "Depressing, isn't it?"[14]

The idea behind the Business Advisory Panel, as the organization became known, was that it would be an ostensibly apolitical group, in that executives who participated would not be expected to endorse Reagan or contribute financially to the campaign. They would simply meet with the candidate, get to know him, learn his ideas about how to promote economic growth, and share their own insights. The Business Advisory Panel would counteract the impression that (as Fuller put it) the "business viewpoint" was not "represented as well as it could be" in the Reagan campaign. The executives who joined the panel included the chairmen, CEOs, and presidents of Procter & Gamble, Morgan Stanley, Pfizer, Merrill Lynch, and the New York Stock Exchange, among others. (The group was so uniformly white and male that one executive made the recommendation that "women and minorities" be invited to join the group.)[15]

The meeting at the New York hotel wasn't just a cheerleading session: Reagan wanted to get the executives' ideas about how the United States could become more competitive in international markets, what to do to encourage new capital investment in business and industry, and how to end the spiral of inflation. Ed Zschau, the president of System Industries, whose political lobbying had been critical in helping to win cuts in capital gains taxes in 1978, asked Reagan if he really thought that he could win the election as an open, enthusiastic supporter of free private enterprise in the year 1980—wasn't public contempt for corporations simply too great?

Reagan responded that he thought that the "1.7 million people" who had lost their jobs in the spring of 1980 would be "very ready to hear that message." He argued that overregulation was hamstringing the American economy and making it more difficult for American corporations to compete overseas. Despite the disagreement of several of the executives, he expressed his support for the Kemp-Roth tax cuts and promised to reduce the size of the federal government to avoid excessively large deficits. He warned that Social Security was dangerously unsound, and he promised to return welfare to the states. Most of all, Reagan swore that he would use the "bully pulpit" of the presidency to spread the faith of the free market—that under his administration the federal government would no longer be "hostile" and adversarial toward business. Government should be "put in proper perspective"—it should not "interfere with the private sector."[16]

The executives who gathered in the Hoover Suite seemed reassured by their time with the former governor of California. There was something exciting about talking to a politician who was as openly, as proudly probusiness as Reagan—someone running for public office who saw free enterprise as a cause and businessmen as heroes. Many of the executives who attended the meeting went on to become active in the campaign, writing to Reagan and his advisers to share their ideas about economic policy. A Bethlehem Steel executive told the *Wall Street Journal* after the meeting that Reagan was an "excellent listener." Another participant described the discussion as thoroughly "refreshing."[17]

The enthusiasm and the promises of mutual support extended both ways. As James Fuller wrote to Edwin Meese in September 1980, "If we win I will assist you in any way you think appropriate including working for, or with, your team. If we lose I would like to be helpful in achieving your personal goals and ambitions. That's an offer that stands!"[18]

Reagan tried to broaden his support in the business world through the Business Advisory Panel. But even before Fuller got involved in organizing executives for Reagan, the candidate drew from the connections to business conservatives that had long sustained his political life. The Executive Advisory Council, a small group that met monthly explicitly to plan strategy for the campaign, was filled with longtime business supporters.

William Simon was the chair of the group. A former senior partner at Salomon Brothers who had served as treasury secretary under Nixon and Ford, Simon was best known for refusing to help New York City when it teetered on the edge of bankruptcy in 1975, arguing that the city had brought its problems on itself through its generous contracts with city workers and its extensive social welfare policies. In 1978 he published a manifesto (ghostwritten by a young acolyte of Ayn Rand) entitled *A Time for Truth,* which called for "a massive and unprecedented mobilization of the moral, intellectual and financial resources" of business to "aid the intellectuals and writers" who were fighting on the side of capitalism.

"The alliance between the theorists and men of action in the capitalist world is long overdue," Simon wrote, adding that he thought "any businessman with the slightest impulse for survival" would help the cause. Friedrich von Hayek wrote a generous foreword to the book. *A Time for Truth* resonated with executives; the National Federation of Independent Business distributed tens of thousands of copies to its members, as did the National Association of Manufacturers, and the Farm Bureau advertised the book in its newsletter. Simon went on to head the Olin Foundation, doing his part to help channel business money toward the support of free-market ideas.[19]

California businessmen were well represented on the Executive Advisory Council: Ed Mills, Jack Hume, Holmes Tuttle (former members of Reagan's kitchen cabinet from his Sacramento days), and the PAC proselytizer Justin Dart all participated. Newer allies from outside the Golden State joined as well, such as Charls E. Walker (a lobbyist who represented companies like Ford, General Electric, and U.S. Steel in Washington), Joseph Coors, A. W. "Tom" Clausen of the Bank of America, Don Kendall of PepsiCo, Richard Shinn of Metropolitan Life Insurance, Walter Wriston of Citibank, and Clifton C. Garvin, Jr., of Exxon. Even John Connally came on board after his own campaign folded.[20]

The members of the council debated campaign tactics and fantasized about Reagan's victory. Would black voters support Reagan because they were drawn to the idea of a 30 percent tax cut? How could PACs best help the campaign? Who among those present might make good cabinet members? In an April meeting, Justin Dart, arguing that they needed to remember to work on congressional elections too so that President Reagan could come in with support in the legislature, urged all the corporate members to purchase and disseminate copies of William Simon's *A Time for Truth* to their employee organizations. These advisers stayed with Reagan through all the upheavals of the campaign, such as the complete change in leadership from the longtime consultant John Sears (deemed by conservatives to be too liberal) to the corporate lawyer William Casey shortly after the New Hampshire primary.[21]

Yet even as he courted business supporters, Reagan managed to project an image of skeptical distance from corporate America. Despite his time as a spokesman for GE, as a Hollywood actor he had in a sense been an entrepreneur. He celebrated the individual risk-taker, the small proprietor, not the lifelong executive or bureaucrat. He was not certain that he wanted to be known as the open candidate of big business. Jude Wanniski, who wrote policy memos for the campaign and helped to brief Reagan on supply-side ideas, commented approvingly (while Connally was still in the race) that Reagan seemed "not at all distressed that John Connally is the candidate of 'big business,'" instead saying that he would be "the candidate of the entrepreneur, the farmer, the small businessman, the independent." Reagan himself told *Fortune* in May 1980 that he didn't care about Fortune 500 companies—the "support I appreciate comes from all those people I shake hands with who have calluses on their hands." The candidate's ambivalence toward being identified with business was so profound that the economist Murray Weidenbaum, who edited AEI's journal on regulation, complained that there was a note of "genuine dislike" for business, especially big business, within the Reagan campaign. When Donald Rumsfeld, then the CEO of the pharmaceutical giant G. D. Searle, met with the editors of *Newsweek,* they were stunned to hear his open advocacy of Reagan, because they claimed not to have met any "Eastern businessman, Fortune 500 caliber" who endorsed the candidate with such enthusiasm.[22]

Reagan did care about corporate support, as the Business Advisory Panel and the Executive Advisory Council made clear, but he tried to demonstrate his loyalties to business in ways that allowed him to emphasize his vision of the market economy as inherently populist. For example, he courted direct-marketing companies such as Amway and Shaklee Corporation. In the late 1970s, President Carter had threatened to reclassify the companies' sellers as employees, requiring the corporations to pay Medicare and Social Security taxes and permitting income taxes to be deducted directly from paychecks. Reagan's letter of support to Gary Shansby, the CEO of Shaklee, in September 1980—insisting that he understood that the "chance to be independent, to start your own business, and to be your own boss is one of the central features and most valuable blessings of our economic system"—was sent out to 2 million Shaklee distributors. Shansby, who also served on the Executive Advisory Council, told Reagan that he would do all he could to work for a Republican victory. Meanwhile, Amway invited Reagan to address the company's distributors at its huge promarket extravaganza rallies.[23]

As his hold on the nomination grew stronger, Reagan started to do more to woo business. In June 1980 the campaign appointed as deputy director for campaign operations William Timmons, who had formerly represented the Business Roundtable as a lobbyist (his accomplishments also included a stint lobbying Congress on behalf of Richard Nixon in a desperate attempt to halt the move toward impeachment). In September the campaign met with public relations executives from Bank of America, Philip Morris, AT&T, Pfizer, Hill & Knowlton, Pillsbury, ALCOA, General Motors, and other companies to talk about the Reagan campaign's public relations strategy ("Make Reagan more simple," the PR executives recommended, saying that he should talk about "jobs," not "capital formation," and identify his campaign with the "future, not just tomorrow, but the remainder of the century"—although they also warned against the perception that Reagan was "glib").[24]

The campaign began to create a network of businesspeople across the country devoted to electing Reagan. Throughout the campaign, Reagan's advisers were fascinated—as William Baroody had been in his efforts to build AEI in the 1950s—with the question of how to use the social power of business, the circles of employees, stockholders, managers, and suppliers, to mobilize political support.

The chairman of Business for Reagan/Bush was William Agee, the youthful CEO of the manufacturing conglomerate Bendix Corporation. Agee was a good friend of Jack Kemp and well integrated into the free-market intellectual world. In the end he didn't play the dynamic role in the Reagan campaign he might have hoped; in the fall of 1980, as the election drew near, rumors swirled about the exceedingly rapid promotion of a beautiful twenty-nine-year-old woman from executive assistant to senior vice president at Bendix. But despite the distraction of the scandal, Agee tried to construct an organization of businessmen spanning the nation to campaign for Reagan. "We must enlist as many American business leaders as we can to join with us in spreading this message to every business leader in every city, town and village in our great country," he wrote in a letter to a Wichita, Kansas, businessman who had joined the campaign. Everyone involved should try to contact as broad a range of people in the business world as possible—the "CEOs of Fortune 500 companies, members of the Young Presidents' Organization, all minority and women business leaders, CEOs of SBA [Small Business Association] supported companies, key corporate public affairs officers." Participants would send chain letters (one activist hoped for no fewer than 1 million) to help build the personal connections that would make up the glue of the campaign. "This is the year when business cannot opt out," read one such letter. "Obviously, all of us favor Reagan's election, but often business people are too busy to vote." Throughout the country, business activists joined Business for Reagan/Bush; progress reports from activists indicated that tens of thousands of chain letters had gone out.[25]

Despite all these projects, top campaign leaders worried about whether they had done enough to encourage corporate participation. Reagan's legal advisers crafted a memorandum reminding business owners that corporate money could be used in "unlimited amounts" to contact shareholders, executives, and administrative personnel: "Many labor unions are spending in the millions of dollars communicating with their members and getting-out-the-vote for Carter. There are more than 25 million stockholders in this country. Corporations can reach their stockholders with a letter from the President in quarterly reports or enclosed with dividends. Not only is this a huge free direct mail program, it is targeted to a group very concerned about the issues discussed." The campaign's lawyers tried to encourage executives to organize transportation pools to take personnel, stockholders, and their families to the polls. William Timmons wondered if John Connally might be enlisted in the final weeks of the campaign to "contact major business leaders to urge they communicate with their management, workers, stockholders and suppliers about the issues in this campaign." There were even plans to send mailgrams to CEOs of the Fortune 500 reminding them to get absentee ballots for executives who might be out of town to guarantee that they would vote, and letters to the chief executives of the one thousand largest companies in the country enumerating point by point all the ways in which Reagan was good for business so they could write letters to their shareholders. But the campaign ran out of time to put these tactics into use.[26]

At a meeting of five hundred small-business owners in early October, campaign representatives discussed the importance of holding meetings with workers to talk about the presidential election: "Employees know that their financial futures are tied to the success of their small business employer—they must know where their employer stands and why the persecutors of small business must be turned out of Washington." Employers should openly express their pro-Reagan views to their workers, and they should also encourage workers interested in politics to talk to each other. "I propose that we recruit as many company Presidents as possible to give us a commitment to personally visit with their employees . . . to tell them why it is important to elect a President who understands the basic economic system that has made this Country great," wrote the head of the Central States Region for Business for Reagan/Bush.[27]

Just as businessmen like the salt tycoon Sterling Morton had dreamed of using the working class to defeat Roosevelt in the election of 1936, so the Reagan campaign did in 1980 to defeat Carter. It is not clear that the campaign was able to follow through on all of these efforts—how many managers actually held political meetings for their workers, for example?—but pro-Reagan businessmen and campaign aides alike were inspired by the idea that executives could use their influence over employees and colleagues to achieve a Reagan victory.

The Republican convention in 1980 was held in Detroit, where the city's deserted factories formed a strange backdrop to the revelry of the delegates. Reagan gave two additional speeches in the city during the 1980 campaign. The first was in May, before a gathering of two thousand businessmen at the Detroit Economic Club (the organization attracted the largest audience in its history for Reagan's speech). At his second address, right before Labor Day, Reagan was a guest at a backyard barbecue hosted by assembly-line auto- and steelworkers in the suburb of Allen Park. Despite the differences in the audience, his message to both groups was the same. The decline of Detroit—the bombed-out windows of downtown and the abandoned buildings and empty lots spreading through the city—was not caused by the automakers, which had for decades been slowly moving production away to low-wage regions and the suburbs while subcontracting out union jobs to small non-union auto parts plants. Nor was competition from Europe or Asia the largest problem. Rather, Detroit's decline was ultimately the responsibility of the federal government, which, with its heavy-handed regulation inspired by the likes of Ralph Nader and the EPA, was strangling the industry. "The U.S. auto industry is virtually being regulated to death," he said in May, calling for "the freedom to compete, unhindered by whimsical bureaucratic changes in energy, environmental and safety regulations." In September he told the autoworkers not to blame Japan for their problems but to turn their rage instead against the bureaucrats in Washington, D.C. (although he also promised to try to negotiate with Japan to slow the flow of imported cars).[28]

But although Reagan tried to inspire both groups with his economic rhetoric, his closest advisers believed that he would need to do more. In particular, they thought that mobilizing employers would not be enough. As Richard Wirthlin, pollster and strategist for the campaign, wrote in one memo, the traditional Republican base was "simply not large enough to win the presidency." The campaign would need to find a way to reach out.[29]

Wirthlin was an entrepreneur who had started his polling firm at his kitchen table in 1964, when a friend who was running for Congress (ironically, on the Democratic ticket) asked for his help. By 1980 the company's roster of clients included companies such as Greyhound, General Foods, Ford, and a variety of retail and supermarket chains in addition to politicians like Reagan. Before Wirthlin went into business, he had been the chair of the Brigham Young University economics department. But although his company did so much work for industry, he wanted to think of ways to appeal to working-class voters. The key to Reagan's victory, the pollster argued in a June 1980 campaign memo, was to break up the coalition that had supported the Democratic Party throughout the postwar years by winning the votes of "Southern white protestants, blue collar workers in the industrial states, urban ethnics, and rural voters."[30]

Wirthlin advised a variety of strategies to win these disaffected, mostly white voters. "People act on the basis of their perception of reality; there is, in fact, no political reality beyond what is perceived by the voters," he wrote. The "quiet, relatively passive" political mood of the postwar years had been destroyed by the upheavals of the 1960s and 1970s—by the "racial revolution of the 1960s, the most unpopular war in American history in Vietnam, the alienation of American youth, Watergate," among other factors. "Neighborhoods" were under attack by "government activity" such as building public housing and busing schoolchildren to different neighborhoods in order to integrate public schools. Families were eroding as women entered the workforce and children moved away from the communities in which they were born to seek employment. "Traditional Americans," he wrote, "are finding themselves beset by a vocal minority who find it chic to denigrate family solidarity, parental respect, and familial intradependence." The result was a tense, fragmented, and disillusioned political atmosphere. But Wirthlin believed that Reagan could transform these social conflicts into political victory.

Voters, he argued, wanted nothing more than to "follow some authority figure." Indeed, Wirthlin suggested that the "resurgence of religious fundamentalism" that had swept the country in the late 1970s was in large part an expression of this desire. Americans longed for a "leader who can take charge with authority; return a sense of discipline to our government; and manifest the willpower needed to get this country back on track." Reagan, he wrote, could present himself as that man, appealing to white voters of the North and South by establishing himself as a defender of neighborhoods and families against the incursions of the government (which often meant racial integration of schools): "Every effort should be made to argue for the preservation of the family and neighborhood without government intervention." He should peel blue-collar workers away from their unions, wooing them with promises of a tax cut and "targeted media messages for populist America." Wirthlin thought that this would work, because "these voters are no longer solely motivated by economic concerns but by larger social issues as well."[31]

The campaign tried to put Wirthlin's advice into action. Betty Southard Murphy, the first woman to serve on the National Labor Relations Board, traveled the country to speak to union leaders and ask them to endorse Reagan. Murphy, a self-described Taft Republican, tried to convince Reagan's advisers not to give up on winning union votes. "The Democrats have no corner on social justice, and we should not allow them to say so," she wrote to the campaign headquarters. "Don't forget, he is the only candidate ever from a major political party who has been a union president," she told a staff member at the George Meany Center for Labor Studies, referring to Reagan's stint as president of the Screen Actors Guild in the late 1940s.[32]

But while Reagan sought with little success to win endorsements from union leaders, he also tried, in Wirthlin's words, to "differentiate between the official position of the unions and the rank and file members of those unions." He reassured the critics of school busing that he opposed "the forced busing of school children to achieve arbitrary racial quotas." He spoke about states' rights at the Neshoba County Fair in Mississippi, in the same town where three young civil rights workers had been killed in 1964. And he tried to frame his economic message in rhetoric that would appeal to working-class Democrats, seeking, as one campaign adviser urged him to do, to show that he was not an "Ivy Leaguer" or a "member of the Eastern establishment," but rather that in many ways he remained a "Roosevelt Democrat who has not abandoned the tradition of the New Deal." Carter, like Herbert Hoover, represented an old, exhausted economic order, while Reagan could stand for "Rooseveltian-type realignment in search of new economic growth" (as another aide put it). Taken together, this was the same kind of strategy F. Clifton White had envisioned for Goldwater in 1964—one that would appeal to white working-class voters afraid of the integration of their schools and neighborhoods by using the language of market idealism combined with resentment. And labor unions and the liberal state were so much weaker in 1980 than they had been sixteen years earlier that the campaign was able to win a great deal of support from those voters, who would become known as the Reagan Democrats.[33]

The Reagan campaign also sought to win the support of conservative Christians. Although Wirthlin had argued that Reagan could easily woo "Southern white Protestants" away from Carter, their candidate in 1976, Reagan was not an obvious candidate for these religious voters. He had signed a bill to legalize abortion in California; he opposed the effort in that state to ban gays and lesbians from teaching in public schools; he had been divorced from his first wife. Still, the Reagan campaign vigilantly sought ways to succeed in the "large Christian vote market," as one note from a supporter put it.[34]

The courting of religious voters began in the summer of 1979. In the middle of August, Reagan met with a group of evangelical leaders, including Ben Armstrong, the head of the National Religious Broadcasters. The pastors asked the candidate: "If you died and you were standing before God at heaven's gate, what reason would you give for Him to let you into heaven?" Reagan replied, "I'd just ask for His mercy," and then proceeded to quote the Gospel of John ("For God so loved the world, that He gave His only begotten Son, that whosoever believeth in Him should not perish, but have everlasting life"). By contrast, John Connally, who met with the evangelicals at about the same time, responded with a joke: "I'd tell Him that if He was letting those other guys in, He ought to let me in too." Reagan wrote a special note to Armstrong afterward, thanking him for arranging the meeting and saying that he felt sympathetic to the concerns the group had expressed "in the area of religious freedom and other social issues." Armstrong was won over.[35]

The evangelical movement was itself gearing up for politics in 1980. Early in the year, Moral Majority had hosted a Key Pastors Meeting in Indianapolis, Indiana, designed to encourage ministers to start to use the pulpit to press for political engagement. All the participants received a thick packet analyzing biblical passages and showing how they could shed light on contemporary politics—always from the conservative perspective. Moral Majority argued that the Bible could be linked to present-day economic concerns. For example, the commandment "Thou shalt not steal" was interpreted as a commentary on inflation, since rising prices effectively stole the value of money itself; on the subject of welfare, the organization suggested that the Bible did not say anything about "government being the ordained provider" and quoted the Book of Proverbs: "The soul of the sluggard desireth, and hath nothing: but the soul of the diligent shall be made fat." A "Program for Political Participation of Church-Going Christians," prepared by Moral Majority or another Christian action group, advised church leaders to engage in an elaborate process of voter registration, candidate assessment, and ultimately voter turnout, including extensive phone banking using church membership rolls to get voters out on election day. The goal was political power. "Such a program run through the churches can produce those votes for the candidate of your choice and after the election, it will be easy to show that candidate why he won and perhaps make the level of commitment even greater to those fundamental moral issues which are so important in our country today," suggested the guidebook.[36]

Robert Billings, the president of Moral Majority (whose first foray into public activism was organizing against the IRS regulations concerning Christian private schools), contacted the campaign in May 1980 to offer his services: "We have felt very keenly that our group has been left out of the political process. Now with the opportunity of doing something on the front lines, our people really get excited." Letters of recommendation for Billings arrived from Jerry Falwell, the Southern Baptist preacher Adrian Rogers, the popular evangelical speaker Tim LaHaye, and even the fundamentalist leader Bob Jones III. (The campaign contacted Jones to make sure that he would encourage fundamentalists to work with Billings. Jones said that he couldn't speak for everyone in the fractious fundamentalist world but that he'd certainly support Billings himself.) The campaign took Billings on board, along with another religious activist, William Chasey, who was less closely aligned with conservative evangelicals but who proposed ambitious plans for turning out the Christian vote.

Chasey wanted Reagan to speak before religious audiences and hoped to supplement the voter turnout efforts of Moral Majority by encouraging pastors to set up voter registration drives and ultimately to take their flocks to the polls to vote. He also planned a "Christians Are Citizens Too Sunday," to be followed up by a "Christian Voters Sunday" right before election day.[37]

Such an aggressive attempt to use the churches to mobilize voters met with some resistance within the campaign. Many staffers were uncomfortable about the influence of the evangelicals. The leadership of the campaign rejected the idea of using the pulpit to turn out votes. Max Hugel, a New Hampshire businessman who was chief operating officer of Centronics Data Computer Corporation before joining the Reagan effort to organize citizen voter groups, insisted that such an attempt could not be publicly associated with the Reagan campaign: "If this is to be done at all, it would have to be done by the Christian movement itself—on their own." And shortly before the election, Billings complained that another staffer had said to him, "I'm afraid of you people. You are making the Republican Party a religious organization and chasing off many of our supporters!" He told Hugel, "Maybe somebody is afraid of us, but I am afraid Reagan will lose without us!"[38]

But despite mutual anxieties about the tight partnership between the Moral Majority and the Reagan campaign, Reagan worked very hard to show conservative evangelicals that he was their candidate. In August 1980 he appeared at the National Affairs Briefing in Dallas, an event organized by the Religious Roundtable, whose leaders included virtually all of the luminaries of the Christian right—Pat Robertson, Jerry Falwell, Tim LaHaye, and various Christian business conservatives such as the Hunt family of Texas. Ministers received special invitations to the meeting, which promised that it would give them "a knowledge about what is really going on in the erratic swings of the economy, the intrigues of international affairs and the domestic crisis which is morally enslaving our country." No longer would the church leaders have to play "voting lever roulette." They could be inside players.[39]

One of Reagan's speechwriters carefully crafted a talk for the evangelical audience in Dallas. In a note to the campaign staff explaining his handiwork, the writer pointed out: "Please note: there are an awful lot of code words, religious allusions and whatnot built into this, which might be missed if one is not close to evangelical religion." But if Reagan didn't comprehend the multilayered speech, not to worry: "It is not important, however, for the speaker to understand each and every one of them. His audience will. Boy, will they ever!"[40]

And they did. The shimmering 105-degree heat of Texas in August did not deter the thousands in the crowd from listening to Reagan's speech in Reunion Arena. At the meeting, attendees received "Christian vote" ratings of congressmen and senators, booklets detailing voter turnout tactics, and pins emblazoned with the word "VOTE," the "T" turned into a cross. (They also got some sage advice from Paul Weyrich, who urged them to target for voter turnout only those people who could be trusted: "I don't want everybody to vote. Our leverage, quite frankly, goes up as the size of the voting population goes down. We have no responsibility, moral or otherwise, to turn out our opposition.") The crowd roared for James Robison, the Southern Baptist televangelist known as "God's Angry Man," whose program had been temporarily suspended in 1979 when he had insisted that gays tried to recruit children to engage in homosexual acts, and who had campaigned successfully on the grounds of free speech for it to go back on the air. "Not voting is a sin against Almighty God!" he told the crowd, exhorting them to take friends to the polls. Condemning the passivity of his people, Robison shouted, "I'm sick and tired of hearing about all the radicals and the perverts and the leftists and the Communists coming out of the closet! It's time for God's people to come out of the closet!"[41]

Reagan spoke right after Robison, the seeming answer to the prayers of the evangelicals: here was the man who would lead Christians back to the White House. Earlier in the day he had met in the Dallas Hyatt Regency with more than two hundred business and religious leaders, including the Texas Rangers owner Eddy Chiles, Jesse Helms, and the Fort Worth industrialist T. Cullen Davis. "We have God's promise that if we turn to Him and ask His help, we shall have it," Reagan told the rapt crowd. "If we believe God has blessed America with liberty, then we have not just a *right* to vote, but a *duty* to vote." Reagan painted the Christian worldview in broad strokes that made clear its commonalities with the larger antistate agenda of his campaign, denouncing the FCC for interfering with religious broadcasting, the IRS for threatening the autonomy of religious schools, and the NLRB for meddling with church employees. Christians had a religious obligation to fight for laws in keeping with their moral code: "When the Israelites were about to enter the Promised Land, they were told that their government and laws must be a model to other nations, showing to the world the wisdom and mercy of their God."[42]

One newspaper described the entire National Affairs Briefing as a "thinly disguised religious pep rally for Ronald Reagan." Reagan's old friend and California associate Herbert Ellingwood, a longtime member of the Full Gospel Business Men's Association, wrote to Reagan after the Dallas meeting was over, telling him that the enthusiastic crowd was committed to "follow up on the suggestions for political action." Ellingwood enclosed a poem that he thought might be inspirational for the campaign:

> *Oh God, help us.*
> *We are a nation of too many laws.*
> *Not too much law . . . but too many laws.*
> *We can handle the lawbreakers,*
> *But who will save us from the lawmakers*
> *Before we overdose on lethal amounts*
> *Of legislation, regulation and litigation . . .*

At such moments in the midsummer of 1980, the distance between the evangelicals and the businessmen seemed very small indeed.[43]

• • •

REAGAN'S FAMOUSLY disorganized campaign in the late summer and early fall of 1980 was filled with missteps, such as his infamous claim that trees caused more pollution than factories (which led protesters to tack signs on trees at Reagan rallies: "Chop Me Down Before I Kill Again"). The polls were flat and inconclusive until after the debates. But in the weeks leading up to the election, the ambivalence that business leaders had expressed about Reagan in the spring disappeared. The *Wall Street Journal* conducted a poll a few weeks before the election which found that 87 percent of chief executives from large corporations supported Reagan. Contrary to the image of Reagan as the champion of small business, he won more support from executives of large companies than from those at small firms (where 67 percent endorsed him) and even medium-sized companies (81 percent). High-profile executives such as General Electric's Reginald Jones, a Business Roundtable leader who had once been a frequent visitor to Carter's Oval Office, spoke pessimistically about the economy's performance under the Democrats.[44]

Meanwhile, in the last weeks before November 4, Carter tried to reaffirm his own free-market credentials. "Every day millions of economic decisions are made in factories, in automobile showrooms, in banks and in brokerage houses, on farms and around kitchen tables where family budgets are being prepared," he told the National Press Club. "These millions of choices are not made by official command, but according to private needs and private individual judgments." He proposed a tax program featuring juicy incentives for investment. The CEO of Caterpillar observed: "Leaving out the Reagan tax cut, there really is a great deal of similarity between the candidates on economics." But none of it was enough to win back for Carter the commitments of businessmen. Even Irving Shapiro of DuPont, who stuck with him to the bitter end, conceded that he knew virtually no other executives willing to back the incumbent president. In the last days before the election, the London bookies, who had been calling for Carter all fall, swung over to Reagan (in Vegas, the odds were 9–5 in favor of the man who had once had a lounge act there). Ultimately Reagan was able to attract enough of the formerly Democratic votes that he needed to take the White House, and he won by a landslide in the Electoral College (489 for Reagan to 49 for Carter), despite holding only a narrow majority in the popular vote—51 percent to 41 percent for Carter and 7 percent for John Anderson, who ran as a third-party candidate after he was defeated in the primary.[45]

THE STOCK market jolted upward when Reagan won the election, prices rising in unmistakable euphoria. Analysts predicted breathlessly that the Dow Jones would soon top 1,000 (which it didn't for two more years—only after the recession of the early 1980s). "We're enjoying a Reagan rally right now," said the manager of corporate bond trading for First Boston. "The market is and should be buoyed by the Reagan victory and the conservative sweep across the country."[46]

Businessmen quoted in the newspapers—despite making the obligatory qualifiers that no single election could work magic—expressed their delight over the victory. "This conservative landslide should provide considerable encouragement for the private sector," cheered Reginald Jones. The chairman of Union Pacific pronounced that he was "ebullient" over Reagan's victory: "He'll be very good for business."[47]

Executives looked forward to tax cuts and deregulation. One *Wall Street Journal* headline for an article about commodities traders read, "Reagan Victory Is Met with Enthusiasm in Hopes of Less Government Meddling." A government affairs adviser for Marathon Oil Company exclaimed, "With Reagan in the White House and the Republicans in control of the Senate, the atmosphere will be go, go, go." A vice president at Paine Webber cheered the victory: "Reagan's going to take the regulatory shackles off the energy industry. Energy companies are going to go bananas." Executives at defense companies were especially thrilled—as one former aide put it, "Those weapons labs have got to be pouring champagne right now"—as their stocks rose in anticipation of a renewed arms race. Donald Rumsfeld, at that time the chief executive at G. D. Searle, told the *Wall Street Journal* that Reagan's tax cuts would "encourage things America needs and eliminate some of the disincentives to productivity, investment, risk-taking, research, development and technological advancement." Even if Reagan spent vast new sums on defense, his economic program would yield such potent results that the "net effect will not be to increase the federal deficit, but to reduce it." Even executives in the beleaguered steel industry were optimistic. "I see the election results as the start of a whole new era of greater productivity and profitability for the steel industry," insisted the CEO of Republic Steel.[48]

The old allies of business conservatism basked in the new glow of a friendly White House. Veterans of GE—some of whom had tried to organize "GE Alumni for Reagan" during the campaign—happily circulated articles about their former spokesman. The Heritage Foundation published a 1,077-page guide to public policy titled *Mandate for Leadership*; Reagan gave a copy to every member of his cabinet at their first meeting. Murray Weidenbaum got the nod to serve as the chairman of Reagan's first Council of Economic Advisers, and Reagan spoke at AEI's Public Policy Week, saying that he wanted to maintain a close "working relationship" with the think tank. The Chamber of Commerce supplied the White House with a list of names of Carter civil service appointees whom Lesher and others thought should be removed from their posts. Reagan spoke at a dinner attended by one thousand activists hosted by the Conservative Political Action Conference. "Had there not been a Barry Goldwater willing to make that lonely walk, we would not be talking of a celebration tonight," he told the crowd. He made special mention of his gratitude to Friedrich von Hayek, Milton Friedman, and Ludwig von Mises—all of whom had been present at the first meeting of the Mont Pelerin Society in 1947—for their intellectual acuity in dark times.[49]

"Does this election mean the end of liberalism as we know it?" a businessman asked the future attorney general Ed Meese at a Chamber of Commerce meeting in December, one month after the election. Even though Meese reminded his audience that liberalism remained potent and threatening and that the liberal forces were gathering for a counterattack, the possibilities evoked by the question lingered in the air.[50]

In the excitement of victory, their shared sense of struggle against the common enemy of liberalism permitted businessmen to gloss over many of their conflicts—about free trade, tax policy, and protections for manufacturing—at least for the moment. They all believed that they were creating a political order in which the role of business had been restored to its proper and central place. They were certain that in the future the state would see its primary responsibility as clearing the way for companies to have the freest possible range of action. They were convinced that the free market had the ability to create economic abundance and moral order simultaneously—that its invisible hand would punish the indolent and reward the entrepreneurs.

In the end, it would prove easier for conservatives to share such a broad and sunny faith when they were out of power. The divisions within the business mobilization—and between the businessmen and the social and religious conservatives—would emerge in time, both in the 1980s and afterward. But the businessmen who exulted in Reagan's election in 1980 could not know what the future held. They did not know what the economic impact of Reagan's policies would be. It was impossible for them to foresee the coming technological changes and the ways in which they would transform industry. No one could expect that the cold war would soon enter its final stages. They did not anticipate the free fall of American manufacturing or the rise of service companies and retail giants organized on the central principle of keeping labor costs low. No one knew that the labor movement would soon enter its prolonged decline. The divisions that remained beneath the surface of Reagan's support would emerge as the crystalline ideology of the free market came to be reduced to actual policies in the years that followed. Nonetheless, the businessmen who cheered for Reagan in 1980 were right to celebrate. They had been a long time in the wilderness. No matter whether they could in reality achieve the full rollback of the state they had long imagined; they were poised to govern at last.

Epilogue

A GREAT TRANSFORMATION of American politics began during the years that Ronald Reagan was in the White House. This might not, at first, have appeared the likely outcome of his two administrations. Conservative activists (the same ones who would in later years celebrate Reagan as a saint) struggled during the 1980s with various disappointments: as president, Reagan did not end abortion, he met with Soviet leader Mikhail Gorbachev, and he failed to eliminate the welfare state or even notably shrink government bureaucracies. And the enthusiasm within the business community that followed his election did not last long, as the economy sank into a deep recession, with unemployment rising to nearly 10 percent in 1982. As the manufacturing belt began to rust over, political conflicts between industrial companies desperately seeking subsidies and protection and those businesses that were able to thrive in global free markets grew more heated and intense. Tensions erupted between the owners of stock—newly confident and aggressive about using their financial power to compel management to do anything to raise returns—and career corporate executives. Today, the economic changes that began during the 1980s have an air of inevitability about them—the advent of globalization, the shift to a service economy. But at the time these transformations proved devastating to many of the manufacturing companies that had once most vociferously protested the New Deal.[1]

And yet over the course of the decade the old skepticism toward business that had been born in the Great Depression and reawakened for a new generation in the Vietnam era finally began to disappear. The economic transformations of the decade would be interpreted through the framework of the free market vision. The 1970s campaigns to revive the image of capitalism among college students bore fruit in the 1980s. Universities created new centers for the study of business themes such as entrepreneurship. Students in Free Enterprise, a group started in 1975 to bring students together to "discuss what they might do to counteract the stultifying criticism of American business," thrived on small college campuses, funded by companies like Coors, Dow Chemical, and Wal-Mart (as well as the Business Roundtable). The group organized battles of the bands, at which prizes would be doled out to the best probusiness rock anthems, helped silkscreen T-shirts with pro-capitalist messages, and created skits based on Milton Friedman's writings, which college students would perform in local elementary schools. In the workplace, the decline of the old manufacturing cities of the North and Midwest and the rise of the sprawling suburbs of the Sunbelt metropolises marked the rise of a new economic culture, dominated by companies such as Wal-Mart and Home Depot and Barnes & Noble.[2]

The Clinton years of the 1990s symbolized the success of the new order, not the restoration of the old. The end of the cold war meant that there seemed no longer to be any real alternative to capitalism; if that was the case, what now stood in the way of unrestrained laissez-faire? In the frenzy that followed, the CEO and the entrepreneur came to be seen as folk heroes, much as the Business Roundtable had once hoped they might—risk-taking daredevils whose brave and courageous acts perennially revolutionized American society. The market was the truly democratic sphere, the state for plodding bureaucrats only. The new economic order was one without a place for unions or much role for the government in shaping economic ends. As president, Bill Clinton accomplished much of what Reagan could not: the dismantling of welfare, the deregulation of Wall Street, the expansion of free trade. Labor experienced no grand revival under the Democratic president; economic inequality continued to widen. Even Barry Goldwater (whose stubborn support for abortion and gay rights in the 1990s put him increasingly on the outskirts of his own party) could express approval of Clinton. As he wrote to the Republican Speaker of the House, Newt Gingrich, "He's a Democrat, but I do admire him, I think he's doing a good job."[3]

What has happened to the business conservatives in this changed world? Many of their oldest institutions still exist today, although some of them seem to have lost their purpose in the world they helped to create, their urgent, embattled tone an echo of an earlier time. Leonard Read died in 1983, but his Foundation for Economic Education is still located in the same outsized mansion north of Manhattan where Read set up shop when he moved to the East Coast from California in 1946. Even though the liberal ideology that FEE once sought to combat has crumbled, the organization continues to profess the "freedom philosophy" it has for sixty years, with the single-minded intensity that has always defined it. FEE still holds regular seminars on the ideas of Friedrich Hayek (who died in 1992) and Ludwig von Mises (who died in 1973). The organization has eschewed direct political engagement, declining to get involved in the Republican resurgence and preferring to exert its influence in the realm of ideas alone, where its leaders continue to believe much work is yet needed. To quote its website, "Despite the end of the Cold War and the demise of the Soviet Empire, too many Americans do not seem to appreciate the very concept upon which the Founding Fathers established the American Republic"—in other words, that of freedom, defined as always by FEE as the freedom of the market.[4]

The Mont Pelerin Society, meanwhile, has held its meetings in recent years in such far-flung locales as Tokyo, Nairobi, and Guatemala. It finds new members by invitation only. The apparent defeat of socialism, the triumph of the market vision around the world, the rise of multinational capitalism—none of this has diminished the organization's sense of the fragile and delicate nature of market society; in this, it remains stubbornly loyal to Hayek's founding vision. Its website—which features a picture of a soaring snow-capped peak—declares that the society remains composed of those people who "continue to see the dangers to civilized society outlined in the statement of founding aims."[5]

Other organizations created by the business conservatives have matured into regular fixtures of the Washington scene. They embody the mundane yet powerful presence of business in the capital and in national politics—the fulfillment, in a quiet way, of the long-ago vision of the Liberty League. The Chamber of Commerce—the organization where Leonard Read and William Baroody got their start and for which Lewis Powell wrote his memorandum—now has 3 million members and spends millions of dollars each year lobbying on everything from opposing paid maternity leave to fighting card-check regulations that would make it easier for workers to organize unions. Under George W. Bush, a Chamber official who had spent his career fighting regulation was appointed to head the Occupational Safety and Health Administration. The Chamber of Commerce's National Chamber Litigation Center is especially active, filing lawsuits to protect business and market principles, and the organization has played a special role in trying to guarantee that business-friendly justices such as Samuel Alito and John Roberts are appointed to the Supreme Court.[6]

In the summer of 2007, the Business Roundtable (which counts among its membership about 160 companies, each represented by a chief executive officer) raised a few eyebrows when it tentatively spoke up in favor of health-care reform. But in most other ways its positions are consonant with those it has long pursued—it has hired consultants to defend high pay for executives, and along with the Chamber and other business groups, such as the National Association for Independent Business, it participated in a broad business coalition organized by the Republican strategist Karl Rove to back the tax cuts advocated by President Bush. And although the influence of the National Association of Manufacturers has declined with that of the American manufacturing sector, making the organization that fought the New Deal in the 1930s a narrower interest group than it once was, the NAM continues to count 14,000 member companies, which it organizes to advocate for weaker environmental regulations, permanent repeal of the "death tax" (estate tax), and new free trade treaties, and to continue the eternal struggle against "efforts by organized labor to restrict the rights of workers."[7]

The conservative think tanks too have grown into stable, respectable institutions, generating a constant if repetitive stream of studies and reports to bolster free-market positions. They provide precisely the kind of intellectual infrastructure for opposing regulation and the expansion of the state that their founders believed was missing in the 1940s and 1950s. The American Enterprise Institute proudly proclaims the slogan Baroody invented when the free-market believers felt they were political outsiders: "Competition of ideas is fundamental to a free society." Its trustees include the former CEOs of American Express, Merck, and ExxonMobil. William Baroody himself never got to see the triumph of the political movement to which he devoted his life; he died a few months before Reagan's election in 1980. (Clarence Manion also died in 1979, after twenty-five years and 1,294 weekly radio broadcasts.) But Baroody's children continued to play their roles in the conservative scene; in the spring of 2007, Michael Baroody, the son of AEI's founder and a NAM lobbyist, was nominated by President Bush to head the Consumer Product Safety Commission (although after much outcry over the idea that someone best known for his staunch opposition to consumer protection could wind up heading the regulatory agency, he withdrew his name). Meanwhile, the Heritage Foundation declares its support for "free enterprise, limited government, individual freedom, traditional American values and strong national defense"; early in 2008 it launched a campaign devoted to the question "What Would Reagan Do?"[8]

It is in the world of labor relations that the vision of the business conservatives has perhaps been most fully realized. Lemuel Boulware died in 1990, at the age of ninety-five. He had moved to Florida, although he still kept in touch with his old company, occasionally corresponding with "Neutron Jack" Welch, the CEO of GE in the 1980s. (After one visit, Welch wrote to him, "Dear Lem, We loved being with you. We owe you. 'Companies don't provide job security—customers do.' That one thought gets you a free lunch every summer.") Herbert Northrup, one of Boulware's protégés in the 1950s who became a professor at the Wharton

School of Business at the University of Pennsylvania, helped to produce a guide for companies on hiring replacement workers titled *Operating during Strikes.* The copper company Phelps Dodge used Northrup's manual during a strike in the early 1980s in which it fired all strikers and hired replacements. The company—like many others, including Greyhound, Continental Airlines, International Paper, the *Chicago Tribune,* and Caterpillar, which replaced strikers to break unions during the decade—was also taking cues from another GE alum, Ronald Reagan, who in 1981 fired and permanently replaced more than 11,000 federal air traffic controllers who went on strike. Over the course of the 1980s and 1990s, the number of major strikes declined sharply, as did the proportion of the workforce represented by unions—one outcome being the return of levels of economic inequality not seen since before the New Deal. The decline of labor was not only institutional: the very *idea* of the working class, as a distinct group with its own interests different from those of its employers, also seemed to recede, yielding to a new vision of workers as entrepreneurs themselves, always engaged in selling their talents, their future tied to the stock market instead of their collective efforts.[9]

In a way, the business conservatives seem to have modernized, as both political parties, as well as so much of the broader culture, now celebrate business and capitalism. Their stridency has given way to a subtler tone; the very success of the market agenda has rendered the old political register of their rhetoric obsolete. Throughout the postwar period, these institutions and the people who created them were engaged in a conscious attempt to mirror and to counter the labor and countercultural political movements that challenged the dominance of business. But as those other social and political movements have been defeated, as the labor movement has dwindled and the left has been pushed back, the idea of a political movement of businessmen, so often referred to and dreamed of by conservative activists, successful in so many ways, has come to seem oddly melodramatic and out of place. Today's institutionalized movement exerts its pressure on political life more quietly and steadily, in a context in which it confronts far fewer opponents than it did in the postwar years.

Yet at the same time the market enthusiasts and the business conservatives will always face a certain political danger, because the world they labor to create cannot be, for most people, the space of freedom that they promise. And if at times they seem to have lost their direction, if the old passions appear now and then to flag, it is worth remembering that the political cause for which they labored has in large part been triumphant: the New Deal has been turned back.

There is little reason to romanticize postwar liberalism. The welfare state it built was fragmented and partial; liberal politicians did not address civil rights or racial segregation or sexual inequality until pressured to do so by popular uprisings; the liberals of the cold war era took the United States into the Vietnam War; the liberal regime proved incapable of coping with the economic problems of the 1970s. But for all its problems, the political economy of the postwar years stands out as an anomaly in American history, produced under conditions of great economic crisis and political instability. The resistance that its central institutions met from businessmen, both openly and in quieter ways, throughout that period only highlights its exceptional nature. And the reasons for its decline lay not only in its inner tensions—although those were real and important—but also in the slow preparation of an alternative agenda by its business opponents.

In a *Forbes* profile of Boulware a year before his death, a journalist wrote, "His ideas were thought reactionary at the time, but Lemuel Boulware has lived to see many of them accepted." The same might be said of the entire community of conservative businessmen and their intellectual and political allies, who devoted their time, money, and political energy to the long struggle against the New Deal.[10]

Acknowledgments

I APPRECIATE THE work of all the archivists at the libraries I visited in the course of writing this book, but I would especially like to thank Beth Hoffman and Nicholas Snow at the Foundation for Economic Education; Jo Jackson at the Jesse Helms Center for Free Enterprise; Carol Leadenham at the Hoover Institution of Stanford University; William LeFeber at the Walter Reuther Library of Wayne State University; Linda Long and Bruce Tabb at the Knight Library of the University of Oregon; Patrick Robbins at the J. S. Mack Library of Bob Jones University; Patrizia Sione at the Kheel Center for Labor-Management Documentation and Archives at Cornell University; Jennifer Sternaman at the Ronald Reagan Presidential Library in Simi Valley, California; and Lynn Catanese, Carol Lockman, and Marjorie McNinch at the Hagley Museum and Library. The archivists at the Rare Book and Manuscript Libraries at the University of Pennsylvania and Columbia University, the Library of Congress, the National Archives and Records Administration, and the Harold B. Lee Library at Brigham Young University were also very helpful. Thanks also to the Business Roundtable, Jesse Helms, and William A. Rusher for permission to quote from their papers, as well as to the family of William F. Buckley, Jr.

My earliest years of work on this project were assisted by an Andrew W. Mellon Fellowship in Humanistic Studies from the Woodrow Wilson Foundation, a Richard Hofstadter Fellowship from the History Department at Columbia University, and a fellowship from the Miller Center for Public Affairs at the University of Virginia. Research grants from the Bentley Library of the University of Michigan at Ann Arbor and the Hagley Museum and Library in Wilmington, Delaware, made trips to those archives possible.

This book began as a dissertation in the History Department of Columbia University, and my dissertation committee—Elizabeth Blackmar, Alan Brinkley, Eric Foner, Joshua Freeman, and Ira Katznelson—provided crucial intellectual guidance for the project in its early stages and beyond. Eric Foner supervised the dissertation, and I am especially grateful to him for his support and critical engagement, as well as for the scholarly example he provides.

The Gallatin School of New York University has been a wonderful intellectual home for the book's completion. I am especially appreciative of the support that I have received from e. Frances White, David Moore, Ali Mirsepassi, Lisa Goldfarb, and Susanne Wofford. Research funds from Gallatin facilited many trips to archives. I am also grateful to all of my Gallatin colleagues for welcoming me into the lively community of the school. Alexander Engel provided critical help as a research assistant, with the aid of a Stephen Golden Faculty Enrichment Grant. I have also learned a great deal from teaching my students about economic ideas and American history; their insights have made me see my own work differently.

Many historians read drafts of the manuscript, in part and in whole. I would like to thank Steve Fraser, Joshua Freeman, Beverly Gage, Bruce Schulman, Elizabeth Blackmar, Pamela Laird, Eric Foner, Nelson Lichtenstein, Julia Ott (and her graduate seminar), and Lauren Winner for their comments and criticism, all of which strengthened the manuscript greatly. I am very grateful in particular to Elizabeth Blackmar and Nelson Lichtenstein for reading a draft of the entire manuscript on short notice at a late stage in the process. I have presented selections from the manuscript at conferences, including those of the American Historical Association and the Organization of American Historians, the Business History Conference, the Cambridge University–Boston University Conference on the Seventies, the Capitalism and Its Cultures Conference at the University of California at Santa Barbara, the Yale Market Cultures Workshop, the Social Science History Conference, and the Tamiment Labor History Seminar, and I have appreciated the comments of the audience members and panelists at all these venues. The New York City Market Cultures Workshop has also been a supportive forum. An early verson of Chapter 5 appeared in Nelson Lichtenstein, ed., *American Capitalism: Social Thought and Political Economy in the Twentieth Century* (Philadelphia: University of Pennsylvania Press, 2006).

I have been very fortunate to work with an amazing editorial team at W. W. Norton. I have learned a great deal from the insights and advice of my editor, Alane Mason, whose careful work on the manuscript truly went above and beyond. Alexander Cuadros provided a great initial set of line edits, and Liz Duvall did excellent work with the copy editing. Alexandra Heifetz and Denise Scarfi were helpful as well in readying the manuscript for publication. Sydelle Kramer, my agent, not only assisted me in crafting the original book proposal but also offered many insightful comments as well as support and guidance along the way.

Finally, I am grateful to the friends and family who supported me in myriad ways while I worked on this book. I would especially like to thank Margaret Adasko, Hermine Hayes-Klein, and Becca Lena Richardson. Beverly Gage, who always reminds me to work with care, has been a wonderful friend throughout graduate school and beyond. I appreciate the enthusiasm and support of the entire Strauss family. I am grateful to Albert and Geraldine Vargo for their welcome and their kindness. Thanks to Elinor Tucker, Eric Tucker, and Laramie and Theodore Palmer for opening their homes to me on research trips. My sister, Jess Phillips-Fein, not only read several chapters of the manuscript and gave helpful feedback but also offered good advice about other aspects of the writing process. My parents, Charlotte Phillips and Oliver Fein, have given a tremendous amount to this project through their deep support and love.

Greg Vargo did so many different things to help me write this book that it is hard to find words for all of them. He accompanied me on many research trips to archives all over the country, and kept me company (at times helping me go through boxes of documents) throughout the days of research in libraries from Wingate, North Carolina, to Provo, Utah, to Simi Valley, California. When he couldn't come along, he gave me music to take with me. He read multiple drafts of every chapter, he talked about the ideas and arguments throughout, and his editorial suggestions and criticism have made the book much stronger than it would have been otherwise. He also came up with the title. But these great gifts of his time and intelligence are really the very smallest part of what he has given to this book: his love, kindness, and generosity have sustained me and brought me joy over the years of its writing, and it is with overwhelming gratitude and love that I dedicate it to him.

Notes

Abbreviations

ACU Papers: American Conservative Union Papers, L. Tom Perry Special Collections, Harold B. Lee Library, Brigham Young University
BGCA: Billy Graham Center Archives, Wheaton, Illinois
BJU: Fundamentalism File, J. S. Mack Library, Bob Jones University
 Guy Archer Weniger Papers
Boulware Papers: Lemuel Boulware Papers, Rare Book and Manuscript Library, Van Pelt Library, University of Pennsylvania
Buckley Papers: William F. Buckley, Jr., Papers, Sterling Memorial Library, Yale University
BRA: Business Roundtable Archives, Washington, D.C.
CHS: Chicago Historical Society
 Clarence Manion Papers
 Sterling Morton Papers
FEEA: Foundation for Economic Education Archives, Irvington, New York
Goldwater Papers: Barry Goldwater Papers, Arizona Historical Foundation, Arizona State University
GRA: Group Research Archives, Rare Book and Manuscript Library, Columbia University
Hagley: Hagley Museum and Library, Wilmington, Delaware
 IDP Papers: Irénée du Pont Papers
 JEC Papers: Jasper Crane Papers
 JHP Papers: J. Howard Pew Papers
 Charles McCoy Papers
 NAM Papers: Papers of the National Association of Manufacturers
 PDP Papers: Pierre du Pont Papers
 Irving Shapiro Papers
 U.S. Chamber of Commerce Papers
Helms Papers: Papers held at Jesse Helms Center for Free Enterprise, Wingate, North Carolina

Hoover: Hoover Institution, Stanford University
- Friedrich von Hayek Papers
- B. E. Hutchinson Papers
- Walter Judd Papers
- Denison Kitchel Papers
- MPS Papers: Mont Pelerin Society Papers
- Edith Phillips Collection
- Henry Regnery Papers

Kheel: Archives Organization Files, Kheel Center for Labor-Management Documentation and Archives, M. P. Catherwood Library, Cornell University

LBJ Papers: Papers held by Lyndon Baines Johnson Presidential Library, Austin, Texas

LOC: Library of Congress
- WJB Papers: William J. Baroody Papers
- Richard Dudman Papers
- William Rusher Papers

Oregon: Special Collections and University Archives, University of Oregon Libraries
- James Ingebretsen Papers
- WCM Papers: W. C. Mullendore Papers
- Peter Steele Papers

NARA: National Archives and Research Administration, College Park, Md.

Powell Papers: Lewis F. Powell Papers, Washington and Lee University

RRPL: Ronald Reagan Presidential Library, Simi Valley, California
- CA-HQ Papers: Peter Hannaford/California Headquarters Papers
- William Clotworthy Papers
- Max Hugel Papers
- Edwin Meese Papers
- William Timmons Papers
- Richard Wirthlin Papers

Shadegg Papers: Stephen Shadegg Papers, Center for American History, University of Texas at Austin

Sligh Papers: Charles Sligh Papers, Bentley Library, University of Michigan

UAW: United Autoworkers Union Papers, Walter Reuther Library, Wayne State University
- Local 833
- Region 10
- Walter Reuther Papers

White Papers: F. Clifton White Papers, Kroch Library, Cornell University

Introduction

1. Ronald Reagan to Lemuel Boulware, n.d., Box 48, Folder 1435, Boulware Papers.
2. Lemuel Boulware to Ronald Reagan, June 15, 1981, ibid.
3. Richard Hofstadter, "Pseudo-Conservatism Revisited: A Postscript," in Daniel Bell, ed., *The Radical Right* (New Brunswick, N.J.: Transaction, 2002), 99.
4. Examples of scholarship on the liberal consensus and business: Kim McQuaid, *Big Business and Presidential Power* (New York: Morrow, 1982), and Robert Collins, *The*

Business Response to Keynes, 1929–1964 (New York: Columbia University Press, 1981). On data on income inequality: Lawrence Mishel, Jared Bernstein, and Sylvia Allegretto, *The State of Working America 2006–2007* (Ithaca, N.Y.: ILR Press, 2006), 54–59; Emmanuel Saez and Thomas Piketty, "Income Inequality in the United States, 1913–1998," *Quarterly Journal of Economics* 118, no. 1 (2003): 1–39.

5. My argument here builds on those of a number of other historians who have challenged the idea of the liberal consensus. For examples of the most important work, see my Bibliographic Essay and Note on Sources.

1. Paradise Lost

1. Irénée du Pont to Michael F. Shannon of the Benevolent & Protective Order of Elks, Aug. 17, 1934, Series J, Box 109, American Liberty League 6–8/34, IDP Papers, Hagley.
2. Thomas Ferguson, *Golden Rule: The Investment Theory of Party Competition and the Logic of Money-Driven Political Systems* (Chicago: University of Chicago Press, 1995), 141.
3. Robert F. Burk, *The Corporate State and the Broker State: The Du Ponts and American National Politics, 1925–1940* (Cambridge, Mass.: Harvard University Press, 1990), 131, 127, 132, 141.
4. Irving Bernstein, *Turbulent Years: A History of the American Worker, 1933–1941* (Boston: Houghton Mifflin, 1971), 217–317.
5. Frederick Randolph, "The American Liberty League, 1934–1940," *American Historical Review* 56, no. 1 (Oct. 1950): 19–20.
6. Irénée du Pont to F. A. Howland, President of National Life Insurance Company of National, Vermont, June 26, 1935, Series J, Box 114, American Liberty League Corporation Contacts, IDP Papers, Hagley.
7. For a description of the products made by DuPont during the 1920s, see Burk, *The Corporate State and the Broker State,* 3.
8. Ibid, 9, 11–15, 28. Burk also highlights the tension between modernity and feudal mystique in the du Pont family.
9. On labor movement figures: Irving Bernstein, *The Lean Years: A History of the American Worker 1920–1933* (Boston: Houghton Mifflin, 1960), 84. On the veneration of business: John Kenneth Galbraith, *The Great Crash: 1929* (New York: Houghton Mifflin, 1997), 170. Galbraith describes a famous *Ladies' Home Journal* article by John J. Raskob, a DuPont executive, encouraging readers to invest in common stocks, titled "Everybody Ought to Be Rich" (ibid., 52). The economic growth of the 1920s, of course, was never as widely distributed as its boosters indicated, or as the absence of political conflict during the decade might suggest. See Charles F. Holt, "Who Benefited from the Prosperity of the Twenties?" *Explorations in Economic History* 14 (1977): 277–289, and Frank Stricker, "Affluence for Whom?—Another Look at Prosperity and the Working Classes in the 1920s," *Labor History* 24, no. 1 (Winter 1983): 5–33. On the "employer's paradise": Bernstein, *The Lean Years,* 144.
10. Arthur M. Schlesinger, Jr., *The Crisis of the Old Order, 1919–1933* (Boston: Houghton Mifflin, 1957), 180.

11. On Whitney, building contractor: Robert S. McElvaine, *The Great Depression: 1929–1941* (New York: Times Books, 1984), 76. On Schwab: Schlesinger, *Crisis*, 180.
12. McElvaine, *The Great Depression*, 75; Louis W. Liebovich, *Bylines in Despair: Herbert Hoover, the Great Depression, and the U.S. News Media* (Westport, Conn.: Praeger, 1994), 107. On Hoover's actions: McElvaine, *The Great Depression*, 69–70.
13. Donald A. Ritchie, *Electing FDR: The New Deal Campaign of 1932* (Lawrence: University Press of Kansas, 2007), 96. Also see Steve Fraser, *Every Man a Speculator: A History of Wall Street in American Life* (New York: HarperCollins, 2005), 411–439.
14. Robert M. Collins, "Positive Business Responses to the New Deal: The Roots of the Committee for Economic Development, 1933–1942," *Business History Review* 52, no. 3 (Autumn 1978): 369–391, discusses the participation of business in the Business Advisory Council. On the NRA: Robert F. Himmelberg, *The Origins of the National Recovery Administration: Business, Government, and the Trade Association Issue, 1921–1933* (New York: Fordham University Press, 1993). On arguments about business support for Roosevelt and the New Deal: Steve Fraser, *Labor Will Rule: Sidney Hillman and the Rise of American Labor* (New York: Free Press, 1991); Colin Gordon, *New Deals: Business, Labor and Politics in America, 1920–1935* (New York: Cambridge University Press, 1994); and Ferguson, *Golden Rule*. Also see Robert H. Jackson, *That Man: An Insider's Portrait of Franklin D. Roosevelt* (New York: Oxford University Press, 2003).
15. Jackson, *That Man*, 16, discusses Roosevelt's sense of surprise at the hostility with which his politics were received. William Leuchtenberg, *Franklin Delano Roosevelt and the New Deal* (New York: Harper & Row, 1963), 122–125 describes the president's ambivalence about welfare.
16. Lizabeth Cohen, *Making a New Deal: Industrial Workers in Chicago, 1929–1939* (New York: Cambridge University Press, 1990); also see Staughton Lynd, ed., *"We Are All Leaders": The Alternative Unionism of the Early 1930s* (Urbana: University of Illinois Press, 1996).
17. S. M. DuBrul to Donaldson Brown, Chairman of General Motors. June 19, 1934, Series 9, Box 109, Folder: American Liberty League June–August 1934, IDP Papers, Hagley; Irénée du Pont to Pierre du Pont, July 10, 1934, Series A, File 771, 1929–1948, "American Liberty League, 1934," PDP Papers, Hagley; On incorporation: Burk, *The Corporate State and the Broker State*, 135; also see George Wolfskill, *The Revolt of the Conservatives* (Boston: Houghton Mifflin, 1962), 25.
18. *American Liberty League: A Statement of Its Principles and Purposes*, quoted in Frederick Rudolph, "The American Liberty League, 1934–1940," *American Historical Review* 56, no. 1 (Oct. 1950): 21; "League Is Formed to Scan New Deal, 'Protect Rights,'" *New York Times*, Aug. 23, 1934, 1; *The American Liberty League: A Statement of Its Principles and Purposes*, Mudd Library, Yale University.
19. Unsigned editorial, "Growing Pains," *New York Times*, Aug. 25, 1934, 12; "Topics in Wall Street," *New York Times*, Aug. 24, 1934, 23; John W. Haverty, "Liberty League Unique in Nation's Political History." *Washington Post*, Sept. 2, 1934, B1; "Roosevelt Twits Liberty League as Lover of Property," *New York Times*, Aug. 25, 1934, 1.
20. On "ravenous madness": William R. Perkins, "A Rising or a Setting Sun? A Study of Government Contrasting Fundamental Principles with Present Policies in Light of Authentic History," address presented before the Sphex Club, Lynchburg, Va., Sept.

1936, Edith Phillips Collection, Hoover. On centralization of power: Jouett Shouse, "The New Deal vs. Democracy," speech on the National Broadcasting System, June 20, 1936, ibid.; also see "The Dual Form of Government and the New Deal," American Liberty League, Sept. 1936, ibid. For league quotes: Randolph, "The American Liberty League," 24, 31. For New Deal bureaucracy: "Federal Bureaucracy in the Fourth Year of the New Deal: A Study of the Appalling Increase in the Number of Government Employees Which Has Resulted from the Attempted Concentration of Power in the Federal Government under the Present Administration," Aug. 1936, Edith Phillips Collection, Hoover.

21. "Shouse Denounces Roosevelt's Plans," *New York Times*, Mar. 31, 1935, 2; "Suit Challenges Security Act Tax," *New York Times*, June 24, 1936, 39.
22. Irénée du Pont to Frank Lovejoy, Mar. 16, 1935, Accession 228, Box 111, Folder: American Liberty League, April–March 16, 1935, IDP Papers, Hagley; Wolfskill, *The Revolt of the Conservatives*, 62–63.
23. Burk, *The Corporate State and the Broker State*, 220, 221; Richard S. Tedlow, "The National Association of Manufacturers and Public Relations During the New Deal," *Business History Review* 50, no. 1 (Spring 1973): 27.
24. On drop in membership: Tedlow, "The National Association of Manufacturers," 29. On "business salvation": Quoted in Richard Walter Gable, "A Political Analysis of an Employers' Association: The National Association of Manufacturers," Ph.D. diss., University of Chicago, 1950, 229. On changing membership: Philip Burch, "The NAM as an Interest Group," *Politics and Society* (Fall 1973): 102.
25. Tedlow, "The National Association of Manufacturers," 31, 33, 36.
26. On NAM lawyers' actions: Howell John Harris, *The Right to Manage: Industrial Relations Policies of American Business in the 1940s* (Madison: University of Wisconsin Press, 1982), 24. On the "Mohawk Valley Formula": Gable, "A Political Analysis of an Employers' Association," 110, and Marc Steven Kolopsky, "Remington Rand Workers in the Tonawandas of Western New York, 1927–1956: A History of the Mohawk Valley Formula," Ph.D. diss., State University of New York at Buffalo, 1986. On defense tactics: "Defend Labor Aim of Industrial Body," *New York Times*, Mar. 3, 1938, 6; Louis Stark, "Third Parties Used in Steel Campaign," *New York Times*, July 22, 1938, 8; Report of the Senate Committee on Education and Labor, *Violations of Free Speech and Rights of Labor: Industrial Munitions* (Washington, D.C.: Government Printing Office, 1939), 46–47, 52–58.
27. S. Alexander Rippa, "The Textbook Controversy and the Free Enterprise Campaign, 1940–1941," *History of Education Journal* 9, no. 3 (Spring 1958): 50.
28. See Mary Sennholz, *Leonard Read: Philosopher of Freedom* (Irvington-on-Hudson, N.Y.: Foundation for Economic Education, 1993), 1–65. Also see Gregory Eow, "Fighting a New Deal: Intellectual Origins of the Reagan Revolution," Ph.D. diss., Rice University, 2007, 109–115.
29. "'Apostles of Hatred' Flayed by Executive," *Los Angeles Times*, Apr. 4, 1931, A11; "Nation's Bankers to Open Annual Meeting Today," *Los Angeles Times*, Oct. 4, 1932, A1; Sennholz, *Leonard Read*, 54–55.
30. George Nash, *The Conservative Intellectual Movement in America Since 1945* (New York: Basic Books, 1976), 17; Sennholz, *Leonard Read*, 55.
31. "William C. Mullendore, President, Los Angeles Chamber of Commerce—1944,"

W. C. Mullendore 10/42–10/47 Folder, Leonard Read Correspondence, FEEA; Eow, "Fighting a New Deal," 117–124; "Bill," n.d., W. C. Mullendore 10/42–10/47 Folder, Leonard Read Correspondence, FEEA.

32. W. C. Mullendore to Leonard Read, May 14, 1934, Box 2, WCM Papers, Oregon; W. C. Mullendore to Leonard Read, July 20, 1938, ibid.
33. Mullendore to Elmo Thompson, VP, First National Bank and Trust Company, Sept. 16, 1938, ibid.; W. C. Mullendore to Leonard Read, Aug. 11, 1938, ibid.
34. For the point about the L.A. Chamber as a precursor to Read's later endeavors at ideological mobilization, I am indebted to Eow, "Fighting a New Deal," 129.
35. Maurice C. Bryson, "The Literary Digest Poll: The Making of a Statistical Myth," *American Statistician* 30, no. 4 (Nov. 1976): 184–85.
36. "Lewis Declares Landon Is 'Puppet': Big Business, Fighting to Bar Revival of New Deal Reforms, Pulls Strings, He Says," *New York Times*, Sept. 20, 1936, 27; Wolfskill, *The Revolt of the Conservatives*, 210–211. On Republican request that the ALL not endorse Landon: Rudolph, "The American Liberty League," 31; Wolfskill, *The Revolt of the Conservatives*, 207.
37. "A Report by the Industrial Division of the Republican National Committee 1936 Campaign," Box 4, Morton Papers, CHS; "Resolution," n.d. and author unclear, ibid.
38. On pay envelopes: Turner Catledge, "Industrialists Fighting Roosevelt by Tax Warning on Pay Envelopes," *New York Times*, Oct. 24, 1936, 1. Employers had been trying to communicate with employees about Social Security and the election in ad hoc ways before the RNC effort; in one case, an employer reportedly circulated a letter among his workers asking each how he or she intended to vote. For Morton quotation: Sterling Morton to B. E. Hutchinson, June 10, 1954, Box 4, Hutchinson Papers, Hoover.
39. Wolfskill, *The Revolt of the Conservatives*, 222–223; "Farley to Finish His Cabinet Term," *New York Times*, Nov. 5, 1936, 2.
40. Burk, *The Corporate State and the Broker State*, 225, 237–238.
41. Unsigned editorial, "The Sticking Point," *New York Times*, Jan. 28, 1937, 24. For tensions among liberals in the late 1930s: Alan Brinkley, *The End of Reform: New Deal Liberalism in Recession and War* (New York: Knopf, 1995), especially 137–174.
42. James MacGregor Burns, *Roosevelt: The Lion and the Fox* (New York: Harcourt, Brace, 1956), 156.
43. Henry Simons, *Economic Policy for a Free Society* (Chicago: University of Chicago Press, 1948), 42; Frank Knight, *The Ethics of Competition and Other Essays* (Freeport, N.Y.: Books for Libraries Press, 1935), 75, 47; Walter Lippmann, *An Inquiry into the Principles of the Good Society* (Boston: Little, Brown, 1937), 280–281; Michael Wreszin, *The Superfluous Anarchist: Albert Jay Nock* (Providence: Brown University Press, 1971), 127–128. Eow, "Fighting a New Deal," provides an overview of the anti–New Deal arguments advanced during the decade, which provided roots for later libertarianism. Knight's essays quoted here predate the 1930s, and he did grow more critical of the New Deal during that decade, but they were still included in a collection of his work published in 1935.
44. On DuPont and unions: Sanford Jacoby, *Modern Manors: Welfare Capitalism Since the New Deal* (Princeton, N.J.: Princeton University Press, 1997), 158–159, 189–190. On DuPont war production: Burk, *The Corporate State and the Broker State*, 278. For quotations: ibid., 283, 281, 287, 282.

45. Burk, *The Corporate State and the Broker State*, 290; Pierre du Pont to Jouett Shouse, Jan. 25, 1950, Box 4, Folder 11, Jouett Shouse Papers (59M61), Special Collections and Digital Programs, University of Kentucky Libraries.

2. Down from the Mountaintop

1. Leonard Read, *The Romance of Reality* (New York: Dodd, Mead, 1937), 10; George Nash, *The Conservative Intellectual Movement in America Since 1945* (New York: Basic Books, 1976), 17.
2. Gregory Eow, "Fighting a New Deal: Intellectual Origins of the Reagan Revolution," Ph.D. diss., Rice University, 2007, 143–144. For Goodrich's help in making contacts for Read, see David Goodrich to Leonard Read, May 1, 1946, David M. Goodrich Folder, Leonard Read Correspondence, FEEA.
3. Leonard Read to Earl W. Benjamin of the Washington Co-Operative Farmers Association, Aug, 9, 1949, Box 34, "FEE Folder 2," JEC Papers, Hagley; "Activities at FEE," Sept. 1963, Accession 1411, Series 1, Box 99, Hagley; "How to Fight Socialism: Notes from FEE," Apr. 15, 1954, NAM Papers, Accession 1411, Series 1, Box 6, Hagley.
4. Jasper Crane to Harry Earhart, Sept. 5, 1947, Box 31, Folder E, 1920–1935, JEC Papers, Hagley.
5. See the biographical statement on Crane at Hagley Museum and Library, Wilmington, Delaware, and "Edward Crane Dies Suddenly," undated news clipping from unknown paper, Box 9, JEC Papers, Hagley. For the physical and personality descriptions: Arthur Newcomb, "Analysis of Mr. Jasper E. Crane," Box 8, "Jasper Crane Biog.," ibid.; this analysis was prepared for the office of Dr. Katherine M. H. Blackford, an employers' adviser, when Crane was thirty-eight years old, in 1919.
6. "Some Observations on the German Economy," talk presented at the Economics Department, Princeton University, May 16, 1938, Box 7, "Addresses, Articles, Publications, Etc. 1930–1948," JEC Papers, Hagley. On Crane and the Liberty League: "Seating List: American Liberty League Dinner," Mayflower Hotel, Jan. 25, 1936, Series A, File 771 1929–1948, American Liberty League 1936, PDP Papers, Hagley. On moral punishment: "The Church and Social Security in Industrial Life," remarks by Jasper E. Crane at Round Table of Institute of Public Affairs, Charlottesville, Va., July 6, 1935, Box 7, JEC Papers, Hagley.
7. George Lipsitz, *Rainbow at Midnight: Labor and Culture in the 1940s* (Urbana: University of Illinois Press, 1994), Chs. 4–6; "Strike of Coffin Makers Brings Shortage," *New York Times*, Jan. 18, 1949, 3.
8. Jasper Crane to Loren Miller, Nov. 27, 1945, Box 51, JEC Papers, Hagley.
9. Isabel Paterson to Leonard Read, Aug. 22, 1945, JEC File, Leonard Read Correspondence, FEEA; Jasper Crane to Leonard Read, Sept. 11, 1945, ibid.; Jasper Crane to Leonard Read, Nov. 26, 1945, ibid.; Jasper Crane to Leonard Read, Mar. 18, 1946, ibid.; Jasper Crane to Irénée du Pont, Nov. 19, 1957, Box 57, JEC Papers, Hagley. Also see Jasper Crane to Isabel Paterson, Aug. 14, 1945, JEC File, Leonard Read Correspondence, FEEA, in which Crane says that he has heard about Read and would be eager to meet him.
10. Jasper Crane to Leonard Read, Sept. 14, 1945, JEC File, Leonard Read Correspondence,

FEEA; "Definitions" read to the National Lay Committee of the National Council of Churches, May 8, 1954, Box 7, "Addresses, Articles, Speeches, Etc. Folder 2," JEC Papers, Hagley; Jasper Crane to Loren Miller, Nov. 13, 1945, Box 51, "Loren Miller, 1945–1946," ibid. Miller, an ardent free-market believer, was well aware of the power of manifestos; he made everyone he hired at the bureau read and agree to abide by a ten-page document setting out his libertarian principles, and he corresponded with Crane about starting an "investment counsel" of wealthy businessmen to help guide their donations to free-market intellectual organizations, an idea that never entirely came together. "Conversation with Loren B. Miller, 3/29/46," ibid. Also see Brian Doherty, *Radicals for Capitalism: A Freewheeling History of the Modern Libertarian Movement* (New York: Public Affairs, 2007), 182.

11. Jasper Crane to Loren Miller, Sept. 14, 1945, and Nov. 13, 1945, Box 51, JEC Papers, Hagley. The description of the "bible" of American liberty also appears in a letter from Crane to Leonard Read, Dec. 11, 1945. Crane went so far as to put together a list of the qualities he felt the "treatise on liberty" might embody; he seemed to hope that Read and others could simply locate a writer for the project. "Treatise on Liberty" memo, Jan. 22, 1946, JEC File, Leonard Read Correspondence, FEEA.
12. On increasing receptiveness to Keynesian economics: Richard Parker, *John Kenneth Galbraith: His Life, His Politics, His Economics* (New York: Farrar, Straus and Giroux, 2005), 163–177, and Robert M. Collins, *The Business Response to Keynes, 1929–1964* (New York: Columbia University Press, 1981). On the AFA president's speech: Charles F. McGovern, *Sold American: Consumption and Citizenship, 1890–1945* (Chapel Hill: University of North Carolina Press, 2006), 337. On the U.S. Chamber of Commerce president's speech: Andrew A. Workman, "Manufacturing Power: The Organizational Revival of the National Association of Manufacturers, 1941–1945," *Business History Review* 72 (Summer 1998): 294. The NAM, as Workman shows, remained more critical of the wartime expansion of the state and sought to find ways to resist the wartime power of unions. See Nelson Lichtenstein, "Class Politics and the State During World War II," *International Labor and Working-Class History* 58 (Fall 2000): 261–274; also see Howell Harris, *The Right to Manage: Industrial Relations Policies of American Business in the 1940s* (Madison: University of Wisconsin Press, 1982).
13. On popular fears: Meg Jacobs, *Pocketbook Politics: Economic Citizenship in Twentieth-Century America* (Princeton, N.J.: Princeton University Press, 2005), 221–231. On the Taft-Hartley Act: "A New Deal for America's Employers," *Business Week,* June 28, 1947; see also Robert Griffith, "Forging America's Postwar Order," in Michael Lacey, ed., *The Truman Presidency* (Cambridge: Cambridge University Press, 1989), and Harry A. Mills and Emily Clark Brown, *From the Wagner Act to Taft-Hartley: A Study of National Labor Policy and Labor Relations* (Chicago: University of Chicago Press, 1950). On the failing labor unions: Lichtenstein, *State of the Union;* Steve Fraser, "The 'Labor Question,'" and Nelson Lichtenstein, "From Corporatism to Collective Bargaining: Organized Labor and the Eclipse of Social Democracy in the Postwar Era," both in Steve Fraser and Gary Gerstle, *The Rise and Fall of the New Deal Order, 1930–1980* (Princeton, N.J.: Princeton University Press, 1989).
14. Alan Brinkley, *The End of Reform: New Deal Liberalism in Recession and War* (New York: Vintage, 1995), 227–264; Ellen Schrecker, *The Age of McCarthyism* (New York: Bedford/St. Martin's, 2002), 45. See Arthur M. Schlesinger, Jr., *The Vital Center: The*

Politics of Freedom (Boston: Houghton Mifflin, 1949), for the classic statement of postwar liberal anticommunism. Also see Jonathan Bell, *The Liberal State on Trial: The Cold War and American Politics in the Truman Years* (New York: Columbia University Press, 2004), for a discussion of the ways in which anticommunism reshaped domestic politics in the immediate aftermath of World War II.

15. David Vogel, "Why Businessmen Distrust Their State: The Political Consciousness of American Corporate Executives," in Vogel, *Kindred Strangers: The Uneasy Relationship Between Politics and Business in America* (Princeton, N.J.: Princeton University Press, 1996) considers the roots of antistate sentiment among businessmen.
16. Alan Ebenstein, *Friedrich Hayek: A Biography* (New York: Palgrave, 2001), chaps. 1–5. For Mises, see Israel M. Kirzner, *Ludwig von Mises* (Wilmington, Del.: ISI Books, 2001), 1–31.
17. Ebenstein, *Friedrich Hayek*, chaps. 6–10. Also see Robert Skidelsky, *John Maynard Keynes: Hopes Betrayed* (London: Macmillan, 1983).
18. On Hayek's circumstances in Cambridge: Ebenstein, *Friedrich Hayek*, 104–127. On the evolution of Hayek's ideas: Friedrich Hayek, *The Road to Serfdom: Text and Documents*, ed. Bruce Caldwell (Chicago: University of Chicago Press, 2007), intro., 1–9.
19. On Mises on the market: Ludwig von Mises, *Human Action: A Treatise on Economics* (New Haven, Conn.: Yale University Press, 1949), 257. For more on the theory of individualism, see Friedrich von Hayek, "Individualism and Social Order," in *Individualism and Economic Order* (Chicago: University of Chicago Press, 1994), 6.
20. Hayek, *The Road to Serfdom*, 224.
21. Hayek, "Individualism and Social Order," 4, 14.
22. Friedrich Hayek, "Why I Am Not a Conservative," in *The Constitution of Liberty* (Chicago: University of Chicago Press, 1960), 398, 399, 400. This aspect of the thinking of Hayek and Mises echoes that of another famous Austrian economist, Joseph Schumpeter. Schumpeter, of course, differed from Mises and Hayek generally—especially in his skepticism about competitive markets (he suggested that all innovation reflected monopoly) and in his argument that capitalism was politically doomed and that socialism was inevitable given the declining faith in the system of the owners of industry and of intellectuals. Hayek rejected the political determinism and despair reflected in the first sentences of Schumpeter's section on capitalism in *Capitalism, Socialism and Democracy*: "Can capitalism survive? No. I do not think it can."
23. On Adam Smith: Emma Rothschild, *Economic Sentiments: Adam Smith, Condorcet and the Enlightenment* (Cambridge, Mass.: Harvard University Press, 2001); Gertrude Himmelfarb, *The Idea of Poverty: England in the Early Industrial Age* (New York: Knopf, 1984); Eric Foner, *Free Soil, Free Labor, Free Men: The Ideology of the Republican Party Before the Civil War* (New York: Oxford University Press, 1970); Amy Dru Stanley, *From Bondage to Contract: Wage Labor, Marriage and the Market in the Age of Slave Emancipation* (Cambridge: Cambridge University Press, 1998). For Sumner quotation: William Graham Sumner, "The Concentration of Wealth: Its Economic Justification," in *Social Darwinism: Selected Essays of William Graham Sumner*, ed. Stow Persons (Englewood Cliffs, N.J.: Prentice-Hall, 1963), 157. Also see David Nasaw, "Gilded Age Gospels," in Steve Fraser and Gary Gerstle, eds., *Ruling America: A History of Wealth and Power in a Democracy* (Cambridge, Mass.: Harvard University Press, 2005).

24. Richard Hofstadter, *Social Darwinism in American Thought* (Boston: Beacon, 1992); James Livingston, "The Social Analysis of Economic History and Theory: Conjectures on Late Nineteenth-Century Development," *American Historical Review* 92, no. 1 (Feb. 1987): 69–95.
25. Quoted in Eow, "Fighting a New Deal," 142.
26. William F. Buckley to Roger Milliken, Mar. 10, 1962, Box 21, Buckley Papers.
27. Hayek, *The Road to Serfdom: Text and Documents,* intro., 1.
28. Henry Hazlitt, "An Economist's View of 'Planning,'" *New York Times*, Sept. 24, 1944 BR1; Hayek quoted in Richard Cockett, *Thinking the Unthinkable: Think Tanks and the Economic Counter-revolution, 1931–1983* (London: HarperCollins, 1995), 101. Also see Theodore Rosenof, "Freedom, Planning and Totalitarianism: The Reception of F. A. Hayek's Road to Serfdom," *Canadian Review of American Studies* 5, no. 2 (Fall 1974): 149–165.
29. On Luhnow and the Volker Fund: Doherty, *Radicals for Capitalism*, 182–183. On Luhnow's meeting with Hayek: Stephen Kresge and Leif Wemur, *Hayek on Hayek*, 127. For Luhnow quotation: Harold Luhnow to Friedrich Hayek, Sept. 7, 1945, Box 58, Folder 16, Hayek Papers, Hoover. Robert Van Horn and Philip Mirowski, *The Rise of the Chicago School of Economics and the Birth of Neoliberalism* (Cambridge, Mass.: Harvard University Press, forthcoming), tells the story of Luhnow and the Volker Fund's role in Hayek's American career in great detail; my analysis here rests on that work.
30. On Luhnow and the University of Chicago: Harold Luhnow to Friedrich Hayek, Sept. 29, 1948; Robert M. Hutchins to Harold Luhnow, Oct. 19, 1948; Harold Luhnow to Robert M. Hutchins, Oct. 20, 1948, all in Box 58, Folder 16, Hayek Papers. On Hayek's personal situation: Hayek to Luhnow, May 9, 1948.
31. Jasper Crane to Loren Miller, Aug. 28, 1945, Box 51, JEC Papers, Hagley; Jasper Crane to Loren Miller, May 21, 1946, ibid.
32. Jasper Crane to Loren Miller, June 3, 1946, ibid.; Jasper Crane to Loren Miller, Nov. 13, 1945, ibid.
33. Mont Pelerin Society membership lists, Box 57, Folders 1–5, MPS Papers, Hoover.
34. François Denord, "French Neo-Liberalism and its Divisions: From the Colloque Walter Lippmann to the 5th Republic," unpublished paper in possession of the author; Van Horn and Mirowski, "The Rise of the Chicago School," 14; R. M. Hartwell, *A History of the Mont Pelerin Society* (Indianapolis: Liberty Fund, 1995), 33.
35. Friedrich Hayek to Jasper Crane, Feb. 7, 1947, Box 73, Folder 1, Hayek Papers, Hoover.
36. Jasper Crane to Friedrich Hayek, Mar. 7, 1947, ibid.; Crane Fundraising Letter, Apr. 25, 1957, Box 52, "MPS 1957, No. 1," JEC Papers, Hagley.
37. Minutes from Apr. 9, 1947, discussion of name of society, Folder 13, Box 5, MPS Papers, Hoover. The discussion of the appropriate name went on for some time. Milton Friedman strongly opposed naming it after individuals, saying instead that abstract principles seemed more important and appropriate. Lionel Robbins commented that the use of a name had a pleasingly "esoteric" nature. And after Karl Brandt suggested "Mont Pelerin Society," Karl Popper responded, "That is meaningless."
38. E. R. Noderer, "Seven Nations Map Freedom Fight in Secret Talk," *Chicago Tribune*, Apr. 3, 1947, 25. Press was barred from attending sessions. The drafted statement, Hayek said, would be "carefully worded so as to contain no information."

39. Friedrich Hayek address to Mont Pelerin Society, Apr. 1, 1947, Box 5, Folder 13, MPS Papers, Hoover. In his comments on "false rationalism," Hayek made special mention of the need to bridge the divide between classical liberalism and Christianity, arguing that "unless this breach between true liberal and religious convictions can be healed there is no hope for a revival of liberal forces."
40. "Statement of Aims," Mont Pelerin Society, Apr. 8, 1947, Box 71, Folder 8, Hayek Papers, Hoover; Nash, *The Conservative Intellectual Movement,* 26. At the time, Friedman expressed a certain doubt about the ability of the society to self-consciously nurture the vision of the free market. If it were to succeed, shouldn't it be able to do so on its own? As he wrote to Hayek, "Our faith requires that we be skeptical of the efficacy, at least in the short run, of organized effort to promulgate it"; Milton Friedman to Friedrich Hayek, Jan. 2, 1947, Box 73, Folder 40, Hayek Papers, Hoover.
41. Jasper Crane to H. B. Earhart, Sept. 5, 1947, Box 31, JEC Papers, Hagley; Jasper Crane to J. Howard Pew, Dec. 28, 1948, Box 52, "MPS 1947–1956," ibid.
42. Friedrich Hayek to Jasper Crane, June 19, 1947, Box 73, Folder 1, Hayek Papers, Hoover; Jasper Crane to Friedrich Hayek, Sept. 5, 1947, Box 52, "MPS 1947–1956," JEC Papers, Hagley; Jasper Crane to Loren Miller, May 23, 1947, JEC File, Leonard Read Correspondence, FEEA; Jasper Crane to Friedrich Hayek, Oct. 17, 1949, Box 52, "MPS 1947–1956," JEC Papers, Hagley.
43. Jasper Crane to Friedrich Hayek, Feb. 29, 1952, Box 52, "MPS 1947–1956," JEC Papers, Hagley.
44. Jasper Crane to Friedrich Hayek, Nov. 21, 1956, ibid.; Jasper Crane to Friedrich Hayek, Dec. 13, 1956, ibid. It is unclear what prompted Crane's reevaluation of the situation. Other businessmen had similar feelings at about the same time; industrialist William Grede, for example, who also helped to organize for the 1958 American meeting, described his disillusionment with "broad public education programs" of the sort carried out by NAM and his new interest in focusing on the "'intelligentsia'—the opinion molding groups," which led to his interest in Mont Pelerin; William Grede to C. S. Rogers, Dec. 13, 1956, Box 74, Folder 15, Hayek Papers, Hoover.
45. Sterling Morton to B. E. Hutchinson, June 10, 1954, Box 4, Hutchinson Papers, Hoover; Jasper Crane to Friedrich Hayek, Dec. 13, 1956, Box 52, "MPS 1947–1956," JEC Papers, Hagley; Membership lists, Box 57, MPS Papers, Hoover. On Goodrich: Dane Starbuck, *The Goodriches: An American Family* (Indianapolis: Liberty Fund, 2001), 318–319.
46. Crane fund-raising letter, Apr. 25, 1957, Box 52, "MPS 1957 Folder 1," JEC Papers, Hagley. The contributors included Irénée du Pont, Pierre du Pont, Lammot du Pont Copeland, and Walter Carpenter, the chairman of the board of DuPont. A small conservative group named the Relm Foundation gave $5,000, as did J. Howard Pew. Jeremiah Milbank, the United Fruit Company, U.S. Steel, the Ford Motor Fund, and the Milliken Foundation each contributed $1,000. The Winchester Foundation contributed $3,000 at the behest of Pierre Goodrich, and the Frederick Nymeyer Foundation, run by a business consultant, gave $1,000. Smaller contributions came from Henning Prentis (of Armstrong Cork Company), Sterling Morton of Morton Salt, B. E. Hutchinson, the Beech Aircraft Corporation, and Grede Foundries, as well as corporate foundations like the Kennametal Foundation. See Fritz Machlup, "Final Financial Statement on Princeton Meeting," May 20, 1959, sent to Jasper Crane,

William Curtiss, John Davenport, Lawrence Fertig, and Friedrich Hayek, Box 78, Folder 1, Hayek Papers, Hoover.

47. F. A. Harper to Jasper Crane, Oct. 1, 1957, and Oct. 2, 1957, Box 52, JEC Papers, Hagley; Jasper Crane to Friedrich Hayek, Nov. 19, 1957, Box 73, Folder 1, Hayek Papers, Hoover; Pierre Goodrich to Jasper Crane, Jan. 4, 1958, Box 52, "MPS 1958 File No. 1," JEC Papers, Hagley; Friedrich Hayek to Jasper Crane, Mar. 3, 1958, ibid.
48. Fritz Machlup to Friedrich Hayek, Jan. 31, 1958, Box 78, Folder 1, Hayek Papers, Hoover; Friedrich Hayek to Fritz Machlup, Feb. 10, 1958, ibid.
49. Jasper Crane to Friedrich Hayek, June 6, 1958, ibid. Fritz Machlup never appreciated the influence Crane had over invitations. A year later, when the society was planning a meeting at Oxford, Machlup wrote to Hayek that Crane wanted to bring people to Oxford: "Personally, I do not believe that the people whom he proposes have in the past contributed a great deal to our meetings, or are likely to do so in the future. It would be my preference to save our funds for more important purposes in the future"; Machlup to Hayek, June 18, 1959, Box 78, Folder 1, Hayek Papers, Hoover.
50. Jasper Crane to John Holmes, May 7, 1958, Box 53, "MPS File No. 2 1958," JEC Papers, Hagley; Jasper Crane to Frederick Nymeyer, Oct. 25, 1957, Box 52, "MPS 1957 No. 1," ibid.; Jasper Crane to Friedrich Hayek, list of individuals and companies to thank, Sept. 19, 1958, Box 53, ibid. He was inspired in part by a letter from the conservative journalist Garet Garrett, in which Garrett imagined what a European would need to see to understand American free enterprise. "He must go to Texas. I can't explain why. It is a statement. He will know why when he has passed through it"; Richard Cornuelle to Jasper Crane, Dec. 6, 1957, Box 52, "MPS 1957 No. 2," ibid.
51. Confidential Memorandum of Delinquencies of A. Hunold, Secretary of the Mont Pelerin Society, in Connection with its American Meeting in Princeton September 8–13, Sept. 17, 1958, Box 52, JEC Papers, Hagley (it is unclear who wrote this document); Jasper Crane to Wilhelm Roepke, Aug. 18, 1960, Box 53, "MPS 1959–1960," ibid.
52. Jasper Crane to Ralph Harris, Feb. 8, 1961, Box 54, "MPS 1961," ibid. Also see Jasper Crane to James A. Kennedy, Dec. 19, 1960, Box 53, "MPS 1959–1960," ibid.
53. Ivan Bierley to Friedrich Hayek, Nov. 16, 1964, Box 58, Folder 19, Hayek Papers, Hoover.

3. Changing the Climate

1. W. C. Mullendore to Leonard Read, Feb. 28, 1946, Box 2, WCM Papers, Oregon; W. C. Mullendore to Leonard Read, Apr. 26, 1949, Box 34, JEC Papers, Hagley.
2. "Longest Utility Strike in History Ends," *Los Angeles Times*, May 12, 1953, A4; W. C. Mullendore to Leonard Read, Mar. 16, 1953, William C. Mullendore, 7/23/51–3/29/54, Leonard Read Correspondence, FEEA; W. C. Mullendore to Leonard Read, Apr. 22, 1953, ibid.; Message to Stockholders, Fourth of July, 1949, Box 4, WCM Papers, Oregon; "Dangers Foreseen in Federal Policy," *New York Times*, Jan. 13, 1944, 27; "Utility Executive Assails U.S. Taxes," *New York Times*, Aug. 13, 1944, 33; Ayn Rand to W. C. Mullendore, May 8, 1949, ibid.; W. C. Mullendore to Leonard Read, Apr. 19, 1947, "Mullendore 10/42–7/47," Leonard Read Correspondence, FEEA.
3. "Foundation for Economic Education: Donors of $500 and Over, Fiscal Year Ending

March 31, 1949," Box 5, Hutchinson Papers, Hoover; Outline of Proposed Activities and Reasons Therefor the Foundation for Economic Education, FEEA.

4. On FEE flyers: FEE Donor Form, Box 20, Folder 1, Hayek Papers, Hoover. Also see Brian Doherty, *Radicals for Capitalism: A Freewheeling History of the Modern Libertarian Movement* (New York: Public Affairs, 2007), 158, for a description of Read's attitude toward fund-raising and FEE's eschewal of tactics such as direct mailings. It should be noted that Read was not quite as cavalier toward fund-raising as this stance might suggest; when FEE was short of funds, he would assiduously do what he could to try to raise money. Also on fund-raising: Mary Sennholz, *Leonard Read: Philosopher of Freedom* (Irvington-on-Hudson, N.Y.: Foundation for Economic Education, 1993), 83.
5. For Read and Mises: George Nash, *The Conservative Intellectual Tradition in America Since 1945* (New York: Basic Books, 1976), 346; Leonard Read to Friedrich Hayek, Mar. 4, 1948, Box 20, Folder 1, Hayek Papers, Hoover; James Beard to Leonard Read, Apr. 1, 1949, Leonard Read Correspondence, FEEA; Jasper Crane to Irénée du Pont, Nov. 19, 1957, Box 52, JEC Papers, Hagley; Friedrich Hayek to Karl Brandt, Apr. 20, 1949, and May 2, 1949, Box 72, Folder 36, Hayek Papers, Hoover.
6. "Strictly Personal," Address by Leonard Read, May 16, 1947, Blackstone Hotel, Commercial Club of Chicago, "Meeting 12/4/46," Leonard Read Correspondence, FEEA.
7. On mockery: James Patterson, *Grand Expectations: The United States, 1945–1974* (New York: Oxford University Press, 1996), 244. On moderation: Dwight D. Eisenhower to Edgar Eisenhower, Nov. 8, 1954, quoted in L. Galambos and D. van Ee, eds., *The Papers of Dwight David Eisenhower* (Baltimore: Johns Hopkins University Press, 1996), available at http://www.eisenhowermemorial.org/presidential-papers/first-term/documents/1147.cfm. On Eisenhower's political vision and government's role: Robert Griffith, "Dwight D. Eisenhower and the Corporate Commonwealth," *American Historical Review* 87, no. 1 (Feb. 1952): 87–122.
8. Griffith, "Dwight D. Eisenhower," 92, 89; Arthur Larson, *A Republican Looks at His Party* (Westport, Conn.: Greenwood, 1974), 121, 1. David Stebenne, *Modern Republican: Arthur Larson and the Eisenhower Years* (Bloomington: Indiana University Press, 2006), looks at Larson's book and career.
9. David A. Horowitz, *Beyond Left & Right: Insurgency & the Establishment* (Urbana: University of Illinois Press, 1997), 267. For Welch's ideas, see Jonathan M. Schoenwald, *A Time for Choosing: The Rise of Modern American Conservatism* (New York: Oxford University Press, 2001), 64–75.
10. My data on the funding of conservative organizations come from the files of the organizations, not from those of the corporations. Generally, corporate records are not available, which makes it hard to measure the significance of their donations to conservative groups relative to the other philanthropic efforts that they may have participated in. However, I am primarily concerned with the meaning of their donations in terms of building the right rather than with the internal donation structure of the companies.
11. On support for McCarthy: Charles J. V. Murphy, "McCarthy and the Businessman" and "Texas Business and McCarthy," *Fortune*, April and May 1954. On the American Security Council: "binder," 1957, for selling the ASC to new members, Box 3, Folder

10, Regnery Papers, Hoover; flyer, "The Need for the American Security Council," ibid.; year-end report for FY ending Mar. 31, 1960, ibid. Also see Fred Cook, "The Ultras," *The Nation*, June 30, 1964. On the Christian Anti-Communism Crusade: Lisa McGirr, *Suburban Warriors: The Origins of the New American Right* (Princeton, N.J.: Princeton University Press, 2001), 99; Rick Perlstein, *Before the Storm: Barry Goldwater and the Unmaking of the American Consensus* (New York: Hill & Wang, 2001), 148–149; Arnold Forster and Benjamin Epstein, *Danger on the Right* (New York: Random House, 1964), 49.

12. Forster and Epstein, *Danger on the Right*, 14, 45; Schoenwald, *A Time for Choosing*, 63–64; Perlstein, *Before the Storm*, 110–119; Gerald Schomp, *Birchism Was My Business* (New York: Macmillan, 1970).
13. Letter from Kenneth Miller, Dec. 1954, along with "The Lockheed Story," Accession 1411, Series 1, Box 1, NAM Papers, Hagley.
14. List of Trustees, Nov. 13, 1958, Box 42, Folder 8, WJB Papers, LOC.
15. "Challenge on Jobs Taken Up by Brown," *New York Times*, Apr. 29, 1936, 14; "Company Reports to Its Jobholders," *New York Times*, Mar. 8, 1938, 26; "Corporate Soul," *Time*, Apr. 3, 1939; Drew Pearson, "Business Interprets Legislation," *Washington Post*, Apr. 14, 1949, 13. Pearson claimed that a congressman from Georgia, Eugene "Goober Gene" Cox, took credit for the idea for AEA and that he had persuaded Eugene Stetson of Guaranty Trust Co. to get involved. Also see Sam Rosenfeld, "From Lobbyists to Scholars: AEI and the Politics of Expertise, 1943–1964," senior thesis, Columbia University, April 2004, 7–21. This senior thesis is the best analysis of AEA, and I rely on it throughout this section.
16. Sam Rosenfeld, "From Lobbyists to Scholars," 21–30; James Allen Smith, *The Idea Brokers: Think Tanks and the Rise of the New Policy Elite* (New York: Free Press, 1991), 175; Report of Select Committee on Lobbying Activities, House of Representatives, 81st Congress, 2nd sess., Dec. 1950, 19–20, Box 11, GRA, Columbia.
17. See James Allen Smith, *The Idea Brokers*, 176–177 for a description of Baroody as a "policy entrepreneur."
18. Myra MacPherson, "The Baroody Connection." *Potomac/Washington Post*, Aug. 17, 1975, Box 102, Folder 4, WJB Papers, LOC. On the political rival: F. Clifton White, *Suite 3505: The Story of the Draft Goldwater Movement* (New Rochelle, N.Y.: Arlington House, 1967), 201–203.
19. William J. Baroody to Harvey Peters, July 17, 1959, Box 40, Folder 4, WJB Papers, LOC.
20. William J. Baroody to William McGrath, Aug. 17, 1954, Box 38, Folder 11, ibid.; William J. Baroody to Allen Marshall, Mar. 17, 1954, Box 20, Folder 2, ibid.; Rosenfeld, "From Lobbyists to Scholars," 34; AEA pamphlet, Carton 2, "Hutch correspondence," WCM Papers, Oregon. Rosenfeld provides an excellent analysis of Baroody's fund-raising strategies and techniques. Also see Rosenfeld for the new slogan as part of Baroody's overhaul of the group.
21. William J. Baroody to Allen Marshall, Aug. 1, 1958, Box 42, Folder 8, WJB Papers, LOC; William J. Baroody to B. E. Hutchinson, July 1, 1954, Box 37, Folder 4, ibid.; William Baroody to Edgar Smith, Sept. 26, 1956, Box 34, Folder 8, ibid.; William J. Baroody to B. E. Hutchinson, Jan. 24, 1956, Box 37, Folder 5, ibid.
22. William J. Baroody to William Taylor, Oct. 27, 1958, Box 56, Folder 1, ibid.; William

Taylor to William Baroody, Oct. 30, 1958, ibid.; William J. Baroody to William Taylor, Sept. 15, 1959, ibid.

23. Sources of Association Support, Meeting of the Board of Trustees, American Enterprise Association, Mar. 13, 1958, Box 42, Folder 8, WJB Papers, LOC; William Baroody to Allen Marshall, Aug. 1, 1958, ibid.; American Enterprise Institute for Public Policy Research Attachment to Form 990-A, Calendar Year 1962, Box 4, Dudman Papers, LOC; Rosenfeld, "From Lobbyists to Scholars," 45. The organization received donations from a wide variety of companies. For example, one description of the group argued that its supporters included "some of the very largest as well as some of the smallest business firms in the country." There was no schedule of dues; companies were asked to give what they could, and gifts ranged in size from $250 to $20,000. "The American Enterprise Association," Samples of Enclosures, n/d, Box 56, Folder 3, WJB Papers, LOC.
24. Draft, Nov. 17, 1958, Box 71, Folder 2, WJB Papers, LOC; "Labor Unions in Modern Society: A Description of the Overall Research Investigation," Confidential Memo presented at Trustees Meeting, Mar. 31, 1959, ibid.; Joseph A. Loftus, "Economist Scores Union Pay Theory," *New York Times*, Jan. 27, 1958, 16; "Labor Rein Urged by Roscoe Pound," *New York Times*, May 20, 1957, 12; "The Fallacies of Consumption," excerpts from G.A. Briefs, "Unionism Appraised," Box 11, GRA; Raymond Moley, "Valley Authorities," and Felix Morley, "Treaty Law and the Constitution: A Study of the Bricker Amendment," ibid. Also see "Expert Decries U.S. School Aid," *New York Times*, Nov. 21, 1955, 32.
25. Rosenfeld, "From Lobbyists to Scholars," 49–52. Also see correspondence with Ralph Harris, Box 55, Folder 4, WJB Papers, LOC.
26. William Baroody to W. T. Taylor, Chairman, ACF Industries, Mar. 27, 1962, Box 59, Folder 1, WJB Papers, LOC; R. Daniel McMichael to C. E. Ford, Aug. 16, 1963, "Hoover Institute and American Enterprise Institute Potential Projects," Box 90, Folder 11, ibid. See Rosenfeld, "From Lobbyists to Scholars," for the argument that AEA sought to position itself as an objective institute.

4. Cultural Politics: Churches, Radio Stations, and Magazines

1. Ayn Rand to Leonard Read, Feb. 23, 1946, Ayn Rand Folder, Leonard Read Correspondence, FEEA. For a discussion of the vexed relationship between Rand and conservatives of the religious-traditionalist school, see Jennifer Burns, "Godless Capitalism: Ayn Rand and the Conservative Movement," in Nelson Lichtenstein, ed., *American Capitalism: Social Thought and Policy in the Twentieth Century* (Philadelphia: University of Pennsylvania Press, 2006).
2. On *Roofs or Ceilings?*: Brian Doherty, *Radicals for Capitalism: A Freewheeling History of the Modern Libertarian Movement* (New York: Public Affairs, 2007), 193. On Rand and Read: Ayn Rand to Leonard Read, Sept. 12, 1946, Ayn Rand Folder, Leonard Read Correspondence, FEEA; Ayn Rand to Leonard Read, Nov. 2, 1946, ibid. See also Jennifer Burns, *Goddess of the Market: Ayn Rand and the American Right, 1930–1980* (New York: Oxford University Press, forthcoming); Gregory Eow, "Fighting a New Deal: Intellectual Origins of the Reagan Revolution, 1932–1952," Ph.D. diss., Rice University, 2007, 145–156; and Doherty, *Radicals for Capitalism*, 190–195. Burns

offers an especially helpful analysis of the reasons Rand had such difficulty working with others. She also tells the story for the first time of the conflict between Read and Rand over the circulation of Rand's document of principles.

3. George Nash, *The Conservative Intellectual Tradition in America Since 1945* (New York: Basic Books, 1976), 144; Burns, "Godless Capitalism," 286. Also see Burns, *Goddess of the Market*, for Rand's popularity among businessmen both small and large.
4. Ronald Wuthnow, *The Restructuring of American Religion: Society and Faith Since World War II* (Princeton, N.J.: Princeton University Press, 1989), 143; Joel Carpenter, *Revive Us Again: The Reawakening of American Fundamentalism* (New York: Oxford University Press, 1997); Elizabeth Fones-Wolf, *Selling Free Enterprise: The Business Assault on Labor and Liberalism, 1945–1960* (Urbana: University of Illinois Press, 1994), 237.
5. J. Howard Pew to Robert H. Crawford, Jan. 31, 1945, Box 8, Spiritual Mobilization Folder, JHP Papers, Hagley; J. Howard Pew to James Fifield, Nov. 10, 1944, Box 6, ibid.; J. Howard Pew to William Rand, Monsanto Chemical Company, Oct. 22, 1947, Box 15, Spiritual Mobilization Folder, ibid.; Pew quoted in Jasper Crane to Leonard Read, Nov. 29, 1946, "Meeting 12/4/46," Leonard Read Correspondence, FEEA.
6. Carpenter, *Revive Us Again*, 172; Sarah Hammond, "'Business Men Working for Jesus': Toward a Historiography of Twentieth-Century American Christianity and Capitalism," paper presented at the Organization of American Historians Annual Meeting, Minneapolis, Apr. 1, 2007; Jeff Sharlet, "Jesus Plus Nothing: Undercover Among America's Secret Theocrats," *Harper's Magazine*, May 2003; Lisa Getter, "Showing Faith in Discretion," *Los Angeles Times*, Sept. 27, 2002.
7. Carey McWilliams, "Battle for the Clergy," *The Nation*, Feb. 7, 1948; James Fifield, "A Letter to Leonard Read," National Industrial Conference Board Binder, Read Papers, FEEA; James W. Fifield, *The Single Path* (Englewood Cliffs, N.J.: Prentice-Hall, 1957), 87, quoted in Eckard V. Toy, Jr., "Spiritual Mobilization: The Failure of an Ultraconservative Ideal in the 1950s," *Pacific Northwest Quarterly* (April 1970): 77–86. Also see Eckard V. Toy, Jr., "Ideology and Conflict in American Ultraconservatism, 1945–1960," Ph.D. diss., University of Oregon, 1965, and Ralph Lord Roy, *Apostles of Discord: A Study of Organized Bigotry and Disruption on the Fringes of Protestantism* (Boston: Beacon, 1953), 285–308, for more on Spiritual Mobilization.
8. McWilliams, "Battle for the Clergy."
9. Edmund Opitz to Henry Hazlitt, July 17, 1953, Box 81, Folder 7, Ingebretsen Papers, Oregon; "Minutes," Nov. 9, 1954, Box 87, Folder 11, ibid.
10. "The Christian's Political Responsibility," *Faith and Freedom*, Sept. 1952; Irving Howard, "The Power of the Individual," in *Faith and Freedom*; Charles Sligh, "Christianity in Business," Box 12, Sligh Papers.
11. Eckard V. Toy, Jr., "Spiritual Mobilization," 83; Pamphlet, 1947, Box 15, Spiritual Mobilization Folder, JHP Papers, Hagley.
12. "Contributions—1955, $100 and over," Box 91, Folder 4, Ingebretsen Papers, Oregon (other corporate donors included Carnation Company, the Firestone Tire and Rubber Company, Goodyear Tire and Rubber Company, Republic Steel Company, and Sun Oil); "Confidential List of Corporate and Corporate Foundation Contributors, January through November 1960," Box 91, Folder 5, ibid. (some of the companies were Firestone, Carnation, Gulf Oil, Sun Oil, General Motors, and U.S. Steel).

13. James Ingebretsen to James Dunkel of Ford Motor Company Fund, Nov. 4, 1954, Box 70, Ingebretsen Papers, Oregon; James Ingebretsen to Corporate Contributions Committee, Mar. 10, 1960, Box 91, Folder 5, ibid.
14. Quoted in Doherty, *Radicals for Capitalism*, 275. The quotes are from Ingebretsen's autobiography, in which he describes his increasingly elaborate (and decidedly non-Christian) spiritual beliefs, including his awakening in 1955 and his powerful sense of identification with a daughter who died as an infant. See James Ingebretsen, *Apprentice to the Dawn* (Los Angeles: Philosophical Research Society, 2003).
15. Doherty, *Radicals for Capitalism*, 280; James Ingebretsen to J. Howard Pew, Dec. 13, 1961, Box 75, Folder S, JHP Papers, Hagley. See Doherty for a discussion of the Spiritual Mobilization set's forays into psychedelics. Also see Toy, "Spiritual Mobilization."
16. J. Howard Pew to James Ingebretsen, Jan. 4, 1962, Box 75, Folder S, JHP Papers, Hagley; Rev. Irving E. Howard, "What Did Jesus Believe about Wealth?" *Christian Economics*, May 3, 1955, "Capitalism" File, Fundamentalism File, W.O.H. Garman Papers, J. S. Mack Library, Bob Jones University; Billy Graham to J. Howard Pew, Mar. 26, 1955, Box 42, JHP Papers, Hagley; Mary Sennholz, *Faith and Freedom: A Biographical Sketch of a Great American, John Howard Pew* (Grove City, Pa.: Grove City College, 1975), 154–155; Billy Graham, *Just As I Am: The Autobiography of Billy Graham* (San Francisco: HarperCollins, 1997), 228. For Pew's contribution to *Christianity Today*: J. Howard Pew to Dr. L. Nelson Bell, Nov. 20, 1956, Box 53, JHP Papers, Hagley.
17. Jennifer Burns, "Godless Capitalism," 271; William F. Buckley to Ruth Alexander, Jan. 26, 1956, Box 1, Buckley Papers.
18. "The Magazine's Credenda," *National Review*, Nov. 19, 1955; Isabel Paterson, "The Southern Breakthrough," *National Review*, Dec. 21, 1955; William F. Buckley, "Why the South Must Prevail," editorial, *National Review*, Aug. 24, 1957. On the labor movement: L. Brent Bozell, "Reuther Schemes for Power," *National Review*, Oct. 20, 1956; Suzanne La Follette, "Labor Against the Workers," *National Review*, Apr. 11, 1956, among others. For more on the *National Review*'s writing about the South, see Joseph E. Lowndes, *From the New Deal to the New Right: Race and the Southern Origins of Modern Conservatism* (New Haven, Conn.: Yale University Press, 2008), 48–54.
19. John Judis, *William F. Buckley, Jr.: The Patron Saint of the Conservatives* (New York: Simon & Schuster, 1988), chap. 1.
20. William F. Buckley to Ruth Alexander, Jan. 26, 1956, Box 1, Buckley Papers.
21. Milliken biography: "Legacies of Leadership: South Carolina Business Hall of Fame," http://www.knowitall.org/legacy/laureates, viewed August 2008; Alan Otten, "Ideas & Men: Virginia Textile Institute Turns Out Both for Industry," *Wall Street Journal*, Mar. 13, 1952, 1.
22. "Union Wins and Loses at Mill," *New York Times*, Oct. 18, 1956, 18; George Ryder, "Milliken: Is He Bigger Than the Law?" *Textile Labor*, Nov. 1956, Box 220, GRA.
23. H. E. Williams of Cotwool Manufacturing Company to William F. Buckley, Apr. 1, 1955 (accompanied by a check for $1,000 made out at Milliken's order to fund a research study on bias at the *New York Times Book Review*), Box 3, Buckley Papers; Felix Wittmer, "New Slants on Best-Sellers," *American Mercury*, Jan. 1956; Roger Milliken to William F. Buckley, Jan. 7, 1955, Box 5, Buckley Papers.

24. Judis, *William F. Buckley, Jr.*, 121; Roger Milliken to William F. Buckley, July 28, 1958, Box 6, Buckley Papers; William F. Buckley to A.W.D. Harris, Nov. 10, 1955, Box 2, ibid.
25. William F. Buckley to Roger Milliken, Feb. 20, 1958, Box 6, Buckley Papers; William F. Buckley to Gerrish Milliken, Apr. 1, 1957, Box 3, ibid. On Chamber of Commerce: Milliken to Buckley, Dec. 29, 1955, Box 3, and Dec. 10, 1957, Box 5, ibid.
26. William F. Buckley to Lemuel Boulware, May 31, 1955, Box 1, Buckley Papers; Sterling Morton to William F. Buckley, Aug. 5, 1957, Box 51, Morton Papers, CHS; William F. Buckley to William Rusher, July 14, 1957, Box 2, Buckley Papers. This letter lists companies whose advertising contracts with *National Review* were on the brink of expiration; Buckley asked Rusher to contact them to renew the contracts. Also see William Rusher to Sterling Morton, Aug. 19, 1957, Box 51, Morton Papers, urging Morton Salt to become a regular advertiser and listing other companies that had decided to do so.
27. William F. Buckley to W. C. Mullendore, Mar. 22, 1955, Carton 1, Buckley File, WCM Papers, Oregon; W. C. Mullendore to Allan Hoover, Dec. 20, 1954, ibid.
28. James Patterson, *Mr. Republican: A Biography of Robert A. Taft* (Boston: Houghton Mifflin, 1972), 152. Taft's politics contained numerous contradictions—he supported Social Security, backed an antilynching law (unlike most Democrats at the time), and lent his name to the charter public housing legislation of the Truman era. Also see Rick Perlstein, *Before the Storm: Barry Goldwater and the Unmaking of the American Consensus* (New York: Hill & Wang, 2001), 1–16, for an excellent discussion and character portrait of Manion.
29. David Horowitz, *Beyond Left and Right: Insurgency and the Establishment* (Urbana: University of Illinois Press, 1997), 216.
30. Justus Doenecke, *Not to the Swift: The Old Isolationists in the Cold War Era* (Lewisburg, Pa.: Bucknell University Press, 1979), 234, 242.
31. Quoted in Arnold Forster and Benjamin Epstein, *Danger on the Right* (New York: Random House, 1964), 121, 129.
32. I. M. Herrmann of Acme Galvanizing Inc., n.d., Box 89, Folder 16, Manion Papers, CHS. Also see the discussion of Manion's strategy of fund-raising from suppliers in Forster and Epstein, *Danger on the Right*, 126–129.
33. Luther Griffith fund-raising letter, Mar. 11, 1960, Box 102, Folder 3, Manion Papers, CHS; Luther Griffith to Clarence Manion, Apr. 14, 1960, Box 68, Folder 5, ibid.; Grieco Brothers fund-raising letter, June 25, 1955, Box 102, Folder 3, ibid.; William Grede fund-raising letter, Dec. 18, 1967, ibid.
34. Undated list, Box 69, Folder 4, Manion Papers, CHS.
35. H. W. Zinsmaster to Clarence Manion, Aug. 29, 1958. Box 4, Folder 9, ibid.; Sterling Morton to Clarence Manion, Aug. 11, 1956, Box 3, Folder 8, ibid.
36. Clarence Manion to William F. Buckley, forwarding note from H. A. Parmalee to Clarence Manion, July 17, 1956, Box 3, Clarence Manion Folder, Buckley Papers.

5. How to Break a Union

1. "The Overhaul of General Electric," *Fortune*, Dec. 1955, 112–116, 234–240.
2. On median family incomes: Lawrence Mishel, Jared Bernstein, and Sylvia Allegretto,

The State of Working America 2006–2007 (Ithaca, N.Y.: ILR Press, 2006), 45, 55. On pension benefits: Samuel Rosenberg, *American Economic Development since 1945* (New York: Palgrave Macmillan, 2003), 78. On health insurance: Jennifer Klein, *For All These Rights: Business, Labor, and the Shaping of America's Public-Private Welfare State* (Princeton, N.J.: Princeton University Press, 2003), 230. On vacations and for Reuther quote: David Brody, *Workers in Industrial America: Essays on the Twentieth-Century Struggle* (New York: Oxford University Press, 1993), 192.

3. "Work Stoppages Involving 1,000 or More Workers, 1947–2007," Bureau of Labor Statistics, http://www.bls.gov/news.release/wkstp.to1.htm; Brody, *Workers in Industrial America*, 204; Lichtenstein, *State of the Union*, 136. P. K. Edwards, *Strikes in the United States, 1881–1974* (New York: St. Martin's Press, 1981), notes that when all strikes are considered (and not just ones with more than 1,000 workers), the late 1940s and early 1950s see a peak in strike activity, which declines later in the decade. Jack Metzgar, *Striking Steel: Solidarity Remembered* (Phildelphia: Temple University Press, 2000), provides a detailed study of the emotional life of a union steelworker and his family in the 1950s.
4. In 1961 Congress held hearings on the new levels of hostility faced by unions at which union supporters outlined many of these problems. See U.S. Congress, Senate, *Hearings Before the Subcommittee on National Labor Relations Board*, 87th Cong., 1st sess., 1961, and James Gross, *Broken Promise: The Subversion of U.S. Labor Relations Policy, 1947–1994* (Philadelphia: Temple University Press, 1995), 153–156, for a discussion of the hearings. Also see Jefferson Cowie, *Capital Moves: RCA's Seventy-Year Quest for Free Labor* (Ithaca, N.Y.: Cornell University Press, 1999), especially 93–95, for the role played by tariffs.
5. Quoted in John S. Saloma III, *Ominous Politics: The New Conservative Labyrinth* (New York: Hill & Wang, 1984), 64. There are probably a variety of reasons that GE was more willing than General Motors to take on the fight. The company may have faced more intense competition from low-cost or non-union producers because of the sheer variety of its product lines, which gave it an extra incentive to contain labor costs. See Ronald Schatz, "The End of Corporate Liberalism: Class Struggle in the Electrical Manufacturing Industry, 1933–1950," *Radical America* (July–Aug. 1975): 189–190, for a discussion of some of the distinctive economic features of the electrical manufacturing industry. And unions at GE were much weaker than those at the auto giants, making it easier for the company to campaign against them.
6. David Loth, *Swope of GE: The Story of Gerard Swope and General Electric in American Business* (New York: Simon and Schuster, 1958), 31–34, 43.
7. Roland Marchand, *Creating the Corporate Soul: The Rise of Public Relations and Corporate Imagery in American Big Business* (Berkeley: University of California Press, 1998), 150–151.
8. Ronald Schatz, *The Electrical Workers: A History of Labor at General Electric and Westinghouse, 1923–1960* (Urbana: University of Illinois Press, 1983), 15.
9. Marchand, *Creating the Corporate Soul*, 151–155.
10. James Matles and James Higgins, *Them and Us: Struggles of a Rank-and-File Union* (Englewood Cliffs, N.J.: Prentice Hall, 1974), 78–88; Schatz, *The Electrical Workers*, 70–74.
11. On executive ideal: Lisa Ann Kannenberg, "The Product of GE's Progress: Labor,

Management and Community Relations in Schenectady, 1930–1960," Ph.D. diss., Rutgers University, 1999, 26, 188–189. On summer camps: Garry Wills, *Reagan's America: Innocents at Home* (New York: Penguin, 1985), 334–335.

12. Elizabeth Fones-Wolf, *Selling Free Enterprise: The Business Assault on Labor and Liberalism, 1945–1960* (Urbana: University of Illinois Press, 1994), 15.
13. Kannenberg, "The Product of GE's Progress," 190–191.
14. Jeremy Brecher, *Strike!* (Cambridge, Mass.: South End, 1997), 245–246. On General Motors strike: Nelson Lichtenstein, *Walter Reuther: The Most Dangerous Man in Detroit* (New York: Basic Books, 1995), 220–248. Also see "Employees of Four Detroit Dairies Strike," *New York Times*, Feb. 21, 1946, 10; "Bus Drivers Strike in Seattle Already Lacking Papers, Phones," *New York Times*, Jan. 12, 1946, 1; "Flint Closes Schools," *New York Times*, Jan. 18, 1946.
15. Matles and Higgins, *Them and Us*, 140–141; Schatz, "The End of Corporate Liberalism," 194, 141.
16. A. H. Raskin, "4,000 Protest at Electrical Plant," *New York Times*, Feb. 21, 1946, 1. The Bloomfield protest was at a Westinghouse plant.
17. H. Walton Clarke, "Massed Philadelphia Pickets Routed by 1,000 Club-Swinging Policemen," *New York Times*, Feb 28, 1946, 1; H. Walton Clarke, "Police Battle 3,500 Pickets in a New Philadelphia Riot," *New York Times*, Mar. 1, 1946, 1.
18. On hot lunches: Matles and Higgins, *Them and Us*, 144. On college students: "Getting First-Hand Strike Information," *New York Times*, Jan. 20, 1946, 4. Students from Mount Holyoke joined a Westinghouse picket line, carrying signs reading "Salary Workers Need $2 a Day Too!" On government support: Matles and Higgins, *Them and Us*, 144. On Bloomfield strike: Lucy Greenbaum, "Townsfolk in Bloomfield Support Strike of Its Electrical Workers," *New York Times*, Jan. 16, 1946, 13. On strikers' children: "Children Form Picket Line," *New York Times*, Feb. 23, 1946, 10.
19. U.S. Congress, Senate, *Testimony before Senate Committee on Education and Labor, Hearings on S. 1661, A Bill to Provide for the Appointment of Fact-Finding Boards to Investigate Labor Disputes*, 79th Cong., 1st and 2nd sess., Part I, 1945–1946, 647, 645, also quoted in Schatz, "The End of Corporate Liberalism," 149; Herbert Northrup, *Boulwarism* (Ann Arbor: University of Michigan, 1964), 21.
20. Schatz, *The Electrical Workers*, 145.
21. Directors' Meeting Notes, Dec. 17, 1954, Box 8, Folder 170, Boulware Papers.
22. On appearance and accent: Thomas W. Evans, *The Education of Ronald Reagan: The General Electric Years and the Untold Story of his Conversion to Conservatism* (New York: Columbia, 2006), 41. On college years and early career: Biographical note with manuscript collection, Van Pelt Library, University of Pennsylvania. On personality: Box 41, Folder 1175, MS Collection 52, Boulware Papers, contains a remarkable unpublished memoir by a Boulware subordinate in which he recalls Boulware's work habits and character. The memoir is not completely reliable, however, in part because the author confesses to being an alcoholic and says that he was frequently quite drunk while he was working under Boulware. On cruise: Biographical note with manuscript collection, Van Pelt Library, University of Pennsylvania.
23. On selling washing machines: "Carey *vs.* Boulware," *Fortune*, Oct. 1952.
24. "Proposed Program of Industrial and Community Relations, 8/1/45," Box 8, Folder 154, Boulware Papers (in a note about the memorandum, Charles Wilson wrote, "A

splendid contribution, I think. Give it wide distribution"); "Questions," n.d. [ca. 1956], Box 9, Folder 181, ibid.; Division Managers Meeting memo, Nov. 17, 1954, Box 8, Folder 170, ibid.

25. Stephen K. Galpin, "Boulwarism: C.I.O. Cries Foul as 'Tough But Fair' Wage Policy Spreads," *Wall Street Journal*, Nov. 3, 1954, 1.
26. Lemuel Boulware to Greg Copeland, Nov. 23, 1960, Box 34, Folder 879, Boulware Papers.
27. Supervisors' Guide to GE Job Information, Accession 5583/1, Box 57, Kheel; *G.E. Schenectady News*, Jan. 14, 1955, State University of New York at Albany Library.
28. Boulware, *The Truth About Boulwarism*, 30–38; Kannenberg, "The Product of GE's Progress," 215; "Highlights of the General Electric Economic Education Program," Accession 5583/4, Box 52, Kheel.
29. "The Lockland Plan: A Case History of a Planned Community Advertising Program" and "The General Electric Louisville Plan: A Case History of GE's Entry into Louisville, Kentucky," Accession 5583/1, Box 57, Kheel (the Louisville Plan won a Certificate of Public Relations Achievement from the American Public Relations Association in 1952); Peter Brimelow, "A Look Back at Boulwarism," *Forbes*, May 29, 1989. Also see "Program for Clergy," Accession 5583/4, Box 53, Kheel.
30. Board of Directors Meeting, 12/14/56, Box 9, Folder 180, Boulware Papers; Lemuel Boulware, "Salvation is Not Free," Accession 5583/1, Box 60, Kheel; Lemuel Boulware, "How Can the Businessman Contribute to Better Government?" address before the National Canners Association, Chicago, Dec. 21, 1959, Box 80, Boulware Papers; Lemuel Boulware, "The Next Round of Wage Increases and What G.E. Is Doing About It Now," Box 8, Folder 165, ibid.; Boulware, "Salvation is Not Free."
31. *Oral History Project: Schenectady General Electric in the Twentieth Century*, Gerald Zahavi interview with A. C. Stevens, IUE/UE Local 301 Collection, Series 3, Box 3, 45, M. E. Grenander Department of Special Collections and Archives, State University of New York at Albany Library; Kannenberg, "The Product of GE's Progress," 199–203. Also see "The Overhaul of General Electric," *Fortune*, Dec. 1955, and Evans, *The Education of Ronald Reagan*, 70–73.
32. John McCarty to Lemuel Boulware, Mar. 29, 1957, Box 2, Correspondence D-G, Steele Papers, Oregon; Peter Steele to Thurston Steele, Apr. 1, 1957, ibid.
33. Memo, Sept. 12, 1956, Box 9, Folder 180, Boulware Papers; *G.E. Schenectady News*, July 15, 1960, M. E. Grenander Department of Special Collections and Archives, State University of New York at Albany Library; Memo, "National Negotiations News," July 1, 1960, Box 10, Folder 196, Boulware Papers; *G.E. Schenectady News*, Sept. 16, 1960, M. E. Grenander Department of Special Collections and Archives, State University of New York at Albany Library.
34. Edward Rumely to Lemuel Boulware, Sept. 12, 1957, Box 49, Folder 1479, Boulware Papers.
35. "Management's No. 1 Worry," *Business Week*, Mar. 23, 1957; Ludwig von Mises, *Human Action* (New Haven, Conn.: Yale University Press, 1949), 779; Friedrich von Hayek, *The Constitution of Liberty* (Chicago: University of Chicago Press, 1960), 275; Jack Barbash, "Union Response to the 'Hard Line,'" *Industrial Relations*, Vol. 1, No. 1, October 1961, 25–38, among other articles in the same issue.
36. Gross, *Broken Promise*, 92–122. Also see Janice A. Klein and E. David Wanger, "The

Legal Setting for the Emergence of the Union Avoidance Strategy," in *Challenges and Choices Facing American Labor*, ed. Thomas A. Kochan (Cambridge, Mass.: MIT Press, 1985), 75–89.

37. Communications Manual for Union Representation Elections, Mar. 11, 1957, "Sample Letter #2," Accession 1412, Series 7, Box 128, "General: January–March 1957," NAM Papers, Hagley; "Example of Company Letter Sent to Employees Before a Union Election," memo, May 29, 1961, Accession 1412, Series 7, Box 130, "Folder: General 1961–1962," ibid.
38. Michael Goldfield, *The Decline of Organized Labor in the United States* (Chicago: University of Chicago Press, 1987), 196; Gross, *Broken Promise*, 137.
39. "Politics and the Corporation," *Fortune*, Oct. 1958, 103; "Let's Give Two Cheers," *Fortune*, Sept. 1958, 102.
40. J. J. Wuerthner, *The Businessman's Guide to Practical Politics* (Chicago: Regnery, 1959), 14; Lester Tanzer, "Business and Elections," *Wall Street Journal*, Oct. 14, 1958, 1; David Galligan, *Politics and the Businessman* (New York: Pitman, 1964), 32–33; Lemuel Boulware, "Politics . . . The Businessman's Biggest Job in 1958," May 21, 1958, speech delivered to Annual Meeting of Phoenix Chamber of Commerce, Accession 5583, Box 60, Kheel.
41. See Schatz, *The Electrical Workers*, and Matles and Higgins, *Them and Us*, for discussions of anticommunism in the electrical workers' unions. On GE: Salvatore Joseph Bella, "Boulwarism and Collective Bargaining at General Electric: A Study in Union-Management Relations," Ph.D. diss., Cornell University, 1962, 249–340.
42. Victor Riesel, "Inside Labor," *South Bend Tribune*, Apr. 18, 1960, cited in Bella, "Boulwarism and Collective Bargaining," 425–426; "Draft of Telegram Subject to Legal and Policy Check," Box 10, Folder 204, Boulware Papers.
43. 10/10/60, Box 10, Folder 204, Boulware Papers. It is unclear whether this pamphlet was produced.
44. "Beyond General Electric," Oct. 14, 1960, Box 10, Folder 205, Boulware Papers; Kannenberg, "The Product of GE's Progress," 270. One employee, Mary Kuykendall, a novice reporter on the staff of the *Schenectady Works News*, posed as the "Bowler's Wife," claiming on radio shows to be a mother whose husband had vanished into the bowling alleys as soon as the strike began.
45. A. H. Raskin, "GE's Labor Formula: Its Technique in Strike May Foster Stiffening in Management's Approach," *New York Times*, Oct. 25, 1960, 31; "Tougher Bargaining: Profits Squeeze Leads Many Firms to Stiffen Stand on Wage Boosts; GE's Success Spurs Trend," *Wall Street Journal*, Nov. 9, 1960, 1; Maxwell Goodwin to Lemuel Boulware, Oct. 25, 1960, Box 37, Folder 1044, Boulware Papers.
46. On price-fixing scandal: Harlan Byrne, "Antitrust Assault," *Wall Street Journal*, Oct. 21, 1960, 1; "Four Executives Start Jail Term," *New York Times*, Feb. 14, 1961, 40; Austin Wehrwein, "G.E. Plans Drive to Avert Rigging," *New York Times*, Mar. 2, 1961, 33; J. Anthony Lukas, "G.E. Agrees to Pay $7,470,000 to U.S. for Price Fixing," *New York Times*, July 28, 1962, 1. On Cordiner: "To All GE Managers and Supervisors," Feb. 25, 1960, Box 10, Folder 201, Boulware Papers (the speech may have been written by Boulware; it is in his papers and in his style); Felix Belair, Jr., "Hearing Is Told Cordiner Knew of G.E. Price Fixing," *New York Times*, Apr. 26, 1961, 1. On NLRB suit: Gross, *Broken Promise*, 187–189. GE immediately appealed, but the Second Court of Appeals upheld the NLRB's decision in 1969.

47. Ronald Reagan, *An American Life* (New York: Simon and Schuster, 1990), 127–128; Evans, *The Education of Ronald Reagan*, 13.
48. Lou Cannon, *Reagan* (New York: Putnam, 1982), 92–94. Also see Ronald Reagan with Richard G. Hubler, *Where's the Rest of Me? The Ronald Reagan Story* (New York: Duell, Sloan & Pierce, 1965).
49. Evans, *The Education of Ronald Reagan*, 62, 59; Wills, *Reagan's America*, 332.
50. *Oral History of Earl Dunckel: Ronald Reagan and the General Electric Theater, 1954–55*, interviewed by Gabrielle Morris, 1982, pp. 11, 10, Bancroft Library, University of California at Berkeley.
51. Ibid., 15; Ronald Reagan to William Clotworthy, June 17, 1980, Clotworthy Papers, RRPL. Reagan once told an interviewer about talking to Cordiner after giving a speech in which he'd criticized the TVA, with which GE had major contracts. Cordiner didn't ask him to withdraw any comments about the government agency, even though TVA officials were upset. Reagan was very impressed by the independence the company afforded him in this instance. But while it does highlight the contradictions within GE's position—on the one hand, opposed to government; on the other, engaging in contracts with the state—it seems likely that Cordiner shared many of Reagan's critiques. The company may still have had its limits: Cannon also suggests that Reagan became too conservative for GE after Kennedy was elected, prompting Reagan to leave the company in 1962. See Cannon, *Reagan*, 95.
52. On the Elks, Rotary, and Chamber of Commerce: *Oral History of Earl Dunckel*, 12. On the California Fertilizer Association: Edmund Morris, *Dutch: A Memoir of Ronald Reagan* (New York: Modern Library, 1999), 302–310. On NAM: Lou Cannon, *Reagan*, 96. Evans suggests that by the late 1950s Boulware pulled Reagan off the plant tour and encouraged him to focus his efforts more closely on speaking to civic and employers' groups. For Reagan on social legislation: "Losing Freedom by Installments," speech given to the Oregon-Columbia Chapter of the National Electrical Contractors Association, Sept. 25, 1961. The organization reprinted the speech with a memo at the front: "We firmly believe that the Electrical Contractor members of our Association are 'Foot Soldiers' in the battle to preserve the free enterprise system in our country." I am grateful to Victor McFarland for sharing with me his copy of this speech. For Reagan on big government: "Encroaching Control," speech delivered at the Annual Meeting of the Phoenix Chamber of Commerce, Mar. 1961, Clotworthy Papers, RRPL.
53. *Oral History of Jacquelin Hume: Basic Economics and the Body Politic: Views of a Northern California Reagan Loyalist*, interview by Gabrielle Morris, 1982, pp. 44–45, Bancroft Library, University of California at Berkeley.

6. Suburban Cowboy

1. J. William Middendorf II to Leonard Read, Aug. 5, 1964, Box 20, Folder 1, Hayek Papers, Hoover.
2. J. William Middendorf II, *A Glorious Disaster: Barry Goldwater's Presidential Campaign and the Origins of the Conservative Movement* (New York: Basic Books, 2006), 4; F. Clifton White, *Politics as a Noble Calling: The Memoirs of F. Clifton White* (Ottawa, Ill.: Jameson, 1994), 74, 112.

3. Middendorf, *A Glorious Disaster,* 17; J. William Middendorf II to Leonard Read, Aug. 5, 1964, Box 20, Folder 1, Hayek Papers, Hoover.
4. Barry Goldwater to Thomas Edison, date unclear but ca. 1923, personal, Alpha Files E, Goldwater Papers. On biography: Robert Alan Goldberg, *Barry Goldwater* (New Haven, Conn.: Yale University Press, 1995), chaps. 1–3, and Rick Perlstein, *Before the Storm: Barry Goldwater and the Unmaking of the American Consensus* (New York: Hill & Wang, 2001,) 17–22; Stewart Alsop, "Can Goldwater Win in 64?" *Saturday Evening Post,* Aug. 24–31, 1963.
5. Barry Goldwater to John Evans, June 27, 1938, personal, Writings, Editorials and Radio Talks, 1939–1949, Goldwater Papers.
6. Goldberg, *Barry Goldwater,* 51–52; Elizabeth Tandy Shermer, "Origins of the Conservative Ascendancy: Barry Goldwater's Early Senate Career and the Delegitimization of Organized Labor," *Journal of American History* (Dec. 2008): 10, copy in possession of the author.
7. Goldberg, *Barry Goldwater,* 49, 48.
8. Ibid, 50; Barry Goldwater to Wes Knorpp at Arizona Republic, May 11, 1939, with editorial, personal, Writings, Editorials and Radio Talks, 1939–1949, Goldwater Papers.
9. Barry Goldwater, "Speech to the Convention of National Tank Truck Carriers," May 5, 1959, Media, 86th Congress, Speeches, Statements, Remarks—What Business Can Do For Government, Goldwater Papers; Personal, Alpha Files, Journals (Thoughts on Senate), ibid.
10. Shermer, "Origins of the Conservative Ascendancy," 18, 40–43; Statement of Barry Goldwater, "The Dime Store New Deal," May 5, 1960, Media, 86th Congress, Speeches, Statements, Remarks—The Dime Store New Deal, Goldwater Papers.
11. Goldberg, *Barry Goldwater,* 71–75, 102; on copper: Barry Goldwater to Dwight D. Eisenhower, Sept. 20 1957, Personal Alpha Files Box E, Eisenhower File, Goldwater Archives.
12. Walter Uphoff, *Kohler on Strike: Thirty Years of Conflict* (Boston: Beacon, 1966), 1–101.
13. Kevin Boyle, *The UAW and the Heyday of American Liberalism* (New York: Cornell University Press, 1995), 64–65; "What Does Reuther Want?" *Saturday Evening Post,* Aug. 14, 1948, 15; Frederick Crawford to Charles Sligh, Sept. 11, 1951, Box 11, Folder Correspondence 9/1–9/18 1951, Sligh Papers.
14. L. L. Smith to executives of Industrial Relations Group, Dec. 6, 1955, Series 5, Box 62 A, NAM Papers, Hagley; Uphoff, *Kohler on Strike,* 162. For Kohler's voice, see Joseph A. Loftus, "Kohler, at Inquiry, Defends Actions in 4-Year Dispute," *New York Times,* Mar. 27, 1958, 1; for his physical appearance, see *Milwaukee Journal,* June 1954, NLRB Records, RG 25, Box 5, Folder 2, NARA.
15. Everett Tate to UAW (Aircraft Staff), June 27, 1957, Box 8, Folder 18, Local 833, UAW; Robert F. Kennedy, *The Enemy Within* (New York: Popular Library, 1960), 262–263.
16. Uphoff, *Thirty Years of Conflict,* 145–146; "For These We Fight," pamphlet on Kohler by the UAW, RG 25, Box 43, NLRB Records, NARA (for photo of strikers in gas masks); "Bathtub Baron," *Ammunition,* June 1954, ibid.; Daily Strike Report, June 21, 1954 (boycott of scab sausage), and Daily Strike Report, June 25, 1954 (cigarettes),

Folder 6, Box 9, Region 10, UAW; "From the Picket Line," *The Kohlerian*, Aug. 12, 1954, 5 (bartender), Folder 22, Box 8, ibid.

17. "Strikebreakers Are Traitors," *The Kohlerian*, Aug. 12, 1954, 5, Folder 22, Box 8, Region 10, UAW; "I Had A Club Myself," Aug. 29, 1955, Folder 4, Box 5, Local 833, UAW; "The Strike That May Never End," *Look*, Nov. 29, 1955, Folder 22, Box 8, Region 10, UAW.
18. Uphoff, *Kohler on Strike*, 183–185, 188; "Kohler Worker Beaten by CIO Strikers Dies; Family Blames Vicious Attack for Death," *Chicago Tribune*, Oct. 28, 1955, 9, Folder 13, Box 8, Local 833, UAW. In this case the assailant, John Guanaca, returned to Michigan. The Michigan governor refused to extradite him to Wisconsin for trial in the Sheboygan area on the grounds that he would not be able to receive a fair trial, which outraged Kohler Company representatives, who saw in this further evidence of the political power of the UAW. Eventually Guanaca returned to Wisconsin for trial, was found guilty of assault, and was sentenced to three years in prison (of which he served eighteen months). David Anderson, "The Battle for Main Street, United States of America: Welfare Capitalism, Boosterism and Labor Militancy in the Industrial Heartland, 1895–1963," Ph.D. diss., University of North Carolina at Chapel Hill, 2002, contains an excellent discussion of the prevalence and meaning of violence, vandalism, and sabotage in strikes in the 1950s between businessmen resistant to the terms of the New Deal order and industrial unions like the UAW (he focuses on the Perfect Circle strike in Indiana, contemporaneous with the Kohler strike).
19. Ray Vicker, "Kohler Boycott," *Wall Street Journal*, Aug. 9, 1956, 1; "Kohler Goods Hauled Away," *Milwaukee Journal*, Aug. 10, 1956, "Citizens' Committee" Folder, Box 14, Region 10, UAW.
20. "Herbert V. Kohler Speaks," speech at Associated Industries of Alabama, Nov. 4, 1955, Folder 7, Box 9, Local 833, UAW; Peter Steele to William Collins, Apr. 9, 1957, Box 2, Steele Papers, Oregon. On Kohler and the *National Review*: William A. Rusher to Sterling Morton, Aug. 19, 1957, Box 51, Morton Papers, CHS. On Kohler and FEE: B. E. Hutchinson to James Ingebretsen, Jan. 23, 1956, Folder 8, Box 109, Ingebretsen Papers, Oregon. On right-to-work speeches: Summary of Talks Made at Atlanta Chamber of Commerce Luncheon Meeting. Lucius Chase speech, July 14, 1957, Folder 4, Box 31, Local 833, UAW.
21. "The Right to Work," Herbert Kohler to Spartanburg Chamber of Commerce, Mar. 21, 1957, Folder 12, Box 9, Local 833, UAW.
22. "The 'Labor Movement' in Action at Kohler," Oct. 20, 1957, Box 88, Folder 5, Manion Papers, CHS; "The Herbert V. Kohler Talk and Mutual Broadcasting System, Inc.," memo, ibid.; L. F. Reardon, "Dear Mr. American Businessman," Nov. 4, 1957, Folder 8, Box 8, Region 10, UAW.
23. W. A. Moncrief to Barry Goldwater, June 24, 1957, Correspondence Folder, Harry Rosenzweig 1, Box Personal, Senate Campaigns, Goldwater Papers; "Reuther Dares Sen. Goldwater," *Washington Post*, Mar. 9, 1958, A2.
24. Senate Select Committee on Improper Activities in the Labor or Management Field, *Hearings Before the Senate Select Committee on Improper Activities in the Labor or Management Field*, 85th Congress, 2nd sess., 1958, 10162–10163, pt. 25; "Smash Hit for the Reuther Troupe," *National Review*, Apr. 12, 1958.

25. R. W. Marvin to Barry Goldwater, Aug. 5, 1958, Correspondence Folder, Harry Rosenzweig 1, Box Personal, Senate Campaigns, Goldwater Papers.
26. Perlstein, *Before the Storm*, 3–16, 43–51.
27. Barry Goldwater to Stephen Shadegg, Sept. 7, 1959, Writings 1938–1965—Conscience of a Conservative—Victor Publishing Company Folder 2, Goldwater Papers; Barry Goldwater to L. Brent Bozell, Aug. 12, 1959, ibid.; Brent Bozell to Clarence Manion, Aug. 17, 1959, Box 68, Folder 4, Manion Papers, CHS; Clarence Manion to Roger Milliken, June 18, 1959, Box 69, Folder 5, ibid.; Minutes Taken at Goldwater Meeting, Jan. 23, 1960, Box 70, Folder 4, ibid.
28. Clarence Manion to Barry Goldwater, July 21, 1959, Writings 1938–1965—Conscience of a Conservative—Victor Publishing Company Folder 1, Goldwater Papers; Clarence Manion to Roger Milliken, June 18, 1959, Box 69, Folder 4, Manion Papers, CHS.
29. Clarence Manion to Barry Goldwater, Mar. 9, 1960, Writings 1938–1965—Conscience of a Conservative—Victor Publishing Company Folder 2, Goldwater Papers; Clarence Manion to Andrew Jergens, Apr. 1, 1960, Box 68, Folder 5, Manion Papers, CHS; Clarence Manion to Adolphe Menjou, Apr. 6, 1960, Folder 4, Box 68, ibid.
30. Barry Goldwater, *The Conscience of a Conservative* (New York: Hillman House, 1960), 1–2, 10–12, 75, 121, 37–38, 122, 93; for Bozell and antimaterialism, see Thomas Sugrue, "In Your Guts You Know He's Nuts," *London Review of Books*, Jan. 3, 2008.
31. John Chamberlain, "The Humane Base of Conservatism," *Wall Street Journal*, June 2, 1960, 10 (Chamberlain was a member of the Mont Pelerin Society). Also see Perlstein, *Before the Storm*, 64–67, for examples of similar reviews and press coverage for the book.
32. On success of *Conscience*: Perlstein, *Before the Storm*, 62. On college campuses: John Chamberlain, "Campus Radicals: Increasingly, They Are Right Wing, Drawn to Goldwater," *Wall Street Journal*, Nov. 3, 1960, 14. On companies buying books: Robert Love to Clarence Manion, Mar. 21, 1960, Folder 4, Box 68, Manion Papers, CHS; Clarence Manion to Roger Milliken, May 6, 1960, Folder 6, Box 68, ibid.
33. Stephen Shadegg to Mrs. Robert Burkham, Aug. 19, 1960, Box 3H504, Shadegg Papers. For the Goldwater speech at the convention, see Perlstein, *Before the Storm*, 95.
34. F. Clifton White, *Suite 3505: The Story of the Draft Goldwater Movement* (New Rochelle, N.Y.: Arlington House, 1967), 30–42; also see "The Goldwater Presidential Nomination: The Reminiscences of F. Clifton White," Oral History Research Office, Columbia University, 1965, 3, 11, Goldwater Papers.
35. White, *Suite 3505*, 44–45; Barry Goldwater form letter, June 6, 1961, Personal, Senate Campaigns—Correspondence Folder, Harry Rosenzweig 4, Goldwater Papers; Reception List, June 21, 1962, Box 3, 1964 Presidential Campaign, Finance Committee Lists 1960–1962, ibid.; Edward M. Keyes to Stephen Shadegg, June 13, 1961, Personal, Stephen Shadegg 1961, ibid.; William Middendorf to Barry Goldwater, Apr. 5, 1963, Goldwater Correspondence, Box 18, White Papers. On executive survey: See letters between Michael Malone (on behalf of Robert J. Kleberg, Jr.) and Donald C. Power of General Telephone and Electronics Corporation, H. W. Balgooyan of American & Foreign Power Company Inc., National Industrial Conference Board, Standard Oil Company of California, John M. Fox of United Fruit Company, and others from the spring of 1963. Not all the letters were positive, of course, and Malone also got

responses from businessmen who were backing Nelson Rockefeller or Kennedy. Also see Robert J. Kleberg, Jr., to Barry Goldwater, May 23, 1963. All in Box 4, Kitchel Papers, Hoover.

36. Peter Clayton Memo, June 25, 1963, Box 8, White Papers. Also see Perlstein, *Before the Storm*, 214, for a description of the memo and its impact on the Republican campaign.
37. Stewart Alsop, "Can Goldwater Win in '64?" *Saturday Evening Post*, Aug. 24–31, 1963; Goldwater, *The Conscience of a Conservative*, 35; Joseph Lowndes, *From the New Deal to the New Right: Race and the Origins of Modern Conservatism* (New Haven, Conn.: Yale University Press, 2008), 71.
38. 8/26/63 Survey, Opinion Research Corporation Folder, Box 9, White Papers; Opinion Research Corporation to F. Clifton White, Oct. 15, 1963, ibid.
39. Stewart Alsop, "Can Goldwater Win in 64?" *Saturday Evening Post*, Aug. 24–31, 1963; J. William Middendorf to Gerrish Milliken, Oct. 15, 1963. Box 5, White Papers; Cabell Phillips, "Tour Enhances Goldwater's Status as '64 Contender," *New York Times*, Sept. 18, 1963, 21; Richard Bergholz, "Goldwater Hits Policies of Kennedy," *Los Angeles Times*, Sept. 17, 1963, 1. Also see Perlstein, *Before the Storm*, 231.
40. Finance Highlights Report 20, Jan. 10, 1964, Box 5, Finance, White Papers; also see Perlstein, *Before the Storm*, 252–255, 257.
41. On contributors: List of Contributors, $500 and up, Jan. 19, 1964, Box 7, White Papers; Businessmen for Goldwater, Acceptances, Sept. 10, 1964, ibid.; Goldwater for President Finance Committee, Apr. 4, 1964, Box 12, ibid,; Memo on finance chair backgrounds, Jan. 24, 1964, Box 7, ibid.; press release, "Gainey Named Finance Chairman of Goldwater Campaign Committee," Jan. 19, 1964; Horace Stoneham to Harry Rosenzweig, June 3, 1964, 1964 Campaign, Harry Rosenzweig File, Goldwater Papers; Bruce Gimbel to Harry Rosenzweig, June 4, 1964, ibid. On Boulware's contribution: Boulware-Goldwater Correspondence, Box 35, Folder 880, Boulware Papers. On Goldwater-Boulware relationship: Barry Goldwater to Lemuel Boulware, Apr. 27, 1978, Box 37, Folder 1040, Goldwater Papers.
42. Melvin Birks to Lester Ruffner, Oct. 28, 1964, 1964 Campaign, Ruffner File, Goldwater Papers; George Melloan, "Playing Politics," *Wall Street Journal*, Feb 17, 1964.
43. Milton Friedman, *Capitalism and Freedom* (Chicago: University of Chicago Press, 1962), 20, 17, 110; Milton Friedman, "The Goldwater View of Economics," *New York Times Magazine*, Oct. 11, 1964; Perlstein, *Before the Storm*, 255–256, 417–418, 420–421, 423; Karl Hess, *In a Cause That Will Triumph: The Goldwater Campaign and the Future of Conservatism* (Garden City, N.Y.: Doubleday, 1967), 28–30.
44. On the convention: Goldberg, *Barry Goldwater*, 202–204. On bumper stickers: 1964 campaign, Box 9, Goldwater Papers. On the Goldwaters: Freedom Special, Mar. 16, 1964, Weekly Reports, March–October 1964, ibid. On Rebel: Freedom Special, May 25, 1964, ibid. On the jewelry: "Poverty Area Inspires Unique Goldwater Jewelry," *Washington Wire*, Sept. 1, 1964, 1964 campaign, Box 5, ibid. On campaign subculture: Rick Perlstein, "Mass Martyrs: What Is Conservative Culture?" *New Republic*, July 3, 2006.
45. Perlstein, *Before the Storm*, 383–387; Goldberg, *Barry Goldwater*, 207.
46. Goldberg, *Barry Goldwater*, 204; Perlstein, *Before the Storm*, 392–393.

47. "The Unconscious of a Conservative: A Special Issue on the Mind of Barry Goldwater," *Fact* (Sept.–Oct. 1964), 60, 46, 41, 24.
48. Richard Hofstadter, "Goldwater and Pseudo-Conservative Politics," in *The Paranoid Style in American Politics and Other Essays* (Cambridge, Mass.: Harvard University Press, 1965), 141.
49. Dr. Charles E. Walker, "A Tax Cut This Winter?" Speech to the Annual Meeting of the Texas Mid-Continent Oil & Gas Association, Dallas, Texas, Oct. 9, 1962, quoted in *Vital Speeches of the Day* 29, no. 4 (Dec. 1, 1962): 104; Kim McQuaid, *Big Business and Presidential Power* (New York: William Morris, 1982), 217; Hobart Rowen, *The Free Enterprisers: Kennedy, Johnson and the Business Establishment* (New York: Putnam, 1964), 275.
50. McQuaid, *Big Business and Presidential Power,* 223–227; Bert C. Goss, "Paradox in Government-Industry Relations: Peace at Top—Strife at Bottom," speech delivered June 5, 1964, quoted in *Vital Speeches of the Day* 30, no. 18 (July 1, 1964): 555.
51. On President's Club: Herbert Alexander, *Financing the 1964 Election* (Princeton, N.J.: Citizens Research Foundation), 9. On Ford: Edwin Weisl to Walter Jenkins, Aug. 7, 1964, Lyndon Baines Johnson White House Central Files, EX:PL, Box 26, LBJ Papers; Jack Valenti to Walter Jenkins, July 15, 1964, ibid. On CEO support: McQuaid, *Big Business and Presidential Power*, 231. On Business Council: Alexander, *Financing the 1964 Election*, 94. It should be noted that in 1964 it was not legal for corporations to give directly to presidential campaigns through PACs. Donations came from individual directors, CEOs, presidents, or other executives. (The Democrats, however, did not hold the loyalties of big business for too long; in 1968, Nixon and the Republicans regained the support of the Business Council executives by a margin of three to one. See Herbert E. Alexander and Harold B. Meyers, "A Financial Landslide for the G.O.P." *Fortune*, Mar. 1970.)
52. Memo from Walter Heller, "Sweet Notes from the Midwest," Dec. 30, 1964, Lyndon Baines Johnson White House Central Files, EX:PL, Box 27, LBJ Papers. Also see David Bazelon, *Power in America: The Politics of the New Class* (New York: New American Library, 1967), 96–102.
53. "Report 1964," Box 11, White Papers.
54. Peter Byrnes to Rita Bree, Sept. 23, 1964, ibid.; John Crowe to campaign, Sept. 19, 1964, Box 3, ibid.
55. Unsigned memo, n.d., Box 4, ibid. Also see Samuel G. Freedman, "The First Days of the Loaded Political Image," *New York Times*, Sept. 19, 1996, H30.
56. Perlstein, *Before the Storm*, 482–483.
57. *Choice,* by the Citizens Committee for Goldwater and Miller, 1964, Arizona Historical Foundation; *The Reporter*, Nov. 5, 1964, Box 3H514, Shadegg Papers; Perlstein, *Before the Storm*, 494–495.
58. Perlstein, *Before the Storm,* 494–496; White, *Suite 3505*, 414–415.
59. "Goldwater-Miller Freedom Special," Oct. 17, 1964, Goldwater for President—Campaign 1964—Freedom Special weekly reports, Goldwater Papers.
60. Pam Rymer to Denison Kitchel, Dean Burch, John Grenier, Wayne Hood, and Sam Claiborne, Research memo, "Goldwater Tour Through the South," Sept. 23, 1962, 1964 Campaign, Goldwater for President 1964 Committee, September–December 1964, ibid.

61. Perlstein, *Before the Storm*, 499–504.
62. Ronald Reagan, "A Time for Choosing," in Kurt Ritter and David Henry, *Ronald Reagan: The Great Communicator* (Westport, Conn.: Greenwood, 1992), 135, 142, 139, 143.
63. Matthew Dallek, *The Right Moment: Ronald Reagan's First Victory and the Decisive Turning Point in American Politics* (New York: Free Press, 2000), 64–69, 71–79; Carl Greenberg, "Ronald Reagan's Kitchen Cabinet," *Los Angeles Times*, Apr. 23, 1967.
64. James Reston, "What Goldwater Lost," *New York Times*, Nov. 4, 1964, 23; "Wax Goldwater Being Put on Ice," *Washington Post*, Nov. 9, 1964, A6.

7. The Attack on the Free Enterprise System

1. Barry Goldwater to Denison Kitchel, Nov. 12, 1968, Alpha Files K, Goldwater Papers.
2. Quoted in David Vogel, *Fluctuating Fortunes: The Political Power of Business in America* (New York: Basic Books, 1989), 57.
3. Gene Smith, "Honeywell Meeting Adjourns After Protest," *New York Times*, Apr. 29, 1970, 71; "It's Face to Face with Dissidents," *Business Week*, May 2, 1970; Vogel, *Fluctuating Fortunes*, 56. Also see "The American Corporation Under Fire," *Newsweek*, May 24, 1971.
4. "Riots at UC Santa Barbara," *Los Angeles Times*, Mar. 1, 1970, F5; "A Life of Love and Freedom," *Fortune*, Apr. 1970, 65; Robert E. Wood, "B of A Acts to Show Students 'The Establishment' Also Cares," *Los Angeles Times*, May 12, 1970, C7; Winthrop Griffith, "The Isla Vista War—Campus Violence in a Class by Itself," *New York Times Magazine*, Aug. 30, 1970, 10; Vogel, *Fluctuating Fortunes*, 57. Also see "Bank of America Hit for 35th Time," *Washington Post*, May 2, 1971, 3. A variety of different organizations took responsibility for the explosions, most of which did not hurt people but only damaged property. On Capitol bombing: John W. Finney, "Bomb in Capitol Does Wide Damage," *New York Times*, Mar. 2, 1971, 1. On demonstrations: James M. Naughton, "700,000 Rally in Capital to End War," *New York Times*, Apr. 25, 1971, 1.
5. Charles Reich, *The Greening of America* (New York: Crown, 1970), 2, 1; Ralph Nader, *Unsafe at Any Speed: The Designed-In Dangers of the American Automobile* (New York: Grossman, 1965), vii; "The American Corporation Under Fire," *Newsweek*. Also see Thomas Byrne Edsall, *The New Politics of Inequality* (New York: W. W. Norton, 1984), 113; Vogel, *Fluctuating Fortunes*; Robert D. Hershey, Jr., "Chase Assailed on World Issues," *New York Times*, Apr. 3, 1970, 51.
6. Bethany Moreton, "Make Payroll, Not War: Business Culture as Youth Culture," in Bruce Schulman and Julian Zelizer, eds., *Rightward Bound: Making America Conservative in the 1970s* (Cambridge, Mass.: Harvard University Press, 2008), 58–59; for the point about students as future members of the managerial elite, 56.
7. Jefferson Cowie, "'Vigorously Right, Left and Center': The Crosscurrents of Working-Class America in the 1970s," in Beth Bailey and David Farber, eds., *America in the Seventies* (Lawrence: University of Kansas Press, 2004), 78; Samuel Rosenberg, *American Economic Development Since 1945* (New York: Macmillan, 2003), 131; Aaron Brenner, "Rank and File Rebellion, 1966–1975," Ph.D. diss., Columbia University, 1996, 41; "Postal Anarchy," *New York Times*, Mar. 19, 1970, 46. Brenner also discusses the increased prevalence of workplace and shop-floor issues in strikes in this period; see 53.

8. On antibusiness sentiment: "America's Growing Antibusiness Mood," *Business Week*, June 17, 1972. On public confidence: Edsall, *The New Politics of Inequality*, 113. On activist businessmen: Marilyn Bender, "Executives' Group Revives, Taking Aim at Congress: Businessmen Against the War," *New York Times*, Jan. 3, 1971, F2; also see John Herbers, "Businessmen Set Antiwar Parley," *New York Times*, Sept. 19, 1967, 11; Gladwin Hill, "1,600 Executives Form Group for a National Antiwar Drive," *New York Times*, Feb. 27, 1968, 9; Robert A. Wright, "Businessmen's Commitment Found Lacking," *New York Times*, May 30, 1970, 30. For Rockefeller quote: "The American Corporation Under Fire," *Newsweek*, May 24, 1971.
9. On meat prices: Deirdre Carmody, "Consumers Scoff at Ceiling and Step Up Boycott Plans," *New York Times*, Mar. 31, 1973, 17; Deirdre Carmody, "Behind the Metropolitan Boycott, a Militant Union," *New York Times*, Apr. 6, 1973, 55; Deirdre Carmody, "Boycott of Meat Ends with a Call for New Protests," *New York Times*, Apr. 8, 1973, 1; "Increase Expected in Deer-Poaching," *New York Times*, Nov. 25, 1973, 104. On truckers' strike: Ron Berler, "Truck Stop," *Chicago Tribune*, Mar. 10, 1974, 48. On fuel crisis: "Empty Tanks," *Wall Street Journal*, Feb. 8, 1974, 1. Meg Jacobs, "Highway Guerillas: The 1970s and the Conservative Turn in American Politics," unpublished essay in possession of the author, is a superb essay treating the independent truckers' strikes and their impact on American politics.
10. Martin Feldstein, ed., *The American Economy in Transition* (Chicago: University of Chicago Press, 1980), 2; Gilbert Burck, "Union Power and the New Inflation," *Fortune*, Feb. 1971; "The U.S. Can't Afford What Labor Wants," *Business Week*, Apr. 11, 1970; Gilbert Burck, "The Building Trades Versus the People," *Fortune*, Oct. 1970; John Davenport, "How to Curb Union Power," *Fortune*, July 1971.
11. John Jeffries, *Justice Lewis F. Powell, Jr.* (New York: Macmillan, 1994), 219. The memo, entitled "Political Warfare," was dated June 30, 1970.
12. Richard Armstrong, "The Passion That Rules Ralph Nader," *Fortune*, May 1971; Jack Newfield, "A Populist Manifesto: The Making of a New Majority," *New York*, July 19, 1971; Alice Widener, "'Total Break With America': The Fifth Annual Conference of Socialist Scholars," *Barron's*, Sept. 15, 1969; Jeffrey St. John, "Memo to G.M.: Why Not Fight Back?" *Wall Street Journal*, May 21, 1971, 8; "Analyzing Youth," *Richmond Times-Dispatch*, July 7, 1971: Powell-Sydnor Correspondence, Powell Papers.
13. Lewis Powell, "Confidential Memorandum: Attack on the Free Enterprise System," Aug. 23, 1971, Powell-Sydnor Correspondence, Powell Papers.
14. Eugene Sydnor to Lewis Powell, Aug. 25, 1971, ibid.; Lewis Powell to Ross Malone, Sept. 13, 1971, ibid.
15. Eugene Sydnor to Lewis Powell, Oct. 22, 1971, ibid.; Eugene Sydnor to Lewis Powell, May 30, 1973, ibid.
16. Jack Anderson, "FBI Missed Blueprint by Powell," *Washington Post*, Sept. 29, 1972, C27; Jack Anderson, "Powell's Lesson to Business Aired," *Washington Post*, Sept. 28, 1972, F2; Fred P. Graham, "Powell Proposed Business Defense," *New York Times*, Sept. 29, 1972, 31.
17. Norman W. Worthington to *Washington Post*, Nov. 9, 1972, A19.
18. John M. Olin to William Baroody, Mar. 22, 1973, Box 60, Folder 8, WJB Papers, LOC. On Pacific Legal Foundation: Jefferson Decker, "The Conservative Non-Profit Movement and the Rights Revolution," paper presented at the American Society for

Legal History, Nov. 18, 2006, 4, in possession of author. On DuPont: Roy Wentz to Charles McCoy and Irving Shapiro, Nov. 2, 1972, Box 7, McCoy Papers, Hagley. Also see Oliver Houck, "With Charity for All," *Yale Law Journal* 93, no. 8 (July 1984): 1415–1563, for a discussion of the Powell memorandum and the nonprofit business law groups. Steven Teles, *The Rise of the Conservative Legal Movement: The Battle for Control of the Law* (Princeton, N.J.: Princeton University Press, 2008), describes the difficulties that business sponsorship created for some conservative public-interest law firms.

19. Marilyn Bender, "Curb Asked on Gifts to Colleges," *New York Times*, Oct. 18, 1973, 71; Donald Kendall, "Adulthood," speech delivered at Commencement, Western Kentucky University, Bowling Green, Ky., May 12, 1972, reprinted in *Vital Speeches of the Day* 38, no. 7 (June 15, 1972): 542; Alan S. Boyd, "Free Enterprise Threatened?," speech delivered before the 29th Annual Conference of the Southern Industrial Development Council, Louisville, Ky., Oct. 14, 1974, reprinted in *Vital Speeches of the Day* 41, no. 3 (Nov. 15, 1974): 75. Also see O'Connor, *Social Science for What?*, 126–127, and Moreton, "Make Payroll, Not War," 55–56. In 1971 the governor of Arizona signed a law mandating that high school students take economics as part of their required curriculum; twenty more states followed suit over the 1970s.
20. Vernon Louviere, "Corporate Reports Speak Up on Public Issues," *Nation's Business*, July 1976.
21. Robert Bork, "Capitalism and the Corporate Executive," n.d., Box 76, Folder 2, WJB Papers, LOC.
22. Sidney Blumenthal, *The Rise of the Counter-Establishment: From Conservative Ideology to Political Power* (New York: Times Books, 1986), 147–165; Irving Kristol, "The Corporation and the Dinosaur," *Two Cheers for Capitalism* (New York: Basic Books, 1978), 69–73.
23. Irving Kristol, "Horatio Alger and Profits," *Wall Street Journal*, July 11, 1974, 8; Lyle R. Mercer to Irving Kristol, Sept. 21, 1976, Box 78, Folder 10, WJB Papers, LOC.

8. Turning the Tide

1. William J. Baroody, "The Corporate Role in the Decade Ahead," speech delivered at the Business Council Meeting, Hot Springs, Va., Oct. 20, 1972, Box 86, Folder 9, WJB Papers, LOC; William J. Baroody, untitled and undated speech, ibid.
2. For descriptions of the new doctrines of rational choice theory that were making their way through academic departments during the decade, see S. M. Amadae, *Rationalizing Capitalist Democracy: The Cold War Origins of Rational Choice Liberalism* (Chicago: University of Chicago Press, 2003), and Hugh Stretton and Lionel Orchard, *Public Goods, Public Enterprise, Public Choice: Theoretical Foundations of the Contemporary Attack on Government* (New York: St. Martin's, 1994). Also see Alice O'Connor, "Financing the Counterrevolution," in Bruce Schulman and Julian Zelizer, eds., *Rightward Bound: Making America Conservative in the 1970s* (Cambridge, Mass.: Harvard University Press, 2008), 148–170. For law and economics, see Steven Teles, *The Rise of the Conservative Legal Movement: The Battle for Control of the Law* (Princeton, N.J.: Princeton University Press, 2008), especially chap. 4 on Henry

Manne, who raised money to support the creation of law and economics programs at the University of Miami and elsewhere with the help of the Sun Oil executive Bill Weston and the Liberty Fund (a foundation started by Pierre Goodrich, the Indianapolis lawyer who was a supporter of the Mont Pelerin Society).

3. Karl Hess, *In a Cause That Will Triumph: The Goldwater Campaign and the Future of Conservatism* (Garden City, N.Y.: Doubleday, 1967), 29; Rick Perlstein, *Before the Storm: Barry Goldwater and the Unmaking of the American Consensus* (New York: Hill & Wang, 2001), 390; F. Clifton White, *Suite 3505: The Story of the Draft Goldwater Campaign* (New Rochelle, N.Y.: Arlington House, 1967), 201–203; William Baroody to Barry Goldwater, Jan. 25, 1965, Goldwater, Personal Correspondence, B-C, Goldwater Papers.
4. Carl Jacobs to William J. Baroody, July 1964, reprinted in Minutes of the Annual Meeting of the Board of Trustees, AEI, Dec. 30, 1964, Box 39, Folder 5, WJB Papers, LOC.
5. White, *Suite* 3505, 201; "Rightist Group Lists Expenses of $421,088," *St. Louis Post-Dispatch*, Jan. 21, 1965, Box 12, GRA; George Rucker to Harry Olsher, Oct. 25, 1965, ibid. Also see Sam Rosenfeld, "From Lobbyists to Scholars: AEI and the Politics of Expertise, 1943–1964," senior thesis, Columbia University, Apr. 2004, 57–60. On Rational Debates: "Updating the American Enterprise Institute," Sept. 1979, GRA Report, Box 11, Folder "American Enterprise Institute 1986," GRA.
6. Stephen Isaacs, "Coors Beer—and Politics—Move East," *Washington Post*, May 4, 1975, 1; Lee Edwards, *The Power of Ideas: The Heritage Foundation at 25 Years* (Ottawa, Ill.: Jameson, 1997), 9.
7. Dan Baum, *Citizen Coors: An American Dynasty* (New York: Morrow, 2000), 84.
8. Isaacs, "Coors Beer—and Politics—Move East."
9. Grace Lichtenstein, "Rocky Mountain High," *New York Times Magazine*, Dec. 28, 1975; Baum, *Citizen Coors*, 91; Lemuel Boulware to Earl Dunckel, June 8, 1983, Box 36, Folder 936, Boulware Papers.
10. Stephen Isaacs, "Coors-Backed Unit Seeks Defeat of Hill 'Radicals,'" *Washington Post*, May 6, 1975, A1; Stephen Isaacs, "Coors Bucks Network 'Bias,'" *Washington Post*, May 5, 1975, A1.
11. James A. Smith, *The Idea Brokers: Think Tanks and the Rise of the New Policy Elite* (New York: Free Press, 1991), 195–198; Edwards, *The Power of Ideas*, 5.
12. Edwards, *The Power of Ideas*, 10; Onalee McGraw, "Secular Humanism and the Schools: The Issue Whose Time Has Come" (Washington, D.C.: Heritage Foundation, 1976); Walter E. Williams, "Government Sanctions Restraints that Reduce Economic Opportunities for Minorities," *Policy Review*, Fall 1977; Jay Van Andel and Richard M. DeVos, "The Government Versus the Entrepreneur," *Policy Review*, Fall 1979; Stephen Isaacs, "Coors' Capital Connection," *Washington Post*, May 7, 1975, A1.
13. Edwards, *The Power of Ideas*, 277–278, 27, 23–25.
14. William J. Baroody to Robert Hornby, Oct. 18, 1977, Box 37, Folder 3, WJB Papers, LOC.
15. Smith, *The Idea Brokers*, 179.
16. Gordon Hodgson to William J. Baroody, Oct. 5, 1973, Box 72, Folder 3, WJB Papers, LOC; David Vogel, *Fluctuating Fortunes: The Political Power of Business in America*

(New York: Basic Books, 1989), 115–120. The revelations of the illegal corporate financing of the Nixon campaign were followed by investigations into the use of corporate funds to influence politics in other countries.

17. See Robert Wingerter to the Board of Trustees, May 28, 1974, Box 56, Folder 5, WJB Papers, LOC; Herman J. Schmidt to all trustees, Sept. 3, 1974, ibid. Even when the drive didn't yield donations, it could be a time to reaffirm the importance of the work. The president of Libbey-Owens-Ford scolded one executive who had turned down his request: "The current business literature seems full of admonitions to top management for more effective involvement in stating and supporting the basics of private enterprise philosophy." See Robert Wingerter to Horace Schwartz, July 9, 1974, ibid.
18. Gordon Hodgson to William J. Baroody re: Energy Project, Oct. 5, 1973, Box 72, Folder 3, WJB Papers, LOC; Morris Lewis to food industry executives, June 19, 1975, Box 46, Folder 1, ibid.; Fund-raising letter from Clarence Adamy, president of the National Association of Food Chains, Sept. 19, 1975, ibid.; John M. Olin to William J. Baroody, Apr. 26, 1976, Box 60, Folder 8, ibid.; John M. Olin to William J. Baroody, Mar. 4, 1976, ibid.
19. Myra MacPherson, "The Baroody Connection," *Potomac/Washington Post Magazine*, Aug. 17, 1975, 202.
20. "Updating the American Enterprise Institute," Sept. 1979, GRA Report, Box 11, Folder "American Enterprise Institute 1986," GRA; Minutes of Annual Meeting of Board of Trustees, May 7, 1975, Box 39, Folder 6, WJB Papers, LOC; William J. Baroody to Leslie Lenkowsky, Mar. 29, 1977, Box 63, Folder 1, ibid.; "Brookings Educational Programs for Business Executives 1974–75," Mar. 17, 1975, ibid. Also see letter to Baroody, signature illegible, Mar. 17, 1975, and Rosenfeld, "From Lobbyists to Scholars," 60–64.
21. Eduardo Canedo, "'Free the Fortune 500': Murray Weidenbaum and the Business Campaign Against Social Regulation in the Late 1970s," paper presented at the Annual Meeting of the Organization of American Historians, Minneapolis, Mar. 29–Apr. 1, 2007, 10; copy in possession of the author.
22. Murray Weidenbaum, *Business, Government and the Public* (Englewood Cliffs, N.J.: Prentice-Hall, 1977), 11; Murray Weidenbaum, "The New Wave of Government Regulation of Business," *Business and Society Review* (Fall 1975): 83; Canedo, "'Free the Fortune 500,'" 7–8.
23. Canedo, "'Free the Fortune 500,'" 11.
24. Sidney Blumenthal, *The Rise of the Counter-Establishment: From Conservative Ideology to Political Power* (New York: Times Books, 1986), 203–206.
25. George Gilder, *Wealth and Poverty* (San Francisco: Institute for Contemporary Studies, 1993), 21.
26. Ibid., 79, 122, 123, 274, 276.
27. Blumenthal, *The Rise of the Counter-Establishment*, 173–178.
28. Johan van Overtveldt, *The Chicago School: How the University of Chicago Assembled the Thinkers Who Revolutionized Economics and Business* (Evanston, Ill.: Agate, 2007), 188–193; David Warsh, *Economic Principals: Masters and Mavericks of Modern Economics* (New York: Free Press, 1993), 192–196; Alfred L. Malabre, Jr., "Arthur Laffer's Influence Climbs a Rising Curve, Although Many Other Economists Flunk

His Ideas," *Wall Street Journal*, Dec. 1, 1978, 46. Also see Blumenthal, *The Rise of the Counter-Establishment*, 176–179.

29. Robert L. Bartley and Amity Shlaes, "The Supply-Side Revolution," in Brian Anderson, ed., *Turning Intellect into Influence: The Manhattan Institute at 25* (New York: Reed, 2004), 33.
30. Blumenthal, *The Rise of the Counter-Establishment*, 192–195.
31. Jude Wanniski, *The Way the World Works* (Washington, D.C.: Regnery, 1978), 51, 42, 49. Jonathan Chait, *The Big Con: The True Story of How Washington Got Hoodwinked and Hijacked by Crackpot Economics* (Boston: Houghton Mifflin, 2007), 27–28, also describes some of Wanniski's strange metaphors about parenting and economics.
32. Jude Wanniski, "The Mundell-Laffer Hypothesis: A New View of the World Economy," *Public Interest* (Spring 1975): 51; Wanniski, *The Way the World Works*, 326; Jude Wanniski, "The No. 1 Problem," *New York Times*, Feb. 27, 1980, A27.
33. Blumenthal, *The Rise of the Counter-Establishment*, 185–186.
34. Edward C. Burks, "Rep. Kemp's Play Can Make Old No. 15 Taxpayers' No. 1," *New York Times*, May 23, 1978, 20; Norman C. Miller, "Tax-Cut Plan Gives GOP a New Issue—And a New Face," *Wall Street Journal*, Sept. 19, 1978, 1; Alfred L. Malabre, Jr., "Arthur Laffer's Influence Climbs a Rising Curve, Although Many Other Economists Flunk His Ideas," *Wall Street Journal*, Dec. 1, 1978, 46; "Democrats Seeking to Stem G.O.P. Tax-Cut Moves," *New York Times*, Aug. 1, 1978, A12.
35. Edward Cowan, "The Roth of Kemp-Roth," *New York Times*, Dec. 7, 1980, F19; Steven Rattner, "Washington Watch," *New York Times*, July 3, 1978, 30; Bruce Schulman, "Slouching Toward the Supply Side," in Gary M. Fink and Hugh Davis Graham, eds., *The Carter Presidency: Policy Choices in the Post–New Deal Era* (Lawrence: University Press of Kansas, 1998), 66.

9. Building the "Business Activist Movement"

1. Douglas E. Kneeland, "Advocates of Free Enterprise Are Teaching Corporations How Best to Use Political Action Groups," *New York Times*, May 14, 1978, 26.
2. "Fumble?" *Time*, Nov. 14, 1949; "Wonder Boy Makes Good," *Time*, Aug. 18, 1958; "Darting Ahead," *Time*, Oct. 22, 1975.
3. *The "Kitchen Cabinet:" Four California Citizen Advisers of Ronald Reagan*, interviewed by Steven D. Edgington and Lawrence B. de Graaf, 1981, p. 38, California Government History Documentation Project, Reagan Era, Oral History Project, California State University at Fullerton.
4. Ibid., 43.
5. Ibid., 42, 47.
6. Neil Ulman, "Business Lobby," *Wall Street Journal*, Aug. 15, 1978.
7. For statistics: David Vogel, *Fluctuating Fortunes: The Political Power of Business in America* (New York: Basic Books, 1989), 193–206. Also see Thomas Byrne Edsall, "The Changing Shape of Power," in Steve Fraser and Gary Gerstle, *The Rise and Fall of the New Deal Order* (Princeton, N.J.: Princeton University Press, 1989), 271. For quote: Philip Shabecoff, "Big Business on the Offensive," *New York Times Sunday Magazine*, Dec. 9, 1979, 34.

8. Arthur M. Schlesinger, Jr., "Laissez-Faire: Planning and Reality," *Wall Street Journal*, July 30, 1975, 10.
9. On liberal Democrats' policies: Jefferson Cowie, "'Vigorously Left, Right and Center': The Crosscurrents of Working-Class America in the 1970s," in Beth Bailey and David Farber, *America in the Seventies* (Lawrence: University of Kansas Press, 2004). On full employment bill: Timothy N. Thurber, *The Politics of Equality: Hubert H. Humphrey and the African American Freedom Struggle* (New York: Columbia University Press, 1999). On tensions within the Democratic Party: Bruce Miroff, *The Liberals' Moment: The McGovern Insurgency and the Identity Crisis of the Democratic Party* (Lawrence: University Press of Kansas, 2007).
10. Steven Rattner, "Big Industry Gun Aims at the Hill," *New York Times*, Mar. 7, 1976, F3.
11. Gerd Wilcke, "DuPont's New Boss: Confidence, a Little Caution and a Keen Sense of Humor," *New York Times*, Dec. 31, 1967, 69; "Patrol to Quit Wilmington Ghetto at Last," *Chicago Defender*, Jan. 21, 1969, 8; "Delaware Guard Called," *New York Times*, Apr. 10, 1968, 37; Ben Franklin, "Armed Guardsmen Still Patrol in Wilmington's Slums, 7 Months After Riot," *New York Times*, Nov. 17, 1968, 80; "Troops Withdraw from Wilmington," *New York Times*, Jan. 22, 1969, 26. On demonstrations: Pittsburgh Area Religion and Race Council to C. Greenewalt, Jan. 8, 1969, Box 12, McCoy Papers, Hagley; R. M. Roger description of visit from delegation from Pittsburgh Area Religion and Race Council, Jan. 10, 1969, ibid.; John Burchenal memo describing the demonstration at New York offices, Jan. 16, 1969, ibid.; Donald Roney memo on picketing demonstrations, Jan. 13, 1969, ibid.
12. F. J. Zugehoer (general counsel) and T. W. Stephenson (director, public relations), memo on Ralph Nader Study for Executive Committee Heads of Departments at Du Pont, Nov. 19, 1970, Box 8, McCoy Papers, Hagley; James Phelan and Robert Pozen, *Ralph Nader's Study Group Report on Du Pont in Delaware: The Company State* (New York: Grossman, 1973), 409.
13. Walter Rugaber, "Nader Study Says du Pont Runs Delaware," *New York Times*, Nov. 30, 1971, 90; "The Raider," *Delaware Today*, Jan. 1972, Box 8, McCoy Papers, Hagley.
14. "How Should Business Respond to Its Critics?" Charles McCoy at the Business Council, May 7, 1971, Box 39, McCoy Papers, Hagley; John Harper to Charles McCoy, Mar. 10, 1972, Box 7, ibid. The other companies were Ford, GE, Gulf Oil, Libbey-Owens-Ford, Procter & Gamble, Reynolds Metal, Standard Oil, U.S. Steel, and Westinghouse. On Washington meeting: Kim McQuaid, *Big Business and Presidential Power* (New York: Morrow, 1982), 284–285; Benjamin Waterhouse, "The Creation of the Business Roundtable and Corporate Activism in the 1970s," unpublished paper in possession of the author, 4–18.
15. James Gross, *Broken Promise: The Subversion of U.S. Labor Relations Policy, 1947–1994* (Philadelphia: Temple University Press, 1995), 234–237; Waterhouse, "The Creation of the Business Roundtable," 4–18.
16. Washington Reps Memo, Apr. 20, 1972, Box 7, McCoy Papers, Hagley; Remarks by Clause Wild of Gulf Oil, March Group on Tax Reform, Sept. 14, 1972, ibid.; Cook Tuthill Nelson Report, Box 6, ibid. The memo urged members to contribute generously to AEI and perhaps even commission AEI to do a study on political disaffection and whether Americans' hostility to business was unique or reflected a broader disillusionment with the establishment.

17. Waterhouse, "The Creation of the Business Roundtable," 21; "Them," *Reader's Digest,* Apr. 1975; "Free Enterprise: Is This Any Way to Live?" *Reader's Digest,* Sept. 1975; Waterhouse, "The Creation of the Business Roundtable," 23–24. The *Reader's Digest* series ran all through 1975; other titles include "You Pay for What You Get" (Oct.); "Why Companies Do Business Abroad" (Nov.); "The Magic of New Products" (Dec.); "Whatever Happened to the Nickel Candy Bar?" (Feb.); and "America's Amazing Success Machine" (July). Also see memo from John Harper to the members of the Business Roundtable, Apr. 16, 1974, Box 6, McCoy Papers, Hagley, describing the financing of the project. (John Harper's remarks to the Business Roundtable annual meeting are not explicitly about the *Digest* ads but reflect the broader approach; John Harper, remarks to the annual meeting, June 16, 1975, Business Roundtable Correspondence, 1975, BRA.)
18. Public Information Committee minutes, Apr. 30, 1973, Business Roundtable Correspondence, 1973, BRA; Richard M. Lee to William J. Baroody, "Contributions to NEP originating from Messrs. Harper and Speer letters," July 30, 1975, Box 72, Folder 5, WJB Papers, LOC; Howard Morgens to John Harper, Mar. 11, 1976, Box 86, Folder 10, ibid. (includes invitation to Baroody to speak at the Roundtable).
19. John Post to the Membership, Feb. 7, 1980, Business Roundtable Correspondence, 1980, BRA.
20. On inflation: John Harper to Alan Greenspan and Council of Economic Advisers, Sept. 24, 1974, Business Roundtable Correspondence Files, 1974, BRA. On food stamps: "Fact Sheet on Food Stamp Legislation," Apr. 12, 1973, Box 5, McCoy Papers, Hagley.
21. Excerpts from Report by Bert S. Cross, chair of Environmental Task Force, Nov. 21, 1973, Business Roundtable Correspondence Files, 1973, BRA; John Harper to the Membership, Nov. 24, 1975, Business Roundtable Correspondence Files, 1975, ibid.; Lewis Foy to members, July 1, 1976, Business Roundtable Correspondence Files, 1976, ibid.; Edgar Speer, Report on Energy, Sept. 14, 1976, ibid.
22. *Roundtable Report,* Dec. 1976; BRA; Benjamin Waterhouse, "Big Business Versus Big Brother: The Slow Death of the Consumer Protection Agency," unpublished paper in possession of the author (a terrific paper that is the first exploration of the Roundtable and the CPA); *Cost of Government Regulation Study for the Business Roundtable, The Report* (New York: Arthur Anderson, 1979), Executive Summary, i. The CPA study wasn't the only time that the Roundtable used survey data in public debates; the organization also commissioned studies by the Opinion Research Corporation on subjects such as unions and inflation. See Box 5, McCoy Papers, Hagley. On the critique of the survey: "Consumer Survey Biased?" *Washington Post,* May 31, 1975, C3.
23. Robert Hatfield to members, June 28, 1976, Business Roundtable Correspondence Files, 1976, BRA; Remarks of Robert Hatfield at Roundtable Annual Meeting, June 16, 1975, Business Roundtable Correspondence Files, 1975, ibid. For a reporter's description of the Roundtable's lobbying strategy sessions, see Walter Guzzardi, Jr., "Business Is Learning How to Win in Washington," *Fortune,* Mar. 27, 1958.
24. Quoted in the *Business Roundtable Report,* June 15, 1973, Box 6, McCoy Papers, Hagley; Thomas Murphy Talk at Annual Meeting, June 12, 1978, Business Roundtable Correspondence Files, 1978, BRA.

25. On EEOC: John Harper to Business Roundtable Members, Apr. 4, 1974, Business Roundtable Correspondence, 1974, BRA. On Panama Canal and Israel: Irving Shapiro to Roundtable Members, Sept. 16, 1977, Business Roundtable Correspondence, 1977, ibid.; "Guidelines for Antiboycott Bill Proposed by Business Organization, Jewish Group," *Wall Street Journal*, Mar. 7, 1977, 5; "Notes: the Business Roundtable and the Anti-Defamation League of B'nai B'rith," Jan. 28, 1977, Box 2, Folder 16, Shapiro Papers, Hagley; C. C. Garvin to Irving Shapiro, Mar. 28, 1977, Box 2, Folder 12, ibid.
26. "The Roundtable's Mission," *Wall Street Journal*, Oct. 6, 1976, 22.
27. On meeting in 1974: John Harper and G. William Bates to members, Sept. 26, 1974, Business Roundtable Correspondence Files, 1974, BRA. For quote about Carter: "Carter Shapes Up a New Deal," *Business Week*, July 26, 1976. On Carter's business connections: Kevin Phillips, *The American Political Report*, July 25, 1976, Box 20, Folder 5, ACU Papers; Eduardo Canedo, "The Origins of Neoliberalism: Jimmy Carter and the Ideology of Deregulation," unpublished paper in possession of the author; Louis Kohlmeier, "The Big Businessmen Who Have Jimmy Carter's Ear," *New York Times*, Feb. 5, 1978, F1; Martin Tolchin, "Carter's Corporate Brain Trust," *New York Times*, July 24, 1978, D1. For Shapiro quote: Irving Shapiro with Carl B. Kaufman, *America's Third Revolution: Public Interest and the Private Role* (New York: Harper & Row, 1984), 35. Canedo's excellent paper sets out a vision of Jimmy Carter as the first neoliberal Democrat, the political and intellectual father of Bill Clinton, and my argument in this paragraph is indebted to its interpretation.
28. Richard Riley to Roundtable Members, Mar. 9, 1978, Business Roundtable Correspondence Files, 1978, BRA; Robert Merry and Albert Hunt, "Business Lobby Gains Power as it Rides Antigovernment Tide," *Wall Street Journal*, May 17, 1978, 1; Juan Calderon, "Small Business Trips Big Labor," *Fortune*, July 31, 1978; Shabecoff, "Big Business on the Offensive."
29. James P. Gannon, "The Old West's New Rightists," *Wall Street Journal*, Mar. 29, 1978, 22; Shabecoff, "Big Business on the Offensive." For a history of the labor law reform bill (which focuses in part on Carter's ambivalence about the legislation), see Gary M. Fink, "Labor Law Revision and the End of the Postwar Labor Accord," in Kevin Boyle, *Organized Labor and American Politics, 1894–1994: The Labor-Liberal Alliance* (Albany: State University of New York Press, 1998), 239–257.
30. Richard I. Kirkland, Jr., "Fat Days at the Chamber of Commerce," *Fortune*, Sept. 21, 1981; Louis M. Kohlmeier, "The N.A.M. and the Chamber Bid for More Power," *New York Times*, June 27, 1976, 87.
31. Kirkland, "Fat Days"; Richard L. Lesher, "Can Capitalism Survive? The Unbelievable Growth of Government Power and Spending," speech delivered at the 143rd Convention of the International Platform Association, Washington, D.C., Aug. 7, 1975, reprinted in *Vital Speeches of the Day* 41, no. 23 (Sept. 15, 1975): 734.
32. N. R. Kleinfeld, "Amway's Direct Sales Foster Zeal, Success and Criticism," *New York Times*, Sept. 17, 1977, 29; Jacqueline Trescott, "Amway: Distributing the American Dream," *Washington Post*, June 9, 1975, B1. For more on Amway, see Nicole Woolsey Biggart, *Charismatic Capitalism: Direct Selling Organizations in America* (Chicago: University of Chicago Press, 1989); Stephen Butterfield, *Amway: The Cult of Free Enterprise* (Boston: South End, 1985).

33. Wilbur Martin, "Amway Founder: A Salesman for Free Enterprise," *Nation's Business*, May 1979; Trescott, "Amway: Distributing the American Dream."
34. "'Invisible Rich' Located," *New York Times*, Jan. 26, 1979, D2; "Amway: Soap Suds and Foam," *New York Times*, Nov. 3, 1974, 27; Martin, "Amway Founder."
35. Kirkland, "Fat Days."
36. Ibid.
37. Ibid.; "The Voice of Business Grows Stronger in Washington," *Nation's Business*, Mar. 1977; Kirkland, "Fat Days"; "National Chamber's Chief Officers," *Nation's Business*, May 1979.
38. "Annual Report for the Young Tells Business Story," *Nation's Business*, July 1977; Vernon Louviere, "Getting Economic Basics Across to Children," *Nation's Business*, Aug. 1977; advertisement for "Economics for Young Americans—Phase II," *Nation's Business*, Aug. 1977; Priscilla Schwab, "Introducing Johnny and Mary to the World of Business," *Nation's Business*, Jan. 1978; Vernon Louviere, "Telling Students the Truth About Business," *Nation's Business*, Mar. 1977. The Chamber described the Economics for Young Americans program as an explicit response to the Powell memorandum.
39. Kirkland, "Fat Days"; William S. Mitchell, "Why Government Neglects the Stockholder," speech delivered at Safeway annual meeting, reprinted in *Nation's Business*, Aug. 1975.
40. On Kilpatrick: James J. Kilpatrick, "Restraining the Public Employee Unions," *Nation's Business*, Feb. 1977; James J. Kilpatrick, "New Hope for Employers Harassed by OSHA," *Nation's Business*, Mar. 1977; James J. Kilpatrick, "The Case Against ERA," *Nation's Business*, Jan. 1975; James J. Kilpatrick, "Rulings that Penalize Private Schools," *Nation's Business*, Sept. 1976. On surveys: "Sound Off Response: More Boos than Hoorays for ERA," *Nation's Business*, Apr. 1975; "Sound Off Response: Prayer in the Schools: An Overwhelming Verdict," *Nation's Business*, Feb. 1975. On tax and deregulation: "Taxpayers in Revolt," *Nation's Business*, July 1978; "Let the Free Market System Work for Energy," editorial, *Nation's Business*, Aug. 1979; "The Social Security Tax Problem," editorial, *Nation's Business*, Oct. 1975.
41. James J. Kilpatrick, "Why Students Are Hostile to Free Enterprise," *Nation's Business*, July 1975; James J. Kilpatrick, "Rulings That Penalize Private Schools," *Nation's Business*, Sept. 1976; Kirkland, "Fat Days."
42. Martin Jay Levitt with Terry Conrow, *Confessions of a Union Buster* (New York: Crown, 1993), 15; John Logan, "Consultants, Lawyers and the 'Union Free' Movement in the United States Since the 1970s," *Industrial Relations Journal*, Aug. 2002, 207. On overall increase in anti-union activity: Robert Michael Smith, *From Blackjacks to Briefcases: A History of Commercial Strikebreaking and Unionbusting in the United States* (Athens: Ohio University Press, 2003), 104–117.
43. Joseph A. McCartin, "'Fire the Hell Out of Them': Sanitation Workers' Struggles and the Normalization of the Striker Replacement Strategy in the 1970s," *Labor: Studies in the Working-Class History of the Americas* 2, no. 3 (2005): 67–92; Joseph A. McCartin, "'A Wagner Act for Public Employees?' Labor's Deferred Dream and the Rise of Conservatism, 1970–1976," *Journal of American History* 95, no. 1 (June 2008): 123–148.
44. "Idahoan Wins Right to Curb U.S. Safety Checks at Plants," *New York Times*, Jan. 17,

1977, 14; Robert Pear, "Tables Turned as OSHA's Targets Are Organized," *Washington Star,* Nov. 18, 1977, Box 90, Folder 2, ACU Papers.

45. John Runft to Gary Jarmin, July 31, 1977, Box 89, Folder 3, ACU Papers. ACU raised over $100,000 to help support the case, more than half the money needed. For money raised for the Barlow case, see Legislative Report, ACU Board Meeting, Feb. 10, 1979, Box 71, Folder 8, ibid. For "more than half," at which point the amount raised was smaller, see John Runft to Gary Jarmin, July 31, 1977, Box 89, Folder 3, ibid.
46. Pear, "Tables Turned"; Guy D. Schein, "When OSHA Knocks At Your Door," Box 88, Folder 5, ACU Papers; Urban C. Lehrer, "OSHA Resisters May Suffer From Bad Advice," *Wall Street Journal,* Oct. 18, 1979, 16.
47. Charles Noble, *Liberalism at Work: The Rise and Fall of OSHA* (Philadelphia: Temple University Press, 1986), 201; Marc Allen Eisner, *Regulatory Politics in Transition* (Baltimore: Johns Hopkins University Press, 2000), 153–169.
48. Robert N. Dobbin, president, Dobbins Metals Products Inc., San Antonio, TX, to George Hansen, July 7, 1978, Box 87, Folder 1, ACU Papers (Hansen, a congressional representative from Idaho, had been recruited by the ACU to act as the public head of the drive); A. Stuart Graham to Robert Bauman, July 2, 1979, Box 89, Folder 8, ibid.; D. Jeffrey Hollingsworth to A. S. Graham, Flick Industries, Sept. 11, 1979, Box 87, Folder 2, ibid.; Robert A. Rader to Gary Jarmin, May 30, 1979, Box 87, Folder 3, ibid.; W. B. Meredith II, Inc., to George Hansen, June 12, 1978, ibid.
49. Gary Jarmin to J. McCullogh, Nov. 14, 1978, Box 87, Folder 4, ibid.; William Speer of Modern Metals Industries of New Jersey to Senator James McClure, Oct. 17, 1977, Box 73, Folder 7, ibid.; J. S. Loe of Phoenix Transit Systems to Gary Jarmin, Feb. 9, 1979, Box 87, Folder 4, ibid.; Robert Milliken of Mount Hope Finishing Company to George Hansen, Feb. 7, 1975, Box 87, Folder 3, ibid.; From Mel Waller of Zirbel Transport, Sept. 15, 1978, Box 73, Folder 7, ibid. Some larger companies did ask ACU for information: Pfizer and Phelps Dodge both requested brochures. See Aldo Osti of Pfizer to ACU, June 16, 1979, and David Killough of Phelps Dodge to ACU, June 22, 1979, Box 87, Folder 4, ibid.
50. Lehrer, "OSHA Resisters May Suffer from Bad Advice."
51. Edwards, *The Power of Ideas,* 37–40; AEI Annual Report 1980, Box 12, GRA.
52. Entry Apr. 27, 1979, Personal Files—Alpha Files—Journals—Politics—Running for Office, Goldwater Papers.

10. Making the Moral Majority

1. Richard Viguerie, *The New Right: We're Ready to Lead* (Falls Church, Va.: Viguerie, 1981), 7. For an excellent discussion of the New Right, see Bruce Schulman, *The Seventies: The Great Shift in American Culture, Society and Politics* (New York: Free Press, 2001), 193–218.
2. James P. Gannon, "Coalition Politics on the Right," *Wall Street Journal,* Jan. 10, 1978, 12.
3. Viguerie, *The New Right,* 32–33; Nick Kotz, "King Midas of 'the New Right,'" *Atlantic Monthly,* Nov. 1978, 52–61.
4. Gannon, "Coalition Politics on the Right"; Kotz, "King Midas," 52–61.
5. Matthew D. Lassiter, "Inventing Family Values," in Bruce Schulman and Julian Zelizer,

eds., *Rightward Bound: Making America Conservative in the 1970s* (Cambridge, Mass., Harvard University Press, 2008), 13–29; Kevin Phillips, *The Emerging Republican Majority* (New Rochelle, N.Y.: Arlington House, 1969), 25–42; Rick Perlstein, *Nixonland: The Rise of a President and the Fracturing of America* (New York: Scribner, 2008), 587; Jonathan Rieder, *Canarsie: The Jews and Italians of Brooklyn Against Liberalism* (Cambridge, Mass.: Harvard University Press, 1985); James Moffett, *Storm in the Mountains: A Case Study of Censorship, Conflict and Consciousness* (Carbondale: Southern Illinois University Press, 1988), 3–25; Paul Cowan, *The Tribes of America* (New York: Doubleday, 1979), 79; Max Fraser, "Blue-Collar Patriots: The New York Hard Hat Riots and the Remaking of Class in America," senior thesis, University of Pennsylvania, 2006, 3–5.

6. See Dan Carter, *The Politics of Rage: George Wallace, the Origins of the New Conservatism and the Transformation of American Politics* (New York: Simon and Schuster, 1995), 425; Alan Otten, "A Thorny New Road for Conservatives," *Wall Street Journal*, Aug. 20, 1976.
7. Richard Viguerie, "Let's Get Union Members to Support Conservatives," *Conservative Digest*, Aug. 1977, 56; Patrick Buchanan, "Why the Right Has Failed," *Conservative Digest*, Feb. 1976, 15; M. Stanton Evans, "Can Reagan and Wallace Get Together?" *Conservative Digest*, Nov. 1975, 29.
8. Patrick Buchanan, "Does Big Business Deserve Our Support?" *Conservative Digest*, Apr. 1977, 6, 11; Richard Viguerie, "Big Business Must Get Back on Track," *Conservative Digest*, July 1977, 56. The retraction of the Ford rumor appeared in *Conservative Digest*, Sept. 1977.
9. Brian Benson, "How Businessmen Can Stop Losing in Politics," *Conservative Digest*, Feb. 1977, 6. For Business Roundtable speech: Thomas A. Murphy, Chairman of General Motors, "Big Business Says: It Isn't the Other Guy's Fault," *Conservative Digest*, Jan. 1977, 24; Publisher's Note, *Conservative Digest*, Oct. 1975, 1. The ad to advertise in the *Conservative Digest* ran in the Oct. 1976 issue.
10. Philip Crane, "The Blue Collar Constituency Is Really Conservative," *Conservative Digest*, Apr. 1978, 6; Ben Stein, "Why I Don't Like Liberals," *Conservative Digest*, Dec. 1976, 40; Joanna Gault, "These Liberals," *Conservative Digest*, Jan. 1976, 31. Michael Kazin, *The Populist Persuasion: An American History* (New York: Basic Books, 1995), argues that George Wallace presented himself as a conservative populist, an image that was picked up by Richard Nixon and later Ronald Reagan. Yet the *Conservative Digest* vision was a little different from Wallace's populism, in that it explicitly sought to join business owners with workers, whereas Wallace really grounded his claims much more explicitly in an appeal to the working class.
11. D. Keith Mano, "The Poor Man's Bill Buckley," reprinted from *New York* in *Conservative Digest*, Dec. 1975, 25; William Rusher, *The Making of the New Majority Party* (Ottawa, Ill.: Green Hill, 1975), 33.
12. Richard Viguerie, "An Alternative Plan," *Conservative Digest*, Aug. 1976, 56; William Rusher to William F. Buckley, Jr., Mar. 16, 1976, Box 121, Folder 9, Rusher Papers, LOC; Statement of Senator Jesse Helms of North Carolina Following the Meeting of the Committee on Conservative Alternatives, Mar. 7, 1975, Box 142, Folder 6, ibid.
13. Ronald Reagan to Lemuel Boulware, Jan. 2, 1975, Box 48, Folder 1435, Boulware Papers; Lemuel Boulware to Ronald Reagan, Dec. 17, 1974, ibid.

14. Lou Cannon, *Reagan* (New York: Putnam, 1982), 197.
15. Stephen Isaacs, "Newcomers' Hopes Are Scuttled at Third-Party Session," *Washington Post*, Aug. 29, 1976, 3; William Rusher to Joseph Coors, Sept. 9, 1976, Box 21, Folder 3, Rusher Papers, LOC. On Maddox's political career: Kevin Kruse, *White Flight: Atlanta and the Making of Modern Conservatism* (Princeton, N.J.: Princeton University Press, 2005), 194–203, 220–229, 230–233.
16. "The New Right: A Special Report," *Conservative Digest*, June 1979, 10.
17. Ernest B. Furgurson, *Hard Right: The Rise of Jesse Helms* (New York: W. W. Norton, 1986), 13. My argument about Helms has been especially influenced by Bryan Thrift, "Jesse Helms, the New Right and American Freedom," Ph.D. diss., Boston University, 2002, and William A. Link, *Righteous Warrior: Jesse Helms and the Rise of Modern Conservatism* (New York: St. Martin's, 2008).
18. On the *Tarheel Banker*: Furgurson, *Hard Right*, 60. On a private school system: Unsigned editorial, "N.C. Has an Educational Choice, But It Isn't Logically 'Private,'" *Charlotte Observer*, Sept. 7, 1955, North Carolina Bankers Association Series, Box 1, Helms Papers; Furgurson, *Hard Right*, 61–62.
19. Jesse Helms to Frank J. Mackey, Dec. 30, 1957, Box 43, Mackey-Helms Letters, Helms Papers.
20. On swimming pools: Jesse Helms to Sterling Booth, n.d., "August-October, 1960," Box 2, City Council Files, Helms Papers. On Manion visit: Furgurson, *Hard Right*, 85. On ECO: "What Is the ECO Getting Started in Public Affairs Seminar?," program description from Raymond L. Hoewing to Jesse Helms, June 22, 1965, Administrative Files, Box 2, ibid. On von Mises: Jesse Helms to Howard K. Smith, Aug. 30, 1971, Administrative Files, Box 2, ibid. On ideal president: Keith Upchurch, "Jesse Helms and WRAL: Alternative Points of View," *Chronicle* (Duke University student paper), Nov. 3, 1970, Administrative Files, Box 43, Helms Papers.
21. Jesse Helms, *Facts of the Matter*, Feb. 14, 1960, transcript, Helms Papers.
22. Furgurson, *Hard Right*, 90, 102; Karen Rothmyer, "Citizen Scaife," in Herbert F. Vetter, ed., *Speak Out Against the New Right* (Boston: Beacon, 1982).
23. See Earl and Merle Black, *The Rise of Southern Republicans* (Cambridge, Mass.: Harvard University Press, 2002); Matthew Lassiter, *The Silent Majority: Suburban Politics in the Sunbelt South* (Princeton, N.J.: Princeton University Press, 2006); Kruse, *White Flight*; and Joseph Crespino, *In Search of Another Country: Mississippi and the Conservative Counterrevolution* (Princeton, N.J.: Princeton University Press, 2007).
24. Pat Robertson, "A Christian Action Plan to Heal Our Land in the 1980s," Pat Robertson's Perspective: A Special Report to the Members of the 700 Club, Fall 1979, Collection 309, Box 29, Folder 6, BGCA.
25. On the Freedoms Foundation: John Conlan to Grady Wilson, Mar. 7, 1962, Collection 544, Box 11, Folder 1, BGCA; John Conlan to Carl F. H. Henry, June 1960, Collection 8, Box 17, Folder 37, ibid. On Christian Citizen: "Report on Progress Toward Christian Citizenship," n.d. but probably early 1962, Box 241, Folder 2, Judd Papers, Hoover; John Wicklein, "Christian Group Aims at Politics," *New York Times*, Feb. 1, 1962; also see Sara Diamond, *Roads to Dominion: Right-Wing Movements and Political Power in the United States* (New York: Guilford Press, 1995), 105.
26. Bob Jones, Jr., to Jerry Falwell, July 29, 1980, Moral Majority File, Weniger Papers, BJU. Jones initially made the claim in a letter to students at Bob Jones University.

27. Susan Harding, *The Book of Jerry Falwell: Fundamentalist Language and Politics* (Princeton, N.J.: Princeton University Press, 2000), 15–16; Jim Montgomery, "The Electric Church," *Wall Street Journal,* May 19, 1978, 1.
28. William Martin, *With God on Our Side: The Rise of the Religious Right in America* (New York: Broadway Books, 1996), 70, 57, 197–202.
29. "Unlimited Fields to Plow," *Journal-Champion,* Jan. 26, 1979, 2; "Why Christians Should Vote," *Journal-Champion,* Oct. 27, 1978, 2. The *Journal-Champion* can be found in the Fundamentalism File at the J. S. Mack Library at Bob Jones University.
30. "America Threatened by Creeping Bureaucracy," *Journal-Champion,* June 9, 1978, 1; Elmer Towns, "A Message to Congress from One Million Readers," ibid.; "Educator Terms Bureaucracy Frustrating," interview of Elmer Towns, editor, with Al Janney, president of the American Association of Christian Schools, ibid., 5.
31. "Why Fundamentalists are Conservative," *Journal-Champion,* Oct. 13, 1978, 2; "America: Still the Best," *Journal-Champion,* July 21, 1978, 2; "A No-Growth America," *Journal-Champion,* Dec. 22, 1978.
32. "Goodbye to the Goodtimes," *Journal-Champion,* Aug. 4, 1978, 2; "America: Still the Best"; Harry Covert, "Achievement and Free Enterprise," *Journal-Champion,* June 1, 1979, 2.
33. Jim Wallis and Wes Michaelson, "The Plan to Save America," *Sojourners,* Apr. 1976, quoted in Daniel Williams, "From the Pews to the Polls: The Formation of a Southern Christian Right," Ph.D. diss., Brown University, 2005, 330; Field Directors Manual, Christian Freedom Foundation, Box 241, Folder 3, Judd Papers, Hoover; Williams, "From the Pews to the Polls," 333–336; Miller, *With God on Our Side,* 200–201; Jerry Falwell, *Listen, America!* (New York: Doubleday, 1980), 72–73.
34. NRB Letter, n.d. (Summer–Fall 1977), Collection 309, Box 29, Folder 4, BGCA.
35. Crespino, *In Search of Another Country,* 237–266, contains an excellent discussion of the fight over private Christian schools in Mississippi and throughout the South.
36. Ibid., 253–254. "Insignificant" was defined as less than 20 percent of the minority school-age population in the school community.
37. "From the Desk of Jerry Falwell," *Journal-Champion,* Mar. 23, 1979, 3; Tim LaHaye, "Is Government Harassing Schools?" *Journal-Champion,* Apr. 6, 1979, 1; "Christian Lobbyist at the Congress," *Journal-Champion,* Mar. 23, 1979, 1.
38. James T. McKenna, "The Internal Revenue Service vs. Christian Education and the First Amendment: A Handbook for Church and Community Leaders," distributed by Christian Voice, Box 80, Folder 3, ACU Papers; Statement by Philip Crane, Oct. 30, 1978, news conference, Box 79, Folder 14, ibid.; ACU Legislative Alert, "IRS Says: Guilty until Proven Innocent," Box 79, Folder 13, ibid.; Unsigned article, "Mobilizing the Moral Majority," *Conservative Digest,* Aug. 1979, 14.
39. Crespino, *In Search of Another Country,* 256; Martin, *With God on Our Side,* 173; "Mobilizing the Moral Majority."

11. The Market Triumphant

1. "NYSE Members Acclaim Reagan on Visit," *Wall Street Letter,* Mar. 24, 1980.
2. Lou Cannon, *Reagan* (New York: Putnam, 1982), 159; Jerry Gillam, "Reagan Says He Feels White Won't Start Presidential Draft," *Los Angeles Times,* Feb. 21, 1968, 3.

3. Cannon, *Reagan,* 145–165, 166–186, 210–226; Garry Wills, *Reagan's America: Innocents at Home* (New York: Penguin, 1985), 355–373; Matthew Dallek, *The Right Moment: Ronald Reagan's First Victory and the Decisive Turning Point in American Politics* (New York: Free Press, 2000), ix–xi, 173–211.
4. Donald D. Holt, "What He'd Be Like as President," *Fortune,* May 1980, 80.
5. Everett Carll Ladd, Jr., "The Unmaking of the Republican Party," *Fortune,* Sept. 1977, 102; William Safire, "As Time Goes By," *New York Times,* Feb. 11, 1980, A19.
6. Herbert E. Alexander, *Financing the 1980 Election* (Lexington, Mass.: Lexington Books, 1983), 193; Edward T. Pound, "Connally Wealth Mostly in Land; Net Worth Is at Least $5 Million," *New York Times,* Jan. 20, 1980, 1; "John Connally: A Man for the Times," *Conservative Digest,* Feb. 1980.
7. Alexander, *Financing the 1980 Election,* 177; Douglas E. Kneeland, "Bush Moves to Sharpen Differences with Reagan," *New York Times,* Mar. 1, 1980, 8; Howell Raines, "Bush's Son Battling Reagan for Votes of Ex-Cubans," *New York Times,* Mar. 8, 1980, 9; Douglas E. Kneeland, "Reporter's Notebook," *New York Times,* Mar. 7, 1980, D15.
8. A. O. Sulzberger, Jr., "On the Issues: John B. Anderson," *New York Times,* Mar. 29, 1980, 9; "Excerpts from Forum in Iowa of 6 G.O.P. Presidential Candidates," *New York Times,* Jan. 7, 1980, B4; Alexander, *Financing the 1980 Election,* 186–187; "Executives Sign Up to Aid John Anderson," *Business Week,* July 7, 1980.
9. Donald Seibert to Business Roundtable members, Nov. 22, 1978, Business Roundtable Correspondence Files, 1978, BRA; Donald Seibert to Business Roundtable members, Nov. 22, 1978, ibid.; *Roundtable Report,* July 1980, ibid.; "Executives' Choice," *Wall Street Journal,* Apr. 1, 1980, 1.
10. Adam Clymer, "Ford Declares Reagan Can't Win; Invites G.O.P. to Ask Him to Run," *New York Times,* Mar. 2, 1980, 1.
11. Dudley Clendinen, "Campaign Report," *New York Times,* Mar. 11, 1980, B12.
12. "The Death of Equities," *Business Week,* Aug. 13, 1979; David A. Rosenbaum, "Social Security Major Issue in Florida as Primary Day Nears," *New York Times,* Mar. 5, 1976. On the bear market: Roger Lowenstein, *Origins of the Crash: The Great Bubble and Its Undoing* (New York: Penguin, 2004), 1–3.
13. John S. R. Shad to Nicholas Ruwe, Jan. 19, 1980, Box 44, CA-HQ Papers, 1980 Campaign Files, RRPL; James Fuller to Edwin Meese, Jan. 16, 1980, Box 16, Meese Papers, ibid.
14. "Reagan Holds Talks with His New Panel of Business Advisers," *Wall Street Journal,* June 18, 1980, 46.
15. James Fuller to Governor Reagan, June 12, 1980, Business Advisory Committee File 2/3, Box 38, CA-HQ Papers, 1980 Campaign Files, RRPL; Minutes of Business Advisory Panel Meeting, June 17, 1980, Box 38, CA-HQ Papers, 1980 Campaign Files, "Business Advisory Council," RRPL.
16. Minutes of Business Advisory Panel Meeting, June 17, 1980, Box 38, CA-HQ Papers, 1980 Campaign Papers, "Business Advisory Council," RRPL.
17. "Reagan Holds Talks with His New Panel of Business Advisers."
18. James Fuller to Edwin Meese, Sept. 9, 1980, Box 149, Meese Papers, 1980 Campaign Papers, RRPL.
19. William Simon, *A Time for Truth* (New York: McGraw-Hill, 1978), 230–233; Minutes of the Coalition for the Preservation of Free Enterprise, Nov. 20, 1979, Box 2, Folder

8, ACU Papers; "Simon: Preaching the Word for Olin," *New York Times,* July 16, 1978, F1. Also see Peter Stone, "Businesses Widen Role in Conservatives' 'War of Ideas,'" *Washington Post,* May 12, 1985, F4. The Olin Foundation had been around since the early 1950s, funded by John M. Olin's fortune derived from a $1 billion complex of chemical, munitions, paper, and realty companies. Following the takeover of campus buildings at Cornell, Olin's alma mater, by radical African American student activists in the late 1960s, Olin decided to focus the work of his foundation on the support of free-enterprise ideas. As he told the *New York Times,* "Business and the public must be awakened to the creeping stranglehold that socialism has gained here since World War II"; Thomas E. Mullaney, "Olin: Staunch Fighter for Free Enterprise," *New York Times,* Apr. 29, 1977, D3. Also see Alice O'Connor, *Social Science for What? Philanthropy and the Social Question in a World Turned Rightside Up* (New York: Russell Sage Foundation, 2007), 132–138.

20. Executive Advisory Committee Current List, July 25, 1980, Box 102, Meese Papers, 1980 Campaign Files, RRPL. Also see William Endicott, "New 'Cabinet': Reagan Men: They're Rich—Self-Made," *Los Angeles Times,* July 10, 1980.
21. Reagan Executive Advisory Committee Minutes, Apr. 4, June 20, and July 25, 1980, Box 102, Meese Papers, 1980 Campaign Files, RRPL. Arthur Laffer served as secretary to the Executive Advisory Committee.
22. Jude Wanniski, "FYI: With Reagan in California," Campaign Planning—Reagan for President Planning, Budget and Personnel, 1/80–2/80, Box 104, Meese Papers, 1980 Campaign Files, RRPL; Holt, "What He'd Be Like as President"; Richard Williamson to Paul Laxalt and Tom Evans, Minutes of Meeting of National Steering Committee on Business, May 13, 1980 [memo dated May 19, 1980], Box 103, "Political Memos, 5/80," Meese Papers, 1980 Campaign Files, RRPL; Jude Wanniski to Edwin Meese, Jan. 18, 1980, Box 114, "Correspondence File—General 1/180–3/80," ibid. Wanniski was reporting on Rumsfeld's conversation.
23. Ronald Reagan to J. Gary Shansby, Sept. 5, 1980, Box 306, Society of Association Executives Folder 1 of 3, Hugel Papers, 1980 Campaign Files, RRPL; John Conlan to Timmons, Meese and Tyson, n.d., Box 343, "Religion-General," ibid.
24. "Meeting with Public Relations Executives," Box 255, Timmons Papers, 1980 Campaign Files, RRPL.
25. William Agee to Samuel Hardage, Sept. 9, 1980, Box 307, "Business—Small Business," Hugel Papers, 1980 Campaign Files, RRPL; To Regional Chairmen from Ronald Weintraub, Sept. 19, 1980, Box 324, "Business Mailings—9/80," ibid.; David G. Price to Don Baldwin, Oct. 10, 1980, Box 323, "Business—Final Report," ibid.; Progress Report, Oct. 16, 1980, Progress Report on Key States, Oct. 17, 1980, and Progress Report, Oct. 10, 1980, Box 325, "Small Business," ibid.
26. To Supporters from Loren Smith, Chief Counsel, Sept. 26, 1980, Box 323, "Corporate Involvement in 1980," Business Finances, ibid.; William Timmons to William Casey, Oct. 3, 1980, Box 255, Timmons Papers, 1980 Campaign Files, RRPL; Mollie Miller to Bob Turnbull, Oct. 2, 1980, Box 324, "Business—Mailings, 10/80," Hugel Papers, 1980 Campaign Files, RRPL; "Draft Letter (Mailgram) to Go to CEOs of Fortune 500 from RR," ibid.
27. Memorandum of proceedings, n.d. [following Oct. 1, 1980], small business meeting at Waldorf-Astoria at which Reagan spoke, Box 307, "Small Business," Hugel Papers,

1980 Campaign Files, RRPL; Sam Hardage to Roger Cohen, Oct. 16, 1980, Box 323, "Business—Final Report," ibid.

28. James M. Perry, "Reagan, in Detroit, Says Auto Industry's Woes Are Due to 'Unionized' U.S. Rules," *Wall Street Journal,* May 16, 1980, 4; Douglas E. Kneeland, "Reagan Promises Auto Workers to Seek a Cut in Japan's Exports," *New York Times,* Sept. 3, 1980, B8.
29. Richard Wirthlin, "Reagan for President Campaign Plan Draft, 6/29/80," 16, Box 177, Wirthlin Papers, 1980 Campaign Files, RRPL.
30. E. J. Dionne, Jr., "The Business of the Pollsters," *New York Times,* June 29, 1980, F1; Wirthlin, "Reagan for President Campaign Plan Draft," 18.
31. Wirthlin, "Reagan for President Campaign Plan Draft," 16, 31, 68, 36, 149.
32. Betty Southard Murphy to William Casey, "Further Development of the Labor Strategy," June 8, 1980, Box 103, Meese Papers, 1980 Campaign Files, RRPL; Betty Southard Murphy to Gordon Cole, Oct. 1, 1980, Box 151, ibid.
33. Wirthlin, "Reagan for President Campaign Plan Draft," 19; Ronald Reagan to William D'Onofrio, Sept. 26, 1980, Box 151, Meese Papers, 1980 Campaign Files, RRPL; Cannon, *Reagan,* 269–270; Rich Williamson to Paul Laxalt, William Casey, and Ed Meese, Sept. 16, 1980, Box 152, Meese Papers, 1980 Campaign Files, RRPL; Dave Gergen to Jim Baker, Bill Casey, Ed Meese, Ron Walker, and Dick Wirthlin, "Marching into Georgia," Sept. 24, 1980. Box 149, ibid.
34. John Conlan to William Casey, Apr. 24, 1980, Box 307, "Christians—File 1 of 2," Hugel Papers, 1980 Campaign Files, RRPL.
35. John Conlan to Select Christian Leaders, Sept. 27, 1979, National Religious Broadcasters Papers, Collection 209, Box 13, Folder 1, BGCA; Ronald Reagan to Ben Armstrong, Aug. 16, 1979, ibid.; Ben Armstrong to John Conlan, Oct. 8, 1979, ibid. Also see Ben Armstrong to John Conlan, Oct. 2, 1979, Collection 309, Box 30, Folder 1, BGCA.
36. Key Pastors' Meeting, Feb. 12, 1980, Box 307, "Christians—File 1 of 2," Hugel Papers, 1980 Campaign Files, RRPL; "A Program for Political Participation of Church-Going Christians," ibid.
37. Robert Billings to Max Hugel, May 23, 1980, Box 309, "Evangelical/Born Again," ibid.; Letters to Max Hugel from LaHaye, Falwell, Jones, and Rogers, ibid.; William Chasey to Elizabeth Dole, undated memo: Reagan-Bush Committee Christian Voter Program, Box 307, "Christians—File 2 of 2," Hugel Papers, 1980 Campaign Files, RRPL.
38. Max Hugel to William Chasey, Aug. 19, 1980, Box 307, "Christians—File 2 of 2," Hugel Papers, 1980 Campaign Files, RRPL; Robert Billings to Max Hugel, n.d., Box 255, "Christians—Evangelicals," Folder 1 of 4, Timmons Papers, 1980 Campaign Files, RRPL. Billings also complained that another staffer had killed the printing of special stationery featuring religious leaders who supported Reagan; Max Hugel to William Timmons and Stan Anderson, Sept. 11, 1980, ibid.
39. Letter from Edward McAteer (president of Roundtable), James Robison (vice president of Roundtable), and Tom Landry (coach of Dallas Cowboys), June 27, 1980, Box 102, "Campaign Planning Committee 1980," Meese Papers, 1980 Campaign Files, RRPL.
40. Bill Gribben to Ed Meese and Bill Gavin, n.d., Box 153, "Memos and Comments Re Speeches," Folder 1 of 2, Meese Papers, 1980 Campaign Files, RRPL.
41. Bill Stall, "Evangelicals Pin Their Faith on Political Action," *Los Angeles Times,* Aug. 24, 1980, A1; Kathy Sawyer, "Linking Religion and Politics," *Washington Post,* Aug. 24,

1980, A12; Howell Baines, "Reagan Backs Evangelicals in Their Political Activities," *New York Times,* Aug. 23, 1980, 8. On Robison's background: William Martin, *With God on Our Side: The Rise of the Religious Right in America* (New York: Broadway Books, 1996), 198–199.

42. "Address by the Honorable Ronald Reagan for the Roundtable National Affairs Briefing," Dallas, 1980, Box 343, "Religious," Hugel Papers, 1980 Campaign Files, RRPL. On attendees: Thomas Ferguson and Joel Rogers, "The Reagan Victory: Corporate Coalitions in the 1980 Campaign," in Ferguson and Rogers, eds., *The Hidden Election: Politics and Economics in the 1980 Presidential Campaign* (New York: Pantheon, 1981), 3.
43. "Without Christ, Jews Are Lost: Baptist Leader," *Chicago Tribune,* Sept. 20, 1980, A11; Herb Ellingwood to Ronald Reagan, Aug. 26, 1980, Box 148, Meese Papers, 1980 Campaign Files, RRPL. The poem is by Reverend Tony Ahlstrom and appeared in *Christian Legal Society Quarterly* in the summer of 1980.
44. Cannon, *Reagan,* 269–303, quote on 289; Frank Allen, "Carter Rating from Business Drops Further," *Wall Street Journal,* Oct. 30, 1980, 33; Steven Rattner, "Executives Leaning to Reagan," *New York Times,* Oct. 13, 1980, D1.
45. Leonard Silk, "'Invisible Hand' in U.S. Outlook," *New York Times,* Oct. 22, 1980, D2; Thomas C. Hayes, "Executives Favoring Reagan," *New York Times,* Oct. 27, 1980, D1; Rattner, "Executives Leaning to Reagan"; "Reagan a 9–5 Favorite in Odds at Las Vegas," *New York Times,* Nov. 5, 1980, A22.
46. Steve Lohr, "Business Counts on Reagan," *New York Times,* Nov. 6, 1980, D1.
47. Ibid.; "Businessmen Look Forward to Cut in Taxes and Regulatory Burden," *Wall Street Journal,* Nov. 6, 1980, 35.
48. "Reagan Victory Is Met with Enthusiasm in Hopes of Less Government Meddling," *Wall Street Journal,* Nov. 6, 1980, 46; Bill Paul, "Energy Executives Are Elated, Expecting Unfettered Growth With Reagan Tenure," *Wall Street Journal,* Nov. 6, 1980, 5; Gene G. Marcial, "Defense Issues Explode as Reagan's Landslide Is Seen Assuring Increased Spending for Arms," *Wall Street Journal,* Nov. 6, 1980, 55; "Businessmen Look Forward to Cut in Taxes and Regulatory Burden," *Wall Street Journal,* Nov. 6, 1980, 35; Lohr, "Business Counts on Reagan."
49. J. J. Wuerthner to Fellow GE Alumnus, July 22, 1980, Box 48, Folder 1436, Boulware Papers; Lee Edwards, *The Power of Ideas: The Heritage Foundation at 25 Years* (Ottawa, Ill.: Jameson, 1997), 47; AEI Annual Report 1980, Box 12, GRA; Philip Shabecoff, "Business Group Sent Reagan Aide List of 'Unsympathetic' Officials," *New York Times,* Sept. 7, 1984, A15; Lou Cannon, "A Look to Future with Vision of Past," *Washington Post,* Mar. 21, 1981, A1.
50. Remarks of Edwin Meese III, Counselor to President-Elect Reagan, Reagan Transition Team Briefing for Corporation and Association Executives, Chamber of Commerce of the United States, Dec. 5, 1980, Series 3, Box 4, U.S. Chambers of Commerce Papers, Hagley.

Epilogue

1. For various accounts of the Reagan years, see Thomas Ferguson and Joel Rogers, *Right Turn: The Decline of the Democrats and the Future of American Politics* (New York: Hill & Wang, 1986); Ernest Julius Englander and Allen Kaufman, "The End

of Managerial Ideology: From Corporate Social Responsibility to Corporate Social Indifference," *Enterprise and Society* 5, no. 3 (Sept. 2004): 404–450; J. Craig Jenkins and Craig M. Eckert, "The Right Turn in Economic Policy: Business Elites and the New Conservative Economics," *Sociological Forum* 15, no. 2 (June 2000): 307–338; Richard Reeves, *President Reagan: The Triumph of Imagination* (New York: Simon and Schuster, 2005); Richard Reeves, *The Reagan Detour* (New York: Simon and Schuster, 1984); Gil Troy, *Morning in America: How Ronald Reagan Invented the 1980s* (Princeton, N.J.: Princeton University Press, 2005); and Sean Wilentz, *The Age of Reagan: A History, 1974–2008* (New York: HarperCollins, 2008).

2. On SIFE: Bethany Moreton, "Make Payroll, Not War," in Bruce Schulman and Julian Zelizer, eds., *Rightward Bound: Making America Conservative in the 1970s* (Cambridge, Mass.: Harvard University Press, 2008), 52–70. On changing economic culture: Nelson Lichtenstein, "Wal-Mart: A Template for Twenty-First Century Capitalism," and Bethany Moreton, "It Came from Bentonville: The Agrarian Origins of Wal-Mart Culture," both in Nelson Lichtenstein, ed., *Wal-Mart: The Face of Twenty-First-Century Capitalism* (New York: New Press, 2006), 3–31, 57–83; Steve Fraser, *Every Man a Speculator: A History of Wall Street in American Life* (New York: HarperCollins, 2005), 525–615.
3. On the economy in the 1990s: Robert Pollin, *Contours of Descent: U.S. Economic Fractures and the Landscape of Global Austerity* (London: Verso, 2003). On "market populism": Thomas Frank, *One Market Under God: Extreme Capitalism, Market Populism and the End of Economic Democracy* (New York: Random House, 2000), 51–88. For quote: Barry Goldwater to Newt Gingrich, June 14, 1995, Alpha Files F–H, Goldwater Papers.
4. http://www.fee.org/tradition/, accessed Apr. 2008.
5. http://www.montpelerin.org/home.cfm, accessed Apr. 2008.
6. Steven Greenhouse, "Clash Nears in the Senate on Legislation Helping Unions Organize," *New York Times,* June 20, 2007; "Paid Leave for Maternity Is the Norm, Except in . . ." *New York Times,* Oct. 6, 2007; Jeffrey Rosen, "Supreme Court Inc.: How the Nation's Highest Court Has Come to Side with Business," *New York Times Magazine,* Mar. 16, 2008; Stephen Labaton, "OSHA Leaves Worker Safety Largely in Hands of Industry," *New York Times,* Apr. 25, 2007.
7. Gretchen Morgenson, "Corporate America's Pay Pal," *New York Times,* Oct. 15, 2006; Jeffrey Birnbaum, "Tax-Cut Supporters Ready for 'World Series of Lobbying,'" *Washington Post,* Oct. 2, 2007; http://www.nam.org, "Bottom-Line Policy Achievements for Manufacturers," accessed Apr. 2008.
8. http://www.aei.org/about/filter.all/default.asp, accessed Apr. 2008; http://www.heritage.org/about/, accessed Apr. 2008.
9. Jack Welch to Lemuel Boulware, Oct. 24, 1985, Box 53, Folder 1636, Boulware Papers; Jonathan D. Rosenblum, *Copper Crucible: How the Arizona Miners' Strike of 1983 Recast Labor-Management Relations in America* (Ithaca, N.Y.: Cornell University Press, 1998), 60–63, 222–226. On changing working-class identity: Jefferson Cowie, "'Vigorously Left, Right and Center': The Crosscurrents of Working-Class America in the 1970s," in Beth Bailey and David Farber, *America in the Seventies* (Lawrence: University Press of Kansas, 2004), 75–107.
10. Peter Brimelow, "A Look Back at Boulwarism." *Forbes,* May 29, 1989, 286.

Bibliographic Essay and Note on Sources

Some readers may wonder why I call these businessmen conservative rather than neoliberal or libertarian. After all, the conservative intellectual tradition in Europe had long criticized the free market, asserting that the competitive ethos promoted an anarchic selfishness which eroded the traditions and organic hierarchies needed for social stability. The men who fought labor unions and the New Deal state, by contrast, celebrated the market with enthusiasm. They had no complaints about materialism perverting religion or virtue. They did not regret that bonds of family or community might be corroded by commercial values. They had no desire to rid the world of new technologies, nor did they envision a revival of small-scale capitalism. They did not claim to stand for social order against the chaos of change; instead, they embraced the forces of transformation. They wanted to empower business, not to reinvigorate lost traditions, and some even wanted to use the state to enforce policies friendly to business or to the market, the hallmark of the neoliberal.

Nonetheless, most of these activists did call themselves conservatives. While it is true that a few still hankered after the old word "liberal," with its associations with the intellectual movement of John Stuart Mill and Adam Smith, many accepted that Franklin Delano Roosevelt had claimed the word and that they could not easily take it back. And their description of themselves as conservatives was not merely a semantic accident. They dreamed of a return to the low-regulation, low-tax economy of the 1920s, or even the late nineteenth century. Like their counterparts in the European conservative intellectual tradition, they feared the power of the state and the threat of economic redistribution. They believed that at the heart of the New Deal and the labor movement was an excess of democracy—that the organization of working-class people into labor unions led to the rise of the welfare state and the perversion of the market economy. They were confident that the trend toward "collectivism" would destroy the United States, that it would have results more devastating than Soviet espionage. They believed that the free market was equivalent to freedom itself, that regulating the marketplace meant surrendering political liberty as well as economic strength. For them, turning back the New Deal was a question not only of the bottom line but of the deepest social principles. Their antipathy toward social democracy is what marks their kinship with the broader conservative tradition, and what makes "conservative" the appropriate term.

THE CONSERVATIVE movement is a complex, diverse force in American life. Many different kinds of people, socially and demographically, have been drawn to conservative political ideas and activism, and the business activists whose story is told in this book were only one part of this larger mobilization. As an intellectual movement it has encompassed a wide variety of schools of thought, ranging from the traditionalist conservativsm of the 1950s to the neoconservatism of the 1970s to libertarianism—ways of approaching politics that can conflict sharply with each other, despite sharing certain common themes.

Historical writing on the conservative movement goes back to the 1950s. Much of the scholarship centers on a debate about the relationship between psychological and cultural politics versus economic interests in the rise of the movement. The articles in Daniel Bell's edited collection *The Radical Right* (New York: Criterion, 1955), which was in many ways the first serious effort to analyze the modern right, criticized the "pseudo-conservative" supporters of Joseph McCarthy (the 1963 edition included Barry Goldwater), arguing that they were driven to make their fantastical, often conspiratorial charges against liberalism because they were possessed by intense anxiety about their status and role in American political life, brought about by sudden, rapid economic changes. Writing at the height of postwar liberalism, these thinkers saw conservatives as a hopeless rear guard, a reactionary throwback that would surely disappear with time.

By the 1980s, it became clear that conservatism was not about to simply die out but that it was instead the ascendant politics of the country, and scholars turned accordingly to examining its history. The next major wave of writing about the conservative movement dealt with the backlash against the social movements of the 1960s. It was focused tightly on the dissolution of the New Deal electoral coalition. In particular, the historians who wrote on this theme focused on the turn away from the Democratic Party by working-class white ethnic voters in the North as well as by white southerners, as these two groups reacted against the Democrats' support for the civil rights movement and to some extent also the challenge to traditional values represented by the sexual revolution, the antiwar movement, and the counterculture. Their work on racism and cultural backlash was very different from that of the 1950s consensus authors, but it did share with the earlier scholarship a tendency to view the shift to the right in American politics as driven primarily by the fears and angers of the working and middle class rather than as a mobilization of the elite. Especially strong works on the social history of the cultural backlash include Ronald Formisano, *Boston Against Busing: Race, Class and Ethnicity in the 1960s and 1970s* (Chapel Hill: University of North Carolina Press, 1991); Jonathan Rieder, *Canarsie: The Jews and Italians of Brooklyn Against Liberalism* (Cambridge, Mass.: Harvard University Press, 1985); and Dan Carter, *The Politics of Rage: George Wallace, the Origins of the New Conservatism, and the Transformation of American Politics* (Baton Rouge: Louisiana State University Press, 2000).

The analysis of the backlash against civil rights has been deepened by the work of scholars such as Thomas Sugrue, in *The Origins of the Urban Crisis: Race and Inequality in Postwar Detroit* (Princeton, N.J.: Princeton University Press, 1996). Sugrue showed that there was in fact no liberal consensus on racial politics in postwar Detroit. Long before the riots of the late 1960s, white Detroiters were engaged in resisting civil rights initiatives in their city. This interpretation yields a very different narrative of the postwar period, not one of declension or a sudden descent into a politics of violence but rather one of incomplete victory and continued conflict throughout the 1940s and 1950s. (For one influential review essay that makes this point, see Gary Gerstle, "Race and the Myth of the Liberal Consensus," *Journal of American History* 82, no. 2 [Sept. 1995]: 579–586.) More recent work on race and the backlash in the South has examined the way in which the southern reaction against civil rights became part of a larger set of struggles over consumption and suburbanization, muting the overt language of racism even as a new rhetoric of meritocracy and individual choice continued to provide the rationale for the perpetuation of racial divisions; see the scholarship of Matthew Lassiter, *The Silent Majority: Suburban Politics in the Sunbelt South* (Princeton, N.J.: Princeton University Press, 2006), and Kevin Kruse, *White Flight: Atlanta and the Making of Modern Conservatism* (Princeton, N.J.: Princeton University Press, 2005).

Much of the early work on the history of the rise of conservatism focused on the breakdown of New Deal liberalism. But another developing body of scholarship in the 1990s focused on the growth of the conservative movement, and specifically the role of grass-roots activism and political ideas in building a challenge to liberalism. The emphasis has moved away from working-class actors and toward the affluent middle-class people who helped build the movement in its early years. Works such as Gregory Schneider, *Cadres for Conservatism: Young Americans for Freedom and the Rise of the Contemporary Right* (New York: New York University Press, 1999); Lisa McGirr, *Suburban Warriors: The Origins of the New American Right* (Princeton, N.J.: Princeton University Press, 2001); Donald Critchlow, *Phyllis Schafly and Grassroots Conservatism: A Woman's Crusade* (Princeton, N.J.: Princeton University Press, 2005);

John Kelley, *Bringing the Market Back In: The Political Revitalization of Market Liberalism* (New York: New York University Press); and David Farber and Jeff Roche, eds., *The Conservative Sixties* (New York: Peter Lang, 2003) all deal with the activists who built a grass-roots conservative politics in the 1950s, 1960s, and 1970s. Rick Perlstein's *Before the Storm: Barry Goldwater and the Unmaking of the American Consensus* (New York: Hill & Wang, 2001) is a comprehensive and vivid history of the 1964 Goldwater campaign as a moment of activist awakening and mobilization.

Another approach that focuses on the forward-looking agenda of the conservative movement—rather than the breakdown of liberalism—emphasizes the role of ideas and intellectuals. George Nash, *The Conservative Intellectual Movement in America Since 1945* (New York: Basic Books, 1979), remains one of the most important works in this tradition. Scholars have also looked at the emergence of the religious right as a distinctive group of activists; for one good synthesis, see William Miller, *With God on Our Side: The Rise of the Religious Right in America* (New York: Broadway Books, 1996). A powerful new treatment of the role of grass-roots religious organizations in building the conservative movement can be found in Darren Dochuk, "From Bible Belt to Sunbelt: Plain Folk Religion, Grassroots Politics, and the Southernization of Southern California," Ph.D. dissertation, University of Notre Dame, 2005.

On the whole, most of the scholars who have dealt with religion and ideas have looked at the activism of conservatives as roughly analogous to that which built the civil rights and labor movements—the work of ordinary people on the ground, carefully organizing through personal contacts. This book suggests that there is something about the conservative movement which fundamentally distinguishes it from the movements of the left: the role played by business. There have, of course, been businessmen who have given financial and political support to liberal or even left-wing causes. But the extent of businessmen's involvement in postwar conservatism, as funders but also as activists, and the role of the workplace as a site of conflict seem to set conservatism apart from these other social movements. The appropriate way to balance the grass-roots aspects of the conservative movement with the role played by institutions such as universities, think tanks, and corporations will be one of the central questions defining the historiography of the movement for some time to come.

The most recent work on the conservative movement has been careful to analyze not only its successes but also its failures and weaknesses. Bruce Schulman and Julian Zelizer, eds., *Rightward Bound: Making America Conservative in the 1970s* (Cambridge: Harvard University Press, 2008), brings together much of the most recent scholarship on the right, looking at how the conservative movement carefully and strategically built coalitions in the 1970s; in the end, the editors suggest, despite its strengths, the conservative movement was in some ways never able to achieve its most ambitious aims. Recent work on the history of ideas in the conservative movement has treated the institutional context in which conservative thought flourished. Steven Teles, in *The Rise of the Conservative Legal Movement: The Battle for Control of the Law* (Princeton, N.J.: Princeton University Press, 2008), looks at the complex interactions between business funders, lawyers, and intellectual entrepreneurs in building the network of conservative legal institutions and thinkers, arguing that business sponsorship of conservative public-interest law firms created problems for the movement, and also that the conservative challenge was never able to overturn the dominance of liberals completely.

THIS BOOK has dealt with the elite dimension of the conservative mobilization. This focus naturally leads to another question: how did free-market economic ideas come to appeal to people outside of the elite? One group of writers—including Thomas Byrne Edsall, *Chain Reaction: The Impact of Race, Rights and Taxes on American Politics* (New York: W. W. Norton, 1991)—has argued that conservatism was made compelling to working-class Americans, even though their economic interests might seem to be at odds with its policies, through the canny political manipulation of racism and also of traditional social and religious values. While my goal in this book has not been to study the working-class response to the ideas advanced by the business conservatives, it does seem that the free-market agenda in and of itself might have provided ways of bridging the divide between economic classes and creating a conservative movement, quite independent of its connection to cultural politics. There is nothing simple or straightforward about the way in which people come to understand their economic interests—such awareness is itself the product of political organizing, as well as of direct experience. The campaigns of the business conservatives to undermine labor unions and liberal institutions and ideas may well have yielded a different understanding among working-class people of their economic interests from that which they held earlier in the postwar period.

The standard popular narrative of the postwar period continues to emphasize basic social comity and agreement in the 1940s and 1950s, shattered only by the social movements of the 1960s and 1970s and the backlash against them. One outstanding scholarly version of this analysis can be found in Alan Matusow, *The Unraveling of America: A History of Liberalism in the 1960s* (New York: Harper & Row, 1986). But many historians have challenged the idea that the postwar period was one of liberal consensus and have sought to explore the ways in which the economic politics of the postwar period continued to be the subject of great controversy and contest. For a few examples of the most important work, see Nelson Lichtenstein, *State of the Union: A Century of American Labor* (Princeton, N.J.: Princeton University Press, 2002), especially Chapter 3; Bruce Nissen, "A Post–World War II 'Social Accord'?" in Bruce Nissen, ed., *U.S. Labor Relations, 1945–1989: Accommodation and Conflict* (New York: Garland, 1990); Elizabeth Fones-Wolf, *Selling Free Enterprise: The Business Assault on Labor and Liberalism, 1945–1960* (Urbana: University of Illinois Press, 1994); Jefferson Cowie, *Capital Moves: RCA's Seventy-Year Quest for Cheap Labor* (Ithaca, N.Y.: Cornell University Press, 1999); Howell Harris, *The Right to Manage: Industrial Relations Policies of American Business in the 1940s* (Madison: University of Wisconsin Press, 1982); Sanford Jacoby, *Modern Manors: Welfare Capitalism*

Since the New Deal (Princeton, N.J.: Princeton University Press, 1997); David Anderson, "The Battle for Main Street, United States of America: Welfare Capitalism, Boosterism and Labor Militancy in the Industrial Heartland, 1895–1963," Ph.D. dissertation, University of North Carolina at Chapel Hill, 2002; Sugrue, *Origins of the Urban Crisis*; David Vogel, "Why Do Businessmen Distrust Their State?" in *Kindred Strangers: The Uneasy Relationship Between Politics and Business in America* (Princeton, N.J.: Princeton University Press, 1996); Tami Friedman, "Communities in Competition: Capital Migration and Plant Relocation in the U.S. Carpet Industry, 1929–1975," Ph.D. dissertation, Columbia University, 2001; David Stebenne, *Arthur J. Goldberg: New Deal Liberal* (New York: Oxford University Press, 1996); Mike Davis, *Prisoners of the American Dream: Politics and Economy in the History of the U.S. Working Class* (London: Verso, 1986); Herman Krooss, *Executive Opinion: What Business Leaders Said and Thought on Economic Issues 1920s–1960s* (Garden City, N.Y.: Doubleday, 1970); David Witwer, "Westbrook Pegler and the Anti-union Movement," *Journal of American History* 92, no. 2 (Sept. 2005): 527–552; Meg Jacobs, *Pocketbook Politics: Economic Citizenship in Twentieth-Century America* (Princeton, N.J.: Princeton University Press, 2005); and Jennifer Klein, *For All These Rights: Business, Labor and the Shaping of America's Public-Private Welfare State* (Princeton, N.J.: Princeton University Press, 2003). There are also several recent works that focus on the southern United States and its contribution to the rise of the national conservative movement, especially the ways in which the backlash against civil rights was able to merge with the rise of a suburban economic conservatism developing across the country: for example, see Joseph Crespino, *In Search of Another Country: Mississippi and the Conservative Counterrevolution* (Princeton, N.J.: Princeton University Press, 2007).

This book builds on this literature, treating the postwar period as one of sustained conflict over labor unions and the regulatory welfare state. Seeing these decades as ones of conflict can help us to understand why the postwar liberal order declined—in some ways, it was less strong than its proponents at the time believed it to be.

While my focus is the history of the conservative movement, this book should also be seen as an engagement with the history of liberalism in postwar America. One of the dangers of writing about the right is that one runs the risk of suggesting that postwar liberalism was more radical than it actually was. In reality, postwar liberalism was deeply contradictory and conflicted. It never created a universal welfare state. Its social policies benefited whites far more than African Americans and so helped to sustain racial inequality, especially in the economic realm. It did not undo inequalities of wealth. It advanced a vigorous anti-Communist agenda, with disastrous results in Vietnam. For one book that addresses some of these problems especially well, see Robert O. Self, *American Babylon: Race and the Struggle for Postwar Oakland* (Princeton, N.J.: Princeton University Press, 2003). The political fears of the business conservatives may therefore appear in many ways unfounded, since liberals never really sought to restrict and challenge businessmen in the way that the business conservatives feared. But at the same time, the limits of liberalism should not keep us from recognizing how threatening even its moderate reforms were to some parts of the business world. The difficulty that the business conservatives had in accepting the liberal order suggests not so much the radicalism of the reforms but rather the extreme tenacity of the opposition.

Finally, there is a rich literature on the role of business in American politics and culture. This book has focused on the political activism of businessmen, but companies seek to influence culture through subtler means as well—for example, through advertising and public relations. Some of the best examples of this literature are Roland Marchand, *Creating the Corporate Soul* (Berkeley: University of California Press, 1996); Karen Miller, *The Voice of Business: Hill & Knowlton and Postwar Public Relations* (Chapel Hill: University of North Carolina Press, 1999); Charles McGovern, *Sold American: Consumption and Citizenship: 1890–1945* (Chapel Hill: University of North Carolina Press, 2007); Lizabeth Cohen, *A Consumers' Republic* (New York: Knopf, 2003), and Pamela Laird, *Advertising Progress: American Business and the Rise of Consumer Marketing* (Baltimore: Johns Hopkins University Press, 1998). Not all businessmen were conservatives, of course; there were also networks of businessmen who organized in support of Keynesian or liberal policies in the postwar years. Kim McQuaid, *Big Business and Presidential Power* (New York: Morrow, 1982), and Robert Collins, *The Business Response to Keynes, 1929–1964* (New York: Columbia University Press, 1981), have looked at the relationship between businessmen and liberalism. The Johnson administration in particular sought to involve businessmen in antipoverty initiatives, and the period in many ways represents the high-water mark for the postwar period of business participation in the liberal agenda; for one article on business in the 1960s, see Cathie Jo Martin, "Business and the New Economic Activism: The Growth of Corporate Lobbies in the Sixties," *Polity*, Fall 1994. Thomas Ferguson, *Golden Rule: The Investment Theory of Party Competition and the Logic of Money-Driven Political Systems* (Chicago: University of Chicago Press, 1995), analyzes the role of money in shaping the political system, while Mark Smith, *American Business and Political Power: Public Opinion, Elections, and Democracy* (Chicago: University of Chicago Press, 2000), looks at how business lobbyists are constrained by public opinion in their political choices. G. William Domhoff, *Who Rules America?: Power, Politics and Social Change* (New York: McGraw-Hill, 2006), considers the central role of the "corporate community" in politics. David Vogel, *Fluctuating Fortunes: The Political Power of Business in America* (New York: Basic Books, 1989), remains the most comprehensive book about the role of business in politics in the 1970s and 1980s.

Despite the wealth of writing on business in American life, few social histories of business have explored companies as social and political institutions that shape the culture and ideology of those who work within them as well as the culture of their broader communities. This book has tried to address this absence in the literature by exploring businessmen as political actors who are moved not only by the short-term pressures and demands of economic rationality but also (like any group) by broader ideological visions. Some other work that moves in this direction includes Steve Fraser and Gary Gerstle, eds., *Ruling America: A History of Wealth and Power in a Democracy* (Cambridge, Mass.: Harvard University Press,

2005), and the work of Nelson Lichtenstein and Bethany Moreton on Wal-Mart; see, for example, their essays in Nelson Lichtenstein, ed., *Wal-Mart: The Face of Twenty-First Century Capitalism* (New York: The New Press, 2006). Of necessity, I have relied primarily on the papers of individuals and of conservative activists and organizations that are already open to the public in archives to write this book. As the manuscript collections of more businessmen and their companies and business groups active during this period become available, it will be possible to deepen the study of these political actors in ways that go beyond what I have been able to do here. I look forward to the new work—especially local studies of business conservatism in specific communities as well as analyses of particular companies and industries—that will emerge in the future.

Selected Bibliography

Government Documents

U.S. Congress. Senate. Committee on Education and Labor. *Testimony before Senate Committee on Education and Labor, Hearings on S. 1661, A Bill to Provide for the Appointment of Fact-Finding Boards to Investigate Labor Disputes.* 79th Congress, 1st and 2nd sessions, 1945–1946. Part I.

U.S. Congress. Senate. Committee on Education and Labor. *Violations of Free Speech and Rights of Labor: Industrial Munitions.* 76th Congress, 1st session, 1939. Report No. 6, Part 3.

U.S. Congress. Senate. Committee on Education and Labor, Subcommittee on National Labor Relations Board. *Hearings Before the Subcommittee on National Labor Relations Board.* 87th Congress, 1st session, 1961.

U.S. Congress. Senate. Select Committee on Improper Activities in the Labor or Management Field. *Hearings Before the Senate Select Committee on Improper Activities in the Labor or Management Field.* 85th Congress, 2nd session, 1958.

Oral Histories

Oral History of Earl Dunckel: Ronald Reagan and the General Electric Theater, 1954–55. Interviewed by Gabrielle Morris, 1982. Ronald Reagan Gubernatorial Era Oral History Series. Bancroft Library, University of California at Berkeley.

The "Kitchen Cabinet": Four California Citizen Advisers of Ronald Reagan. Interviewed by Steven D. Edgington and Lawrence B. de Graaf, 1981. California Government History Documentation Project Reagan Era, California State University, Fullerton, Oral History Project.

Selected Bibliography

Books

Amadae, S. M. *Rationalizing Capitalist Democracy: The Cold War Origins of Rational Choice Liberalism.* Chicago: University of Chicago Press, 2003.

Auerbach, Jerome. *Labor and Liberty: The La Follette Committee and the New Deal.* Indianapolis: Bobbs-Merrill, 1966.

Baum, Dan. *Citizen Coors: An American Dynasty.* New York: Morrow, 2000.

Bell, Daniel, ed. *The Radical Right.* New Brunswick, N.J.: Transaction, 2002 [1955].

Boulware, Lemuel. *The Truth About Boulwarism: Trying to Do Right Voluntarily.* Washington, D.C.: Bureau of National Affairs, 1969.

Blumenthal, Sidney. *The Rise of the Counter-Establishment: From Conservative Ideology to Political Power.* New York: Times Books, 1986.

Burk, Robert. *The Corporate State and the Broker State.* Cambridge, Mass.: Harvard University Press, 1990.

Cannon, Lou. *Reagan.* New York: Putnam, 1982.

Carter, Dan. *The Politics of Rage: George Wallace, the Origins of the New Conservatism and the Transformation of American Politics.* New York: Simon and Schuster, 1995.

Cockett, Richard. *Thinking the Unthinkable: Think Tanks and the Economic Counter-revolution, 1931–1983.* London: HarperCollins, 1995.

Collins, Robert. *The Business Response to Keynes, 1929–1964.* New York: Columbia University Press, 1981.

Cowie, Jefferson. *Capital Moves: RCA's Seventy-Year Quest for Cheap Labor.* Ithaca: Cornell University Press, 1999.

Crespino, Joseph. *In Search of Another Country: Mississippi and the Conservative Counterrevolution.* Princeton, N.J.: Princeton University Press, 2007.

Doenecke, Justus. *Not to the Swift: The Old Isolationists in the Cold War Era.* Lewisburg, Pa.: Bucknell University Press, 1979.

Doherty, Brian. *Radicals for Capitalism: A Freewheeling History of the Modern Libertarian Movement.* New York: PublicAffairs, 2007.

Ebenstein, Alan. *Friedrich Hayek: A Biography.* New York: Palgrave, 2001.

Edsall, Thomas Byrne. *The New Politics of Inequality.* New York: W. W. Norton, 1984.

Edwards, Lee. *The Power of Ideas: The Heritage Foundation at 25 Years.* Ottawa, Ill.: Jameson, 1997.

Evans, Thomas W. *The Education of Ronald Reagan: The General Electric Years and the Untold Story of His Conversion to Conservatism.* New York: Columbia University Press, 2006.

Falwell, Jerry. *Listen, America!* New York: Doubleday, 1980.

Ferguson, Thomas. *Golden Rule: The Investment Theory of Party Competition and the Logic of Money-Driven Political Systems.* Chicago: University of Chicago Press, 1995.

Ferguson, Thomas, and Joel Rogers. *Right Turn: The Decline of the Democrats and the Future of American Politics.* New York: Hill and Wang, 1986.

Fifield, James. *The Single Path.* Englewood Cliffs, N.J.: Prentice Hall, 1957.

Fones-Wolf, Elizabeth. *Selling Free Enterprise: The Business Assault on Labor and Liberalism, 1945–1960.* Urbana: University of Illinois Press, 1994.

Forster, Arnold, and Benjamin Epstein. *Danger on the Right.* New York: Random House, 1964.

Furgurson, Ernest. *Hard Right: The Rise of Jesse Helms.* New York: W. W. Norton, 1986.
Galligan, David. *Politics and the Businessman.* New York: Pitman, 1964.
Gilder, George. *Wealth and Poverty.* San Francisco: Institute for Contemporary Studies, 1993.
Goldberg, Robert Alan. *Barry Goldwater.* New Haven, Conn.: Yale University Press, 1995.
Goldfield, Michael. *The Decline of Organized Labor in the United States.* Chicago: University of Chicago Press, 1987.
Gross, James. *Broken Promise: The Subversion of U.S. Labor Relations Policy, 1947–1994.* Philadelphia: Temple University Press, 1995.
Harding, Susan. *The Book of Jerry Falwell: Fundamentalist Language and Politics.* Princeton, N.J.: Princeton University Press, 2000.
Harris, Howell John. *The Right to Manage: Industrial Relations Policies of American Business in the 1940s.* Madison: University of Wisconsin Press, 1982.
Hartwell, R. M. *A History of the Mont Pelerin Society.* Indianapolis: Liberty Fund, 1995.
Hayek, Friedrich. *The Constitution and Liberty.* Chicago: University of Chicago Press, 1960.
———. *Individualism and Economic Order.* Chicago: University of Chicago Press, 1948.
———. *The Road to Serfdom.* Chicago: University of Chicago Press, 1944.
———. *The Road to Serfdom: Text and Documents.* Edited by Bruce Caldwell. Chicago: University of Chicago Press, 2007.
Heath, Jim. *John F. Kennedy and the Business Community.* Chicago: University of Chicago Press, 1969.
Hess, Karl. *In a Cause That Will Triumph: The Goldwater Campaign and the Future of Conservatism.* Garden City, N.Y.: Doubleday, 1967.
Himmelstein, Jerome. *To the Right: The Transformation of American Conservatism.* Berkeley: University of California Press, 2000.
Hodgson, Godfrey. *America in Our Time: From World War II to Nixon, What Happened and Why.* Garden City, N.Y.: Doubleday, 1976.
Horowitz, David A. *Beyond Left & Right: Insurgency & the Establishment.* Urbana: University of Illinois Press, 1997.
Jacobs, Meg. *Pocketbook Politics: Economic Citizenship in Twentieth-Century America.* Princeton, N.J.: Princeton University Press, 2005.
Jacoby, Sanford. *Modern Manors: Welfare Capitalism Since the New Deal.* Princeton, N.J.: Princeton University Press, 1996.
Judis, John. *William F. Buckley, Jr.: The Patron Saint of the Conservatives.* New York: Simon and Schuster, 1988.
Kazin, Michael. *The Populist Persuasion: An American History.* New York: Basic Books, 1995.
Kirzner, Israel. *Ludwig von Mises: The Man and His Economics.* Wilmington, Del.: ISI Books, 2001.
Klein, Jennifer. *For All These Rights: Business, Labor, and the Shaping of America's Public-Private Welfare State.* Princeton, N.J.: Princeton University Press, 2003.
Knight, Frank. *Freedom and Reform: Essays in Economic and Social Philosophy.* New York: Harper & Brothers, 1947.
Kristol, Irving. *Two Cheers for Capitalism.* New York: Basic Books, 1978.
Kruse, Kevin. *White Flight: Atlanta and the Making of Modern Conservatism.* Princeton, N.J.: Princeton University Press, 2005.

Larson, Arthur. *A Republican Looks at His Party.* Westport, Conn.: Greenwood, 1974.

Lassiter, Matthew. *The Silent Majority: Suburban Politics in the Sunbelt South.* Princeton, N.J.: Princeton University Press, 2006.

Levitan, Sar A., and Martha R. Cooper. *Business Lobbies: The Public Good and the Bottom Line.* Baltimore: Johns Hopkins University Press, 1984.

Lichtenstein, Nelson. *State of the Unions: A Century of American Labor.* Princeton, N.J.: Princeton University Press, 2002.

Link, William A. *Righteous Warrior: Jesse Helms and the Rise of Modern Conservatism.* New York: St. Martin's Press, 2008.

Lippmann, Walter. *An Inquiry into the Principles of the Good Society.* Boston: Little, Brown, 1937.

Lowndes, Joseph E. *From the New Deal to the New Right: Race and the Southern Origins of Modern Conservatism.* New Haven, Conn.: Yale University Press, 2008.

Marchand, Roland. *Creating the Corporate Soul: The Rise of Public Relations and Corporate Imagery in American Big Business.* Berkeley: University of California Press, 1998.

Martin, William. *With God on Our Side: The Rise of the Religious Right in America.* New York: Broadway Books, 1996.

McGirr, Lisa. *Suburban Warriors: The Origins of the New American Right.* Princeton, N.J.: Princeton University Press, 2001.

McQuaid, Kim. *Big Business and Presidential Power.* New York: William Morris, 1982.

Middendorf, J. William II. *A Glorious Disaster: Barry Goldwater's Presidential Campaign and the Origins of the Conservative Movement.* New York: Basic Books, 2006.

Mises, Ludwig von. *Human Action.* New Haven, Conn.: Yale University Press, 1949.

Nash, George. *The Conservative Intellectual Movement in America Since 1945.* New York: Basic Books, 1976.

Northrup, Herbert. *Boulwarism.* Ann Arbor: University of Michigan Press, 1964.

O'Connor, Alice. *Social Science for What? Philanthropy and the Social Question in a World Turned Rightside Up.* New York: Russell Sage Foundation, 2007.

Perlstein, Rick. *Before the Storm: Barry Goldwater and the Unmaking of the American Consensus.* New York: Hill & Wang, 2001.

Read, Leonard. *The Romance of Reality.* New York: Dodd, Mead, 1937.

Rowan, Hobart. *The Free Enterprisers: Kennedy, Johnson and the Business Establishment.* New York: Putnam, 1964.

Roy, Ralph Lord. *Apostles of Discord: A Study of Organized Bigotry and Disruption on the Fringes of Protestantism.* Boston: Beacon, 1953.

Saloma, John S. III. *Ominous Politics: The New Conservative Labyrinth.* New York: Hill and Wang, 1984.

Schoenwald, Jonathan M. *A Time for Choosing: The Rise of Modern American Conservatism.* New York: Oxford University Press, 2001.

Schomp, Gerald. *Birchism Was My Business.* New York: Macmillan, 1970.

Schulman, Bruce. *The Seventies: The Great Shift in American Culture, Society and Politics.* New York: Free Press, 2001.

Sennholz, Mary. *Faith and Freedom: A Biographical Sketch of a Great American, John Howard Pew.* Grove City, Pa.: Grove City College, 1975.

———. *Leonard Read: Philosopher of Freedom.* Irvington-on-Hudson, N.Y.: Foundation for Economic Education, 1993.

Simons, Henry. *Economic Policy for a Free Society.* Chicago: University of Chicago Press, 1948.

Smith, James Allen. *The Idea Brokers: Think Tanks and the Rise of the New Policy Elite.* New York: Free Press, 1991.

Smith, Robert Michael. *From Blackjacks to Briefcases: A History of Commercialized Strikebreaking and Unionbusting in the United States.* Akron: University of Ohio Press, 2003.

Starbuck, Dane. *The Goodriches: An American Family.* Indianapolis: Liberty Fund, 2001.

Stebenne, David. *Arthur J. Goldberg: New Deal Liberal.* New York: Oxford University Press, 1996.

———. *Modern Republican: Arthur Larson and the Eisenhower Years.* Bloomington: Indiana University Press, 2006.

Stretton, Hugh, and Lionel Orchard. *Public Goods, Public Enterprise, Public Choice: Theoretical Foundations of the Contemporary Attack on Government.* New York: St. Martin's, 1994.

Teles, Steven. *The Rise of the Conservative Legal Movement: The Battle for Control of the Law.* Princeton, N.J.: Princeton University Press, 2008.

Tilman, Rick. *Ideology and Utopia in the Social Philosophy of the Libertarian Economists.* Westport, Conn.: Greenwood, 2001.

Uphoff, Walter. *The Kohler Strike: Its Socio-Economic Causes and Effects.* Privately printed, 1935.

———. *Kohler on Strike: Thirty Years of Conflict.* Boston: Beacon, 1966.

Viguerie, Richard. *The New Right: We're Ready to Lead.* Falls Church, Va.: Viguerie, 1981.

Vogel, David. *Fluctuating Fortunes: The Political Power of Business in America.* New York: Basic Books, 1989.

———. *Kindred Strangers: The Uneasy Relationship Between Politics and Business in America.* Princeton, N.J.: Princeton University Press, 1996.

Wanniski, Jude. *The Way the World Works.* Washington, D.C.: Regnery, 1978.

White, F. Clifton. *Politics as a Noble Calling: The Memoirs of F. Clifton White.* Ottawa, Ill.: Jameson, 1994.

Wills, Garry. *Reagan's America: Innocents at Home.* Garden City, N.Y.: Doubleday, 1987.

Wolfskill, George. *The Revolt of the Conservatives: A History of the American Liberty League, 1934–1940.* Boston: Houghton Mifflin, 1962.

Wreszin, Michael. *The Superfluous Anarchist: Albert Jay Nock.* Providence, R.I.: Brown University Press, 1971.

Journal Articles and Chapters in Books

Akard, Patrick. "Corporate Mobilization and Political Power: The Transformation of U.S. Economic Policy in the 1970s." *American Sociological Review* 57 (October 1992): 597–615.

Bartley, Robert L., and Amity Shlaes. "The Supply-Side Revolution." In *Turning Intellect into Influence: The Manhattan Institute at 25,* edited by Brian Anderson. New York: Reed, 2004.

Burch, Philip. "The NAM as an Interest Group." *Politics and Society* 4, no. 1 (Fall 1973): 97–130.

Burns, Jennifer. "Godless Capitalism: Ayn Rand and the Conservative Movement." In

American Capitalism: Social Thought and Policy in the Twentieth Century, edited by Nelson Lichtenstein, 271–291. Philadelphia: University of Pennsylvania Press, 2006.

Collins, Robert M. "Positive Business Responses to the New Deal: The Roots of the Committee for Economic Development, 1933–1942." *Business History Review* 52, no. 3 (Autumn 1978): 369–391.

Cook, Fred. "The Ultras." *The Nation,* June 30, 1962.

Cowie, Jefferson. "'Vigorously Right, Left and Center': The Crosscurrents of Working-Class America in the 1970s." In *America in the Seventies,* edited by Beth Bailey and David Farber, 75–106. Lawrence: University of Kansas Press, 2004.

———. "Nixon's Class Struggle: Romancing the New Right Worker, 1969–1973." *Labor History* 43, no. 3 (2002): 258–283.

Englander, Ernest, and Allen Kaufman. "The End of Managerial Ideology: From Corporate Social Responsibility to Corporate Social Indifference." *Enterprise and Society* 5, no. 3 (September 2004): 404–450.

Fink, Gary M. "Labor Law Revision and the End of the Postwar Labor Accord." In *Organized Labor and American Politics, 1894–1994: The Labor-Liberal Alliance,* edited by Kevin Boyle, 239–257. Albany: State University of New York Press, 1998.

Griffith, Robert. "Dwight D. Eisenhower and the Corporate Commonwealth." *American Historical Review* 87, no. 1 (February 1982): 87–122.

———. "Forging America's Postwar Order." In *The Truman Presidency,* edited by Michael Lacey, 57–88. Cambridge: Cambridge University Press, 1989.

Lassiter, Matthew D. "Inventing Family Values." In *Rightward Bound: Making America Conservative in the 1970s,* edited by Bruce Schulman and Julian Zelizer, 13–29. Cambridge, Mass.: Harvard University Press, 2008.

Martin, Cathie Jo. "Business and the New Economic Activism: The Growth of Corporate Lobbies in the Sixties." *Polity* (Fall 1994): 49–76.

McCartin, Joseph A. "'A Wagner Act for Public Workers': Labor's Deferred Dream and the Rise of Conservatism, 1970–1976." *Journal of American History* 95, no. 1 (2008): 123–148.

———. "'Fire the Hell Out of Them': Sanitation Workers' Struggles and the Normalization of the Striker Replacement Strategy in the 1970s." *Labor: Studies in the Working-Class History of the Americas* 2, no. 3 (2005): 67–92.

Moreton, Bethany. "Make Payroll, Not War: Business Culture as Youth Culture." In *Rightward Bound: Making America Conservative in the 1970s,* edited by Bruce Schulman and Julian Zelizer, 52–71. Cambridge, Mass.: Harvard University Press, 2008.

Rippa, S. Alexander. "The Textbook Controversy and the Free Enterprise Campaign, 1940–1941." *History of Education Journal* 9, no. 3 (Spring 1958): 49–58.

Rothmyer, Karen. "Citizen Scaife." In *Speak Out Against the New Right,* edited by Herbert Vetter, 22–37. Boston: Beacon, 1982.

Rudolph, Frederick. "The American Liberty League, 1934–1940." *American Historical Review* 56, no. 1 (October 1950): 19–33.

Schatz, Ronald. "The End of Corporate Liberalism: Class Struggle in the Electrical Manufacturing Industry, 1933–1950." *Radical America* (July-August 1975): 189–190.

Schulman, Bruce. "Slouching Toward the Supply Side." In *The Carter Presidency: Policy Choices in the Post–New Deal Era,* edited by Gary M. Fink and Hugh Davis Graham, 51–71. Lawrence: University Press of Kansas, 1998.

Sharlet, Jeff. "Jesus Plus Nothing: Undercover Among America's Secret Theocrats." *Harper's Magazine,* March 2003, 53–64.

Tedlow, Richard S. "The National Association of Manufacturers and Public Relations During the New Deal." *Business History Review* 50, no. 1 (Spring 1976): 25–45.

Toy, Eckard V., Jr. "Spiritual Mobilization: The Failure of an Ultraconservative Ideal in the 1950s." *Pacific Northwest Quarterly* (April 1970): 77–86.

Witwer, David. "Westbrook Pegler and the Anti-union Movement." *Journal of American History* 92, no. 2 (September 2005): 527–552.

Workman, Andrew. "Manufacturing Power: The Organizational Revival of the National Association of Manufacturers, 1941–1945." *Business History Review* 72 (Summer 1998): 279–317.

Dissertations, Theses, and Unpublished Articles

Baltakis, Anthony V. "Agendas of Investigation: The McClellan Committee, 1957–1958." Ph.D. dissertation, University of Akron, 1997.

Bella, Salvatore Joseph. "Boulwarism and Collective Bargaining at General Electric: A Study in Union-Management Relations." Ph.D. dissertation, Cornell University, 1962.

Brenner, Aaron. "Rank and File Rebellion, 1966–1975." Ph.D. dissertation, Columbia University, 1996.

Burns, Jennifer Louise. *Goddess of the Market: Ayn Rand and the American Right, 1930–1980.* New York: Oxford University Press, forthcoming.

Canedo, Eduardo. "'Free the Fortune 500': Murray Weidenbaum and the Business Campaign Against Social Regulation of the Late 1970s." Paper delivered at Annual Meeting of the Organization of American Historians, Minneapolis, March 31, 2007.

———. "The Origins of Neoliberalism: Jimmy Carter and the Politics of Deregulation." Paper delivered at the Policy History Conference, Charlottesville, June 4, 2006.

Decker, Jefferson. "The Conservative Non-Profit Movement and the Rights Revolution." Paper delivered at the American Society for Legal History Conference, Baltimore, November 2006.

Eow, Gregory. "Fighting a New Deal: Intellectual Origins of the Reagan Revolution." Ph.D. dissertation, Rice University, 2007.

Gable, Richard Walter. "A Political Analysis of an Employers' Association: The National Association of Manufacturers." Ph.D. dissertation, University of Chicago, 1950.

Hammond, Sarah. "'Business Men Working for Jesus': Toward a Historiography of Twentieth-Century American Christianity and Capitalism." Paper presented at the Organization of American Historians Annual Meeting, Minneapolis, April 1, 2007.

Jacobs, Meg. "Highway Guerrillas: The 1970s and the Conservative Turn in American Politics." Unpublished essay.

Kannenberg, Lisa Ann. "The Product of GE's Progress: Labor, Management and Community Relations in Schenectady, 1930–1960." Ph.D. dissertation, Rutgers University, 1999.

Kolopsky, Marc Steven. "Remington Rand Workers in the Tonawandas of Western New York, 1927–1956: A History of the Mohawk Valley Formula." Ph.D. dissertation, State University of New York at Buffalo, 1986.

Rosenfeld, Sam. "From Lobbyists to Scholars: AEI and the Politics of Expertise, 1943–1964." Senior thesis, Columbia University, April 2004.

Shermer, Elizabeth Tandy. "Counter-Organizing the Sunbelt: Right-to-Work Campaigns and Anti-Union Conservatism, 1943–1958." *Pacific Historical Review*, forthcoming (February 2009).

———. "Origins of the Conservative Ascendancy: Barry Goldwater's Early Senate Campaigns and the De-legitimization of Organized Labor." *Journal of American History*, forthcoming (December 2008).

Thrift, Bryan. "Jesse Helms, the New Right and American Freedom." Ph.D. dissertation, Boston University, 2002.

Van Horn, Robert, and Philip Mirowski. "The Rise of the Chicago School of Economics and the Birth of Neoliberalism." Cambridge, Mass.: Harvard University Press, forthcoming.

Waterhouse, Benjamin. "Big Business Versus Big Brother: The Slow Death of the Consumer Protection Agency." Paper presented at the Annual Meeting of the American Historical Association, Atlanta, January 2007.

———. "The Creation of the Business Roundtable and Corporate Activism in the 1970s." Paper presented at the Charles Warren Center Workshop on the Political Economy of North America, May 2004.

Williams, Daniel. "From the Pews to the Polls: The Formation of a Southern Christian Right." Ph.D. dissertation: Brown University, 2005.

Index